GAMEFACE

The Kick-Ass Guide for Women Who Love Pro Sports

- -

Erica Boeke *and*
Chris De Benedetti

Distributed by Macmillan

FIRST EDITION

Designed by Jason Snyder

Library of Congress Cataloging-in-Publication Data

Boeke, Erica.
  Gameface / by Erica Boeke and Chris De Benedetti. — 1st ed.
    p. cm.
  Includes bibliographical references and index.
  ISBN-13: 978-0-7535-1328-6 (alk. paper)
  ISBN-10: 0-7535-1328-5 (alk. paper)
  1. Sports—Social aspects—United States. I. De Benedetti, Chris. II. Title.
III. Title: GameFace.
  GV706.5.B63 2008
  306.4'83--dc22

                    2008023256

To our parents and siblings,
who inspired our love of sports and writing.

- -

Our heartfelt thanks to the following people for their blood, sweat, tears, time, brains and support: The entire Boeke and De Benedetti clans, Lisa Grubka, Ken Siman, Angela Woodall, Mary Pender-Coplan, Edmund Brady, Vicki Shapiro, Deborah Baer, Daniella Wells, Tracy & Chris Stewart, Tricia & Kevin Smith, John Baer, Patrick Lavergne, Joe Kulesa, John Gizzi, David Balutanski, Amy Messano, Mark Veeder, Michael Schroeder, Matt & Ginny Hautau, John & Artemis Patrick, Anne Woodard, Camilla Davidsson, Ian Martin, Tim Trevathan, Andrew Kilbourn, Leslie Russo, Diana Boric, Jenny Bowman, Kiersten Geiger, Mary Nolan, Liz Small, Theresa Mullen, Chef Kenny Callaghan, Chef Jody Williams, Adeena Sussman, Michael Green, Judi Rosenthal, Sandy Missakian, Robyn Gordon, Beccy Gordon, Vicki Michaelis, Heidi Durrow, Kristi Klemmer, Nicole Capobianco, Anna Maria Verniero, Paul Lukas, Dave Kopay, Gary Clark, Chris Bull, Phil Villapiano, Mitch Oellrich, Bonnie Oellrich, Billy Bean, Lindsy McLean, Robert Lipsyte, Alex Abramovich, Howard Bryant, Marvin Miller, John Hoberman, Ken & Sharon Ruettgers, Leilani Münter, Dock Ellis, Lon Rosen, Sam Green, Dave Zirin, Dr. Denise Garibaldi, Rob Dennis, Don Buchholz, Steve Waterhouse, Dion Rich, Todd Mintz and Terry Cannon.

CONTENTS

INTRODUCTION

WHY *GAMEFACE*? ONE SUNDAY MORNING, AS I FLIPPED THROUGH channels searching for a good pregame show to prep me for Game Day, it suddenly dawned on me: every sports channel featured a selection of loud, large, opinionated men—a number of them ex-football players—bickering, ridiculing each other, and rifling off stat after stat after stat . . . after stat. At that moment, I realized that these guys were not speaking to me. They were speaking a foreign language. They were part of some sort of clique or club—and it was a club that I had no interest in joining. I knew there were other women out there who found that these sports shows—along with newspapers, magazines, websites, and pretty much all pro sports coverage—were filled with lots of information we didn't really care about, in a voice that didn't speak to us.

Now, I don't have a diehard sports husband or boyfriend at the moment, nor am I watching sports in order to catch one. Quite simply: I love sports. My female friends love sports. We talk about big games and plays. We meet at sports bars and attend games together, where yes, we pay attention to what's going on. We talk about which player is kicking ass and why—and yes, also which player is dating whom. We talk about a great new sports movie in theaters. We talk about a particular sports scandal, and these days, there are a lot to choose from. Loving sports doesn't consume our lives, but sporting events are a big part of our lives. Year-round: Super Bowl. Spring Training. March Madness. Opening Day. The Masters. The Kentucky Derby. The Stanley Cup. The NBA Finals. The World Cup in 2006 (and soon in 2010). Wimbledon. The Australian/French/US Opens. The English Premier League. Baseball's Pennant Races. NASCAR's Chase for the Cup. Preseason Football. The World Series. *Sunday Night Football. Monday Night Football. Thursday Night Football.* Playoffs. Super Bowl. Lather. Rinse. Repeat.

My love affair with sports started as a kid, when I first walked into a Major League Baseball stadium, holding my dad's hand and gazing at the greenest grass I had ever seen. It was the first time, at age 7, that I realized what "larger than life" meant. I couldn't believe that I was in the same stadium as the legendary players and icons whom I had only seen on TV or on baseball cards. But now here they were, live and in person. (Please note that this was during the pre-reality show era when fame was actually an achievement. To see these amazingly talented athletes in person was truly a big deal in Pittsburgh, Pennsylvania, circa 1976.) When these heroic athletes swung that bat or leaped gracefully in the air to catch an impossible line-drive far over their heads, I felt that I was witnessing something incredible. Magic, in fact. I also felt that I was one with all of those fans around me, like we were all in this together. I noticed every detail of my surroundings: The smell of hotdogs. The way the peanut man threw bags to fans in the stands. The various cheers and clap patterns that everyone seemed to know. I paid close attention to the rituals of the game: Having my dad teach me how to mark a ground-rule double on the scorecard. Getting the prize at the bottom of the Cracker Jack box, back when the prizes were actually good. Feeling the butterflies in my stomach, nervous that my team wouldn't win. These moments stay with you. And these moments undoubtedly caused my lifelong love affair with sports.

These days, I love the all-day rituals of Sundays during football season. I get choked-up on Opening Day in April. I keep my NASCAR earplugs in my treasure box. I have been known to spend a perfectly sunny day in a dark and dank Sports Book in Vegas. Every summer, as I'm on the 7 train heading out to Flushing Meadows, I get as excited to see the stars of the US Open as I was to see Justin Timberlake or U2 at Madison Square Garden. I even usher for a Minor League baseball team for a paltry $35 a game. But guess what? I get paid to go to the ballpark! You see, watching sports is still magical to me. It's the only event or performance these days where no one can spoil the ending for you. No one has downloaded it before you. No one has a bootleg copy. No one knows how the game is going to turn out, because it ain't over 'til it's over. And there's always that chance that you'll witness history. Even watching games at home, with family and friends gathered around, breathlessly waiting to see who wins and who loses—to me, this is *real* reality TV. (You mean to tell me that you really thought Bret Michaels and his *Rock of Love I & II* ladies were unscripted and the outcomes were not pre-determined?!) Sorry to pull the curtain back on Oz, people, but there are very few true mysteries left in life these days. The only ones I can think of are love and sports.

Call me naïve. Tell me that the big business of sports is taking the mystery away. But I maintain that even with all of its scandals and problems, there is still so much to savor and celebrate when it comes to sports. Especially for women. There are heroes. Underdogs. There are poor sports and class acts. And of course, there is drama. On the field and off. If you haven't noticed, women in particular love to witness— and be a part of—drama. But sometimes the pure and simple drama of sports is overshadowed by the sheer volume of statistics and factoids that many male sports fans seem to love so darn much. This language— consisting of slugging percentages and career rushing yards and much more minutiae—almost creates a secret code of acronyms and abbreviations that makes some women feel like they will never really be a part of "the club." In sports bars, around water coolers, in the stands, on websites, many men are constantly trying to prove that they know more about sports than everyone else. And they do it to other guys, not just women. This type of guy is always trying to establish himself as the ultimate expert on football or Jeff Gordon or the Celtics or whatever his particular passion is.

My sister and I walked into a sports bar this past football season, proudly wearing T-shirts from our favorite team. We hadn't even ordered a beer yet, when a guy walked up to us and started quizzing us on whether we knew the first *and* last name of the Steelers' new coach, asking us if we knew who the top-five rushers of all time were, challenging us to name at least five current members of the defense and the offense. I could hear the *Jeopardy* theme song playing inside my head.

I said to him, "First, who is Mike Tomlin? Second, who cares about the other stuff? And third, what year did the Steelers merge with the Eagles to become the Steagles, just for one season, because most of the players in the league were fighting overseas in World War II?" He didn't know. I did: 1943. And thankfully, this got him to leave us alone so we could enjoy our game in peace.

It's okay. No harm, no foul, because I'm not really concerned with that stat-head guy. I am content to talk to my family and girlfriends about sports. And my enlightened guy friends, who listen to my reflections and opinions, rather than try to test me on the numbers. In my world, sports bring people together—uniting them in a common cause and a lively conversation. And that's why I wanted to form my own club.

Welcome to *GameFace*—a club where you'll never be tested and you'll never have to prove you know more than the next guy . . . or girl. You'll also never be talked down to. And above all, you'll never be subjected to too much pink. *GameFace* brings the juicier stories to the forefront and celebrates all the things that women love about sports. But don't worry. We're not too soft and fluffy. We'll call people out and name names. We'll cover everything that we feel a female sports fan would be interested in—everything from our profile of the best National Anthem performance in history to the larger implications of how marketing and big business is affecting sports. Our stories are designed to enlighten, engage and entertain female sports fans. Our voice is smart and saucy, not condescending and cloying. We don't go for the obvious angle, instead we opt for the revealing angle. Rather than speaking to some over-media-trained ballplayer, hearing his repeated denials of steroid use, we talk to the mother of a young college student who killed himself after years of using steroids. Instead of hearing the canned statements from an NFL player in the middle of a sex scandal, we interview a woman who conducts workshops and skits for NFL rookies, trying to teach them to make smart choices. We will, however, take a break from being the Woodward and Bernstein of the sports world every once in a while to provide you with fun stuff, like great sports-related trips around the globe, our favorite tailgating recipes from guest chefs (and even our moms), and tales of how we finagled our way into the pit at a NASCAR race.

Notice that I switched from "I" to "we" matter-of-factly there in the last paragraph. Yes, I hatched this idea, but then decided that it would be a lot more fun to have a partner in crime. Someone to be the Maris to my Mantle. The Kareem to my Magic. The Rice to my Montana. The Venus to my Serena. So I recruited someone who I felt could speak this language just as well as I could. Someone who I have known for decades. Someone with whom I have discussed, ad nauseam, over many beers, both the hopeful and the disheartening sports stories of the day. Someone who, as a kid, would also dance with siblings to *Soul Train,* just before the Saturday Game-of-the-Week came on the tube. Someone who measures the love of sports by stomach butterflies and tears shed over a team, rather than stats.

And interestingly enough —despite my tales of tears, butterflies and pre-game dancing to *Soul Train*—this person happens to be a man. I often tell people that instead of throwing a ball like a girl, he watches sports like a girl. (And when those statements are made by someone of the female persuasion, both are meant as huge compliments.) There is no doubt that his take on sports is unusual. He loves the stories, the lore and the drama of sports, probably more so than your average guy might admit. Sure, he's got friends who can spew Michael Jordan's career stats in their sleep— and he can certainly hold his own in those circles—but memorizing stats is not something this guy is too concerned with. He doesn't have time for that. He's too busy reading about some obscure player from the '70s or exploring the overriding societal implications of publicly funded ballparks. His name is Chris De Benedetti. He is a reporter and a natural storyteller. His lifelong love affair with sports has caused his heart to be broken several times—another thing that gives him a unique perspective. In fact, Chris has repeatedly vowed to never again watch a sporting event of any kind because sports are getting too commercial and focused on the almighty dollar. But even though he has denounced baseball, football and basketball forever, at least seven times according to my records, he comes back every time. Because Chris' love runs deep, just like mine. He loves the unlucky losers. He loves rebellious characters. He loves teams filled with misfits and motley characters. To this day, he will look wistfully in the air, stating that he loves the smell of cigarette smoke on a hot day, explaining that it reminds him of childhood games spent at the Oakland Coliseum surrounded by his team's hard-living fans. And these smoke-filled, sunny days bring goose bumps to his arms and tears to his eyes. (I told you he watches sports like a girl!)

Throughout *GameFace,* Chris and I will present our collective take on what we consider to be some of the most fascinating issues and stories in sports. You'll find that sometimes we disagree, and you'll feel like you're spending the day with Dave and Maddie on *Moonlighting.* Other times, I get a bit too girlie on Chris and he nearly gives up on me altogether (namely, 3 on fashion and 8 on sports wives and girlfriends). And there are a few times that I simply don't invite Chris along, because I want a girls-only experience (the Phoenix NASCAR race in 4; he's still a little miffed). And there are times that we split up completely to present a topic from two distinct perspectives (the highly divisive 10, on the pros and cons of sports marketing.) But throughout it all, together we dig deep into all types of sports-related topics—even the uncomfortable ones—with an honest, opinionated and balanced look at things, from both a female and a male perspective. In other words, we keep each other's inner-Neanderthal and inner-Gloria Steinem in check.

Now that you know why *GameFace* exists, you may wonder to yourself, "Why hasn't anyone done anything like this before?" or "Where have you two been all my life?!" I feel your pain—for years I have been craving a resource for female sports fans like myself, but all of the prior attempts to target women like us have completely missed the mark. And I think I know why. Many people have bought into various stereotypes about female fans that quite simply, are completely off base. The result has been a series of magazines, TV shows and websites that try to be everything to everyone. Instead, they appeal to no one. (Chris grew up

with three sisters—remember the *Soul Train* dancing?—so he can easily join me in shattering some stereotypes here.) Follow along as we
debunk a few myths and attempt to inform the misinformed:

Women sports fans are all jocks themselves: Not true. Certainly
some female sports fans did play sports in high school and college, but
there are many who never really played sports all that much, and yet
identify with the guts and the glory of professional sports. And even if
female fans are into fitness now—whether we run, do yoga, or kayak—
we would not go to the same resource to check out sports scores as we
would to find out about the latest running shoes or new yoga poses.
Men wouldn't, why would we?

***Women sports fans don't really understand the game, and basi-
cally choose their team by picking the one with the "cuter" uniform:*** We may not fill our brains with as many numbers as some male
fans do, but we appreciate the intricacies of the game, understand its
complexity and appreciate the larger implications of sports. We get it.
Most of us just aren't quite as obsessive about it as some of our male
counterparts. (Try this analogy: You know how most men memorize
every line of every guy-flick ever made, such as *Caddyshack* or *Anchor-
man*, whereas women can describe the overall plot of the movie? There
is a direct correlation in sports.) As for that insulting uniform stereotype: Haven't we proven by now that women are capable of loving—and
understanding—sports? Please do not insult us by insinuating that we
just choose teams with the "prettier colors"—although we will say that
we do enjoy critiquing those aforementioned uniforms, as a kind of
sport unto itself. (See 3 on fashion, please.)

***Women sports fans are obsessed with male athletes' bodies and
all they care about is looking at their butts in tight pants:*** Sure,
women sports fans don't mind that there are some fine looking men in
sports, and we loved posing the "Would you rather shag Tom or Eli?"
question to our friends during the weeks leading up to the 2008 Super

Bowl. (Erica's answer: Tom Brady. Chris: Gisele Bündchen.) But women also love players for their hearts and minds and characters and gravity-defying skills. While some men are trying to portray us as sex fiends for watching a football game or trying to keep us out of the locker room because we are trying to sneak a peek at some guy's package, they might want to explore the homoeroticism of men patting their teammate's butts and showering together post-game, hmmmm?

Women sports fans are also just as passionate about women's professional sports: Nope, sorry. The majority of female sports fans we know follow male professional sports. Women don't automatically follow female sports, just because we're women. Let's call it the "Hillary Clinton Effect." For those women who do follow women's leagues like the WNBA and Women's Soccer, there are great resources devoted to fans of these sports. But there are lots of us who are all about men's pro leagues, so when you're talking sports to us, please don't automatically include a profile on Mia Hamm. (Don't think we're going to just gloss over this issue. In 6, we explore why many fans, male and female, don't follow women's sports.)

Female fans wish that chicks played in the pros, competing head-to-head against men: Chris, I'll take this one myself. I'm going out on a limb here and stating for the record that there are some physical feats that men can do that women can't—like transform our bodies into beefy, 300-lb. defensive tackles who can then sack beefy 250-lb. quarterbacks. I consider myself a feminist and believe in Equal Rights and Equal Pay for women, and I know some of you ladies out there will disagree with me and think that women *can* do anything a man can. But I am of the belief that each sex has its own set of strengths and weaknesses, and there are certain sports in which women simply cannot compete against men at the same level. So in these pages, you're not going to be reading about the woman who wants to become the first female hockey player in the NHL. There are sports, however, where women *can* compete head-to-head against men on an even playing field. And for us, that's when things get really interesting. You'll see it in auto racing (go, Danica!) and in tennis (hello, Billie Jean King, Martina Navratilova and the Williams sisters), and more and more these days in golf (we're watching you, Michelle Wie . . . and Annika Sorenstam, why are you retiring?!) We're also interested in women in the business world who choose to devote their careers to professional male sports. Here, we'd like to see a bit more equality. You can read more about that in 6, as well.

Now that we got that out of the way, we hope by now you know what *GameFace* is, and what it is not. But before we jump right in, we want you to check out this stat. (Yes, we just spent several pages convincing you that women hate stats, but this is a *meaningful* stat.) According to a study by *Psychology Today,* more than 50% of men consider themselves knowledgeable about sports. Less than 20% of women do. That's a stat that we'd like to change. And this is the true mission statement of *GameFace,* not to get too *Jerry McGuire* on you. But really, we are here to look at sports in an entirely new way. We're here to provide women with an outlet to celebrate sports the way they like to. We are here to start a different conversation at a sports bar, that doesn't lead to an I-know-more-than-you-do competition. Because we think there's always more to learn. For women and for men. That's another reason we love sports. There's always some fascinating player you never heard of (Dock Ellis, 13). A sport you never thought you'd be into (auto racing, 4). Some crazy fan that you forgot about (Rainbow Man, 3). And then you read about this character, and it takes you back to a moment in time. To that greenest field you've ever seen. To the ring in the Cracker Jack box. To the butterflies in the stomach. And that love affair is rekindled once again.

So we invite you to sit back, crack open a beer (fine, make it a low-carb beer, if you must), and let us tell you some stories. We think you'll laugh, probably get angry at a thing or two, and definitely get a few goose bumps, as you remember why you love sports as much as we do. You may even find yourself regaling that stat-spewing guy at the water cooler with some of our tales that convey the thrill of victory and the agony of defeat, as well as the mouthwatering scandals and the sweet, magical moments that only sports can deliver. And by the end of this book, you'll be breathless, more knowledgeable and thrilled that there is finally a voice that speaks intelligently to the female sports fan. Finally, a voice of our own. (No pink jersey required.)

Erica & Chris

P.S. If you like what we have to say and want to add your own voice to the crowd, visit our website at GoGameFace.com.

ERICA'S DISCLAIMER:

For this and all other properties that are a part of the GameFace franchise, I must state, for the record:

I love the Pittsburgh Steelers to the very core of my being. Up until January 5, 2007, Bill Cowher was, to me, the male ideal. I plan to name my first child—boy or girl—Franco Harris Boeke. However, I vow to remain unbiased toward any of the teams who have royally screwed us over, including, but not limited to: those dirty, foul, nasty 1976–1979 and 1996 Dallas Cowboys; the Baltimore Ravens who always give us trouble in our own house; our Ohio rivals the Bengals and Browns; as well as those m*ther-f*cking 2002–2005 New England Cheaters Patriots, who were FINALLY stopped in 2007. Thank you, New York Giants, my new second-favorite team. I promise to put all of that baggage aside. Come on, I'm a member of the press! Unbiased is my middle name.

Next, I love the Pittsburgh Pirates circa 1974-1980 and get chills when I hear the Sister Sledge song, "We are Family." I can be unbiased here because this team has not been decent since the early '90s. However, I must state for the record that if anyone ever tries to dispute that there has ever been any better team on the field than Willie Stargell, Dave Parker, Omar Moreno, Phil Garner, Bill "Mad Dog" Madlock, Bert Blyleven, Ed Ott, Manny Sanguillen, Kent Tekulve, John Candelaria: I will crush you. I will also try to be really fair about not hating the 1990-1992 Atlanta Braves when they cock-blocked the Pirates from the World Series three years in a row, causing hardcore heartache and disappointment, but teaching me fairly early on that anyone you love will just sorely disappoint you in the end. Moving on . . .

Dear reader, you also should know that my first job out of college was as a writer for the *San Francisco Giants* magazine. The Giants are my favorite baseball team and I do love their New York roots, as well as their amazing ballpark—where you can get chowder in a bread bowl, great microbrews and even better Napa Valley and Sonoma County wine (see 9). But I don't like the fact that you might need a blanket and hot chocolate during a game in July, if the fog has rolled in. From working in the front office for nearly four years, I know first-hand that Barry Bonds is not very nice, but his dad was a lovely, sweet man. Willie Mays? Not the nicest guy. Dusty Baker? The best. (I once hit a line drive at Dusty's head, wearing heels and a skirt during batting practice, after he teased that I wouldn't be able to hit.) Again, I will try to hide my disdain for the Atlanta Braves, although they robbed the Giants of a possible World Series appearance in 1993. The Giants had won 103 games that season; the Braves had won 104. The entire season came down to one final game, against our arch-rivals: the dreaded Los Angeles Dodgers. And sadly, tragically, heart-breakingly, the Giants blew it. It was the first time in history a team had won 103 games and had not made it into the playoffs. They lost the pennant race, back in the days when pennant races still actually existed, back in the days before Wild Cards. This was devastating for all of us in the front office—especially because we were madly preparing for the possibility of postseason play, only to have our entire lives come screeching to a halt. But truly the most devastating thing was that it was the closest I would ever come to getting a World Series ring. (Yes, everyone on the staff, even a lowly associate editor like I was, gets a ring if the team wins the Championship. Sigh.)

But, onto happier memories. I have already mentioned that I am an usher (I prefer the title "usherette") for the brand new Lehigh Valley IronPigs, the Triple-A Minor League affiliate of the Phillies. Their record at press time is 5-29, the worst in their league (maybe in any league), so

I'm sure no one hates me at this point. Perhaps they pity me. But I will say that Coca-Cola Park—where the Pigs play and the fans "oink"—is absolutely beautiful. Plus, my dad also works as an usher for the team, leaving us both feeling feel like kids with the coolest summer jobs, ever.

Continuing on with my confessions: I also have an affinity for the Pittsburgh Penguins, along with the Chicago Cubs and the Chicago Bears (for my mom). I have a mild affection for the New York Yankees (for my dad), as well as the Arsenal football club (for my sister), but really I root for any team with Cristiano Ronaldo—go Man U!

Along these lines, I must also confess that I had a childhood crush on Broadway Joe Namath, lusted after Burt Reynolds in *The Longest Yard* and *Cannonball Run,* was fixated on former Steeler Lynn Swann's ass (even as a young child), adored Wayne Gretzky (and still do), and harbored a secret fantasy about former Giant Will Clark and the visiting team's dugout. And I can't help but lust after the oh-so-predictable David Beckham and Andy Roddick. I can't help it. I'm only human.

And now, I have saved the most humiliating admissions for last. Pitcher Tom Glavine during those obnoxious Braves years? Dirty thoughts. Pats quarterback Tom Brady? Filthy thoughts. It's really difficult to curse a team to eternal damnation when you're strongly attracted to one of its star players. See, this is something men don't have to deal with. It's so black and white for them. They never have conflicting, inappropriate feelings that are tearing them up inside. (Actually, maybe they do, but they'll never admit it!) But I haven't felt this wrong since I was lusting over Prince William at Princess Di's funeral. Don't worry, my semi-Catholic upbringing allows me to balance guilt and lust pretty easily. I can deal with it, if you can.

There you have it. My biases. My weaknesses. My heart is officially on the sleeve of my Steelers jersey. I will do my best to fight these prejudices for you, dear reader, and provide a completely objective overview of these sports. I swear on Pittsburgh Pirate legend Roberto Clemente's grave.

CHRIS' DISCLAIMER:

For this and all other properties that are a part of the GameFace franchise, I must state, for the record:

At the end of *Speed*, Dennis Hopper tells Keanu Reeves that only poor people are called "weird." The wealthy, in contrast, are merely "eccentric." It's just like that with bad-boy athletes, isn't it? If you're a team of individuals and you lose, you're labeled as weird, flaky or bums. But the teams that play on their own terms and win, and keep winning, those guys are called "characters."

I was blessed—and a little cursed—to grow up in the '70s and early '80s watching Oakland sports teams like that. Teams that didn't just win, they *dominated* with a long-haired, hard-partying, motley crew of egomaniacal semi-criminals who simply hated to lose. And that was just the team owners!

That's right. My teams were led by some serious characters—whether it was Raiders owner Al Davis' stewing in a luxury box, dreaming up his next lawsuit or intra-league feud while clad in a pompadour haircut and silky white Raiders sweatsuit, or then-Warriors owner Franklin Mieuli sitting courtside wearing a Sherlock Holmes cap and puffing on a pipe. Or Charlie Finley alienating his best A's players while advocating orange baseballs, loud uniforms, something called the "designated runner," and a motorized rabbit that would pop out of the ground to give baseballs to the home plate umpire. (True story.)

You get the picture. With these freaks as my introduction to sports, it's no wonder that—as much as I like seeing my team score more than the other guys—I like the story behind the game even more.

So, yes, it's true. I love—and I mean LOVE—going to 66th Avenue and Hegenberger Road in Oakland, and watching Raiders and A's games at "that li'l ol' bullring," as former Raiders QB Kenny "The Snake" Stabler used to call the Coliseum. I also root for the once sad-sack Warriors who play next door at Oracle Arena, even though I grimace every time I have to call it the "Oracle Arena."

It's also true that I worship the *Azzurri,* the Italian National socce team who won their fourth World Cup title in 2006, putting them second in the world behind only Brazil for World Cup titles. And as a guy whose boyhood idol was Julius "Dr. J" Erving, the Philadelphia 76ers will always have a special spot in my heart.

Conversely, I have a lengthy list of athletes and teams that I despise more than Bill Belichick does Eric Mangini. Erica and I can bond on our hatr- . . . okay, "hate" is too strong. We intensely dislike (much better) the New England Patriots, and my football rivals list also includes the Broncos, Chiefs and Erica's Steelers (sorry, I can't get over that "Immaculate Reception"). As an A's fan, I really can't stand the Yankees, Red Sox and the Angels. Same goes for the Celtics and Lakers, thanks to my old 76ers-rooting days.

For soccer, you'll never find me rooting for Manchester United or Italy's top club teams, Juventus and AC Milan—teams that I consider to be the Yankees and Red Sox of the Mediterranean.

So, there it is, my official rooting list. But don't worry. It's my job to be unbiased and objectively tell the whole story. It's like the Hippocratic Oath that doctors take, without all that life-and-death pressure stuff. I promise, on the grave of former Raider and B-movie actor John "The Tooz" Matuszak, that is what I'll do while writing *GameFace.*

ING CAUGHT WITH YOUR
PA TS DOWN: *Sports Sex Scandals*

WHY DON'T WE JUST START WITH THE TOPIC THAT EVERYONE wants to read about first? Every day you open the paper and there's a new sports-related sex scandal. A recent story described a Pittsburgh Steelers rookie, living off the earnings of a hooker and acting as her pimp. That article hardly raised an eyebrow—probably because he's not a big-name player. But some days, the headlines are bigger than others. And as they say, the bigger they are, the harder they fall. Kobe Bryant will forever be tied to the 2003 rape allegations from his 19-year-old accuser in Vail. Tom Brady will always be known as the conservative, Catholic quarterback who left the pregnant and gorgeous model-turned-actress Bridget Moynahan in 2007 for supermodel-turned-bad-actress Gisele Bündchen. Isiah Thomas will eternally be linked to the $11.5 million sexual harassment suit in which he lost. And of course, who can forget the legendary tales of Magic Johnson and his wild pool parties, or Wilt Chamberlain and the 20,000 notches on his belt (that must be one big belt!). "Yes, that's correct, twenty thousand different ladies," Chamberlain wrote in his memoir. "At my age, that equals out to having sex with 1.2 women a day, every day since I was fifteen years old."

The list of athletes and sex scandals goes on and on and on. But before we start disparaging all of these sex-crazed athletes, there is certainly enough blame to go around. Yes, pro players have big money, enormous fame and larger-than-life egos. Why wouldn't they have sex with 1.2 women per day if they could? But who the hell are these women sleeping with all of these athletes? It boggles the mind that anyone associated with sports can get laid any night of the week. From her days at the Giants, Erica remembers that even the coaches and front-office guys got plenty of female attention whenever they went out or traveled with the team. Even the announcers. Even the scouts. And even the umpires. There is one legendary story—probably an urban myth—of a married umpire who took a groupie back to his hotel room, shagged her and woke up (claiming he was drugged) only to find that his World Series ring was stolen. Whether or not that tale is true or not, we know that in all cases, women aren't merely blameless victims. The notion of the Gold Digger goes back thousands of years and unfortunately, many women perpetuate this stereotype.

WE AIN'T SAYIN' SHE'S A GOLD DIGGER . . .

Not all of these ladies are Gold Diggers, per se. But their stories should be lessons to all Gold-Diggers-in-training. Some are cautionary tales, while others provide how-to guides for women looking to snag a rich athlete and end up with half of his money. But be sure to read 8 on the realities of being a sports wife and/or girlfriend before you embark on your mission.

1. ANNA BENSON: *Married to Pitcher Kris Benson*

Anna gets the number-one spot not just because she's provocative and crazy, but mostly because she's a self-proclaimed Gold Digger (it's her World Series of Poker nickname). She has also made ridiculous public statements about her sex life—embarrassing her husband and possibly costing him his job with the Mets, who reportedly traded Kris to the Orioles because they couldn't take Anna anymore. Could it be because she told Howard Stern that if her husband cheated on her, she would sleep with the entire Mets roster? Or was it because she told *FHM* magazine that if Kris ever won the Cy Young Award he could have anything he wanted, such as "50 free times up the ass"? Or was it because she wore a too-sexy Mrs. Santa suit to the children's holiday party? She filed for divorce in early 2006 but less than a week later, asked for reconciliation. Maybe after she reconsidered her finances. She gets our award as the Goldest Gold Digger of them all. (Update: Kris Benson was signed to the Phillies for the 2008 season and there is a chance he will be playing a game or two for the Lehigh Valley IronPigs, where Erica is an usherette. She will be on the lookout for Anna!)

2. TAMI AKBAR ANDERSON: *Married/Divorced Retired Basketball Player Kenny Anderson*

Tami Akbar Anderson, former cast member of *The Real World: LA,* who now goes by Tami Roman, claims she had a tough childhood in which she and her mother spent some time on the street, and Tami didn't get to go to her prom or graduation. (Check out tamiroman.com to read her riveting story. And what is it with these ladies having their own websites to share things like their poetry with the world? We don't care and your poetry is really bad. And your site has typos.) Anywho, she also announces on the site how hurt she was when Kenny cheated on her (she claimed that she didn't know he was a famous NBA player when they met). Obviously distraught, Tami divorced him, took a big chunk of his assets, talks smack about him on her site, and now rides around in a car with vanity plates that read: "HISCASH."

3. JEAN STRAHAN: *Married/Divorced New York Giants Defensive End Michael Strahan*

After six years of marriage, Michael Strahan filed for divorce, accusing his wife of stealing his money. However, experienced Gold Digger Jean had an ironclad pre-nup. She tearfully told the court tales of her husband's philandering, including a whirlwind weekend with a woman named Cupcake D'Oliveira. Then Jean implied that her husband's relationship with TV's Dr. Ian Smith (currently the medical/diet expert on VH1's *Celebrity Fit Club*) was more than just a friendship. "You could say an alternative lifestyle sprouted," she said. Michael Strahan laughed at the allegations, but the judge was sympathetic to Jean and awarded her $14 million, more than half of Michael's net worth. He is appealing and wants to pay her just $6 million. So in case she doesn't get the full amount, Jean recently hosted a yard sale in the front of their 30-room mansion, where she sold fancy cocktail dresses, as well as a few of her ex-husband's jerseys, commemorative photos, a bronze football statue and, gasp, some of his wide-screen Tvs. (Any woman knows that the way to really hurt a man is to sell his electronics.)

4. KIMBERLY BELL: *Mistress of SF Giants' Superstar Barry Bonds*

Actually, Kimberly Bell needs to go to Gold Digger U. to learn how to do it right, but we like her because she's spiteful! Kim, honey, you're supposed to marry these athletes without a pre-nup, and take half! Her first mistake was to start dating Barry when he was still married to first wife Sun. After they divorced (in which Sun, another novice Gold Digger, did sign a pre-nup and received a fraction of the slugger's fortune), Kimberly and Barry had a good run of it and dated for a few years. She thought she was on the road to becoming wife numero two. Instead, Bonds said that, because of media pressure, he had to marry a black woman. Enter Liz Watson, who is indeed black and who married Bonds in 1998. Barry felt bad for Kimberly and agreed to buy her a house in Arizona, where the Giants go for Spring Training. How convenient! She uprooted her life, moved to Arizona and the two continued their relationship until 2003, when the steroid scandal started heating up and Barry basically disappeared. She claims that he never completely paid for the house, leaving her heartbroken, alone and saddled with a mortgage. Now, what is that they say about a woman scorned? Barry reportedly offered her $20,000 to walk away and sign a confidentiality agreement. She scoffed at his offer and did what any self-respecting, fledgling Gold Digger would do: wrote a tell-all book and testified in court that Bonds indeed used steroids. She also posed in *Playboy* in November 2007, where she was quoted as saying Bonds threatened to chop off her head and leave her body in a ditch. She also revealed that Bonds had backne, shrinking testicles and was lousy in the sack. Hey, a girl's gotta eat.

5. JUANITA JORDAN: *Married/Divorced NBA Legend Michael Jordan*

She's not officially a Gold Digger, but we are including her because her split with the Greatest Basketball Player of All Time is now the Largest Divorce Settlement of All Time. In November 2007, Juanita was awarded a record $168 million from MJ. But we say that for the 17 years of bullshit she put up with from His Royal Airness, Juanita has earned every penny. The two married when they were young and she has suffered through reports of cheating (including a recent paternity scandal), his retirement/comeback revolving door and his legendary gambling habit. Plus, she's a class act, divorcing him amicably and leaving with her integrity intact. In our book, Juanita is in the Gold Digger Hall of Fame and should serve as an example to all of those aspiring young opportunists out there.

But really, maybe we all are a little to blame for holding these players up to a double standard. On one hand, we want them to be these aggressive, fierce competitors. Lord knows that we love a good fight, in every sport. What is better than the dugouts emptying and two teams coming to blows? Or two hockey players dropping the gloves and going at it, *mano a mano*? Or a basketball player heading to the stands to kick some fan's ass? In football, every single play has the potential to end someone's career. Aggressive conduct makes for exciting games, gets the crowd going and, of course, sells tickets. So how can we expect these guys to be vicious and violent, and then flip a switch and be upstanding citizens in every aspect of their lives? They're supposed to give to the community, speak nicely and articulately to the media, be exemplary husbands/fathers, be amazing at what they do and never make a mistake. Ever. How many of us can live up to those standards?

Okay, but before we get too philosophical and let these guys off the hook, let's take a look at some of the more sensational sex scandals in sports. We'll quickly snap back to reality and realize that we're really not just scrutinizing these fellas for minor transgressions. These scandals are pretty astonishing—either the act itself or for how stupid they were to get caught.

JUICIEST SEX SCANDALS OF ALL TIME

1. MIKE TYSON: We already know that this freakydeak likes to nibble on ears. Just ask Evander Holyfield. But after he made Robin Givens' life a self-proclaimed living hell during their one-year marriage from '88 to '89, Tyson was convicted of raping Desiree Washington, Miss Black Rhode Island, in an Indianapolis hotel in 1991. He served three years of a six-year sentence in prison.

2. JOSE CANSECO AND MADONNA: Two sexy superstars, in the prime of their careers, hooking up for a one-night stand in 1991. Big deal, right? But wait, Canseco was married at the time and his wife Esther was at home 3,000 miles away when the big slugger was spotted leaving Madonna's Manhattan apartment at 4 a.m. Oops. Canseco said they just talked. But so did Esther's attorney. They divorced not long afterward. And in light of Canseco's recent tell-all books, *Juiced* and *Vindicated*, accompanied by his buffoonish behavior as he made the rounds in the media, all we can say is, "Madge, what were you thinking?!"

3. STEVE GARVEY: All you need to know about this scandal is stated in this real bumper sticker: "Steve Garvey is not my Padre," making light of this former San Diego Padre's various transgressions. First Garvey had a messy divorce from Cyndy Garvey. Then he knocked up two women at the same time in the late 1980s. Hey, he didn't commit any crimes, but when you're a (supposedly) squeaky clean ambassador of baseball with political aspirations (they even named an LA-area school after him), then you're fair game. And Garvey's special brand of infamy just won't go away. Almost 20 years later, whenever an overly fertile athlete gets into trouble, the Garvey jokes pop up all over again.

4. WADE BOGGS: The Red Sox singles hitter was a master at swinging the stick. In baseball, that is. He was an excellent hitter for average and a superstar before the Steroids Era. But if only he was as selective with women as he was with pitches. The married father's image lost some luster when his longtime Southern California mistress, Margo Adams, filed a $12-million palimony suit against Boggs in 1988. The case was tossed out less than a year later, but not before putting a big ol' Clinton-sized stain on his reputation.

5A. DALLAS COWBOYS' "WHITE HOUSE" SCANDAL: When brash wide receiver Michael Irvin was arrested for drug and gun possession in the mid-'90s, the lid got blown off the team's notorious party pad, where Texas-sized orgies reportedly took place. The place was called the "White House," which sounds way better than "drug-addled brothel."

5B. "THE GOLD CLUB" SCANDAL: Membership sure *did* have its privileges. This Atlanta strip joint would let star athletes from all sports (the NBA's Patrick Ewing, baseball's Andruw Jones and the NFL's Terrell Davis) have sex with their strippers for free, figuring that having celebrity athletes there would attract other paying customers. Problem is, the club owners were caught funneling money to the mob. All the fun and games ended in the 2001 criminal trial.

5C. "THE LOVE BOAT" SCANDAL: In October 2005, a group of Minnesota Vikings rookies treated veteran players to a crazy, sex-o-palooza boat cruise. But the guys didn't really think this one through. The captain of the boat and other crew members started spilling the beans about the raucous and raunchy behavior that took place on the Lido Deck—including lap dances, sex toy use and oral sex. Next thing you know, then-quarterback Daunte Culpepper and three teammates, Bryant McKinnie, Moe Williams and Fred Smoot (supposedly the mastermind of the entire idea), were charged with various infractions. More than a dozen other players were allegedly on board during the party, but only Smoot and McKinnie were fined the equivalent of one game's pay.

6. FRITZ PETERSON AND MIKE KEKICH: In keeping with the tradition of the CBS show, *Swingtown* (which has nothing to do with swinging bats), these two best friends and Yankee pitchers had the brilliant idea to not only swap wives back in 1973, but also to swap families. They traded wives, kids, pets, houses—prompting Yankees GM Lee MacPhail to tell the press, "We may have to call off Family Day." Mike Kekich and Marilyn Peterson didn't work out as a couple, but Fritz Peterson and Suzanne Kekich ended up getting married. (We have to ask, was this whole harebrained scheme Fritz's idea to begin with?!) They had four more kids together, and remain a couple. And now, oddly, Fritz is an evangelist.

7. MAX MOSLEY: This is a new one, but destined to be a classic. You may not have heard of this guy, but he's a powerhouse in the international racing scene. The 67-year-old millionaire is the president of the International Automobile Federation, the body that governs Formula One. According to a British tabloid in April 2008, he hired five prostitutes to engage in "a depraved Nazi-style orgy in a torture dungeon." Apparently, one of the prostitutes had a hidden camera, which captured all the twisted details, including Mosley barking out orders in German at the hookers—some dressed in Nazi uniforms, others dressed in striped prisoner outfits. Also in the video, one of the prostitutes commanded Mosley to take his clothes off so she could inspect him for lice. And if that's not weird enough for you, Mosley's British parents were well-known Nazi sympathizers who had a special guest of honor at their wedding in 1936: Adolf Hitler. Many sponsors, drivers and high-level executives are calling for his resignation. At press time, he has apologized, but refuses to step down.

Although these juicy scandals might be entertaining for us, they are undoubtedly bad for business. And these days, technology makes it easier than ever to catch these guys in the act. How could Max Moseley have known that one of the hired hookers brought a hidden camera to the party? Or how could have catcher Paul Lo Duca predicted that his 19-year-old mistress would brag about their affair on her Facebook page—undoubtedly contributing to the ballplayer's split from his wife, a former *Playboy* model? Regardless of how we find out about them, these scandals sell newspapers, and tarnish the reputations of the leagues and their teams. And when reputations get tarnished, sponsorship dollars are in jeopardy. This is why each sport goes to great lengths to prevent these scandals in any way possible.

Sex Scandal Training Camp to the rescue! Each of the major sports leagues host training camps, where they teach the new players about life as a professional athlete—from how to manage their finances, how to handle themselves with the media, and yes, how to safeguard themselves from dangerous Gold Diggers, Groupies and Baby Mamas. These programs are not necessarily teaching sensitivity and awareness of women's issues, nor are they preaching that players shouldn't cheat on their wives or not sleep with thousands of women. But they are helping them to make better decisions and possibly save them from the pitfalls of fame—not to mention the long arm of the law.

Sex Scandals 101

Ahhh, remember your first job orientation? Benefits. 401K. Health insurance forms. Directions to the bathroom. Good luck. Don't you wish you had a week-long symposium on how to survive in the workplace? Perhaps it should have started with a guest speaker teaching newbies that it's never a good idea to take your top off at an after-work happy hour, even if someone shouts "Simon Says" first. And then maybe another speaker could have yelled at these fragile young newbies, *Scared Straight*-style, about not getting too drunk and soiling themselves at the company holiday party. Then a diva-turned-homeless person could have stood at the podium and warned them, with world-weary eyes and a trembling voice, not to spend their entire paychecks on fancy dinners or Marc Jacobs' bags—no matter *how* cute the purse might be. A PR expert could have then shared horror stories of accidentally blogging about her sexual exploits on MySpace.com—only to have a prospective boss see it and decide not to hire her, but ask her out instead. Yeah, that would have been real nice.

In retrospect, maybe we all should have been pro athletes. Aside from the big signing bonus and enormous contract, their bosses do things right, most of them anyway. These green and naïve rookies get to participate (in some cases, *have* to participate) in intensive training camps to prepare them for what's to come. These in-depth seminars can run from four to six days. and for the most part, upper management takes them very seriously. Thanks to guest speakers, ex-players and top executives, these would-be stars are taught very important life lessons, like learning how to invest in mutual funds, to think about a career after pro sports, and yes, how to face that dangerous creature: woman.

Each January, MLB's Rookie Career Development program reaches about 90 players who are deemed most likely to make it to the big leagues the following season, as selected by each team's General Manager. For some reason, their program seems less intense than those of the NBA and the NFL. It's the shortest of the training camps, and yes, they do cover topics like media, finance, alcohol, tobacco and drugs, and umpires—but they break into teams and compete for prizes such as baseball cards, video games and licensed MLB apparel. ("Whoopee, now can we go to the strip club?") This is undoubtedly because the structure of the Minor League system makes this type of training a little tough to do. And it sure would be expensive and kind of silly to put the hundreds, perhaps thousands, of Minor League players of all ages through a program, when most of them will never play a day in the majors. So instead, we suggest giving them each a *Bull Durham* DVD and calling it a day. It would be cost effective, entertaining and very educational in the proper treatment of Baseball Annies.

The NHL training isn't as formal. Individual teams hold their own Prospect Development Camps, focusing on nutrition and training. And when any controversial issues arise—such as racism—they do call mandatory team seminars. A few years ago, some players were dropping the "n"-bomb in reference to black players on the ice and even the "f"-bomb in reference to French players (calling them "frogs"). So NHL execs decided it was time for everyone to participate in a diversity program. But even though the NHL has had its share of image problems—brutal on-ice fights, gambling scandals, various Russian players with a penchant for underage girls, and the hiring of a hit man by one hockey player to kill his agent—at this point in time, they don't seem to see a need for a formal rookie training program. Or maybe they can't afford it (some NHL rookies have to pay their own way to attend these camps). And when you think about it, rookie hockey players aren't exactly rolling in dough, sporting bling, cruising around the streets of Edmonton in Escalades, and jetting off to Vegas with Nelly, á la Pacman Jones, are they?

The WTA (Women's Tennis Association) opts for a mentoring program for emerging tennis stars. Every young player who is 18 or under and ranked in the Top 100 of singles is assigned to a retired or veteran player who acts as her mentor. Rather than a formal training camp, these mentor/mentee duos spend two years interacting via email, phone, at tournaments, etc. Their older counterparts help guide these rookies on the importance of the public and their fans.

As for our friends over at NASCAR, they don't have formal training for new drivers; they leave that up to the individual teams or sponsors. Because when all is said and done, all of this really does go back to image and sponsorship dollars. Leave it to NASCAR to tell it like it is: "The system of sponsorship in NASCAR creates a self-policing environment," said NASCAR Director of Business Communications Andrew Giangola in a recent article in *License!* magazine. "Our athletes are independent contractors, and most have extensive sponsor commitments in their contracts. So if a driver were to engage in any behavior that a sponsor deemed inappropriate, that driver would be out of a ride pretty quickly."

The fact of the matter is that teams in the NBA and NFL have just paid handsomely for their rising young stars—more handsomely than the other sports. And their sponsors want squeaky-clean reputations in order to keep pouring millions into the leagues. So they will spend a lot of money to protect their most precious commodities. According to a *New York Times* article on the Rookie Symposium, the annual NFL rookie gathering costs upwards of more than $750,000.

And the lives of these young NBA and NFL players are decidedly different than the other sports: the minute a young football or basketball player is signed, the spotlight is immediately shining on him. He's got a pile of cash, old friends and distant cousins coming at him asking for a loan or trying to get them to invest in some cockamamie idea, and suddenly a bunch of chicks all over him—whether he's married or not.

In the NBA, post-Kobe Bryant, the rookie training program is a big deal. The NBA has been holding their Rookie Transition Program since 1986, longer than any other professional sport. Every September, for six full days they cover everything from computer training to gambling, and from challenges facing international players to challenges facing the 20-and-under set. In the NBA, there is constant follow-up; they assign a player development group that visits specific teams, and this same group also visits rookies at home to reinforce their message.

In the NFL, post-Rae Carruth (the former Carolina Panthers wide receiver found guilty in 2001 of conspiring to murder his girlfriend, who was eight months pregnant), they know they have an image problem as a league of thugs and criminals. And more recently, thanks to guys like the aforementioned Pacman Jones and the 10 Cincinnati Bengals who were arrested within a 14-month period from 2006-2007, the league is once again under major scrutiny. Toss in our animal-abusing pal Michael Vick and you have a recipe for a PR catastrophe. This is why training these rookies and helping them make better decisions is more important than ever before.

Since 1997, the NFL has required all new players to attend a five-day Rookie Symposium held in June, where these 200+ athletes learn everything about life in the NFL. They get the basics, like 401K and benefits and taxes, but they also have in-depth training in real-life situations. Situations like overbearing parents, baby mamas, domestic abuse, bar brawls, drug use and abuse, as well as leeches, false friends and people who are going to try to rip them off. And if they miss the symposium—even a day of it—they pay a fine. A $25,000 fine. Speakers include professionals in specialized fields, along with current and former NFL players who have experienced these situations first-hand. Throughout the training, rookies will hear from players who got burned by scams and have scary stories to tell, as well as drug addicts, guys in bankruptcy and convicted criminals there on special permission from their parole officers. In 2006, the NFL included an openly gay speaker in their diversity session—former NFL defensive tackle Esera Tuaolo—for the first time in the program's history.

But of all of the issues players face, there seems to be a recurring theme: women and sex.

According to the *Times* article, one of the first speakers to talk to the players during the Symposium is Sandra McDonald, a renowned AIDS activist specializing in educating the black community. She starts her seminar by passing out bananas and teaching these men—grown men—how to put condoms on bananas. Some snicker, but she brings them back to reality when she talks about Magic Johnson, and shows them close-up shots of herpes sores and gonorrhea and syphilis. They ask her things such as whether or not they can get AIDS from oral sex? Or if a woman uses KY jelly, will it burn a hole in a condom? According to the article, sometimes Sandra also has to hit them over the head with the obvious. Like telling them that you can't always tell if a beautiful woman has AIDS by looking at her.

Next, it's time for skits. It's a challenge to present this information in a professional manner that won't get ridiculed, and in a useful manner that will actually resonate with these guys. For this tricky undertaking, the NFL (as well as the NBA and NHL) turns to ZINC Sports Consulting. This troupe of actors and experts specialize in skits, role-play and interactive Q&A sessions—many of which are consistently ranked the most popular and helpful by the players.

Heidi Durrow is a writer/actress and former lawyer who has worked for ZINC for eight years. Her unique background helps her not only act in the skits, but also facilitate the Q&A sessions afterwards. "I've played the girl at the club, the girlfriend with a child that the athlete's no longer with," Durrow says, "And I'm so old now that I often play the mother!" She emphasizes that the ZINC troupe is not there to tell these guys how to behave, but to reinforce that life is all about choices, decisions and consequences. (This is ZINC's oft-repeated mantra that the players will have embedded deep into their brains by the end of the symposium.)

"We are not Dr. Phil, handing out answers," Durrow says. "We present situations they might find themselves in and give them a chance to think about how they would handle it." In one scenario they affectionately call "the Barbecue Scene," the actors portray family members at a gathering, where everyone at the party is asking the player for something—one needs money for school, another has an investment idea, and then the player's mama has a few ideas about how junior should spend his money. "Usually what we do is perform a scene and have it end terribly," Durrow continues. "Then we let the players discuss answers among themselves. One of the players will then come on stage and re-do the same scene to come up with a better ending."

In another skit, Durrow plays the role of the common-law wife. The player in the scene decides to kick his live-in girlfriend out, and Durrow's character tells him that he better reconsider because she's already seen a lawyer and knows she's entitled to half his worth. The players collectively boo at Durrow. Overall, despite a few jeers here and there, Durrow says the players are very respectful, and that ZINC workshops provide a professional environment to discuss these tricky topics. "We allow them to speak like professionals about women in a way that they probably are not used to in a macho male environment," she says. "They don't have to just do the locker room talk."

Collectively, the group shares ideas on how to talk to family members and how to choose friends and lady-friends wisely—and what the consequences are of not making the right choices. Sometimes, through the group dynamic, the decisions they come up with are not great, Durrow concedes. According to the *Times* article, some players suggest that having two cell phones—one for their wife and one for their girlfriends—is a good solution to some issues that arise. Others recommend lying about being professional athletes to women they meet at clubs. (One player mentioned that he tells women that he is a garbage collector until he gets to know her better. P.S. When's the last time you met a hot, muscular garbage man wearing lots of bling and buying you drinks in the VIP section of a club? Are these chicks really that dumb? Don't answer that.)

Now, time-out please. Here's where it's hard not to jump on a soap box and scream that these men should not be sharing tips on having two phones and lying to women! Rather, these guys should be learning to respect women and to never beat up their wives/girlfriends or lock them out of the house half-nude or throw cookies in their wives' faces like Frisbees (shout-outs to Allen Iverson and Jason Kidd, respectively).

Is it hard, as a woman, to hear these types of responses? "If we get smart-ass answers like keeping two phones, we ask them questions and interrogate them," Durrow says. "We say, 'That's a choice. You made the decision. And what are the consequences?' It's important to have them think about it and not accept easy answers and take the easy way out."

Yes! Go, Heidi! Go, women! But then Heidi describes her very first NBA session and it's clear that things are not that simple.

"The first time I did the NBA session, we were at a really isolated hotel, far away from a big city," she said. "The first night, it was kind of a weird feeling to be one of two women at the end of the day, down at the hotel bar. But then on Tuesday, there were a couple more women. And the next day, a couple more. By Thursday, there were more and more women at the bar. I realized that somehow the word was getting out, and they were here to meet these players. In the middle of nowhere . . . It's upsetting for me as a woman to see other women responding in that way."

Combine the presence of predatory women with the pressure to be fierce, brutal competitors—do you have a toxic combination?

"We did one of the sessions at an NFL training facility and I thought to myself, this is like when you visit a prison if you're a woman," Durrow says. "There is a lot of aggressive energy there. That's their sport, being a competitive aggressor is really important to their jobs. And then they are supposed to turn that off and go change diapers and not respond to whatever it is that's not good for them. It's not that I'm giving them an out, but it is a challenge. And this is why they need a forum to talk to each other sensibly, and regularly."

This is exactly what the NFL is proposing. In 2007, NFL commissioner Roger Goodell ramped up these training sessions, requiring yearlong rookie training and an expanded annual life-skills program for all players. So maybe there's hope for better choices, decisions and consequences for all players.

After watching Durrow play the role of Gold Digger, Baby Mama, Common-Law Wife and even overbearing Big Mama, none of these players would actually ask her out or hit on her when the sessions were over and they were hanging down at the hotel bar, right? "Well, people have approached me. But I tell them that I'm married and in my work capacity. I really try not to appear socially around them unless I'm with other actors in the troupe. It's just inappropriate," she said. "I do think that being married was a plus when I was hired, though!" Good thing someone's acting appropriately around here.

So beyond these Sex Training programs, what can really be done about athletes and sex scandals? Isn't it just human nature? You can try to teach these guys to stay out of trouble. Some will listen, some won't. You can hope that women will start respecting themselves and not throw themselves at men just because they are famous and have money. Perhaps Oprah can start a self-esteem camp for celebrity and athlete groupies after she's done building schools in Africa?

For now, all we can do is sit back and wait for the next scintillating scandal to unfold, so we can decide who was at fault, secretly judge them, decide that we're better than them and announce that we'd never do anything like that.

MOST FERTILE ATHLETES: THE BABY DADDY HALL OF FAME (OR SHAME?)

If you're looking to become an athlete's baby mama yourself (who isn't?) you should cut out this list of our Fertile Five and keep it in your wallet. But beware—not all of these stories have happy endings and not all of these ladies got "half." Read and proceed with caution . . .

1. CALVIN MURPHY: *NBA Hall of Famer & Accused (But Acquitted) Child Molester*

Okay, this guy is fertile—it is reported that he has 14 illegitimate kids by nine different women—but he's also been accused of sexually abusing children. Murphy has three daughters with his wife Vernetta, none of whom ever accused him of abuse. But then five of his daughters from three different women claimed that Murphy sexually abused them as children. He denied these charges, stating that they were banding together in an effort to get money from him—and one of the daughters did admit she was lying. A jury took less than two hours to acquit Murphy, but he lost his job with the Houston Rockets after working there in some capacity for 35 years. He currently hosts his own show on an ESPN Radio affiliate in Houston and is a mentor for the NBA, undoubtedly sharing his cautionary tales with up-and-coming players.

2. TRAVIS HENRY: *NFL Running Back & Victim of Severe Condom-Phobia*

He's not even 30 yet and this bucking Bronco has an astounding nine children with nine different baby mamas. He seems committed to being a good dad, and has gone broke paying child support for all of these women. (Henry apparently was not paying attention during the banana/condom segment of the symposium.) In 2007, he tested positive for drugs with the Broncos, but wasn't suspended. (Apparently, he missed the drug section of the symposium, as well.)

3. SANTONIO HOLMES: *NFL Wide Receiver & Former Fertile College Student*

This current Steeler went to The Ohio State University, but left school a year early and was taken in the first round of the 2006 NFL draft. He also left behind two co-ed baby mamas, with whom he has three children. He was also arrested for domestic violence in 2006, so if you decide to pursue Santonio, better take some Tae Bo classes first.

4. EVANDER HOLYFIELD: *Former Boxing Champ & Holder of Many Baby Daddy Titles*

It's true, Evander Holyfield married a college student back in 2003 and they now have two kids. But in 1998, he announced that he has nine other illegitimate children out of wedlock. Wowza. The man obviously has a high sperm count and a low brain-cell count—the perfect combination for aspiring baby mamas. Sure, he has been accused of using steroids and HGH that keep him fighting well into his 40s, but he's loaded and still doing product endorsements, so he won't end up being a dead-beat dad.

5. SHAWN KEMP: *Former NBA Star & Drug Abuser*

At least Kemp, who fathered seven children with six different women—according to a 1998 *Sports Illustrated* article—did so before he got married. Now he's married with three more kids, but he still has problems. He struggled with a weight problem that kept him out of the NBA at times, during his playing days. He has also struggled with drugs. In 2001, he went to rehab, before it was trendy, but it didn't work. In 2005 he was busted when marijuana and cocaine were found in his car, and he was nabbed for another marijuana possession in July 2006. So ladies, he might not be the top choice for baby daddy material. But he's renowned for his virility and fertility, so we salute him.

But hey, men aren't the only ones making tawdry headlines. Check out this unbelievable story about two professional—and profane—cheerleaders!

SIS-BOOM-BI?: CHEERLEADERS GONE WILD

Hey, NFL owners! It's 2 a.m., do you know where your cheerleaders are? Unfortunately for the Carolina Panthers, everyone knew where two members of their cheer squad were one drunken night in 2005. Renee Thomas and Angela Keathley were arrested at a Tampa nightclub for doing what is nearly every guy's dream. But it was the NFL's nightmare. Thomas and Keathley, two female Panthers cheerleaders, were accused of having sex in a ladies bathroom stall—with each other. And they probably could have left the nightclub with no problems, except that Thomas punched one of the women waiting to use the bathroom. That's when the cops showed up.

The trouble started at Banana Joe's nightclub late one Saturday evening, the night before the Panthers played the Tampa Bay Buccaneers. Those inside the ladies room noticed that Keathley was standing on top of a toilet with her head visible above the stall, while Thomas' legs were facing forward inside the stall, according to the Tampa police report. One witness said Keathley was "making facial expressions and noises," which led her to believe that the cheerleaders were having sex. Someone else in line looked over the stall door and confirmed that, yep, sex was indeed being performed. The line of women waiting for the stall, meanwhile, grew ugly as some of the women called the cheerleaders "whores" and yelled for them to hurry up. That's when the cheerleaders finally left the stall and Thomas, whom police described as being "extremely intoxicated," angrily threw two punches at a woman. To make matters worse for Thomas, she gave police a fake name, telling the Tampa cops that she was "Kristen Owen"—a fellow cheerleader who was nowhere near the incident.

Thomas and Keathley lost their cheerleader jobs, and got their names splashed onto every newspaper in the country. But they both avoided prison time by taking a plea bargain with a probation sentence, while Thomas also had to perform 50 hours of community service and pay a fine. Banana Joe's, of course, somberly shrunk away from the notoriety in a respectful way. Wait, no they didn't! The nightclub embraced the controversy the very next weekend by announcing that anyone—male or female—dressed as a cheerleader would get into the club for free. Hey, at least *somebody* benefited from this mess.

2 GAMEFACE GREATEST HITS: *Sports & Music*

A SONG BLARED FROM THE FENWAY PARK LOUDSPEAKER just as Red Sox left fielder Manny Ramirez stepped into the batter's box. This has been the norm since the late-1990s, when Major League Baseball first allowed players to choose their own special "at-bat song." But on this day in September 2002, the colorful, often flaky Ramirez chose a tune that has never been played in any ballpark since. That's because the lyrics to *Good Times,* Ramirez's audacious decision for an at-bat song, are all about the joys of smoking pot. It also contains a line that features what the Associated Press called a "12-letter profanity." (Could it be the one that begins with an *M* and ends with an *R*?) Most players choose either hard-charging rock music or hip-hop that has been double-checked by team employees, but this at-bat song somehow fell through the cracks. Suddenly a fun, modern tradition had turned into a PR nightmare for Ramirez and the Red Sox organization, and maybe an unexpected headache for parents who just wanted to enjoy a ballgame. One moment you're teaching your little daughter about balls and strikes, and the next moment she's asking, "Mommy, what's a bong?" Bad times all around.

A similar moment happened in April 2004 when a profanity-laced version of *Party Up,* by recording artist DMX, played at Philips Arena during an Atlanta Hawks basketball game. Likewise in November 2003, an Atlanta Falcons halftime show, according to the Associated Press, featured an R-rated song titled *Never Scared*. It was performed by Atlanta rapper Bone Crusher, who in the song reportedly talks about shooting someone in the head. Inappropriate music—it's fannnnnntastic!

In all of these cases, the team front offices responded to the controversies by quickly going into standard damage-control mode: offering apologies that the offensive lyrics ruined the ballgame's "family atmosphere," while vowing that the error would not be repeated.

Obviously, the union of music and sports today, like any marriage, isn't always perfect. If those examples above weren't proof enough, then check out the five volumes of *Jock Jams,* the CD collection of obnoxious stadium anthems. (But you don't have to listen to them. Really. Just trust us.) In fact, plenty of these well-intentioned moments over the years have ranged from the memorable to the mind-boggling, from the infamous to the incredible: Roseanne butchering the National Anthem at a San Diego Padres game. The Chicago Bears' classic *Super Bowl Shuffle* video. And the NFL turning equal parts classy (Ella Fitzgerald, 1972), controversial (Janet Jackson, 2004) and corny (Carol Channing, 1970 and 1972) when picking its Super Bowl halftime performers.

One of the earliest incarnations of halftime acts were those old-fashioned marching bands. While they're still very much a part of high school and college teams' pomp and circumstance, the pro leagues mostly have gotten rid of them, foregoing tradition for the marketing value of pop music. Why? Because these leagues want to entertain you better and simultaneously make themselves more money. Good enough goals, but there's a reason why that saying about good intentions and the road to hell has become a cliché. Just look at the seemingly endless parade of delusional athletes who think they can crossover and be just as successful at hitting vocal notes as they do curveballs, with about one-tenth of the practice. Isn't that idea as ridiculous as a singer thinking he can train for a few months and still make a pro sports team? (Wait, Marvin Gaye and Garth Brooks both tried that? Um, never mind!)

Still, to our amazement and nonstop laughter, far too many athletes have attempted to forge a musical career. Despite an endless list of failures, they keep trying. And trying. God, do they keep trying. In fact, the hip-hop generation in recent years has been the worst offender. Allen Iverson, Ron "Tru Warier" Artest, Kobe Bryant and many, many more have cut rap albums in the last 10 years, although Iverson's was never released. (Insert sigh of relief here.)

But let's not pick on just the NBA. Hall of Fame Steelers quarterback Terry Bradshaw released four country and gospel albums in three different decades. Boxer Joe Frazier had a fairly long stint as a nightclub singer, even though critics jabbed him worse than George Foreman used to.

At the same time, not all of the athletes/artists are laughably bad. Cincinnati Reds pitcher Bronson Arroyo released a decent alt-rock album featuring the big-haired free spirit on guitar. Also, ex-Cincinnati Bengal lineman Mike Reid doesn't perform, but he writes country songs for some of Nashville's top acts. He even won a Grammy Award in 1983, and one of his ditties, *I Can't Make You Love Me,* sold six million copies when Bonnie Raitt recorded it. Yep, there have been hits and there have been misses. But our absolutely favorite sports-and-music moment is Marvin Gaye's soulful performance of the National Anthem at the 1983 All-Star Game. This is the story of that timeless performance.

BEST NATIONAL ANTHEM EVER

Some say the 1960s that we remember today—revolutionary social changes, legendary political protests and groundbreaking music—didn't really begin until the JFK assassination in 1963. Likewise, our image of the 1980s—featuring a surge in patriotism and newfound optimism (not to mention Debbie Gibson album sales)—didn't really start until the 1984 Summer Olympics. America dominated those Los Angeles Games, spawning more flag-waving than a Toby Keith concert. Without question, *those* 1980s started in Los Angeles. Except that we believe they actually began there at a different sporting event, more than a year *before* the Summer Games. In our eyes, it all started Feb. 13, 1983, with *The Star-Spangled Banner,* performed before the NBA All-Star Game.

Hoops legends such as Magic Johnson, Larry Bird, Moses Malone and George "Iceman" Gervin came to The Forum in Los Angeles that day to thrill a star-studded group of fans. But basketball would have to take a back seat because the man of the hour there wasn't even an athlete. It was Motown legend Marvin Gaye, who took center stage with a stirring performance of the National Anthem that is considered by many, including us, to be the best version ever. With it, he took a typically blasé Southern California crowd and instantly electrified them. From the outset, the All-Star Game spectators warmed to the song's slow drumbeat, which sounded much like *Sexual Healing,* his comeback hit single at the time. Within seconds, some fans were applauding and screaming "Whoo!" in unison at the end of some lyrics.

"Between the second and third lines of the anthem, our entire section arose *en masse* and began clapping to the beat, which we continued to do for the rest of the song," wrote blogger Todd Mintz, who attended the game at age 15. "For what seemed like hours, we weren't in the Fabulous Forum . . . we were in the pews of Marvin's church."

It's true. By the song's conclusion, the fans were cheering and swaying to the melody as if they were testifying at the biggest Baptist service LA had ever seen.

Wait, don't you have to be a madman to risk making the National Anthem sound like *Sexual Healing*? Yep, pretty much. In author Nick Tosches' biography on Dean Martin, he calls the crooner a *menefreghista,* slang-ish Italian that means, "one who simply does not give a f-ck." Well, Gaye was such a *menefreghista,* he made Dean Martin look like Donny Osmond. Gaye was accustomed to standing up to authority figures, whether it was his own troubled father, powerful record producers who placed profits over artistic principles, and even America's leaders, whom he chastised in his groundbreaking 1971 album, *What's Going On?*

So, maybe it's not surprising that he decided to sing *The Star-Spangled Banner* set to an R&B beat from a drum machine. It was a risky move—and Gaye knew it. Just 15 years earlier, during the 1968 World Series between St. Louis and Detroit, he had sung a traditional, straightforward National Anthem. But just a few days later, Detroit fans booed singer Jose Feliciano for delivering a heartfelt but offbeat version. After that controversy, anthem singers learned to avoid risking the bad press and they mostly just played it safe and straight.

That is until Gaye strolled to the Forum's center court that day. He was dressed almost like a conservative politician, having arrived in a blue suit and tie and mirrored aviator sunglasses. No one could see his eyes. They didn't have to. All they had to do was listen. A magical moment was coming.

Thing is, the performance almost didn't happen at all. The Lakers initially hired Lionel Richie, who was pop music's biggest star at the time. But for some reason NBA Commissioner Larry O'Brien rejected him, according to Lon Rosen, then the Lakers' director of promotions. So the team next hired Gaye, one of Rosen's favorite singers. The day before the All-Star Game, however, things got dicey. Gaye and Rosen got into an argument at rehearsal over the length of the singer's version, which was to last five minutes. Rosen told him that was way too long because CBS had allotted only two minutes for the TV broadcast. The singer got angry. "He was really disturbed with me," said Rosen, now a William Morris Agency exec in Beverly Hills. "He wouldn't talk to me, he wouldn't even look at me."

Finally, Rosen caught a break. The players were practicing there at the same time, and NBA star Julius "Dr. J" Erving came over to play peacemaker. Erving, also a big Gaye fan, was able to convince the temperamental singer that the shorter version would work. "Julius just said, 'Let's get this done, the players wanna hear it,'" Rosen said.

The next day, Rosen was still nervous as game time approached, and Gaye gave him plenty of reason to be. The performer arrived at 12:25 p.m., almost an hour late, and barely in time to walk on court and sing. "Remember, this was before cell phones, so there was no way to contact him," Rosen said. "I had an usherette standing by getting ready to sing in case he didn't show up."

Gaye, of course, brought the house down with his amazingly soulful performance, which lasted a manageable two minutes and 35 seconds. Then, true to his enigmatic image, he just walked out of the building, declining to watch the game he had just energized. "It was almost a surreal experience," Rosen said.

The crowd loved it. But not everyone did. "When it was done, I thought I was fired," Rosen recalled. "Commissioner O'Brien just screamed at me, 'That was the most disrespectful thing I've ever heard!'"

But Rosen's boss, Lakers owner Dr. Jerry Buss, quickly reassured him that he thought it was great. In the ensuing weeks, however, the Lakers received so many complaints from viewers, Rosen had to craft an official apology letter just to respond to all of them. One phone call he didn't mind getting came from Gaye himself, who warmly thanked Rosen for setting it all up.

Neither of them knew it then, but that rendition was one of Gaye's last TV performances. His late arrival that day helped cement his reputation for the kind of erratic behavior that today would embarrass Amy Winehouse. Yep, he had personal demons, and his mental state grew even more fragile years later, after the tragic death of his singing partner (and rumored lover) Tammi Terrell in 1969. Gaye was so distraught at Terrell's funeral that he reportedly talked to her casket as if she were still alive. It got even weirder. For a time, he reportedly moved to Hawaii and lived in a bread truck. (What the . . .?) Then he tried out for the Detroit Lions at the age of 30. Despite his serious training, Marvin was no Marvin Harrison—he didn't make the football team. But he invited his new friends, Lions players Lem Barney and Mel Farr, to join him in the recording studio. You can hear them talking in the beginning of *What's Going On?*, an album that he made to shake his depression. And in our view, any song that begins with a Detroit Lion saying, "This is a really groovy party, man!" has to be considered a classic. The critics and the public thought so, too. It was a huge hit. He enjoyed a few more hit albums before losing creative steam in the late '70s.

Gaye scored a big comeback with the release of *Sexual Healing* in 1983, but the renewed success would be short-lived. There were good reasons, after all, why author David Ritz's biography on Gaye was titled, *Divided Soul*. But in a way, it's fitting that a troubled, outspoken artist like Gaye could give a performance that symbolized a nation finally healing its wounds from past political fights. His All-Star Game vocals did just that, in our opinion. Just like only Nixon could go to China, maybe only a searingly honest artist like Marvin Gaye—who grew up in racial segregation in Washington, D.C.—had the credibility to tell a scarred nation that it might be cool to be patriotic again, and that it was okay to drop the cynicism and trust America's beautiful promises once more. This was the same guy, after all, who was the first to mix commercial R&B and politics successfully with *What's Going On?* And with that, he gave the black community a voice on the radio airwaves that matched what radical political groups like the Black Panthers were expressing on the streets.

But with his special National Anthem, Gaye was singing a tune very different from what he used to. It was one that celebrated America after his generation had spent years idealistically questioning it. And he was doing it to the beat of a different drummer, literally; this time with a distinctly black sound that was heartfelt and hopeful. He wasn't saying it loud, as James Brown had urged. But he was, in his own way, repeating the latter half of the Brown lyric: I'm black and I'm proud.

"It reminded me of Jimi Hendrix's anthem at Woodstock," Kareem Abdul-Jabbar told the *Los Angeles Times.* "Marvin changed the whole template and that broadened people's minds. It illuminated the concept, 'We're black and we're Americans.' We can have a different interpretation [of the anthem], and that's okay."

For Rosen, the performance then and now has universal appeal. "There were no color barriers with Marvin Gaye," he said. "The white players and black players both loved it."

Intentional or not, Gaye delivered a performance that signified a shift in the nation's mood. America was about to get its swagger back. A year later, the US dominated the 1984 Summer Olympics, kickstarting the decade's positive tone of patriotism and economic good times. Regardless of one's opinion of Ronald Reagan, he was re-elected president in a landslide that year, and flag-waving commercial jingles popped up on our TVs faster than you can say *Born in the USA*. If those Summer Olympics were the nation's "main course" for this feel-good era, then Gaye's anthem had set the table.

We're not saying this story has a fairytale ending, of course. A year after the performance, Gaye's life would end in bizarre tragedy. He was shot dead by his father after one of their many arguments. And many would say that America certainly didn't exactly live happily ever after, either. But his brilliant performance that day will never be forgotten. And, at the very least, it changed the way *The Star-Spangled Banner* was sung at sporting events forevermore.

The anthem likely affected the players that day, too. Erving, seemingly inspired by the blazing vocals of his favorite singer, went out and scored 25 points in 28 minutes, winning All-Star Game MVP honors. In November 1986, about two and a half years after Gaye was killed, Erving was finishing his own incredible career with the Philadelphia 76ers. He and the Sixers were in Oakland to play the Golden State Warriors, and he addressed the sold-out crowd during this stop in his "farewell tour" to NBA fans. Erving remarked how Oakland and the Bay Area had always appreciated great artists. He then ended his speech with an unmistakable reference to a Gaye song: "So in the words of my favorite artist, let's get it on."

The hoops superstar then dramatically dropped the microphone and headed to center court to start the game. The crowd roared in approval. And for one brief but wonderful moment, the world of NBA basketball and the music of the late Marvin Gaye had intersected once again.

GREATEST NATIONAL ANTHEM PERFORMANCES

1. MARVIN GAYE, NBA ALL-STAR GAME *Los Angeles, February 1983*

What else is there to say? It was soulful, cool and even sexy. This is the greatest version ever. And maybe the only one that also would be perfect for a make-out session.

2. KELLY CLARKSON, NBA PLAYOFF GAME *Boston, April 2005*

A straightforward, workmanlike version. But her all-world pipes and an emotional big-game crowd make this great effort an easy choice.

3. WHITNEY HOUSTON, SUPER BOWL XXV
Tampa, January 1991

The nation had just gone to war in the Persian Gulf, and an unusually boisterous Super Bowl crowd channeled their patriotism and anxiety into Houston's vibrant, flawless rendition.

4. THE GRATEFUL DEAD, SAN FRANCISCO GIANTS OPENING DAY
San Francisco, April 1993

Enjoying Jerry Garcia, Bob Weir and co. harmonize nearly perfectly in front of an adoring hometown crowd is about as American as mom, apple pie and marijuana. Well, two out of three ain't bad.

5A. DIXIE CHICKS, SUPER BOWL XXXVII   *San Diego, January 2003*

A great rendition sung by one of our favorite groups just before the Buccaneers throttled the Raiders to win the franchise's first NFL title. Erica likes the performance because she admires fiery lead singer Natalie Maines, while Chris likes it because it was the last Raiders game he watched with any kind of optimism.

5B. MAURICE CHEEKS/NATALIE GILBERT, BLAZERS VS. MAVERICKS PLAYOFF GAME   *Portland, April 2005*

If this one doesn't put a lump in your throat, check your pulse. Natalie Gilbert, then a 13-year-old Portland eighth-grader with a great voice, forgot the words while singing before a 20,000 fans at a playoff game. But her personal hell turned heartwarming when Blazers coach Maurice Cheeks quickly joined her at mid-court, singing with her (as the crowd joined in) until she recovered and finished strong. Gilbert immediately hugged the coach, who reportedly told her: "Don't worry, kid, everyone has a bad game every once in a while."

WORST NATIONAL ANTHEM PERFORMANCES

1. ROSEANNE, SAN DIEGO PADRES GAME *San Diego, July 1990*

Ever crack a joke you thought was harmless but actually offended the entire room? Roseanne has. Her "joke" on *The Star-Spangled Banner* only lasted a few minutes, but it will live forever in infamy. And the "room" in her case was a stadium filled with thousands of fans. She sang the National Anthem unforgivably off-key, and then grabbed her crotch and spit, trying to parody ballplayers' bad habits. All she did was offend the entire country so much that President George H.W. Bush issued a statement condemning her.

2. CARL LEWIS, CHICAGO BULLS VS. NEW JERSEY NETS GAME *Chicago, April 1993*

We don't want to jump to conclusions, but if the crowd laughs *at* you during the National Anthem, things might not be going so well. Welcome to Carl Lewis' nightmare. The Olympic track star did an okay job with this one until his voice cracked halfway through, drawing derisive laughter from fans. Moments later, Lewis actually paused for a second before delivering some lines, as if he was afraid to hit—and miss—certain notes. It didn't last 20 minutes, it only felt that way.

3. STEVEN TYLER (AEROSMITH), 85TH INDIANAPOLIS 500 *Indianapolis, May 2001*

Can you crash and burn at the Indy 500 without getting in a car? Tyler's version wasn't as bad as Carl Lewis', but it was close. Not only did the Aerosmith frontman struggle to hit some high notes in front of the patriotic racing fans, he also made the almost sacrilegious choice to change the lyrics from "home of the brave" to "home of the Indianapolis 500."

4. R. KELLY: BERNARD HOPKINS VS. JERMAIN TAYLOR MIDDLEWEIGHT BOXING MATCH *Las Vegas, December 2005*

Can't fault a guy for trying, right? Unless his name is R. Kelly. R&B's favorite alleged pedophile, already in trouble with the law, tried to rework the National Anthem with a fast, upbeat melody, replete with two couples salsa dancing behind him in the middle of the ring. Kelly, who was booed when introduced, had no luck in getting the crowd to clap along. Oscar De La Hoya, standing inside the ring, actually looked scared at what was occurring. HBO cameras, sensing disaster, spent most of the song trained on anything but Kelly, as his attempt at Marvin Gaye-like inspiration fell brutally short.

5. LEE GREENWOOD: CLEVELAND BROWNS FOOTBALL GAME
Cleveland, September 2006

The country singer whose bread and butter is the ultra-patriotic tune, *Proud to Be an American,* had an amazingly hard time hitting the anthem's tougher notes before a sold-out Browns crowd on this day. On the home-made videotape of this performance that's bouncing around the Internet, one fan can be heard asking sarcastically, "Who is this, Carl Lewis?" For a vocalist, there is no bigger insult.

ATHLETES WHO TRIED TO CROSS OVER INTO MUSIC

Where does it start, this dubious idea that rock (or rap/country/jazz) music will be a hot seller if a famous athlete—painfully untalented or not—is the "musician"? NBA and NFL stars such as Shaq, Ron Artest and Deion Sanders have cut at least one rap album each within the past decade, which makes them either delusional or shrewdly ambitious. Maybe they're both. Even Kobe Bryant recorded a hip-hop CD titled *Visions* in 2000. None of these albums did very well, and Kobe's chances of becoming a hit rapper are as slim as his being elected president of N.O.W.

Do these albums get made due to a number of bad decisions by managers and advisors who only want to strike while the fire is hot? Or are they smart for using this strategy to squeeze a few more apples from the money tree? You can almost envision an athlete's "people" talking in the conference room before a record deal is struck: "Kobe is the best player on the Lakers, who probably have 10 million fans. If only 10% of those schmucks buy this crap, then we have a platinum album. Do the math, baby!"

The trend is going global, too. Tony Parker is the quiet point guard who is as well known for being Eva Longoria's husband as he is for winning NBA titles with the San Antonio Spurs. But Parker, already accused of going Hollywood with his actress wife, now may be "going Paris"—by way of Compton. Huh? Let us explain. Parker is one of the classiest pro athletes around and one of a handful of French stars playing in the NBA, which makes him an unlikely choice to be an aspiring hip-hop artist. But, *oui, oui,* it's true. Parker released a French-language rap album in early 2007, simply titled TP, his initials. The album has timeless classics such as *Pourquoi Je Rappe?* and *Effet Papillon,* which probably won't be popping up on a Nelly LP soon. Honestly, we're not sure if this Parker album shows that the NBA truly is a global game, or if it's a simple, chilling sign that the Apocalypse is near. Given that Oscarwinner Jamie Foxx makes a guest appearance—along with a French rapper named Booba—we're officially leaning toward the Apocalypse.

Closer to home, there's Allen Iverson and his rap CD *Misunderstood.* The 2001 album was never released. Why? Probably not because of the profane and misogynistic lyrics; those are standard features of a lot of music these days. Nope, the kicker here was most likely the gay slur that appears in the lyrics of the song *40 Bars.* We're no music critics, but when civil rights groups and NBA Commissioner David Stern both are criticizing your prose, it's probably time to stick to your day job. Former New York Mets outfielder Lastings Milledge got himself into similar hot water in 2007. Milledge appeared on a hip-hop recording titled *Bend Ya Knees,* which had lyrics with the kind of language that would have gotten Don Imus fired—again! Six months after the Mets front office denounced the song, they traded Milledge to the Washington Nationals.

And don't forget about Deion Sanders. He was a football player. He was a baseball player. He was a hedonist. Then he was a Bible-thumper. What he was *not* was a rapper. Only he didn't get the memo. So, he recorded *Prime Time* in 1995, a hip-hop album named after—who else?—himself and his flashy nickname. Would you expect a guy so self-absorbed that he named his kids Deion Jr. and Deiondra to stop there? We didn't, either. In 2005, he re-released the same songs as club re-mixes, which only proved that any bad idea can always be made worse. . . with another bad idea! Speaking of bad ideas, Sanders and his family star in their own reality show, called *Prime Time Love,* which premiered on Oxygen in early 2008.

Meanwhile, here is a stranger-than-fiction story that doesn't need to be invented. MC Hammer never made the leap from sports to music or vice versa. The future multimillion-album seller was actually immersed in both worlds at a very young age. Hammer—real name Stanley Burrell—was literally plucked from the Oakland Coliseum parking lot by A's owner Charlie Finley. Finley was known for being mercurial—that's fancy talk for "arrogant, cheap and psycho." The eccentric owner was impressed by Burrell's dance moves, and he hired the teenager on the spot as a team employee. But it wasn't just any old job. Incredibly, he made the youngster a team Vice President. A's players gave Hammer his nickname because he looked just like a young Hammerin' Hank Aaron, the former Home Run King. Some of those players were the first investors in Hammer's hip-hop tapes, which he sold from the trunk of his car on Oakland's streets in the earliest days of his recording career. The rest—including Hammer's wild success, followed by his sad and surprising bankruptcy—is sports-music history.

Today, Hammer is on the rebound. He is one of the business partners in a start-up company called DanceJam.com, which is a YouTube-like website for dance videos. Perfect for a guy whose life was changed forever when he was "discovered" as a kid after merely showing off his dance moves.

SUPER BOWL HALFTIME PERFORMANCES

Looking over the rosters of past Super Bowl Halftime Show performers can be more entertaining than some of the performances themselves. Don't get us wrong. The shows have gotten much better in the past five years, when notoriously uptight NFL honchos finally loosened up and caught up (mostly) with the times. Any sporting event that invites Prince to its big game—with all the potential for "His Purple Royal Badness" to misbehave—as the NFL did in 2007, has become pretty cool. Prince didn't disappoint, either. He got revenge on the Foo Fighters, who once covered Prince's *Darling Nikki* against his wishes, by singing their *Best of You* during that halftime show. Prince even generated a touch of eyebrow-raising controversy by placing his phallic-shaped guitar between his legs and silhouetting it behind the stage curtain in a suggestive way. But for a lot of years, this type of hip artist was the exception, not the rule.

During the Super Bowl's first couple of years, when it was known as the "AFL-NFL World Championship Game," we'll give the NFL's leaders a mulligan. Those games took place in the late 1960s, long before league officials in any sport sought a fusion between popular music and sports. Even so, they acquitted themselves well by a) following old-fashioned tradition by getting a college marching band, and b) making an admirably pointed statement about civil rights by hiring the marching band from Grambling University, an all-black university. Doing that may sound obvious now, but in many parts of the country, the late 1960s was no more tolerant a time than the late 1860s. Even in this subtle way, the NFL deserves credit for doing the right, forward-thinking thing at a critical time in our nation's history.

Unfortunately, the shows weren't always that cool. For almost 30 years, we argue, they were mostly a cavalcade of crap. Want proof? How can you explain Anita Bryant? Carol Channing—twice? New Kids on the Block? Enrique Iglesias? Helen O'Connell? Chubby Checker? And something called the Los Angeles Super Drill Team. (Fill in easy porn joke here: ____)

To be fair, there were occasional highlights: Ella Fitzgerald, Tony Bennett, Stevie Wonder and James Brown each performed. But besides these rare bright spots, nearly every act hired between 1970 and 1999 was so lame, there must be only two plausible scenarios to explain it:

1) Lawrence Welk chaired the selection committee, or 2) The über-wholesome group Up With People—which sang soulless covers of hit songs at several halftimes—had nude photos of the commissioner. We're not accusing the NFL of wanting to bore people to tears and ruin their TV ratings during these years. But if that was the goal, mission accomplished.

However, the NFL has finished strong in the last handful of years. In addition to Prince, they've featured U2, The Rolling Stones, Paul McCartney, Tom Petty, Mary J. Blige and Aerosmith. Okay, except for Blige and U2, they're all past their respective primes. But at least these are quality acts that still possess an acceptable level of cool. By hiring them, the NFL demonstrated that it still has the kind of savvy marketing skills that have made pro football America's most popular sport.

(See, we made it through without mentioning any "wardrobe malfunctions." It *can* be done.)

Worst Super Bowl Halftime Performances

1. Up With People: Too bad they weren't down on crap. This conservative nonprofit of volunteers ruined big sporting and political events all over the country by singing and dancing to saccharine-sweet versions of pop songs. What's amazing is that Up With People did the halftime show a mind-boggling four times within eleven years. Where was drug-testing in the NFL offices when we needed it?

2. Michael Jackson: The year was 1993 and it was the end of that era known as: "God, Michael is creepy, but at least he's not a pedophile." But all of that changed a few months later, when accusations were made about Jackson's alleged "inappropriate" behavior with kids. Did we mention that his halftime performance was dedicated to the children of the world? We'll just go on to the next one . . .

3. Blues Brothers & ZZ Top: The Blues Brothers without John Belushi? That's like *American Idol* without Paula Abdul. They may be wasted and unintelligible, but it's just not the same without them. Remember when the Blues Brothers were part of the "Not Ready for Prime Time Players?" Now they're just the "Past their Prime Time" players. Sure, Jim Belushi tried his best to fill his big bro's shoes and an aging Dan Aykroyd worked hard to be Elroy Blues again at this 1997 big game. But watching this was like seeing your uncles perform in a PTA talent show. In between cringing, you're just left wondering: "People used to think this was funny?"

4. *Carol Channing:* Hey, it was the early '70s. Great rock bands like The Who and The Stones were in their prime. So were R&B gods like Al Green and Curtis Mayfield. So, of course the Super Bowl halftime act in 1970 and '72 was . . . Carol Channing?!? Yes, it's true. The campy, gravel-voiced Broadway singer was hired twice in a span of three years. In the words of Li'l Jon: What?!

5a. *Chubby Checker:* One look at the 1988 entertainment roster leaves you with one thought: What 150-year-old man was in charge of booking the talent? How else to explain the presence of one Chubby Checker doing *The Twist* for the millionth time in front of a slack-jawed public. Checker, the 1950s icon whose only other hit 30 years previous was the groundbreaking sequel, *Let's Twist Again,* was joined by The Rockettes dancers and 88 grand pianos. Unless Checker hijacked a time machine and crashed the party from 1955, fans should have definitely gotten their money back.

5b. *Janet Jackson/Justin Timberlake:* Sorry, we broke our promise. After giving it some thought, we had to put it on this list, didn't we? The wardrobe malfunction. Nipplegate. Blah, blah, blah. We know it's been talked to death. But the sad truth is, if Ms. Jackson just had kept her top on, we all would have been spared one million lame Jay Leno/Robin Williams jokes, not to mention the FCC's subsequent wrath on fairly innocuous shows such as Howard Stern's.

SPORTS TEAM SONGS: THE GOOD, THE NOT BAD AND THE AWFUL

The Good:

1. SUPER BOWL SHUFFLE: The *Citizen Kane* of sports songs—this 1985 Chicago Bears rap video changed everything. Now can they please change it back? Kidding! (Sort of.) Winners of Super Bowl XX, this Bears team is one of the best NFL teams ever. And this video is a classic. It's a 1980s music time capsule and proof that plenty of white AND black people can't dance to save their lives.

The Not Bad:

2. SAN DIEGO SUPER CHARGERS: This late 1970s disco classic just barely pre-dated MTV, so there's no video. But here's our suggestion for one: We want the whole Chargers team to dress like Ponch and/or Jon from *ChiPs* and roll into Qualcomm Stadium on motorcycles while this tune blares from the speakers. Who wouldn't be a Chargers fan after that?

The Awful:

3. THE BASEBALL BOOGIE: This simply must be seen to be believed. We're not as shocked that this 1986 LA Dodgers rap video actually happened, as we are that Pedro Guerrero, who appears prominently in a pink satin jacket, didn't pay millions to have the tape destroyed. Not that other ex-Dodgers, such as Bob Welch, Jerry Reuss and Mariano Duncan come off any better. We love the B-list celebrities they recruited to appear in it: Is that really Ed Begley Jr.? Mayor Tom Bradley? What, Alf wasn't available? Like all groundbreaking songs, there is something to be learned here. We're just not sure what it is, other than that Orel Hershiser dances like a guy who's waited too long for the bathroom.

4. WE WEAR THE SILVER, WE WEAR THE BLACK: It should have been called "When the Raiders Jumped the Shark." This 1987 Raiders rap video not only was a shameless rip-off of the Chicago Bears' hit song, it also officially ended the Raiders' 20-year run of dominance. And they have never really gotten the magic back. We would blame it on Los Angeles if, you know, we actually could admit they ever moved down there in the first place. Look for a young Matt Millen doing an air guitar solo while wearing a Tommy Lee-like black wig. The whole thing is such a train wreck that . . . okay, let's watch it again.

5A. UNIVERSITY OF ARIZONA BASKETBALL TEAM: Picture your worst karaoke moment ever captured on tape. Then picture, to your horror, that it is publicly replayed for you over and over again. Welcome to Tom Tolbert's hell. Tolbert co-hosts a sports talk radio program on KNBR in San Francisco, where listeners often razz the NBA journeyman for the rap song he made with hoops teammates at the University of Arizona. Another 1987 copycat of the Chicago Bears hit, this college team featured Tolbert and another future NBA pro, Sean Elliott. But Tolbert will never live down punctuating his last line with a primal scream: "Huhhhhhh!" More like . . . Huh?

5B. THE GRABOWSKI SHUFFLE: Mike Ditka rapping and dancing? It's true, and we have the videotape to prove it. Best of all, it's not even the funniest part of this video about "Grabowskis," Ditka's term of endearment for hard-working overachievers. Ditka was still the revered coach of the Chicago Bears when this classic was filmed. It starts with Ditka picking his "Grabowskis" from a stadium filled with extras so hyper they must be on Red Bull—or something harder (It was the '80s, after all). Then it inexplicably ends in a nightclub where Ditka's multicultural group of "Grabowskis" rap about their blue-collar exploits, while audience members work extremely hard to show just how much doggone fun they're having! Amazon.com lists its release date as 1991, but this is pure-and-concentrated 1980s kitsch. This era was clearly a Golden Age of mind-blowingly cheesy team rap videos, and this one does not disappoint at all.

WORST JOCKS WHO
MOONLIGHTED AS "MUSICIANS"

1. SHAQUILLE O'NEAL: His first rap single, released in 1993, was called *I'm Outstanding*. Listeners could have sued him for false advertising. O'Neal had five (!) albums in the '90s, and they all fell as flat as his free throws. They included *Shaq Diesel* (whatever that is, the price is surely dropping) and *Shaq Fu: The Return*. His last one in '99 is inexplicably titled *Greatest Hits*. Which raises a question that Buddhist monks for years will ponder: If you've had zero hits, how can you have any greatest hits?

2. TERRY BRADSHAW: Look up the words "unintentional comedy" in the dictionary, and there must be a picture of this Louisiana good ol' boy turned Steeler quarterback looking forlornly out the window. It's actually a country album cover from the '70s called *I'm So Lonesome I Could Cry*. Which sounds a lot better than I'm So Talent-less I Could Cry, doesn't it?

3. STEVE YEAGER, JERRY REUSS, JAY JOHNSTONE AND RICK MONDAY: After winning the 1981 World Series, someone made these LA Dodgers an offer they couldn't refuse: to record Queen's *We Are the Champions*. Problem is, when appearing on the Solid Gold TV show, their vocals were as out-of-tune as the leisure suits the quartet sported were out-of-date. They called themselves the "High 5," an appropriate name being that there were only four of them. Hmmm, four guys who hang out together all the time in a locker room doing a Queen song—I'm sure the irony was lost on them.

4. JOE FRAZIER: This boxer's band was called The Knockouts (Get it? Get it?). Maybe they should have called it Punch Drunk. Or better yet, Unanimous Decision, because critics were unified in their views on the second career of Ali's nemesis: Smokin' Joe can't sing.

5. TROY HUDSON: This NBA backup point guard has had a rough year. He had a career-threatening injury to his hip in December 2007. But a few months before that, he released one of the worst-selling rap albums of all time. It was titled *Undrafted*. But given that it reportedly sold 78 copies in its first week, maybe he should have called it *Unwanted*.

ATHLETES TURNED GOOD MUSICIANS

1. WAYMAN TISDALE: The 12-year NBA power forward (1985-97) and college All-American is now an easy-listening jazz guitarist who regularly tours with his band. Chris once saw Tisdale in concert where onstage he yelled, "Hello, Windsor County!" Problem was, he was in Sonoma County. But it's cool. His instrumental version of Smokey Robinson's *Cruisin'* is almost as smooth as his low-post moves in his prime.

2. JACK MCDOWELL: You would expect a guy nicknamed "Black Jack" to have a wild side, right? Former American League Cy Young winner Jack McDowell not only is a decent guitarist, he also recorded a few CDs with his alternative band, Stickfigure. He befriended Eddie Vedder at the peak of both of their fame in the mid-'90s. Perhaps trying to inject some street cred into his Stanford grad image, McDowell was once arrested for starting a brawl in a New Orleans bar while he and Vedder were hanging out.

3. LENNY DINARDO: Who? Yep, the Oakland A's pitcher isn't exactly a household name. But he is an accomplished musician who plays guitar in an indie rock band. DiNardo and fellow ex-Red Sox pitcher Bronson Arroyo were known for jamming onstage with rocker/Red Sox general manager Theo Epstein when they played in Beantown together.

4. BERNIE WILLIAMS: He had a great run with the Yankees. But don't worry, the All-Star outfielder has a promising second career now that he's retired. Williams, born in Puerto Rico, is a respected classically trained guitarist who has released his own album, *The Journey Within*. Williams has a wide range of musical interests: jazz, Brazilian, pop and Latin sounds, and some guy named Paul McCartney recently signed him to the ex-Beatle's label.

5. PAUL O'NEILL: During his baseball career, the fiery outfielder won the hearts of baseball fans with his on-field passion—first with the Cincinnati Reds and then with the New York Yankees. But O'Neill was an even bigger fan of John Mellencamp. On New Year's Eve in 1998, the then-Yankee had a dream come true at Indianapolis' Murat Theater, where O'Neill, a pretty good amateur drummer, played onstage with his rock star hero. "I was more nervous than . . . in the World Series," O'Neill told the *New York Daily News*.

ONE SHINING MASHUP

There are two kinds of people in this world: Those who love *One Shining Moment,* and those who don't. CBS first used the song after the 1987 NCAA Men's College Basketball Championship, setting it to a video montage of tournament highlights. It's been a tournament-ending tradition ever since. Some love the song's old-fashioned wholesomeness, and believe it's perfect for an amateur sport consisting of peach-fuzzed college kids. Still others think the tune is too schmaltzy and grew outdated almost immediately after it was introduced. Even if you're in that more cynical camp, *One Shining Moment,* just like politicians, hookers and the designated hitter, has stuck around long enough to be respected.

But in 2008, CBS offered a smart promotion for college hoops fans just as the tournament began. Fans could go to a special "*One Shining Moment* Mashup" page on NCAA.com, where for the first time ever they could create their own 50-second video of tournament highlights.

It was a surprisingly hip idea from CBS and the NCAA, a normally staid duo. The March Madness mashup page was a very cool way to advertise the tournament. It also gave a modern nod to the YouTube generation while retaining the original song penned by songwriter David Barrett. Here's to hoping that the tournament's video mashup becomes as much of an annual tradition as *One Shining Moment.*

But we also suggest a musical mashup contest, where DJs mix a hip-hop song with *One Shining Moment,* like they did with Jay-Z and The Verve to create a blended tune called *Bittersweet Dirt Off Your Shoulder.* We'll go first: How about doing a mashup with Eminem and call it *One Shining Mosh?* See, it's not so hard. Take it and run with it, CBS. That one was a freebie.

3 WHERE PURPLE DOES NOT REIGN: *Sports & Fashion*

WHEN ORLANDO BROWN WENT TO PLAY FOR THE BALTIMORE Ravens after spending his entire career with the Cleveland Browns, he said: "I hated putting on that purple uniform, and I hated that raven bird." Who can blame him? No one looks good in purple (except for Prince). This is why we hate all teams that feature purple in any way, shape or form. The irony is that Orlando Brown longed for the orange and brown of Cleveland. Now that's a color-combo that only Brownies can pull off.

Team colors and uniforms, along with team mascots and logos, serve many purposes. They are an attempt to intimidate the competition, instill confidence in their team and, ultimately, shape the character of a team. John Madden even felt that certain numbers on uniforms carried certain attributes: 12 meant a leader with charisma and 22 always signified speed, while 16 showed a bit of softness—tell that to Joe Montana.

Sports uniforms can be traced back to uniforms on the battlefield, allowing everyone to know immediately what side you were on. Remember the Red Coats? How about the Blue and the Gray? In baseball, players in the late 1800s were required to wear matching socks, hence the White Stockings (now Sox) and Red Stockings (now Reds). These days, unis are much more elaborate, and have become enduring symbols of beloved teams. Some we wish were a little less enduring, like the Tampa Bay Bucs of the '70s, with their cheesy winking pirate, and the Houston Astros rainbow jerseys that were worn, surprisingly enough, well past the '70s.

For our fashion chapter, it would be very easy to simply rank the best and worst looking uniforms in each league. We'll do a little of that, but we feel that this is a completely subjective debate, and also feeds into the insulting theory that women choose teams based on how "cute" their uniforms are. We have bigger, more fashionable fish to fry. There are burning, uniform questions that we've been struggling with for years.

1. Why do these teams change their uniform designs so damn often? Is it just to gouge consumers and make them buy new stuff year in and year out, just like in the fashion world? One year it's low-rise skinny jeans, the next it's high-waisted with a full leg! Who can keep up?

2. For all of the changes that are made, why don't uniforms look better? With Dolce & Gabbana designing AC Milan uniforms in Italy, and Stella McCartney designing fashions for Adidas, why is the American sports world so backwards when it comes to fashion?

3. Why is it that some leagues are strict with adherence to uniform regulations and others more lax—like Major League Baseball? "Paging Manny Ramirez. Please report to the commish's office to explain why you are wearing pajama bottoms to work."

4. Although some leagues seem to have evolved and incorporated high-tech fabrics into their uniforms, why are baseball players— the boys of summer—still wearing double-knit, polyester pants? Why do they have to wear this hot, itchy, heavy fabric for a good five+ hours per day, 162 games per season—many of which are played during prime sun hours?

5. And why, oh why, do female fans have such few choices when it comes to attractive sports fan apparel? And why do these manufacturers think that the only color women like is pink?

To get to the bottom of these pressing questions, we went to some experts in the field of professional sports uniforms. The first person we turned to was Paul Lukas, the mildly obsessive mind behind the Uni Watch website. In his daily blog known as Uni Watch, Lukas chronicles every detail of every uniform on the planet—from font size to stitch color and from the underbill of a player's hat to the cleats on his shoes. Every day, he documents even the most minute of changes in unis on his site UniWatchBlog.com, and he periodically files lengthier trend pieces for ESPN.com. To be fair, he describes Uni Watch as "The Obsessive Study of Athletics Aesthetics," so he knows he's a bit on the fanatical side. And he's not alone. His site receives 15,000 hits per day—meaning he has quite a few fellow uniform fanatics.

After spending countless hours on his site, using it as a valued resource, we thought Lukas would be the perfect person to ask about some of our burning questions about uniforms. (We knew we had found a kindred spirit, too, as he shared our huge disdain for purple.) In agreeing to do the interview, Lukas did, however, make it clear to us that he considers himself an expert in design, rather than fashion. In fact, he asked us not to refer to the f-word when it came to his site. Fair enough, we said. And we headed to Brooklyn to meet the man behind Uni Watch.

Lukas is a thin, spectacled guy with a goatee. He's more of a Brooklyn-type hipster than your typical sports junkie. He opened the door quickly, then rushed back to his computer. "Sorry guys, we're going to have to make this quick. There's breaking news going on right now." Breaking news in the uniform world? Unless some baseball player dropped his drawers last night during the playoffs, we couldn't really think of anything that might be considered "breaking news." We were wrong.

Lukas explained that Manny Corpas, a pitcher for the Rockies, was being investigated for illegally doctoring the baseball in a playoff game the night before. Apparently, Corpas was seen pouring water or soda onto his jersey, rubbing dirt on it, and was then accused of touching the damp area before throwing a pitch. Breaking news, indeed!

For the first half of the interview, we learned a lot about how Lukas had started out in product and package design, has always been obsessed with details, and he then turned his critical eye on unsuspecting uniforms. First he had a column in the *Village Voice,* then *Slate,* and now writes his daily blog and ESPN.com pieces. Every weekday by 10:15 a.m., Lukas posts his blog on breaking uniform news, and his followers spend the day vigorously debating his commentary. When we asked how many women followed his column, thinking that the aesthetics of uniforms were something women could sink their teeth into, Lukas said he didn't know exactly. "Very few. I would say one to two percent," he said. "If I ever thought I was going to get laid doing Uni Watch . . . that's not going to happen."

Tempted to discuss this further, but knowing we had limited time, Erica changed the subject, "So why do these teams change their unis so often?" Lukas explained that back in the old days, uniforms rarely changed. "But it was TV coverage that changed uniforms the most significantly over the years," he told us. "We can thank Charlie Finley who, in 1963 when baseball games started being televised, changed the A's colors to their current gold and green. That changed everything." Teams began choosing vibrant colors and bold logos and that greatly affected the look of uniforms of today. The branding of a team was born. And now, as team unis are presented on HD televisions and all over the Web, the look and feel of each team's logo and uniform is tinkered with more than ever. "But," Lukas continued, "many changes are an attempt to sell more merchandise." This is why you'll see teams adding alternate and throw-back jerseys to rack up more sales. To be fair to the teams, big changes in the uniform, color scheme or logo usually happen for a reason—like an owner change, a new stadium, or when a team is in a slump and needs to freshen up their look. Many teams harken back to a more successful period in team history, and they try to emulate those colors or logos.

Ten minutes left. "Okay, then with all of these changes in uniforms all the time, why aren't there any fancy pants designers in American sports?" we asked, mentioning our friends Dolce & Gabbana and Stella McCartney. Lukas told us that since 2002, the US Olympic team's uniforms were designed by a fashion designer—Roots, out of Canada. Erica did know this, but she doesn't really consider Roots a "designer." And yes, we all found it ironic that the US went to a Canadian company to outfit the team. (Maybe that's why for the 2008 Olympics, all-American designer Ralph Lauren designed the team's togs.) "No, like real designers, like Marc Jacobs or DVF or Zac Posen!?" Erica asked. Knowing that the f-word is not Lukas' forte, we'll forgive him for his lack of depth here. He did recall, though, that back in 1980, there was a spread in a now-defunct magazine called *Inside Sports* that contained baseball uniforms designed by Geoffrey Beane, Oscar de la Renta and Halston, modeled by the likes of announcers Phil Rizzuto, Jack Buck and Harry Caray. "The results, rather predictably, were pretty brutal," Lukas wrote in his blog. And thankfully the uniforms were never used during play.

"In the late '80s, Alexander Julian designed the Hornets uniforms," Lukas told us. "He started the teal/purple craze, now denounced by the Diamondbacks." Great, thanks Alexander Julian. After further research, we discovered that Julian also ~~ruined~~ designed unis for the UNC Tar Heels, before moving on to Minor League baseball's Oklahoma Red-Hawks and Charlotte Knights. He then shifted to auto racing, where he designed fire suits for Mario and Michael Andretti—which included teal, purple, salmon and ochre armbands at the Indy 500. All those who think these colors should be nowhere near any sport of any kind, raise your hand. Okay, you can put your hand down and continue reading.

But this did get us thinking that the NBA is the only pro sports league that seems open to more input from fashion designers. Aside from Julian, Oscar-winning costume designer Eiko Ishioka created the Houston Rockets unis and renowned menswear designer Jhane Barnes created the Orlando Magic uniforms. And in 2004, Mark Cuban, Dallas Mavericks owner and certified loose cannon, enlisted the help of Sean Combs, a.k.a. P. Diddy, to design the Mavs' away unis. The green and blue creations aren't that different silhouette-wise from regular basketball uniforms, but the font and design are a bit more modern than most, and the team still wears these unis. (The Mavs have always been a bit daring. In 2003-2004, they actually wore a silver uniform, made of Nike's Dri-FIT Shimmer, giving them a metallic finish.) To the NBA, we say: Great work. Although we really are traditionalists at heart, we do like to see things shaken up a bit once in a while.

Back to Lukas: Time was ticking. Next, we wanted to know which leagues were the most strict when it came to unis. Lukas said that the NFL is the strictest of the leagues, followed by the NBA—remember the ban on bling in 2005? "The NHL has more issues with equipment. They are strict about things like hockey sticks, and whether they are regulation or not," Lukas said. And despite a few flare-ups in recent years, including Red Sox manager Terry Francona being questioned about wearing a pullover rather than his uniform top, and Derek Bell being told that he couldn't wear his ridiculously oversized jersey as a tribute to his hip-hop fan-base, Lukas agreed that Major League Baseball is the most lax of all the pro leagues.

And why is the NFL so strict? Mostly to ensure that their corporate sponsors—such as Reebok, who reportedly paid the NFL $250 million in 2002 for a 10-year licensing deal—are represented well on TV. If players start wearing their uniforms any way they want, sponsors are not happy.

To ensure that uniform regulations are enforced, the NFL employs a uniform inspector at each stadium. This inspector checks each player's sock height, pants length, and, above all, that they're not wearing any logo that is not affiliated with the NFL. And if they are, the uniform inspector can enforce fines—from $5,000 for an untucked jersey or a sock violation, to $100,000 for wearing an unlicensed logo during Super Bowl week. (The one thing they really haven't been able to regulate is football players' hair, despite an attempt by the Kansas City Chiefs at the 2008 Owners Meetings to bring the issue to the forefront. Many think this should be an individual's decision, or even a team-by-team decision. Maybe some NFL coaches need to think about adopting George Steinbrenner's zero-tolerance when it comes to long hair and facial hair that extends below the lip on his Yankees).

Here are a few interesting NFL uniform scandals to note:

▶ Back in 1986, Bears quarterback Jim McMahon wore an Adidas headband, which was unlicensed by the NFL. He was warned not to wear the headband in the playoffs by then-commissioner Pete Rozelle. So what did McMahon do? He wore a plain headband on which he wrote "Rozelle," showing just who actually owned him: the NFL. He was fined $5,000, but if a player were to try these antics this year, he would undoubtedly fined upwards of $100,000. Just ask Chicago Bears linebacker Brian Urlacher, who had to pay $100,000 after he was spotted drinking VitaminWater and wearing a VitaminWater hat during Super Bowl Media Week in 2007. Urlacher is a spokesman for the product, but it is not a sanctioned NFL sponsor. Busted.

▶ In 2004, Broncos QB Jake Plummer was threatened with a $30,000 fine for wearing a sticker on his helmet honoring former teammate Pat Tillman, the Army Ranger who was killed in Afghanistan. While Arizona Cardinals players (Tillman's former team) were allowed to wear the stickers for the entire season, other NFL teams were only allowed to wear the decal for one week. Plummer wanted to wear his longer. And he did wear it for an extra week. After a very public back-and-forth, Plummer agreed to remove the sticker and the NFL waived the fine, agreeing to let Plummer film public service announcements in honor of Tillman and show them in stadiums across the country the weekend after Veterans Day. The NFL also donated $250,000 to build the first USO facility in Afghanistan, named after Tillman.

▶ In 2007, several Atlanta Falcons players were fined for uniform violations concerning former Falcons QB Michael Vick, recently convicted for running a dog-fighting ring. Two players wore black under-eye strips that said "MV-7" in support of their jailed quarterback, and one wore a shirt under his jersey that said, "Free Mike Vick"—a shirt that was revealed to TV cameras after he scored a touchdown. In total, the fines added up to $47,500. We can only hope that the NFL takes that money and donates it to the ASPCA or something. (The NFL states that it pools the money from uniform violations and donates it to charity.)

The NBA can be tough on uniform violations, too. In 2006, they banned tights, which some players said helped their circulation and prevent muscle strains. Only players with a doctor's note are able to wear the leggings. Prior to that, the NBA regulated short length, and as we mentioned, in 2005 they banned bling. This was all part of a new dress code that is enforced any time a player is on team or league business—meaning at a game, traveling to or from a game, at a special event or appearing anywhere on behalf of the team. Taken directly from the NBA website, the following is a list of items that players are prohibited from wearing while on team or league business:

▶ Sleeveless shirts

▶ Shorts

▶ T-shirts, jerseys or sports apparel (unless appropriate for the event—e.g. a basketball clinic—team-identified and approved by the team)

▶ Headgear of any kind while a player is sitting on the bench or in the stands at a game, during media interviews, or during a team or league event or appearance (unless appropriate for the event or appearance, team-identified and approved by the team)

▶ Chains, pendants or medallions worn over the player's clothes

▶ Sunglasses while indoors

▶ Headphones (other than on the team bus or plane, or in the team locker room)

Baseball players, on the other hand, do have a lot more freedom of expression. Sure, Major League Baseball has gotten a bit more strict these days, demanding that players remove flags of their home countries from their shoes, hats and bats, and wear only MLB-authorized brands (even if it's a lucky T-shirt). But compared to other leagues, baseball's fashion police are pretty lax. Players can wear necklaces. They can write anything they want on their gloves. And they have much more leeway in how they wear their uniforms: Socks can be showing or not. Pants can be worn right below the knee with stirrups, or loose and baggy.

We are all about free speech, we are all about individual rights, but it's called a UNIFORM for a reason. They are supposed to be UNI-FORM. Uniforms are part of the heart and soul of a team. And although we are shocked that we are typing the following words, we hereby make our plea to Major League Baseball to be more strict and stringent, like your pals over at the NFL and NBA, and regain control of your league! You can leave things like facial hair up to the individual team management, but please, pretty please with sugar on top, stop the insanity with these baggy pajama bottoms and regulate the pants. If you don't, it's clear that the next step will be footie pajamas with trap-drawers in the back. And that, Commissioner Selig, is just too much to bear. You don't have to mandate that players wear actual stirrups—although we'd really, really like it. Right Juan Pierre? (He's the stirrup-wearing outfielder for the Dodgers.) Instead, players could do what A-Rod does and just wear knee socks and fold their pants up a bit. We don't want to take away individual freedoms—we just want players to respect the game and baseball's grand tradition. And not look like buffoons. That's all.

All that being said, we wouldn't mind mixing things up a bit *every once in a while*. If we owned the Yankees or Mets, here's what we would do: No facial hair whatsoever, except handlebar moustaches, like Rollie Fingers, or Brandon Flowers of The Killers, in the "When You Were Young" video. All jerseys would be required to fit properly and not be oversized. Pants must fit well, also—no pajama bottoms. And each player would be required to wear stirrups or knee socks. No jewelry or bling whatsoever. You are at work, and the dress code is part of being at work. Wear that other stuff on your own time. And in September, in conjunction with Fashion Week, Erica would arrange for a guest designer to create special uniforms that the team would wear for the entire week, without Chris knowing, of course. (Imagine Zegna doing a new take on Yankees pinstripes!) Erica would drug Chris and then have the team participate in a runway show in New York City's Bryant Park, and in turn, she would have all of the fashionistas out to the ballpark for a game. Can you imagine seeing all of these haute couture characters, sitting right behind the dugout—*Vogue*'s Anna Wintour with her signature cropped bangs and sunglasses, accompanied by one of her sporty pseudo-boyfriends, like Roger Federer, LeBron James or her new Vogue intern Sean Avery . . . the cast of *Project Runway,* with Heidi Klum, Michael Kors and Nina Garcia . . . and don't forget the entire cast of *America's Next Top Model,* including Tyra, Nigel and J. Alexander, wearing a sports-themed headdress. Again, is that too much to ask? (Chris would answer, but Erica has him bound and gagged in an undisclosed location.)

Well, actually, maybe it is too much to ask. Especially from Major League Baseball. They do allow baggy pants, but they're really not into shaking things up. At least when it comes to fabric choice.

With just two minutes remaining with Lukas, we pressed on: "The NFL, NBA and NHL have all incorporated new high-tech fabrics, and as a result, we've seen an evolution in their uniforms. But why do these baseball players still wear double-knit polyester pants?!" we demanded.

"Well, the fabrics are certainly not as hot as the wool people wore in the 1950s," Lukas told us. It was in 1970 that the Pittsburgh Pirates became the first team to sport the solid-polyester double-knits that we have today, he continued.

That was nearly 40 years ago, we thought. We still wondered why these guys were sporting polyester, when we can hop over to Lululemon and get the most fabulous yoga pants that are lightweight, stylish and wick moisture away? Well, Erica wondered about that while Chris looked out the window.

"The double-knits are lighter, easy to clean, less expensive," he told us. "But I'd like to see them in natural fibers. I hate the way synthetic fibers look. I don't care if they're comfortable. I want them to look good." It reminded us of that *Seinfeld* episode when George talked Steinbrenner into letting the Yankees play in cotton. (Unfortunately, the unis shrunk after one washing, and tore as the Yankees played.) In his blog, Lukas does cover the ill-fated attempt by the White Sox to wear shorts in the first game of a 1976 double-header (the players hated them, and changed into pants for the second game), as well as the Minor League Hollywood Stars pin-striped shorts worn for warm-weather games for two seasons. (Guess no one thought about sliding?) And with that, our uni man Lukas had to go return to his breaking news.

However, we still had a few remaining questions about sports uniforms and fashion. So we headed straight to the source—directly to the very people who manufacture these uniforms. We headed to Majestic Uniforms in Bangor, Pennsylvania—population 5,319.

Driving through the rolling green hills of rural Pennsylvania, you certainly don't feel like you're heading to the place where most MLB uniforms are manufactured. You feel like you're driving to some cute B&B or to a gun convention. But pulling into the driveway of the Majestic headquarters, we were impressed. We were equally impressed by Nicole Capobianco, the Director of Club Outfitting.

But first, a little history. Capobianco's grandmother started an apparel company called Maria Rose Fashions back in the 1950s, where they mainly manufactured women's blouses. In 1976, her father took over the business, and moved away from women's apparel and shifted toward Little League uniforms, calling the company Majestic Athletic. Pretty soon, their hand-stitched uniforms made their way to the pros, and they were granted their first license from Major League Baseball in 1984. In 2000, Majestic was granted exclusive on-field uniform rights from the MLB and by 2005, Majestic became the sole provider of authentic, hand-sewn jerseys for all 30 teams. "We were competing against the Nikes and Adidas' of the world," Capobianco said. But the fact that they were a family-owned business probably helped them secure the MLB contract. Baseball, at its core, retains that small, mom-and-pop feel, that emphasis on family and tradition. Well, for the most part.

In a move that might just reflect baseball's shift to fancy new stadiums, ridiculously paid players and highly lucrative sponsorship deals, Majestic Athletic was recently acquired by Vanity Fair, the world's largest clothing manufacturer. Although Vanity Fair has roots in rural Pennsylvania, too—it was first established as the Reading Glove and Mitten Manufacturing Company in 1899—it now owns dozens of brands, including Lee Jeans, Vans, The North Face, Nautica, Seven for All Mankind Jeans and John Varvatos, who, in a fusion of sports and fashion, is doing a sportswear line for Converse. Hmmm, so much for mom-and-pop. It seems that Capobianco and her brother, who is the Director of Global Baseball Operations, will stay on at Vanity Fair, but their father, Faust Capobianco III, retired. "The sale was emotional, especially for my father," Nicole Capobianco said. "But the opportunity presented itself to partner with a company with a lot of resources." Vanity Fair's resources include an NFL licensing deal. When asked if Majestic is interested in expanding to the NFL, she replied, "Absolutely." Thus far, the daily operations—and small-town feeling of Majestic—has remained unchanged. And we hope it stays that way.

After meeting with Capobianco in her cozy office, surrounded by family photos, newspaper clippings, a sketch of Mark McGwire and a rack of new jerseys waiting to be unveiled, we drove just under a mile to the warehouse where the uniforms are hand-sewn. We passed a light blue and pink sign that still said "Maria Rose Fashions" and entered the facility, which consisted of rows and rows of little elderly ladies (probably the only ones who still know how to sew these days). Each was perched at her sewing machine, some of which were decorated for a favorite team, or with cobwebs and spiders for the upcoming Halloween holiday.

This tight ship is run by Anna Maria Verniero, who has worked at Majestic since she was 19 years old. "It's the only job I've ever had," Verniero says. "I didn't know anything about sewing when I started here. I could barely speak English!" Anna Maria, originally from Sicily, is now 57. She is barely five feet tall, and seems younger than many of her employees. But she's tough. "Good thing you got here now to see the ladies in action," she said. "We are almost taking our 30-minute lunch break."

We hated to interrupt them, because they were so efficient—especially with Anna Maria strolling through the aisles, looking over their shoulders. But we were able to ask them a few questions between stitches. We were fascinated by what we found out.

How many years have we watched these ballplayers on TV, having no idea that these uniforms were all hand-stitched? (So are the jerseys you buy down at your local sports store; look for the Majestic "Authentic" label.) We had no idea that Capobianco and her crack team of three uniform outfitters go to Spring Training in Arizona and Florida each year and measure each player on each team as if they were getting fitted for a custom-tailored Italian suit. (Erica asked if Capobianco needed any additional crew members to be on the measuring team. The answer was a polite, but firm, "No.") They have a one-week window of opportunity, in which they measure each team's entire 40-man roster, and they have just a few hours per team. They punch all of the data into their laptops and send it back to Anna Maria and the crew in Bangor, who then have about three weeks to get the uniforms ready. And some teams have more sets of uniforms than others, like the New York Mets with their seven uniform variations. And on top of that, each player has special requests: Bonds and Sosa preferred elastic around their sleeves and some players request no elastic at the bottom of their pants (we know who you are Manny and Pedro!).

Aside from the regular season unis, there are special throwback unis, commemorative patches to be put on, postseason apparel for division champs and, of course, the World Series champion. It's definitely busy all year—but the spring is crunch time for sure.

So we thought we'd ask Capobianco for her take on why ballplayers wear the damn polyester pants?! "It's about durability," she said. "Each player is issued two road jerseys, two home jerseys and two alternate jerseys, so the fabric has to be durable and withstand not only running and sliding, but also the laundry." We were struck by the fact that one of the main reasons they're stuck in polyester is it's the only fabric that will stand up to Tide?! "Yeah, that and another reason is that baseball is tradition-based," she continued. "Anything too fashion-forward would not work. We're still living in a double-knit world." Capobianco went on to share with us some new fabrics being unveiled for on-field use—a Cool-Base TM jersey for warm-weather play, and a Therma-Base TM fleece warm-up jacket for those cold early-season or postseason nights. They were indeed innovative, but will only be used for jerseys and warm-ups. Not pants. Not yet.

On the way out, we asked Capobianco about women's sports fan apparel. Why so much pink? "We're not involved with the actual design," she said. "We're part of bringing what's on paper to life." She did point out that everything Majestic makes is available in a women's cut. There has definitely been progress in female fan attire, but not enough, according to Erica.

With that, we challenge designers to come up with better female sports fan apparel. The NFL partnered with Reebok this year—you might remember their TV commercial featuring female New York Giants fans, decked out in cute, sporty apparel, doing secret Giants handshakes as they arrive at their girlfriend's apartment to watch the game . . . and then dissing the lowly New York Jets fan who is the last to arrive? Cute ad. Too bad the clothes weren't as cute. Erica ordered two tops from the new collection. First, the order took six weeks to arrive, and upon arrival, both tops were boxy and ill-fitting. She sent them back. Alyssa Milano also has a new line of clothes out, sanctioned by Major League Baseball. It's definitely great to see different styles, fun fabrics and less pink, but her line is a bit too clubby for our taste. Maybe because Alyssa is a Dodger fan and she's based in LA she can wear spaghetti strap tops like this—but on the East Coast, during football season, we ain't wearing tube tops. Right, Chris? Chris?

Erica thinks she is speaking for a lot of women when she begs and pleads for someone to create a line of well-designed, team-branded sportswear that fits a woman's body, is not boxy or clubby, and is not necessarily pink. Never mind, we'll just do it ourselves. Look for a GameFace apparel line, coming soon to a stadium near you! (NFL, MLB, NBA, NHL—have your people call our people.)

JUST SAY YES TO THE SUIT

In 2006, Coach Mike Nolan of the San Francisco 49ers asked the NFL if he could wear a suit during games, rather than the mandated Reebok-branded apparel. To that request, we say "Hell, yeah!" Nolan told officials that he wanted to sport a suit to honor his father, Dick Nolan, who served as coach of the Niners from 1968 to 1975. Back then, it was common for coaches to wear suits—remember Dallas Coach Tom Landry and his fedora? We like it. We like the fact that NBA coaches wear suits today. It's respecting the game. It's a nice tradition. And it sure as hell beats Belichick in those heinous cut-off hoodies.

Jack Del Rio of the Jacksonville Jaguars followed suit (pun intended) and also requested an exemption. In 2006, the NFL decided that the coaches could wear Reebok-created suits for two home games. In 2007, they were allowed to wear suits at all home games, and this time, Reebok hired Joseph Abboud to design a line of formal suits for them, called the "Joseph Abboud Coaches Collection." According to their press release, the collection mixes formalwear with athletic fabrics and features details that include each team's uniform colors. Unfortunately, Nolan's team didn't benefit too much from his snappy new wardrobe—in 2006, they finished 7-9, and in 2007, 5-11. However, in 2007, Nolan was named as the 11th Best Dressed Man in the World by *Esquire* magazine, behind Barack Obama, Jay-Z, Tom Brady and, oddly, Hamid Karzai, the Technicolor-caped president of Afghanistan.

FASCINATING FACTOIDS ABOUT UNIFORM STRATEGY

In baseball, home jerseys are white and away jerseys are gray. That stems back from the old days when players on the road might not be able to launder their unis, so gray helped hide dirt better. (See, it's all about the laundry!) But in football, there is more strategy that goes into choosing which jersey to wear on any given Sunday. The home team always gets to choose their jersey first, then the visiting team acts accordingly. If the home team wears white, visitors must wear dark and vice versa. Now, say you are Jacksonville and you're playing an early-season day game at home, against a team used to playing in cold weather. You choose white unis so the northerners are forced to wear dark jerseys in the heat and humidity. Or, say you are playing a home game on a real grass field. Some home teams would opt for dark uniforms, making their opponent wear white so that the grass and mud stains will give the appearance of a battered and beaten team.

THE GOOD, BAD & THE UGLY

By now, you all know how we feel about the Astros and the Buccaneers unis, but let's not dwell in the past. We all have our "*GQ* Regrets" moments that we'd like to forget. Instead of ranking our favorite uniforms by sport—which is what everyone likes to do—here we present our not-at-all-comprehensive, Mr. Blackwell-esque list of the best and worst dressed individuals/teams/cheerleaders/mascots/fans in sports. (I'll tackle this list solo, since Chris has lost interest and went to make himself a sandwich.)

The Best

TOM BRADY: Let's face it. He's a fine looking man and has had stylish models dressing him for years.

CHICAGO BEARS: Their look is classic and hasn't changed much in decades. That's why I like it. And they wear orange with style, while so many other teams do it wrong. Orange, navy and white. Classic. Da Bears. Don't screw with 'em.

TIKI BARBER: He made the transition perfectly from player to commentator to *Today Show* contributor—and guest star on *Project Runway*! His wife is a publicist for Ermenegildo Zegna, so he is always looking quite dapper. (I'm glad he looks good on the outside, because I'm pretty sure he's crying on the inside since he retired one season short of a historic Super Bowl win with the New York Giants.)

OAKLAND RAIDERS: Love the simplicity of the silver and black. It's classic. And menacing. No one messes with the Raiders. Even with a bad record, they're still badass.

ROGER FEDERER: We already mentioned Roger and his faux-girlfriend Anna Wintour. Word on the street is that she helped him style the all-black tuxedo look. Can't wait to see what he wears on the runway court next.

THE WILLIAMS SISTERS: Love their style or hate it—at least they have style! Women's tennis outfits have the potential to be so fun, but most of the female tennis pros just wear their stuffy tennis whites and call it a day. With their vibrant colors, crazy-ass style and over-the-top bling, the Williams sisters bring an excitement to the court that is only matched by their exceptional skill.

1976-1986 PITTSBURGH PIRATES: That black pillbox hat with the gold horizontal stripes is pretty cool all by itself, but what was even cooler was that team captain Willie Stargell gave "Stargell Stars" to players to wear on their hats for game-winning hits and plays.

MONTREAL EXPOS RED, WHITE & BLUE CHAPEAU: Speaking of hats, the Expos wore a hat that featured varying panels of red, white and blue from 1969 to 1991. Very cool.

ANGELS HALO CAP: The last hat I'll discuss is very old school and also very cute. The California Angels wore navy caps with a red bill—and a thin white halo around the top of the hat—from 1961 to 1970. Wasn't life, and their team name, so much simpler then?

NY YANKEES: Love 'em or loathe 'em, you can't deny that pinstripes are classic.

NEW YORK JETS: Something about that deep green and crisp white screams Joe Namath. Oh, maybe that's me screaming Joe Namath's name. From Broadway Joe to the current Gang Green, gotta love this classic look of the J-E-T-S.

TONY PARKER: Hmmm, sensing a trend here. All of the fine-looking and stylish men have fine-looking and stylish wives who dress them. Tony is another one of them. Great work, Eva!

BOSTON CELTICS: Love the leprechaun, and classic green and white. See, I'm not completely biased against Boston.

AC MILAN: D&G design plus Italian men equals *molto* chic, in my book.

DALE EARNHARDT, JR., PRIOR TO 2008: I happen to like Budweiser's fine array of products as well as the color red, so Junior had made the list—up until now. His distinctive red car and fire suit has been replaced by a hodgepodge of sponsors and colors, dominated by Mountain Dew Amp and the National Guard. The result? A mess.

DALLAS COWBOYS: The simplicity of the lone star on their helmet is all they really need. But the fact that their cheerleaders used to appear regularly on *Love Boat,* still wear those cute little vests with the blouses that tie in the front, and refer to themselves as the DCC (Dallas Cowboy Cheerleaders, natch), proves that the Big D, and its blue, silver and white, is here to stay.

THE SAN DIEGO CHICKEN: Okay, not exactly stylish, but our fine-feathered friend still looks good after all these years, used to be a co-star of *The Baseball Bunch,* and deserves kudos for putting mascots on the map.

PHYLLIS GEORGE: Here she is . . . Miss America . . . and the first female host of *The NFL Today*. She might be pushing 60, but she's still chic, gorgeous and was once married to famed producer and womanizer Robert Evans. Although her stint as a morning news anchor on CBS proved to be disastrous (according to *Time* magazine, she reported that Andrew Loyd Weber was the composer of "Jesus Christ Superstore," and in a live interview with a Chicago man and the woman who falsely accused him of rape, George encouraged the two to hug, on air), don't forget that she also hosted *Candid Camera* and started her own chicken company, called "Chicken By George"! That's why I put her after the San Diego Chicken.

TIED: Pam Oliver/Melissa Stark: Rain, snow, sleet or hail, these sideline announcers seem to always look stylish, no matter what mother nature has in store.

HOWIE LONG: Okay, the flattop is a bit passé, but he is a sharp dressed man, even in those big-and-tall suits. Plus, he just seems like a nice guy. And that never goes out of style.

MARIA SHARAPOVA: Inspired by the bold Williams sisters, Sharapova has moved into their territory, trying more fashiony tennis looks, including her trademark dangly earrings. She's definitely subtler than Venus and Serena, but I give her points for trying to shake up this sometimes-stuffy sport.

BURT REYNOLDS: Okay, I just threw Burt in here, but think about how great he looked in *The Longest Yard,* not in *Boogie Nights,* Okay?

BOSTON BRUINS: Love the black, gold and iconic "B" on the front of their uniforms—and the fact that their mascot is a bear named "Blades the Bruin."

GREEN BAY PACKERS: The classic green and gold . . . Brett Favre . . . need I say more? Oh yes, I do: Those rubbery cheesehead things are not part of this stylish listing.

THE BECKHAMS: This might be controversial, but I say that Becks and Posh are fashion icons. Yes, they both have had some questionable moments—like when Becks wore the kilt and Posh's entire mid-'90s Spice Girl period. And even though Victoria Beckham and Paris Hilton tied for first place on Mr. Blackwell's 2007 worst-dressed list, I feel strongly that both Posh and Becks take risks and ignore criticism, and that's what fashion is all about. (Plus, Posh's appearance in the Marc Jacobs campaign, with her legs dangling out of the bag, was brilliant!)

NOTRE DAME: First, "Notre Dame" is French for "Our Lady," so anything French gets style points. Second, they're the Fighting Irish, so they have a leprechaun, too—and a fighting one at that. But it's the classic navy and gold, with a green jersey for special occasions, that earns them a spot on this list. And I really like the fact that they have been known to change jerseys at halftime. You see, style-leaders are always trying to reinvent themselves.

PAT RILEY: Okay, he might be aging, but he is still a *tres* sexy coach in a *tres sexy* coach suit.

The Worst

THE OREGON DUCKS: While I applaud their attempt to be different, this yellow/green/treadmarks/knickers/metallic helmets/bare legs nonsense is too much to take. Nike, which was founded by two University of Oregon alums, is responsible for these crazy-looking unis.

DENVER BRONCOS: Their logo is too stylized. It's like a stallion, not a bronco. But what I hate most is the orange swish that starts right under the armpit and goes all the way down to the knee. Again, orange and blue, like the Bears. They could be classy. Instead they tried to go too modern and just plain tried too hard.

MICHAEL IRVIN/DEION SANDERS/SHANNON SHARPE: Three very different men, with strangely similar tastes in suits. Former Cowboy Michael Irvin is always in trouble, whether it's drugs, sex scandals or being booted off ESPN. But you'll always find him in some monstrosity of a suit, or a full-length fur. Neon Deion played baseball and football simultaneously and was undoubtedly one of the most versatile athletes of our time—he could also be a pretentious and flashy a-hole, with a taste for neon-colored zoot suits, with long Delta Burke jackets. And former Bronco/Raven Shannon Sharpe is currently a commentator on *NFL Today*. He has been blasted by media critics, but I find his blunders funny and somewhat endearing. However, I find his fashions quite heinous, including one very memorable bright mustard suit. He is improving lately, and I hope he soon leaves Irvin and Sanders behind. Maybe he needs a well-dressed lady in his life? Maybe he should go on that *Millionaire Matchmaker* show?

MID-'70S TO MID-'90S HOUSTON ASTROS: Any uniform with red, orange and yellow horizontal stripes and nicknames like "Rainbow Gut," "Popsicle Uniform" or "Tequila Sunrise" deserves to be retired—and ridiculed.

MINNESOTA T-WOLVES: The trim on their jersey looks like fangs and the font of their logo looks like the font used in *Teen Wolf*—meaning, it's not scary. Were you scared by *Teen Wolf*?

ANDY RODDICK: Baggy clothes with his hat slightly off-center. Take a page out of Federer's style book, Andy, and maybe you'll get your mojo back. Wearing the classic looks of Lacoste *should* help. However, I will say that I like the fact that these baggy, flowing clothes allow us all to see his bare stomach every time he serves.

RAFAEL NADAL: Capri pants? Ass-picking? Rafa is many things: exuberant, exhilarating, passionate. Unfortunately, fashionable is not one of these things.

TONY STEWART & CREW: Not your fault Tony, but I just do not like that Home Depot orange. In fact, orange is right up there next to purple. It's fine as an accent color, but should not be the color of your fire suit AND your car! What I do like, though, is the fact that Tony grew out his hair in early 2008, and the entire NASCAR community is up in arms, complaining that he looks like a hippie!

SAN DIEGO PADRES ARMY FATIGUE UNIFORMS: I like the tribute to the troops, but do you have to wear a camouflage jersey? It looks ridiculous. Plus, it's not really fair because the other team can't see you.

WASHINGTON WIZARDS: First, you have that unfortunate name that has very little to do with basketball and has everything to do with Dungeons & Dragons. Second, you have to wear jerseys in that unfortunate color: You call it corn, I call it maize.

EAGLES CHEERLEADERS: Their cheerleading outfits look like white sports bras with matching white boy-short underwear—both have just a little black and green trim. Can we please try harder here? It's plain. And it's just plain ugly.

COLORADO ROCKIES/LA LAKERS/LAKER GIRLS/BALTIMORE RAVENS/MINNESOTA VIKINGS/KANSAS STATE/UNIVERSITY OF WASHINGTON/JAMIE MCMURRAY & CREW: Very different teams, one thing in common: Purple. Sorry Jamie McMurray and your purple Crown Royal car. The only thing remotely fashionable here are the Laker Girls' gold lamé outfits with just a little touch of purple (they're not really fashionable, they're just so over-the-top that they're kind of cool).

AL DAVIS: Sure, he has "Pride and Poise" but this controversial owner of the Raiders does not have "Style and Subtlety." He may have been the originator of bling, but his has nothing to do with hip-hop. He also has poor taste in eyewear, and certainly wouldn't have petitioned the NFL to allow him to wear a suit on the field—as he loves to wear his silky Raiders warm-up jackets. (Thank goodness Chris is still busy making that sandwich!)

CRAIG SAGER: This TBS and TNT announcer reminds me a bit of Herb Tarlek, the sales guy from WKRP, but since his bio says he is "known for his colorful attire," it means he's doing it on purpose. This doesn't make it any better, but at least he's self-aware.

STEELY MCBEAM: Part of what makes the Steelers great is the fact that they don't need stupid gimmicks. No cheerleaders. Just football. Terrible Towels were about as gimmicky as the Steelers ever got. It all started back in 1975, when famed announcer Myron Cope (who recently passed away) told fans to bring yellow dish towels from home and wave them during a playoff game. But in 2007, when the team celebrated their 75th Anniversary, they came up with this huge-headed mascot that is supposed to be a steel worker. A steel worker with an enormous head. First of all, mascots should not be humans. Second, the thing is ugly. Third, according to a *Pittsburgh Post-Gazette* poll, more than two-thirds of respondents found the mascot to be an unnecessary addition. Fourth, ESPN commentator Tony Kornheiser said Steely McBeam sounds like a porn star name.

TIED: Lesley Visser/Andrea Kremer/Bonnie Bernstein: Love you ladies, you are trailblazers. You have truly paved the way. But it also appears that you are alums of the Hillary Clinton School of Fashion and need to cut down on the vibrantly colored polyester suits from Dress Barn, circa 1987.

CINCINNATI BENGALS: Those stripes. On the sleeves and the pants and the helmets. Enough with the stripes. Although I have dissed orange, I do think that black and orange can work at times. Think Halloween! Think scary! Instead, with the stripes, you get Tony the Tiger—who is GRRRRREAT! Not scary.

LISA GUERERRO: According to the media, bloggers, and us, Guerrero was atrocious as an NFL sideline reporter and left people begging for the disastrous Eric Dickerson to return to the show. Lisa is currently a correspondent for the trashy TV show *Inside Edition* and her taste in clothes is questionable at best (maybe she borrowed that PURPLE Delta Burke trench coat from Deion Sanders?) And then she went and posed for *Playboy*, losing any remaining credibility she might have had left as a journalist. She does have one fashionable accessory—an attractive husband, former ballplayer Scott Erickson. (Chris, back from his sandwich and reading over my shoulder, says: You know you are just being hard on Lisa because you are jealous of her fashionable accessory. To which, I say: Shut it!)

CLEVELAND BROWNS: The brown and orange do not work unless you are a Brownie or work at Burger King. End of story.

BARON DAVIS: Thanks to this Golden State Warriors star, the NBA is going to have to add a new clause to their dress code: *Players may not wear fedoras adorned with actual bullets to any NBA-sanctioned event.*

SUNDERLAND AFC: This European footie club plays in the Premier League, and is based in Northeast England. That's all jolly good and all, but their red and white vertical stripes look like a bucket of Kentucky Fried Chicken—or maybe it just touches a nerve with me because it looks an awful lot like my TGIF waitress outfit I wore in the early '90s?

MIAMI DOLPHINS & THEIR STADIUM: Orange. Teal. And more orange. Orange is the new purple, people.

NASHVILLE PREDATORS/ATLANTA THRASHERS: Tie for the worst logos in NHL history. I'm not even sure what either of these logos are supposed to be. And that's not good really, when talking about logos.

THE RAINBOW WIG GUY: Remember that odd guy in the '70s who showed up in the stands of every major sporting event, dancing strangely, wearing the multi-colored wig and holding signs that said John 3:16? His real name is Rollen Stewart. It all started out as something wacky to do that might make him famous. Then Rollen Stewart found Jesus. Unfortunately, he did not find a stylist. He ended up taking a hotel maid hostage in LA and had plans to assassinate two US presidents. He's in prison now and no longer wears the wig, but instead, an *all orange* jumpsuit. Need we say more?

4 THAT'S RACIN'!:
A Crash Course in Motor Sports

NOT TO PULL A JERRY SEINFELD, BUT WHAT'S THE DEAL with NASCAR? As sports fans originally from the East and West coasts with no Southern roots to speak of, we kind of didn't get it. At all. But there was something about this often-stereotyped sport that intrigued us. Maybe it is the sport's rabid fan base—it's the number-one sport in brand loyalty of fans and it's the number-two rated sport on TV, behind the NFL. Or it could be NASCAR'S super-savvy marketing—they sell more than $2 billion in licensed sales per year. Or perhaps it's the emergence of these young, strapping drivers, who appear everywhere from romance novels and soap operas to music videos and Page Six. Or, possibly it's the fact that lots of women love NASCAR—they have nearly a 50% female fan base. Or maybe because it's a sport that regularly features the terms "Happy Hour" and "Silly Season." Regardless, we had to know more.

When we started, we didn't even know the difference between NASCAR and Indy Racing and Formula One (F1). We had a lot to learn. So we immersed ourselves in the sport and are here to share this late-breaking news: NASCAR—and auto racing on the whole—just might be the coolest sport we haven't been watching. Now we're hooked. And we want to take you along for the ride . . .

First, NASCAR fans don't necessarily like Indy fans. And vice versa. NASCAR-types think that Indy drivers are F1 wannabes and complain that Indy is filled with non-Americans who are just practicing for the big-time (more than half of Indy drivers are from foreign countries.) Indy drivers, on the other hand, think their cars are more technologically advanced and more challenging to drive. They think NASCAR is for the unrefined. They think NASCAR is filled with big, clunky stock cars, big egos and redneck fans. Indy fans think they are Chardonnay, while NASCAR fans are beer. Oh, and F1 thinks that they are Champagne, and everyone pretty much agrees about that.

Here, for those of you new to auto racing like us, we detail the difference between stock car racing (NASCAR) and open-wheel racing (Indy/CHAMP and Formula One):

STOCK CAR RACING

Stock cars are very similar to the cars we drive (from the outside anyway) and NASCAR is the home of stock car racing in America—the acronym stands for National Association for Stock Car Auto Racing. As of 2008, the types of cars driven in NASCAR are: the Ford Fusion, the Toyota Camry, the Chevrolet Impala, and the Dodge Charger. And 2008 is the first full season that all of the NASCAR racing teams have used the Car of Tomorrow (which sounds like a ride at Disneyland, but is really a new, safer car that many of the drivers dislike. They started developing the car in 2001, after the death of Dale Earnhardt in the Daytona 500, and you'll now see it referred to as the Car of Today). Whether or not today's drivers like the CoT, the vehicles can still reach speeds upwards of 180-200 mph, and drivers compete on five types of tracks—short tracks, intermediate, speedways, superspeedways and road courses (see below for an explanation of each). Their season is a long one, from February through November, and consists of 36 races. After the first 26 races, the top 12 racing teams qualify for "The Chase," and that's when things get really exciting!

Although the first NASCAR race was held in the '40s and IndyCar racing has been around much longer, NASCAR has taken over as the most popular type of auto racing in America. This is due to savvy marketing, the fact that the drivers are primarily home-grown boys with huge followings, and because the cars they drive are familiar, and allow people to feel like, "Hell, maybe I could drive my Chevy Impala like that in a NASCAR race." NASCAR has also lapped Indy racing because there has been a rift between the two open-wheel series in the US, and while these two had been busy fighting for 12 years, NASCAR slipped in and has completely dominated the US auto racing scene ever since. More on that later.

Here's the scoop on the different types of tracks that host NASCAR races.

Short Track: An oval-shaped track that is less than 1 mile in length.

Speedway: An oval-shaped track that is between 1 mile and 1.5 miles in length.

Intermediate Speedway: An oval-shaped track that is between 1.5 miles and 2 miles in length.

Superspeedway: An oval-shaped track that is greater than 2 miles in length.

Road Course: A racing circuit that keeps the drivers guessing—these courses are comprised of left- and right-hand turns, as opposed to an oval, which is comprised exclusively of left-hand turns.

OPEN-WHEEL RACING

Open-wheel cars are quite different than your typical stock car. They are lighter, more technologically advanced and have open cockpits, so you can see the drivers better. Open-wheel cars don't have fenders, so the drivers can't bump into each other like they do in NASCAR. And they're faster. These cars can typically can reach speeds of 230—240 mph. Drivers in the open-wheel series race mostly on ovals, but sometimes on road courses and street courses. We love to think of these guys racing around city streets, and it reminds us of that old movie *The Great Race,* starring Jack Lemmon and Tony Curtis.

Up until very recently, there were two types of Open Wheel series in America: CHAMP cars (formerly called CART) and IRL (Indy Racing League). For many years, CART used to be the only open-wheel series in the country. But in 1994, Tony George, owner of the Indianapolis 500, formed the Indy Racing League, and it's been a Hatfield/McCoy-type feud ever since. To many, the split has forever damaged open-wheel racing in America, allowing NASCAR to step in and take over as the most popular racing in the country. In fact, NASCAR's Daytona 500 race now gets higher TV ratings than the venerable Indy 500. The split has also caused some sponsors to defect to NASCAR, or forced them to choose between CHAMP and IRL. The result? Open-wheel racing is not as lucrative for drivers as NASCAR. This is why some of the top CHAMP and IRL drivers have jumped ship for NASCAR, including Dario Franchitti (Mr. Ashley Judd), Sam Hornish, Jr., and A.J. Allmendinger. So in March 2008, CHAMP and IRL finally put their differences aside and merged back into one entity. Only time will tell if these two warring factions—now both under the IRL umbrella—will reunite seamlessly, once again attracting sponsor money and big-name racers in an effort to topple the mighty behemoth known as NASCAR. That's a race that will be fun to watch, too.

FORMULA ONE (F1)

As we mentioned before, F1 is the Champagne of open-wheel racing—it's the most prestigious racing series in the world. The F1 series, also known as Grand Prix races, take place all over the world on racing circuits or on closed city streets. The cars are extremely fast (they regularly go more than 220 mph), are more advanced than stock or Indy cars—and some say, more dangerous. The Grand Prix races have been around since the 1920s, and F1 has always been filled with drama, intrigue, sabotage, spying—juicy stuff. The biggest complaint about F1 is that only a few racing teams dominate the series, which is why German driver Michael Schumacher won the world championship seven times. *Bo-ring.* But luckily, he retired in 2006 so some others have a chance these days. Plus, some people have the same criticism of NASCAR, so there.

Success in F1 has always proven to be rather elusive for Americans. Mario Andretti and a handful of others in the '60s and '70s had respectable F1 performances, but in 1993, Michael Andretti (Mario Andretti's son, natch) tried to break into the F1 ranks. After completing only three laps in his first three races, it was evident that Andretti couldn't really master the F1 cars, after racing stock and Indy cars back in the US He left after one season.

Between 1993 and 2006, there were no US drivers in F1, until a young Californian named Scott Speed made his debut at the Bahrain Grand Prix in 2006. (When we first learned of his name, we thought for sure he was a character in either *Speed Racer* or Hanna-Barbera's animated *Wacky Races* series, featuring Peter Perfect and Penelope Pitstop. We were wrong.) Speed, who won the Red Bull driver search in an attempt to bring American talent to F1, didn't do so well in the Champagne division. He scored no points for team Toro Rosso (that's Italian for Red Bull) in 2006 or 2007, causing tempers to flare. In July 2007, after Speed crashed in the first turn of the European Grand Prix in Nurnburg, Germany (along with a lot of other drivers, we might add), Toro Rosso Team Principal Franz Tost lost his cool. Back in the pit, Speed claims that Tost sucker-punched him in the back, grabbed his neck and knocked him around a bit, and later denied it to the media. Needless to say, Speed is no longer participating in F1 races. He'll be driving in the ARCA Re/Max series in 2008, which is a training ground for would-be NASCAR drivers. Good luck and Godspeed, Speed!

TRIPLE THREAT

One guy who seems to have a good handle on racing in all three racing series is Colombian Juan Pablo Montoya. He used to drive in the CART series and in the IRL (in fact, he won the CART championship in his rookie year and went on to win the Indy 500 the next year). He then spent six years as an F1 driver where he did well, even winning the Monaco Grand Prix. But when he made the controversial move from F1 to NASCAR in 2006, he became the first ever to do so. He was mocked by the snooty F1 community, and many NASCAR fans felt that he took away a spot from a young, homegrown up-and-coming stock car driver. And while Montoya didn't exactly dominate in his first full NASCAR season in 2007—six top-ten finishes, a $4.8 million paycheck and "NASCAR Rookie of the Year" honors is certainly nothing to sneeze at. Plus, we like him because he flipped the bird at a live camera crew, resulting in a $10,000 fine from the conservative NASCAR folks. So JP Montoya is a bad boy and a badass, and we officially endorse him as one of our favorite drivers. Amen. (Oh yes, we also learned that there is a lot of prayer involved in NASCAR. More on that later.)

Racer Girls

We have mentioned this, but it's worth bringing up again. Another thing we like about American racing is that it's the only sport where men and women actually compete against each other in the same league and under the same conditions. While there are no female NASCAR Sprint series drivers, there are a few women in the pit, including trailblazer Nicole Addison. She was part of NASCAR's "Drive for Diversity" program, developed to increase participation by women and other minorities at the professional level, both in the pit and on the track.

Open-wheel racing has been more welcoming to lady drivers. Danica Patrick is the pre-eminent female race-car driver in America. In 2005, Patrick's first year in the IRL, she became only the fourth woman to qualify and race in the Indy 500—after women like Janet Guthrie, Lyn St. James and Sarah Fisher paved the way. And she truly is the most famous female racer of our time, just ask her fan club of Danica Maniacs. Despite her strong performance in the IRL since 2005, including winning "Rookie of the Year" award that year, she still gets trashed by some fans, some of the media and even some of her fellow drivers. Some claim that her minority status and even her low body weight has given her advantages that other similarly talented male drivers wouldn't have—although they changed the weight requirements in 2008, so people should consider the playing field level. There was talk in 2006 of Danica moving to NASCAR, which caused Ed Carpenter, a fellow IRL driver, to tell a Nashville radio station, "I think Danica's pretty aggressive in our cars . . . I mean, you know especially if you catch her at the right time of the month." Nice. To be fair, he did go on to say, "But I think she'll hold her own." We are hoping that her thrilling win in the Twin Ring Motegi Race in Japan in April 2008—making her the first woman ever to win an IndyCar race—will shut some of her critics up, once and for all.

Regardless of ignorant comments like these, the fact that women are competing against men—and winning—is pretty exciting. Besides, women are used to being told we can't do something. We just ignore people and keep on keepin' on. It's what we do. Just ask Leilani Münter. Another female race driver, who doesn't quite fit in the "mold," but she just might be the next big thing.

LEILANI MÜNTER: MAVERICK ON THE TRACK

Leilani Münter is still fairly new to the racing world, which naturally makes her something of an outsider. But that's not a bad thing. In fact, bucking the status quo is a familiar habit for the racing maverick. First, Münter—a former NASCAR ARCA series driver, NASCAR.com correspondent and current IndyCar driver—is one of the sport's small number of female racers. Sure, there are others, including Milka Duno from the Indy Pro Series, and drag racers such as Ashley Force. But auto racing still is mostly a man's world. Then add the fact that Münter (pronounced "Moon-ter") is as passionate about the environment as she is about her racing career and, well, you get the picture: She is more like Bobby Kennedy than NASCAR legend Bobby Allison.

But 32-year-old Münter has long been trying to fuse her two passions. In March 2008, she took that mission to Washington D.C. to lobby Congress in support of a bill that would cut emissions and ease global warming. She spoke to national decision makers, including Sen. Elizabeth Dole (R-North Carolina) and Sen. Richard Lugar (R-Indiana). "(Lugar) said he's a big race fan and he had all these stories from the Indy 500," said Münter.

It was the best of both worlds for her. She was able to use her racing career as an avenue to fight pollution. Can a self-described "tree hugger" truly merge those two worlds? We'll see. But Münter, who clearly likes big challenges, damn sure is going to try. And she's doing just that on the Internet, where her racing website (leilanimunter.com) has a link to what she calls her "eco site" (carbonfreegirl.com). Listed there is her personal mantra, which captures her life philosophy in just seven words: "Life is short. Race hard. Live green."

The "science nerd," as she calls herself, has a Bachelor's degree in biology from the University of California, San Diego (which is, incidentally, Chris and Erica's alma mater. Go, Tritons!). But this "science nerd" wants to bring more environmental awareness to motor sports, a heady goal given that the industry is based on gas guzzling. She posted ideas on her blog on how auto racing can be more green, suggesting that they race with biofuel or place more recycling facilities at speedways. Judging by the blog's reader comments, it may take some time to open minds fully within the industry. "I got some good responses, and I also got people saying I've been brainwashed by Al Gore," she said with a laugh.

Another way she stands out from the crowd is her movie-star looks. Before she raced cars, Münter was a stand-in for actress Catherine Zeta-Jones for movies such as *Traffic* and *America's Sweethearts*. Her beauty obviously can be a blessing in a sport so dependent on media interest and corporate sponsors. Just look at Danica Patrick, who appeared in the traditionally risqué GoDaddy.com Super Bowl commercial, and further sexed-up her image by posing in a bikini in the 2008 *Sports Illustrated* Swimsuit Issue. Münter has mined some of the same eye-candy territory. *Men's Journal* magazine called her America's "Sexiest Race Car Driver," *FHM* magazine named her the "Hottest Woman in NASCAR" and *Playboy* once offered her big bucks to pose nude.

However, she turned Hef down. *Italian Vogue* is more her speed, and Münter's environment-themed photo spread appeared in the European glamour magazine in January 2008. At the same time, her good looks may also work against her. "I feel like I'm fighting to be taken seriously," she said. "You just have to prove that you're there for the right reasons. You have to be able to do both—drive well and sell the product."

Male drivers, such as driving legend Rick Mears, have shown her a lot of support, Münter said. Still, she sometimes faces chauvinist attitudes that are as old as A.J. Foyt. She has heard the occasional snide comments from male drivers. And a reporter once wrote that she had a better chance of being sent into outer space than winning a race. But Münter shrugs at such negative talk. The good news is that there are plenty of fans rooting for her and other female drivers today, especially young girls inspired by them. "It's cool because you feel like you're encouraging girls to do something out of the ordinary," she said. "When no women race, the only woman who little girls see is the trophy girl."

Meanwhile, "the gender thing" may also be a mixed bag. When she loses, Münter faces more scrutiny because she's a woman. But when she does well, she gets more recognition, such as when she placed fourth in qualifying for the First Convenience 100 at the Texas Motor Speedway. When she performed impressively there a second time, finishing seventh in the 2004 contest, the racing world started to take notice and Münter was thrilled with that strong showing. "It's about small steps, right? "she said. "Even if I never win a race, I felt at that moment that I belonged, that I accomplished what I wanted to."

Münter made her Indy Pro Series debut at the Kentucky 100 in August 2007, making her just the fourth woman ever to race in the Series. In that open-wheel contest, she was nearly running in the top five when she hit the wall and smashed her car, which prevented her from finishing. No matter. She shook it off and, one month later, she bounced back from a spinout in the Chicagoland 100 and finished 13th. Münter's ultimate goal is to race fulltime, but she will need to land a major sponsor before that happens. Until then, she said she will keep chasing her dream, driving part-time and competing in the bigger Indy races. "When I pull that helmet and visor down, it's almost like the whole world disappears, and the car and I become one," she said. "I'm so focused I tune out the rest of the world. It's an amazing feeling."

Perhaps it's not surprising that Münter identifies with rebels. That includes her brother-in-law, Bob Weir of the Grateful Dead, the iconic counterculture rock band. She credits Weir for being one who inspired her to try to make a difference in the world. Racing industry insiders cautioned that her public environmental work might hurt her career. But Münter did it anyway, staying focused on the personal goals that already have taken her from the nation's most famous speedways to the halls of Congress.

"I'm sure there are companies who viewed me as 'an eco, tree-hugger, vegetarian chick,'" she said, gently laughing. "But I'm really glad I did it because I can be myself and stay true to my beliefs."

So we've been learning a lot about the ins and outs of racing, identifying with some rebels and underdogs and shattering some stereotypes along the way. We knew there was something about racing we liked! The next step? Experience NASCAR for ourselves, firsthand.

A Day at the Races

In an attempt to completely immerse ourselves in NASCAR, we attended three races in 2007—the first in the Poconos in Pennsylvania, the second in Dover, Delaware, and the last in Phoenix, Arizona. The cool thing is that each track has distinct characteristics, in terms of the track itself and also the atmosphere and ambiance (if you can call it that).

When NASCAR rolls into town, it's like having your city host the Super Bowl. Festivities are going on from Thursday to the big race on Sunday. There are concerts, cook-offs, performances and tailgating. Lots of tailgating. People drive their RVs and campers in, find a good spot—in the Poconos, fans actually park their RVs in the middle of the racetrack—and then they hang out. For days. Maybe even all week. NASCAR races have more attendees than we have ever seen at any other sporting event in our lives. A typical NASCAR race day will see upwards of 200,000 to 300,000 people, including ticket holders and tailgaters (compared to a sold-out Yankee game with 57,000 fans, or a sold-out New York Giants game with 80,000 fans). It's pretty overwhelming. But we are pleased to report that between our first race and our third, we learned how to do things right. We want to share with you the "Dos and Don'ts" of attending a NASCAR race.

THE POCONOS: A DAY OF "DON'TS"

We did not spend all week in the Poconos in mid-August, as alluring as that sounds, but instead, attended the big NEXTEL race (as of 2008, it's now called the SPRINT series) on Sunday. The SPRINT series is the highest level of competition, where you'll see all the big-name drivers: Jimmie, Tony, Jeff, Dale, Jr., etc. The day before the big race, there is the BUSCH series (as of 2008, it's called the Nationwide Series), the minor leagues of NASCAR. There is also the Craftsman Truck series, and several other "touring" divisions, with guys eventually hoping to get a spot in the SPRINT series.

But we were there to see the big names, so Sunday was our day. (FYI, most of the SPRINT races are on Sundays, with an occasional Saturday night race, but these are few and far between). We drove through the winding, backwoods roads of Pennsylvania to get to the track before 9 a.m. to avoid traffic and wander around. That may have been the only thing we did right. Yes, we were early, but we were not prepared. We had no tailgating supplies. No chairs. No sweet "Freedom Rock" soundtrack to rock out to. No confederate flag hanging from our antenna. So there we were, four hours before the race began, wandering around and trying to bum food and beer off people in their Rvs. These people knew what they were doing. They had been there for a week. We stood out like sore thumbs, and these diehards were not very responsive. (Probably because we were with a mixed group of men and women—something tells me that a couple of chicks alone could have gotten all the beer and dogs their little hearts desired.)

Desperate for some sort of alcoholic beverage and pseudo-meat substance, we decided to enter the racetrack to grab our own food and booze—and were in for a big shock. Who knew that Pennsylvania has some strange liquor laws that don't allow them to sell beer at the event, despite the fact that Budweiser, Jim Beam and Jack Daniels are all sponsors?! The good news is that attendees can bring their own 12" x 12" coolers into the event, which basically means each person (over 21) can bring their own 12-pack. The bad news is that we did not have a cooler or 12-pack, and because our car was stuck in the middle of a field— completely blocked in by all of the RVs and cars around us—we were screwed. Plus it was Sunday and the Puritanical state of Pennsylvania doesn't sell booze on Sundays. NASCAR WITHOUT BEER!? COULD IT BE DONE? Yes. It probably wasn't as fun, but it led to more accurate reporting, we suppose.

Another shock for us was that despite its reputation as a "white trash" or "redneck" sport, NASCAR is not cheap. The lowest ticket was $50-$60 for the Sunday race. You can buy a package for the entire weekend, which brings the daily cost down a bit, but between the tickets and food, it certainly costs more than taking your family of four to the baseball game.

So sans beer and our wallets $50 lighter, we begrudgingly we entered the racetrack, purchased some bad hotdogs and sodies, and proceeded to the sponsor area, where our jaws dropped wide open.

Sure, we all know that sponsors slap their names all over the cars and the drivers' racing uniforms, but we had no idea how elaborate the sponsor area was at the actual NASCAR races. We've all been to pro sports games where we're bombarded with advertising and logos, but only at NASCAR can one sing in a Old Spice-branded shower in front of hundreds of people in order to win a T-shirt! And only at NASCAR can one climb into a fake US Army tank and pretend one is in combat, in order to get free, Army-branded dog tags! And only at NASCAR can one try to get a free sample of Prilosec, the official heartburn medicine of NASCAR, in order to combat the aforementioned bad hotdogs, only to find out that there is some rule about giving out free drugs. Instead, one receives a Prllosec keychain, which incidentally does not help combat heartburn.

What did make us feel better was the opportunity to buy branded merchandise from our favorite driver. Inside the track, you can find all of the hats, shirts, die-cast cars and other swag you could ever want. (FYI, NASCAR takes a cut of nearly everything sold inside the racetrack—from the two Dale, Jr. Budweiser hats we purchased, to the several bags of Kettle Corn we consumed during our eight plus hours at the racetrack). But sponsors play a big part in every NASCAR fans' life. For instance, if you love Tony Stewart, you best be prepared to have a huge-ass Home Depot logo on your head or chest. Most fans don't mind this. In fact, the reason so many sponsors want to get in on the NASCAR action is that these fans actually buy products/items based on the drivers that they like. For instance, if you do love Tony Stewart, you would not be caught dead in a Lowe's store, because that would mean that you were supporting Jimmie Johnson. You are Home Depot, all the way, baby.

This even applies to the cars we talked about earlier—Ford, Dodge, Chevrolet and Toyota. Fans will buy cars based on what their favorite NASCAR personality is driving. Or some fans cheer for a specific car manufacturer, meaning they'll root for every driver in a Ford. There's an old NASCAR saying that goes: "Win on Sunday, sell on Monday." It does seem that this particular audience is extremely responsive to advertising, and that's why the sponsors are king at NASCAR. They put up the bucks that make this all possible—they pay for the cars, the crews, the purse money. And this is why the drivers suck-up to their sponsors more so than any other sport. After the race, the drivers will spend a big chunk of their time taking photos with their various sponsors—donning a different hat for each sponsor, posing with a different executive from each company. And if you have ever heard a driver interviewed, pre- or post-race, you can bet they'll refer to their sponsors, one way or another. Take Dale Jarrett for instance. This well-respected NASCAR driver retired in early 2008, after a rather disappointing finish in Bristol. He finished in 37th place to end his 24-year career, and his final quote in the press was: "Well, it wasn't the finish I would have liked, but I'm able to go out with the best sponsor in the business in UPS." These drivers (unlike Chris) sure do know the importance of the sponsors, and maybe this is more pronounced because NASCAR is more of an individual sport. It's hard to imagine any of our other sports heroes kissing sponsor ass like this—except for maybe Michael Jordan.

So back to the Poconos. After wandering around this fantastically elaborate and expensive sponsor section, it was time for pre-race festivities, so we headed toward the bleachers. First, there's the patriotic segment, where a man with a deep, operatic voice sang *God Bless America* and *America the Beautiful*. Then there was a short military parade, paying tribute to our nation's troops, complete with tanks and a fly-over by some military planes. Next, it was prayer time, when a preacher of some sort gave a rather lengthy prayer, which to be honest, caused our minds to wander a bit as we looked down at the hundreds of beer cans that had already fallen through the openings of the bleachers. (It must be noted that another Sunday tradition is that the drivers and their families attend church services on Sunday mornings together, prior to the race, no matter which track they are racing). Next, it was celebrity appearance time. We were welcomed by Chris Tucker, promoting his latest release, *Rush Hour 3*, and announcing in a very exaggerated, cartoony voice: "Gentlemen, start your engines!" (We must also note that in the middle of rural Pennsylvania, and despite the "Drive to Diversity" program, Chris Tucker might have been the only African-American person we saw the entire day.)

So, adrenaline was running through our veins. Our hearts were pounding. THIS WAS OUR FIRST NASCAR RACE! So the gentlemen started their engines and the race began. The pace car started out and the drivers fell in line according to their pole position, which is the order in which the cars line up, determined by their qualifying heats in the days prior to the big race. Before we knew it, the cars were whizzing around in circles on this tri-oval shaped superspeedway, when we learned another surprising thing about racing: it's not a very social event. In fact, it's anti-social. Many people rent or buy headsets, which allow you to listen to the conversations between your favorite driver and his pit crew. And if you don't do that, earplugs are highly recommended, as the noise of the cars driving around is absolutely deafening. Yep, about four hours of deafening noise and no talking. The only social interaction takes place when people are high-fiving or chest bumping their neighbors when there is a crash. (Or when Erica was poking her sister, trying to get her to look at the eight male, shirtless Virginia Military Institute students in front of us, who were crushing beer cans against their foreheads and flipping off Tony Stewart every single time he came around the track, which turned out to be about 220 times.) The only thing really to do is to repeatedly apply sunscreen, watch drunk people wearing T-shirts with obscene sayings like one that featured the outline of a woman's breasts and the phrase: "Caution: Bumps Ahead," and wait for drivers to crash and/or "swap paint" with each other, meaning bump into each other. Unlike the open-wheel racing series where the cars are delicate and the driving more precise, in NASCAR, drivers purposely bump into each other and have even been known to drive toward competing pit crews in the pit! That's something fun to watch for! There are also rumors of sabotaging cars and fixing races. And some drivers (ahem, Tony Stewart) have even accused Big Brother NASCAR of waving false caution flags in order to rig the race. He even compared NASCAR to professional wrestling—alluding to the races being fixed—and got fined $10,000. Add Tony to our list of favorite drivers.

Truthfully, about two hours into the race, we were ready to go. Although we loved our first NASCAR experience, we had been there since before 9 a.m. and had about enough. But as you'll recall, we were trapped. There was no way to get out of the "parking field." And we found out that people don't leave NASCAR races early. They hardly even leave their seats during the race. You are all there waiting for the payoff—you are there to see who wins. So we had no choice but to stay. Until the bitter end. And this was our next mistake. If you can't leave early, you'd best be prepared to stay late. This is why people have these damn Rvs. The night after the race is a big party, too. You stay, you drink, you do more tailgating. But we were anxious to get out of there right after the race. After all, we had a two-hour drive ahead of us and it was a Sunday night. We had to work the next day. Instead, we sat in traffic. The worst traffic we have ever encountered in our lives. It took more than three hours to get out of the parking field. Then another two hours to go through the winding roads of rural Pennsyltucky, back to the main highway. Then another two hours to get back to New York City. It was such a tease to spend the entire day watching these stock cars racing at speeds of nearly 200 mph and then be sitting there, nearly motionless, for seven hours. We vowed to never do NASCAR again. Ever.

It Ain't Over 'Til it's Dover

So imagine our surprise, just a month later, when we decided to go to Dover, Delaware, for another race. Maybe it was the heat and we were out of our minds. Maybe we were slowly getting hooked on NASCAR, and excited to see what the heck went on at the so-called "Monster Mile," a one-mile, oval-shaped short course in the middle of nondescript Delaware. Maybe we just loved sitting in traffic. With each race we attended, we learned even more. (Tip: if you go on nascar.com, they list each of the races and have fan guides to how to best deal with each raceway.) In Dover, we did not park in the NASCAR-sanctioned parking lot, but instead paid $10 to park in a nearby K-Mart. We're glad we did. If not, we would have missed walking through booths of wacky NASCAR knick-knacks, including the Dale Jr.-branded Santa figurines, the confederate flag-print aprons (is Delaware considered the South?), and even a signed, framed *Talladega Nights* poster, perfect for any living room! (Attention NASCAR fans: Don't you know that entire movie made a complete mockery of you!?)

However, there were some great things about Dover: First, they sold beer. Tall boys of Bud Light. Second, there is a casino at Dover, overlooking the backstretch of the racetrack. And what's more, the casino is air-conditioned and you can actually hear each other during the race! We talked our way into a restaurant area and peeked out the floor-to-ceiling windows onto the track for a while, pretending we were waiting for some friends, until we were asked to leave by an elderly lady with white hair. Erica asked a few questions that she didn't really care to know the answers to, like, "How long have you worked here?" and "What's the menu like?" just to buy us some more time in the air conditioning. But unfortunately, white hair lady had enough of us. We were sent back to the steamy stands. Good thing our tickets weren't bad. They cost us $65 each and we were right across from the pit. It was there that we saw a few interesting things: First, a man wearing a trucker hat that featured soft-sculpture, 3-D women's breasts on the bill of the cap. We took a picture, while his wife/companion shook her head in disgust (at him, not us . . . we think). On the flip side, we watched as a security guard told a drunk woman that she was standing too close to the track area, and, without words, she lifted up her top and flashed him—*Girls Gone Wild* style—in response. Her plan did not work and he did not let her get closer to the action! Good man! After an hour or two of people-watching and crash-hoping, we were so paranoid about the traffic that we high-tailed it back to K-Mart and sped away, laughing all the way home at all the suckers who would be stuck for hours! But as we were driving home and listening to the race-day coverage on the radio, we realized that those diehard fans had the last laugh. We missed everything! First, the winning car, driven by Carl Edwards, didn't pass inspection! Next, there was a spectacular 10-car crash! And last but not least, there was a fight in the pit (right across from where we were sitting), which featured Kyle Petty getting in Denny Hamlin's face, causing Hamlin to yell: "Don't smack me on the helmet! You smack me on the helmet, and I'm going to punch you in the face." Whether or not this was a true fight, or one just staged for our benefit—we missed everything. This is why people don't leave early and instead chill in the parking lot, listening to the post-race analysis. Ahhh, foiled again.

PHOENIX: WHERE WE PHINALLY PHIGURED IT ALL OUT!

But alas, the season was not over for us—well at least one of us. Chris, since this was a girls-only trip, Erica will take it from here:

The last stop on the summer NASCAR tour: the Phoenix International Raceway, another one-mile short track. And as they say, the third time was definitely the charm. It was here that I (Erica), along with my well-connected female friends Tracy and Tricia, figured out how to *really* watch a NASCAR race. The first step was to somehow befriend a NASCAR driver. Or befriend the sisters of a NASCAR driver, in our case. Turns out that Tracy and Tricia had a connection with the sisters of Robby Gordon, one of NASCAR's black sheep.

Why a black sheep, you ask? First, Robby Gordon is outspoken against anything he doesn't like about NASCAR (or anything else for that matter). Second, he can be openly aggressive at times (Robby once got out of his car after a CART race and kicked the Ford logo, in an apparent slam at the maker of his car). And last, he is a rebel, trying to make a name for himself amongst the more powerful and established racing teams. He's controversial because he has complained more than a few times that NASCAR has treated his team unfairly—either by issuing unusually harsh penalties or manipulating flags to affect the outcome of the race. Lots of fans don't like him. But in 2008, he found out that lots of fans love him, too. After a severe penalty at the beginning of the 2008 season in Daytona, Robby made it abundantly clear that NASCAR inappropriately penalized his team when they docked them 100 points and $100,000. Legions of fans stood by him and showed their support. And in an unprecedented move, NASCAR reversed its decision. Score one for the underdog. And you know how much I love underdogs. Especially underdogs who invite me and my plugged-in friends to hang out at their tricked-out trailers.

But first, I decided that we needed to get access to the pit. No more of this sitting in traffic, buying crappy tickets. I wanted to experience NASCAR as a VIP. So I emailed the Phoenix International Raceway people and requested press passes. Obviously, because I was writing a book, this was easier for me than it would be for you, dear reader, but I do have a useful tip for you. On the day of the race, when we drove up to the racetrack, we didn't have any credentials at all, we hadn't even picked them up at the press booth yet. So we kept telling every sheriff and security guard that we encountered that we were with the press. The key was to be confident and act like we knew where we were going. It also helped that we told the authorities, "We're also close, personal friends of Robby Gordon." Oh, and it helped that all of us had pretty big cans. (Our editor wasn't sure if "cans" meant big breasts or big butts, so let me clarify: we had pretty big guns, knockers, racks, jugs, melons, bazookas and/or gazongas. Hope that helps.) So thanks to our big gazongas, we made it all the way up to the entrance of the track. I mean, we literally parked outside the entrance of the track. After the "parking field" experience in the Poconos and the K-Mart lot in Dover, I was nearly in tears. This was absolutely unheard of and we were high-fiving our sheer brilliance more than we would have if Jimmie Johnson, Jeff Gordon and Dale Earnhardt, Jr. all crashed in the very last lap! (By the by, if you're not up for bullshitting your way into a good parking spot, our hotel offered guests the option to book a round-trip helicopter ride for just $150 each. That's also a good way to avoid annoying traffic, scary sheriffs and lying.)

Meanwhile, back at the racetrack, we finally picked up our highly coveted press credentials. We each received a "Cold" pass, meaning we could only hang out in the pit up until one hour prior to the race. If we had a "Hot" pass, we could have hung out there the whole time. Regardless of whether you're hot or cold, there is a dress code for the pit. You must wear long pants, closed-toed shoes and no tank tops—you need some sort of sleeves. These rules were designed to prevent some hoochie-mama Pit Lizards or Helmet Lickers, as NASCAR groupies are called, from inflicting their slutty ways on the purity of NASCAR. And just for the record, the fact that we used our voluptuous bazookas to help us get a better parking spot does not make us sluts or hoochie-mamas, right? RIGHT?!!?

So when you're down in the pit, you see the crews working fast and furiously. Be careful not to get in their way, as they're pushing the cars over to be inspected by officials. You also see the media swarming, trying to get the scoop from the pit crew, or catch a glimpse of driver drama. And you see groups of sponsors being given guided tours around the facilities. You're also likely to see a few NASCAR celebs hovering. In Phoenix, we saw "The King," Richard Petty himself, walking around. The pit is definitely the place to be. But, we were "Cold," remember? So we had to get out of the pit an hour before the race. This was almost as humiliating as being escorted out of the Dover casino!

Sure, we could have hung out in the stands or checked out the Van Halen cover band with the rest of the riff raff (please remember that in the past two races, we *were* the riff raff). But instead, we were invited to hang out at our new BFF Robby Gordon's trailer, parked just outside of the track overlooking the third turn. It was there that we met up with one of Robby's sisters, Beccy. She was relaxing outside a huge blue horse trailer, surrounded by friends and family, and next to a big barbecue pit, loaded with various sizzling meats. There were coolers all around, filled with beer and bevies. "This is tailgating, baby!" I thought. We had finally arrived.

We headed into the horse trailer, which obviously had been visited by MTV in a recent episode of *Pimp My Horse Trailer*. This place was boy central—several big-screen TVs, leather furniture, fur throws all around, video games, a big master bedroom, and Robby's current lady-friend. But the best part of this boy palace was the race viewing room, perched over the third turn. We sat on leather bar stools at an oval table, with a perfect view of the race, not to mention air conditioning and near silence! Plus, the room was stocked with food and drink, and we got to hang out with Beccy and her boyfriend, Ryan Hunter-Reay, an IRL driver. Beccy even gave me a lug nut that came off of one of the cars when she was down in the pit. I wore it as a ring. This was a special moment. I had finally mastered NASCAR.

We realize that many of you may not be able to befriend a driver or his sisters, but here are some tips for navigating your own NASCAR adventure:

HOW TO MASTER NASCAR

1. Do your homework by researching the racetrack and figuring out the best way to get there.

2. Do find out what you can bring into the track with you and what you can't. Do find out if it's BYOB!

3. Do plan to arrive early and stay late. Don't suffer through traffic; make the most of your time there.

4. Do try to bullshit your way to a better parking spot. Just try it. The worst thing that can happen is they say no. OR . . .

5. Do take a helicopter if you can afford it.

6. Do go with a group of girls if you can. (Sorry, Chris!)

7. Do make a weekend out of it. Stay in a fun hotel (find out where the NASCAR people are staying). Plan a great dinner. Get some spa treatments. See the sights. See our Travel for more ideas.

8. Do buy the earplugs. It's really freaking loud.

9. Do try out the headsets. They're not cheap (around $50 a day or $70 for the whole weekend), but it's really cool to hear the guys talking to their pit crews.

10. Do go with an open mind. Sure, there's a lot of wackiness, but there's also a lot to enjoy. Talk to other fans before the race. Find out why they love NASCAR. Choose a driver to follow, based on the sponsors: maybe you love Toyotas, love to eat Cheerios, love to shop at Target, or maybe you're trying to quit smoking with Nicorette. Do allow yourself to get into it. And above all, do smash a beer can against your head. Better yet, smash it into some shirtless VMI dude's head.

And before we leave the track, here's a guide to what the different color flags mean during the race:

Green: The start of the race.

Yellow: Caution—slow down or hold your position.

Black: Pull into the pit to consult with your crew.

Black with a white stripe: This lap is not being scored because the driver failed to obey a black flag.

Red: Stop!

Blue with a yellow or orange stripe: Driver must move to another lane; slower traffic should move over.

Yellow with red stripes: There is oil on track.

White: Drivers are entering the last lap.

Black and white checkered: The race is over, let the post-race tailgating begin!

Last but not least, if you're in the pit and you hear the phrases "Happy Hour" or "Silly Season," just laugh and high-five someone. Just kidding. Here's what they mean:

Happy Hour: The last practice before the big race—usually the late afternoon practice on Saturday, just prior to the Sunday race.

Silly Season: The period toward the end of the current season when teams are likely to announce driver, crew or sponsor changes. There's a lot of speculation at this time, and there are many wild predictions based on little more than rumors. But it's how diehard fans get through the off-season, which is really only a couple of months. Guess that's why it's so silly.

PETROSEXUAL ALERT

Let's assume that we have won over your hearts and minds about the thrill of NASCAR and that we've turned you into a complete Petrosexuals (this is a British term that means someone who is obsessively into automobiles. It's taken from "petrol," the word the Brits use for gasoline). You may now start obsessively following the individual drivers, and their juicy personal lives! You will soon realize that NASCAR is home to more drama than you can handle—family drama, relationship drama, driver drama, baby mama drama, even daddy-died-and-now-you're-feuding-with-your-step-mama drama (shout out to Dale Earnhardt, Jr., please see 7 for more).

Each week, fans—especially female fans—want to be kept up on the latest pit action. They need to know which driver's girlfriend is "in or out" (insert Heidi Klum accent here), they need to find out what trouble the wives will be stirring up, and learn which celebs the drivers have been seen canoodling with. A great resource is the "Tall Glass of Milk" website, written by pop-culture blogger Jen (her last name is unknown). She is completely plugged in and has the scoop on who is dating whom, who is snubbing whom, and who is blanking whom. Check it out at drinkthis. typepad.com/answer_this. And if it's your ultimate goal to snag a NASCAR driver for a hook-up/boyfriend/husband, check out *The Girls' Guide to Winning a NASCAR Driver,* written by Liz Allison, Nashville Sports Radio Host, wife of the late Davey Allison, daughter-in-law of Bobby Allison and a former TV reporter for NASCAR races. In other words, she would know how to go from Pit Lizard to Victory Lane, baby.

One woman you don't want to take advice from is Angela Harkness. Check out this twisted tale, which sounds like it could be the plot of one of those silly NASCAR Harlequin romances, except it's true. Follow along as Angela (a.k.a. Fatemeh) goes from stripper to NASCAR owner to fugitive, while leaving a trail of death and destruction in her path. You can't make this stuff up . . .

THE ART OF HARKNESS

How a Scheming Stripper and her Lover Scammed NASCAR

The story that NASCAR would rather forget is too strange and juicy to stop telling. It's got everything. Sex. Crime. Lies. Booze. Strippers. Fugitives. Race. Suicide. Prison. Infidelity. It also has a strange mix of locales: Iran. Los Angeles. Texas. Daytona. Dubai. And another insulated world not understood by many: NASCAR racing. Last but not least it has what every great story needs: A scary villain. Enter this tale's leading lady: Angela Harkness (a.k.a. Fatemeh Rayford, a.k.a. Fatemeh Hiddavsadeh). She obviously has called herself a lot of things. People called her a lot of other names, too. Monster. Sociopath. Femme fatale. Black Widow. Ya' know, all the stuff that might hurt your chances of winning PTA "Mom of the Year." A stripper from Iran might have been the least likely choice to take NASCAR for an expensive ride. But this is Angela's true story—even if she hasn't always stuck to it.

Pole dancing is a bit like NFL football. It can be a lucrative way to use your body. But as a career, it's got the shelf-life of a Paris Hilton CD. Just ask Angela, who by 2001 was stripping at an old Austin, Texas, nightclub called The Yellow Rose, according to *Car and Driver* magazine. She was then just 25, but she'd already had plenty of drama in her short life. She had been married twice, was the single mother of a little girl, and her second husband killed himself. She was hoping for better luck in Texas. It was there that she met Gary Jones, a Wells Fargo Bank vice president who, by most accounts, is a nice, intelligent guy. Seemed that way, anyway. Soft-spoken, African-American and chubby, he had a disarming smile and a pleasant, bespectacled face.

But he was living a double life. He was a frequent customer at The Yellow Rose, and he took a liking to this new dancer. Except for her peroxide blond hair, she was different from the rest. She was more buxom and hard-bodied than naturally pretty. She spoke English well, but it was with some weird, exotic accent. Even her imperfections were kind of cool. She had a slight overbite, and her two front teeth had a gap like the supermodel Lauren Hutton. Yep, Jones liked this new stripper, Angela Harkness. He liked her so much they started an affair, even though Jones was married. An even bigger problem was that he secretly had taken out a bunch of shady bank loans under other people's names, digging himself a criminally deep financial hole. After he teamed up with Angela, that hole only got deeper. Angela just wanted upward mobility fast, and she got it. After bailing on the stripping biz, her second move was to get Jones to think bigger. Or cheat bigger, anyway. He used to follow Angela into The Yellow Rose; now she got him to follow her into the bank, where he fraudulently secured her more than a quarter of a million dollars. But they weren't done.

They started a NASCAR team called Angela's Motorsports in 2002 and they decided to race in the Busch Series (now the Nationwide Series), which, as we mentioned, is sort of like the undercard to NASCAR's Sunday main event. They needed a sponsor and Jones found Rick Barton, president of a small online travel company called WiredFlyer.com, to partly fund the venture. However, deadlines loomed for all of Jones' debts, which eventually totaled more than $1 million. So, when they started Angela's Motorsports, they gave themselves no margin for error. It was madness. It was practically doomed from the start. And you know what? It almost worked. As they approached the end of 2002, remarkably and briefly, they had all the makings of a legit NASCAR operation. Jones and Angela hired a veteran driver and experienced crew leaders, and they got off to a promising start. Angela's Motorsports tested their car at Daytona in January 2003, and they were the fastest team. They were primed to be a Cinderella story. But then it all started to unravel.

Jones and Angela told everyone back at the office that Barton and Wired-Flyer.com would fund the whole shebang, according to *Car and Driver* magazine. At the same time, they told Barton a different story—that they were about to land a big fish in Texas to be the primary sponsor. That never happened. Even worse, they never came up with a Plan B to keep it all going if they never found a bigger backer (they didn't), or if Barton didn't have the money (he definitely didn't). It wasn't long before the crew looked to be paid by Barton, who was upset when he learned the crew thought he was screwing them out of money. Even with all their lies, if Jones and Angela had been able to land a deep-pocketed sponsor at the 11th hour, they actually might have pulled it all off. But they didn't, and things got even worse. Within months of the team's first race, Barton's WiredFlyer.com went under and Angela's Motorsports was officially out of business. Not long after, the stress got to Barton. In July 2003, he died of a heart attack at the age of 48.

After that, the last pieces fell rather quickly. FBI agents arrested Jones for his 16 illegitimate loans and he was indicted in September 2003. And the NASCAR scheme surely wasn't helping his case.

Neither was his partner-in-crime. She sent the cops after her lover and testified against him in exchange for a lighter sentence. Jones was convicted of four felony counts, and was sent to prison for nearly four years. He was released in late 2007. Incredibly, Angela was going to get off easy, if not totally unscathed. All she had to do was plead guilty to a lesser felony, serve a brief time in jail, and she could move on. But she never showed up in court for the sentencing. Instead, she went on the lam, leaving town as a criminal fugitive wanted by the US Marshals.

At that point, two groups that everyone loves to hate—cops and reporters—got involved and did some digging. They found that Angela Harkness was an even bigger con artist with an even shadier past than they thought. In fact . . . (cue the music: dum-dum-duh!) . . . they found out that Angela Harkness wasn't even her original name! Turns out she was born Fatemeh Karimkhani, a *Maxim* magazine story recounts, and is the daughter of a former general in the old Shah of Iran's military. The corrupt Shah was toppled by Islamic fundamentalists when Angela was a toddler, and her family eventually fled to Germany. By the mid-'90s, she was known as Angela and worked at a strip joint called The Candy Cat in Canoga Park, California, a San Fernando Valley suburb. That was where she met attorney Dion Harkness. They married in 1999 and had a daughter. They also had a reportedly stormy relationship that mixed alcohol, cocaine and violent fights. About two years after his wedding day, Dion Harkness was found shot to death in a hotel near Palm Springs. The authorities ruled it a suicide. One of the notes he left read: "Angela has ruined my life," according to *Maxim*. Soon thereafter, she turned up in Texas, where she and Jones met. The rest is NASCAR history.

So, now the feds knew about her past, but they really, really wanted to catch her in the present. Sure enough, the Lone Star Fugitive Task Force (think Chuck Norris with more guns and less facial hair) tracked her down in Dubai, in the United Arab Emirates. She'd gone from the Texas Gulf Coast to the Persian Gulf. Using her childhood name, Fatemeh Karimkhani, she lived quietly for awhile, scraping by as a hair stylist until authorities arrested her in May 2005. However, they had to release her because the United States and the United Arab Emirates had no extradition treaty with each other. So, she and her young daughter Lisha stayed in Dubai, and in legal limbo, for almost two years. Then one day in early 2007, a US Marshal picked up the phone and was stunned to hear Angela's voice on the other end. She wanted to come back, turn herself in and serve her time. Or maybe Fatemeh Karim-khani just missed Angela Harkness. Whatever the reason, she was arrested as soon as she landed in New York, and soon thereafter was sentenced to three years and four months in prison. Until then, her daughter is being cared for by relatives.

NASCAR since has instituted its "Drive for Diversity" program, designed to promote future female and minority owners, drivers and employees. Some question whether or not it screens those groups with more scrutiny than others. But NASCAR says the program's goals are sincere. In 2004, it added Magic Johnson to a committee dedicated to broadening the sport's diversity. NASCAR might have too quickly welcomed Jones and Angela into the fold, it has been reported, in part to prove it has an open mind. But that theory fails to mention that NASCAR long ago approved minority and African-American ownership when some of the other professional sports leagues couldn't be bothered with it. For example, neither MLB nor NFL can claim to have minority ownership, save for Mexican-American Arte Moreno, who owns MLB's Los Angeles Angels of Anaheim. Neither league has had an African-American owner. But NASCAR has.

Until 2010, Angela will live behind bars. If history is an indicator, she is already working to put a plan in motion as soon as she is out. Maybe prison life now isn't so different from a childhood that saw her family trapped in their own country, or when she spent years dancing at dingy strip joints. She eventually got herself out of those places, so why should jail be any different? Her destiny in a life that resembles a B-movie seems to always involve two concepts: Being stuck in a prison of some kind, and plotting a scheme to escape it. Lord knows what she has in mind for a sequel. Grab the popcorn and watch along with us.

So that we don't leave you with a bad taste in your mouth when it comes to women and racing, we went to end this with a bit more on our racing pals Robyn and Beccy Gordon. The sisters of Robby Gordon were not only were instrumental in bringing us into the NASCAR fold, but they also introduced us to a completely different brand of competition—off-road racing. While it's not as commercial and overblown as NASCAR and CHAMP/Indy, it's kind of an underground movement. And for true racing fans who live and breathe the sport, and who are not into kissing up to sponsors and the "professional wrestling" allegations—this is the most exciting form of racing around.

Off-road racing is something the entire Gordon family has had in their blood for generations—from their dad "Baja Bob" Gordon and their brother Robby Gordon, to the Gordon sisters, who, along with their friends, have formed All-American Girl Racing, featuring all-girl racers, all-girl pit crew . . . all girls, all the time! And they did so without help from their famous NASCAR brother, thank you very much. Check out AllAmericanGirlRacing.com for details on their next off-road adventure.

But first, here is a little background to whet your whistle about a couple hard-core, off-road races:

The Baja 1000: This 1,000-mile race is held every November and goes from Ensenada down to La Paz, in Baja California, Mexico. It's the longest continuous, point-to-point race in the world, and it all started back in 1967. If you've ever spent any time in Mexico, you know that in many parts of that country, anything goes. The rules are: there ain't no rules. So just imagine an off-road race where anything goes. And just imagine 200,000+ fans, lining the desert course, nothing between them and vehicles racing by at extremely high speeds. As insane as it may sound, many talk of the mystical quality of this race. It's beautiful. It's dangerous. It's full of surprises. The only thing to expect is the unexpected. And to many, the spirit of this off-road adventure is what's lacking in modern-day organized racing.

Everyone pays the same entry fee, and the prize money is meager compared to current standards. But it's not about the money. This is a race for glory alone. And the chance to come back with a million stories that will keep you going until next year.

Anyone can enter the Baja 1000 and they can race any vehicle they want—from a Rolls Royce to a Winnebago and everything in between—although most entrants ride motorcycles, quads, trophy trucks, buggies, and even old VW bugs. Some people try to power through and drive the entire 1,000 miles themselves, while others put together teams of drivers. Some teams span three generations, some include professional NASCAR drivers (Robby) with their fancy trailers and helicopters, and many just consist of amateurs from SoCal and Mexico, a few using their last dime to cover fuel costs. There are all-girl teams (Robyn and Beccy have competed before), and a fierce woman (as Christian from *Project Runway* might say) named Anna Jo Cody who completed the 2006 race solo on a motorcycle. And, yes, there are even celebs. Back in the '60s, you'd find tough guys like Steve McQueen and James Garner racing. These days, you'll find McDreamy (Patrick Dempsey) and Monster Garage dude/Sandra Bullock's husband (Jesse James).

So McDreamy and Jesse James, along with 1,200 other racers, have 32 hours to complete the grueling 1,000-mile course, taking their lives in their own hands on all sorts of crazy terrain. Throughout the course, they'll find themselves speeding along narrow, winding mountain roads, heading down a cliff to make a break for the coastline, and keeping the pedal to the metal as they power through the notorious silt, which is like driving through a bottomless pit of baby powder (except it doesn't smell as nice). And it's not just the terrain that presents challenges. Try avoiding herds of goats milling about in the middle of the road. Try getting back on track after some mischievous locals decided to move the course markers, or built a jump in the course to see how your bike could handle it. Or try to avoid a gunshot or two from local ranchers who are not happy you are driving through their property. (This is pretty rare, but has been known to happen.) Talk about a wild ride . . .

The Dakar Rally: Started in 1978, the Dakar is a race from a major European city down to Senegal in Africa, and it's thought to be even more dangerous than the Baja 1000—especially with the terrorist threats and political overtones that are now endangering the future of the race (oh yeah, and endangering the lives of the drivers!).

Whereas the Baja course finds racers driving straight through, the Dakar includes 15 grueling days of roughly 500-mile stages, with forced rest-stops. This adds up to a nearly 6,000-mile course, running from a major European city (usually Paris, but sometimes Barcelona or Lisbon) all the way down to Dakar, Senegal, in Africa. This race is for serious entrants only. The entry fee is much higher for racers, and the purse is higher, as well. The course is unmarked, but drivers are given a guide-book. Drivers can use a GPS, but only as a compass. There are specific classifications for each type of vehicle, and you'll find more than 500 off-road motorcycles, cars and trucks competing. Roughly 20% are professional drivers (again, Robby Gordon has been a competitor), while 80% are amateurs. In 2007, it is reported that one million spectators followed the Dakar through Portugal.

The challenges in this course are again difficult terrain that varies from volcanic rock to the desert, herds of wild animals, the possibility of testy locals, and in 2008, terrorism. Just hours before the race was to begin in January 2008, the French-run Dakar was cancelled for the first time in 30 years, because of Al-Qaeda threats in Mauritania, where eight of 15 stages of the race were to be held. After a family of four French tourists were killed in December 2007, and direct threats were made against the Dakar, the organizers said they had no choice but to cancel the race. The last-minute decision left many drivers, including our pal Robby Gordon, furious. Sure, he lost more than $4.5 million because of the cancellation. But more than the money, he just wanted to race. He thought the organizers should have had a Plan B (and Plan C, D and E) in case something like this might to happen. In response to the cancellation, Gordon said in a statement, "Us racers, we like to race.

Just get creative . . . Do something to keep the show in place and save face . . . I can't believe they gave up that easy." He also said some other things that are just not appropriate for print.

The organizers of the Dakar, who incidentally also run the Tour de France, pulled together a race through Central Europe in April 2008, in which Gordon, along with many of the would-be Dakar competitors, participated—especially because much of their equipment was still over in Portugal. The Dakar organizers have also planned a race in Argentina and Chile in January 2009. Still, there are hard feelings from many of the racers, as they were forced to incur costs associated with the cancellation, as well as disappoint many of their sponsors who paid big bucks to participate in the original Dakar race. As we wait for the drama to unfold, we'll just sit back and crank up the song *500 Connards Sur la Ligne de Départ* on iTunes. The French song is a harsh criticism of the Dakar, claiming that these rich jet-setters are spending ridiculous amounts of money to participate in this over-the-top race as Africans live in poverty around them. Translated to English, the title of the song is *500 Assholes at the Starting Line.* (But we're sure they're not talking about our friend Robby!)

Whew! For a couple of latte-sipping, martini-swilling writers who love to ponder our navels as we sit, brooding, in tiny cafés on the East and West Coasts—we found a lot to love about good old NASCAR and auto racing on the whole. Next time, we're definitely taking a chopper and finding a way to get our hands on a couple of "Hot" passes. We'll see you in the pit!

5 CURSES, FOILED AGAIN!:
Curses & Superstitions

- -

FOR ALL OF THE RULES AND STATS FOUND IN SPORTS, MUCH
is left to the imagination. Would the 1972 Dolphins have beat the 2007
Pats? How many home runs would Babe Ruth have hit if he had access
to 'roids? Even Fantasy Leagues are based on pretending you're a team
owner, putting together your dream-team of players. It's no wonder that
fans and players alike have used their imaginations to concoct silly curses
that seem to have plagued our teams for decades, or wacky superstitions
designed to end a streak of bad luck, or keep their lucky streak going. Or
are these curses real? And do these superstitions work? You be the judge.

THE CURSE OF JESSICA SIMPSON:

We love the fact that during the 2007 season, she was being called Yoko
Romo. We also love the fact that Tony Romo's teammate Terrell Owens
told the press, "Jessica Simpson is not a fan favorite—in this locker
room or in Texas Stadium," after the Cowboys' 2007 loss to Philadelphia. And we love the fact that the *New York Post* sent a Jessica Simpson
look-alike to the Dallas/Giants game to distract Romo—and that Perez
Hilton fell for the ruse. Now before we completely buy into this curse
thing, however, we must note that Romo also had a horrible game when
former girlfriend Carrie Underwood was in attendance—so it could
just be the "Curse of Tony Romo's Penchant for Hot, Yet Somewhat
Ditzy Blondes." But whether or not Tony and Jessica are even a couple
anymore, we still think there's something to the Jessica curse and we
think it may extend beyond football. Just ask the following men if they
think there is anything to this Jessica curse business, and you may hear
a resounding "HELL, YEAH!": Nick Lachey, John Mayer, Dane Cook,
Johnny Knoxville, Owen Wilson, Adam Levine, Bam Margera, and the
list goes on . . .

Curse of the Bambino:

From 1920 to 2004, the Curse of the Bambino is all any Boston Red Sox fan could talk about. (Actually, sportswriters really started talking about the curse in 1986 when the Red Sox collapsed against the Mets in the World Series). But the history of the curse can be traced back to 1920 when the Red Sox sold Babe Ruth to the Yankees. Prior to the sale, the Red Sox completely dominated the sport—winning five out of the first 15 World Series match-ups. After the sale, the Yankees emerged as one of the most dominant sports teams ever and went on to play in 39 World Series, winning 26 of them. As we all know, the Red Sox did not have a win in this entire 86 years. Until 2004, that is. Many fans over the years had attempted to break the curse. Some zany antics included putting a Red Sox cap atop Mount Everest, having professional exorcisms at Fenway, repainting the "Reverse Curve" sign on Storrow Drive to say "Reverse the Curse," and even pushing a piano once owned by Ruth into a pond near his farm in Sudbury, Massachusetts.

Some claim the curse was broken on August 31, 2004, when a foul ball, hit by Manny "Baggy Pants" Ramirez, flew into the stands and hit a 16-year-old kid named Lee Gavin in the face, knocking out two teeth. The kid was a life-long Boston fan who just happened to live on Babe Ruth's old farm in Sudbury. (Insert *Twilight Zone* music here.) That same day, the Yankees suffered their worst loss in team history, beaten 22-0 at home by the Cleveland Indians. Others claim that the curse was broken in September 2004, during a concert at Fenway by Jimmy Buffett, who performed a curse-breaking ceremony, accompanied by a witch doctor and a Babe Ruth look-alike.

In 2004, the Red Sox faced the Yankees in the American League Championship series. After losing the first three games, and trailing 4 to 3 in the bottom of the 9th inning of Game 4, the Red Sox came back to win that game, as well as the next three. The Red Sox then went on to beat the St. Louis Cardinals to win the World Series in a four-game sweep. But it was that dramatic ALCS battle that was one of the most exciting match-ups in history—a truly fitting ending to this 86-year curse. And whether you love or hate the Red Sox or the Yankees, it was a baseball-lover's dream.

THE CURSE OF THE BILLY GOAT:

In 1945, during Game 4 of the World Series between the Chicago Cubs and the Detroit Tigers, Billy Sianis—a Greek immigrant and Chicago tavern owner—showed up to the game with two box seat tickets, one for himself and one for his goat. Some sources claim the goat's name was Murphy. Sianis was very close to the goat you see, Murphy had fallen off a truck and wandered into the tavern (which is now known as The Billy Goat Tavern) and Sianis helped nurse him back to health. So he brought Murphy down to the game with a sign pinned to his back that read "We Got Detroit's Goat." Funny times down at good old Wrigley, right? Most people thought so. Sianis and the goat paraded around the field, to much applause, and then were escorted to their seats. A little later in the game, Cubs owner Phillip Knight Wrigley ordered Sianis and Murphy to be ejected from the stadium, stating that the animal smelled and was bothering other fans. Sianis was outraged and placed a curse on the Cubs, stating that they would never win another pennant or play in a World Series at Wrigley because the Cubs had disrespected his goat. The Cubs ended up losing the 1945 series, and Sianis wrote Wrigley a letter saying, "Who stinks now?" And apparently, the curse stuck. The Cubs still haven't won a National League Pennant (despite coming really close in 2003 and at least winning their division in 2007) and have not played in a World Series. In fact, they haven't won a World Series since 1908.

There have been multiple attempts to bring goats out to Wrigley to break the curse, including one attempt by some Cubs fans who tried to bring a goat into Minute Maid Park in Houston in 2003. They were denied access. Billy Sianis' nephew claims that the only way the curse will be lifted will be when the Cubs organization demonstrates a true affinity for goats, letting them on the field because they like them, not just for a publicity stunt.

And in 2003, it looked like the Billy Goat curse was on the verge of being reversed. In a playoff game at Wrigley against the Marlins, the Cubs were just five outs away from winning the National League Pennant and heading to the World Series. But that's when infamous fan Steve Bartman tried to catch a foul ball, preventing Cubs outfielder Moises Alou from making the catch. Moises slammed down his glove in frustration and looked to the ump to call interference. But he didn't. The Cubs lost their mojo and the game, and the Marlins went on to win the World Series. Bartman had to be escorted out of the game by security as fans shouted and threw things at him. The Governor of Illinois jokingly (we hope) told the *Chicago Sun-Times* that Barman "better join the witness protection program." The Governor of Florida, a one Mr. Jeb Bush, offered Bartman asylum in his state and he was even offered a job with the Marlins. But the lifelong Cubs fan and Little League coach apologized in a heartfelt statement, turned down all of the offers and shied away from the publicity—donating any gifts he did receive to the Juvenile Diabetes Research Foundation in the name of Ron Santo, a former Cub-turned-broadcaster who suffers from diabetes.

However Chicagoans were not done with the Bartman ball quite yet. The guys from Harry Caray's restaurant group bought the ball in an auction, publicly exploded it and then took the remains, boiled them down and put the steam from the remains into a pasta sauce. (Leave it to the food-loving city of Chicago to somehow take a sports curse and turn it into an eating extravaganza.) The seat that Bartman sat in during the ill-fated foul ball attempt (section 102, seat 113) is now a tourist attraction at Wrigley, as they continue their tradition as lovable losers.

And apparently, the curse stays with players after they leave the Cubs. Some think that former Cubs go on to play on teams that do win the World Series—including Lou Brock, Rick Monday, Dennis Eckersley, Greg Maddux and Mark Grace. And conversely, there are those who think that former Cubs bring the curse to their new team—including Bill Buckner, Mitch Williams and Mike Krukow. Hmmm, Mike Krukow, that reminds us that he has a curse of his own . . .

THE KRUKOW KURSE:

Aside from the ex-Cub factor, many Giants fans believe that it's their hometown announcer Mike Krukow who is responsible for the fact that the San Francisco Giants have not won the World Series since 1954, back when they were the New York Giants. Before each season, Kruk talks about the Giants chances on his radio show—each year saying that the team ultimately has a chance to win the World Series. Believers think that the year that he does not make this claim is the year the team might actually win.

Another factor the Giants might be facing is the Barry Bonds curse. The city of Pittsburgh thinks that their Pirates are cursed, as the team has not made a postseason appearance since Bonds left, just before the 1993 season. And Barry certainly did not help the Giants win a Series during his entire stint in San Francisco—although they did make it to the series in 2002 and lost to the Angels. But with Barry now indicted and on the verge of retirement, maybe both curses will be put to rest. One can only hope!

THE CHUNKY SOUP CURSE/THE MADDEN CURSE/
THE *SI* COVER CURSE:

We're lumping all three of these together because they are all similar: If you appear in a Chunky Soup ad, on the cover of the Madden NFL video game or on the cover of *Sports Illustrated*—you will be injured, fail miserably and/or fade into obscurity. There are examples up the wazoo of these curses coming true, from Chunky Soup spokesman and Steelers QB Ben Roethlisberger crashing on his motorcycle, to Atlanta QB Michael Vick on the cover of Madden NFL in 2004, the season he got injured the day after the game hit store shelves . . . and we all know what happened in the years that followed.

As for the *SI* curse, there are plenty of examples across all sports, back from the very first issue in 1954 when Braves' Eddie Matthews appeared on the cover and broke his hand that very week, which contributed to the Braves downfall and failure to win the pennant. The curse extended to Anna Kournikova, who never won a singles title in her career after appearing on the cover of *SI* in 2000. And even in 2007, Brett Favre graced the cover and saw his dream season cut short by the Wild Card Giants at what was supposed to be an easy playoff win at home on the frozen tundra.

Now, do these curses exist? Skeptics say that it makes sense that someone at the pinnacle of their career would get all sorts of attention and sponsorship deals, and with the high chances of getting hurt during any given game, it's more like an inevitable occurrence than a curse. For Chunky Soup and Madden, it does seem odd that not one player seems to have escaped "the curse." And back at good old *SI,* they wrote an article in 2002 where they explored their own jinx and evaluated more than 2,400 covers. They found that nearly 40% of the athletes featured on the cover had something "unhappy happen afterwards." If you're an athlete and you think there's a 40% chance of something "unhappy" happening, our guess is that you're not posing for that cover. And that's just what happened in 2002 when the SI editors asked QB Kurt Warner to appear on the cover of the jinx issue, posing with a black cat. Now keep in mind that Warner wears the number 13, so the guy can't be that superstitious, right? Wrong. He turned down the cover and the black cat appeared solo. Don't worry, Kurt, we believe in the jinx, too. Hear that *SI*? Do NOT, we repeat DO NOT put us on your cover! (Obviously we're kidding, *SI*. Call our agent. Set it up. Seriously.)

THE CURSE OF BILLY PENN:

Back to cities that think they are cursed because their teams are lousy. As a rule, we don't buy into recent curses that involve things like architecture and that are based on "the sports gods" getting all riled up because a building was constructed higher than another building. But that's what Philly fans believe has caused their teams to suck. Back in March of 1987, a towering skyscraper named One Liberty Place was built in downtown Philly. The new structure exceeded the height of City Hall, a domed building topped with a statue of William Penn, the city's founder and the "Absolute Proprietor" of the state of Pennsylvania. Under what was known as a "gentleman's agreement" that was made hundreds of years ago, no building in the city was to ever be constructed higher than City Hall. Apparently in the '80s era of Gordon Gekko-esque deals, things like "gentleman's agreements" went out the window in favor of tall buildings and big profits. And now, many more skyscrapers have been built downtown.

Now these Philly folks are serious. They think this curse extends to all sports in the city—football, baseball, hockey, pro and college basketball, and even horse racing, as Smarty Jones based in nearby Bensalem, failed to win the Triple Crown in 2004. So in June 2007, some ironworkers building the latest skyscraper in the city took matters into their own hands. In constructing Comcast Center, which is now Philly's tallest building, the workers hoisted the final beam to the top of the skyscraper—and on it, they placed a small figurine of William Penn, along with an American flag, proving that no building would rise above Billy Penn. At least for a while.

NEW YORK RANGERS CURSE:

After a hockey team wins the Stanley Cup, each member of the winning team can take the Cup wherever they want for 24 hours. Unlike other sports, where they make a new trophy every year, there is only one Stanley Cup (well, there's a replica in the Hall of Fame, so technically, there is more than one). But the trophy is passed from winning team to winning team—meaning that this old Cup has made the rounds, from the White House to children's hospitals and from bars (where it might be filled with booze and the whole joint sips out of it) to a player's home (where he lets his dog eat out of it). All of these antics leave us craving a bottle of Purell, and wondering about this Rangers curse . . .

It all started back in 1940, when the New York Rangers won the Stanley Cup. It is reported that the team execs had just paid off their mortgage on Madison Square Garden, so they burned the mortgage document in the bowl of the Cup. Many feel that this act desecrated the sanctity of Lord Stanley's Cup—and cursed the team. In 1994, more than 50 years later, the curse was finally broken, as the Rangers finally reclaimed the Cup, led by team captain Mark Messier. This meant that the Stanley Cup could then be trotted around New York City by the various players. First, it made an appearance on *The Late Show with David Letterman,* then it showed up at a parade down Broadway. Next, a stop at McSorley's Bar, then it ended up strapped into a cop car in a seat belt, and finally to a Yankees game to sit in Steinbrenner's luxury suite. But the Cup's antics were not over just yet. Captain Mark Messier then took the Stanley Cup to Scores, a strip joint on the East Side, where our dear sweet Cup became a part of the on-stage show. Grab the Purell, people! In fact, we think Purell should sponsor the Stanley Cup! We are officially putting a NEW curse on the Rangers for the next 50 years— because if having strippers writhe all over the Cup is not desecration, we don't know what is! (For the record, Chris does not think strippers writhing all over the Cup is that bad and he does not support Erica's newly instituted curse.)

THE CURSE OF THE ASTROTURF:

Everyone hates AstroTurf. But Houston fans have another reason to hate it. The blasted stuff, first called ChemGrass, just might be responsible for Houston's dismal performance on the field. AstroTurf found fame and fortune when the Houston Astrodome was first built, bringing baseball indoors and fake grass to the forefront. Boo on both. In all 35 years at the Astrodome—from 1965, the year the Astros were born, to 2000, when they moved to a new park—the team never played in the World Series. And some up-and-coming young stars, who could've been contenders, found their careers cut short, thanks to the Curse of the Turf. In 1980, the Astros' All-Star pitcher J.R. Richard suffered a stroke during a light workout day, when the team wasn't even playing. He never pitched another Major League game. In 1984, another promising player, shortstop Dickie Thon, was hit in the face by a fastball, breaking his orbital bone and changing his career forever. Once thought to be a perennial all-star, Thon continued to suffer from depth perception problems and never fully regained all of his skills. Toss in the disastrous 1991 trade of Astros outfielder Kenny Lofton and the insulting low-ball offer the team's execs made to legendary pitcher Nolan Ryan, causing him to finish out his career with the Texas Rangers—and you've got yourself a string of bad luck and bad decisions, turf or no turf.

Regardless, the Astrodome now sits empty after once being declared the "Eighth Wonder of the World"—a declaration that came from Astros management, of course. Love or hate its tacky '60s design, the Astrodome is a historic landmark, being the first domed stadium in the world. There is talk of remodeling the structure and building a luxury hotel in its place, but for now it remains an eyesore. As for the Astros, in 2000 they moved into a new ballpark with a retractable roof, hoping their luck would change. However, the name of the ballpark was Enron Field. So in many ways, their new ballpark has a dark past, too.

And they can change the name to anything they want—Minute Maid Park or "The Juice Box"—we still smell curse. Because when you have someone like the now-deceased Enron CEO and Chairman Kenneth Lay throw out the first pitch in your brand new ballpark, to be remembered for posterity—there's got to be some residual bad karma floating around. Maybe that's why the Astros finally got to the World Series in 2005 and lost to the White Sox, who had a pretty bad curse to overcome themselves. We think the Astros now face the Curse of Kenneth Lay. You heard it here first, folks.

THE CURSE OF THE BLACK SOX:

We're not going to spend too much time on this scandal, because the "Pox on the Sox" has lifted, with the White Sox 2005 World Series win against the aforementioned Astros. But if you want to know more about the Black Sox scandal of 1919—when Shoeless Joe Jackson and the rest of his crooked teammates threw the World Series, allowing Cincinnati to win and lots of gamblers who had money on the fixed game to get rich—rent one of our favorite sports movies, *Eight Men Out*.

VERY SUPERSTITIOUS

There are many rituals that players abide by to make sure luck is on their side. If there's a no-hitter being pitched, whatever you do, do not mention it to the pitcher. In fact, don't even talk to the pitcher. Same goes for hockey if there's a possibility of a shutout. Just avoid talking to the goalie at all costs. Some players have lucky shirts, special socks or auspicious underwear. (Ask Jason Giambi about his lucky gold lamé thong.) Some of these clothing items go unwashed and unchanged for days . . . weeks . . . we'll stop right there. Even the greatest players have quirky little rituals that help them gear up for a big game: Michael Jordan used to wear his UNC basketball shorts under his Bulls shorts while playing in the NBA, Tiger Woods always wears red on Sundays and Wayne Gretzky used to tuck one side of his NHL jersey into his pants.

Back on the baseball diamond, players carefully walk over the baselines when taking their positions on the field. And some ballplayers have strange relationships with their bats—talking to them, getting them blessed by priests, kissing them, even sleeping in the same bed with them before a big game. (Keep it clean, people!)

Racecar drivers have an aversion to green cars and the number 13, both reported to be unlucky. But they also avoid peanuts, of all things. Apparently, an old racecar driver (who no one can really identify) would share his shelled peanuts with other drivers at the track, and whoever ate them would crash. That old driver ended up crashing and dying himself. The result? No peanuts in the pit. It's an unspoken rule.

But we also like learning about quirky, individual superstitions. Here are a few of our favorites:

LUCKY FOOD:

If some players have a good game, they will repeat the same breakfast and lunch they had that day over and over again, for luck. Third baseman Wade Boggs, for instance, ate chicken before every single game he played. And back in the day, Lou Gehrig's mother sent a jar of pickled eels—Gehrig's favorite food—to the Yankees clubhouse. After Gehrig shared it with Babe Ruth and the rest of his teammates prior to a game, they went on a hitting frenzy. After that, the team didn't go out on the field without sampling some pickled eels, until their streak was over. (And rumor has it that Ruth used to mix the pickled eels with a quart of chocolate ice cream.)

LUCKY HYGIENE HABITS:

Former White Sox left fielder Minnie Minoso was in a slump. He needed to change things up. Therefore, after a hitless game, he got in the shower fully dressed—wearing his uniform, his hat, his cleats—in an attempt to wash that bad luck right out of his hair, and out of his uni. The next day, he got three hits—and after the game, eight of his teammates joined him, fully dressed, in the shower. And in another strange custom that involves hygiene, or lack thereof, several baseball players actually pee on their hands. Some say they do so to toughen up the skin, while others claim it gets rid of blisters, and still others just do it because it's a psychological trick that they think will help their game. Although urine is sterile, studies show that it actually softens hands. But don't tell that to outfielder Moises Alou, pitcher Kerry Wood or catcher Jorge Posada, who told Slate.com, "You don't want to shake my hand during Spring Training." We'll remember that, Jorge, and we won't.

UNLUCKY HOOKERS:

Some have lucky thongs or pickled eels, but Eugene Robinson thought that visiting a local hooker brought luck. At the time, Robinson was a free safety with the Atlanta Falcons, returning to the Super Bowl for his third time. The night before the big game, he would once again resort to his tried-and-true Super Bowl tradition of paying a local hooker for a blowjob—sneaking out of his room after bed check. But in 1999, his tradition wasn't quite as lucky as in prior years. Rather, it seemed quite unlucky that the prostitute he paid $40 to for oral sex happened to be an undercover cop. And it was unlucky that Robinson—who had been up all night waiting in the police station—played horribly in the game,

helping to contribute to the Falcons' loss. And his publicist undoubtedly thought it was unlucky that the morning before Robinson carried
out his "local hooker" tradition, he received the Bart Starr Award from
the Christian group Athletes in Action for his "high moral character."
Maybe he should try eating chicken.

LUCKY WIVES & GIRLFRIENDS . . . & MISTRESSES:

Sometimes, sports wives and girlfriends get into the act. Pittsburgh
Pirate pitcher Bob Friend's wife always wore the same exact dress to
the ballpark when her husband was pitching, while renowned pitcher
Tom Seaver's wife Nancy carried a special ring and other lucky trinkets
to help her hubby—then pitching for the Mets—beat the Orioles in the
1969 Series. But back to Wade Boggs. He claims that his batting average
improved when his longtime mistress, our old friend Margo Adams,
came to games sans underwear.

LUCKY LITTLE PEOPLE:

There's no tactful way to say this, so we'll just come out and say it: Pedro
Martinez and the Red Sox had their very own "Rally Little Person" in
2004—a one Mr. Nelson de la Rosa, who stood at 28 inches tall. Some
say this good-luck charm helped lead them to their first World Series
win in 86 years. Although Pedro claims he is not superstitious, he says
that he met de la Rosa, also from the Dominican Republic, and the two
became friends. Martinez began inviting de la Rosa to games during the
2004 season, bringing his buddy into the clubhouse, scooping him up
in his arms. Oddly enough, the games that Nelson attended were games
the Red Sox ended up winning. "He's our lucky charm now . . . The guys
are falling in love with him," Pedro said in an interview with MSNBC.
Nelson remained by Pedro's side through the thrilling ALCS championship, traveling to New York, and even taking photos with adoring fans.
Nelson became a celebrity in his own right—even though he already
sort of was one, as he had appeared in *The Island of Dr. Moreau* with
Marlon Brando and was a popular actor in the Dominican Republic. So
there you have it: Nelson, the lucky little person who brought the team

good fortune and helped them reverse the curse. He even appeared with Pedro in the World Series celebratory parade in Boston. Life was sweet for Pedro, Nelson and the entire Red Sox nation.

Until the offseason. That's when Pedro left the Red Sox for the Mets. (At least he didn't commit the ultimate betrayal like Johnny Damon did when he went to the Yankees.) But Pedro not only left town, he also dissed his former team, and worse, he dissed Nelson de la Rosa. Actually, according to Nelson, it is more accurate to say that Pedro broke his heart. In a news conference with Pedro's new team, Martinez said that he didn't believe in good luck charms and said, "That was just a trick." He then picked up another little person who *happened* to be in attendance at the press conference and referred to Nelson as a "palm-sized pipsqueak." (Maybe Pedro is just trying to fit in with all of the other so-called rude New Yorkers?) Nelson stated that he had become a free agent. He said he remained true to the Red Sox, but that if another Dominican player on the Mets wanted him, he would be there. He also said he would go to the Yankees, if asked. Unfortunately, before he got a chance to represent another team, Nelson died of heart failure in 2006 at the age of 38. So listen up, Pedro, you over-sized pipsqueak! We think your treatment of Nelson could be the very reason the Mets imploded in 2007. The Curse of Nelson de la Rosa. It is on.

Lucky Slump Busters:

According to former Cubs and Diamondback first-baseman Mark Grace, some ballplayers who are going through a hitting slump solve the problem by embarking on a "slump buster." Brace yourself for this one. A "slump buster" is when a ballplayer goes out to a bar and finds an overweight, ugly woman, then sleeps with her—effectively ending his slump.

Erica's response? FYI, fellas, many of us ladies do a variation of this when trying to end a sexless streak. We go out to a bar, sleep with the *hottest* guy we can find, and then decide we have our mojo back. We're just not sure why you are forced to choose unattractive people? Oh yeah, we're chicks. We can get laid any day of the week. Sorry!

6 LEVELING THE PLAYING FIELD: *Women & Sports*

WHEN IT COMES TO WOMEN AND THE ROLE THEY PLAY in professional sports, we've come a long way, baby. Sort of. In 1952, Major League Baseball Commissioner Ford Frick formally banned all women from playing on a professional baseball team. The ban still stands. Other professional sports leagues have similar restrictions. Fine. We can't play. We get it.

But over the past 50 years, women have made great strides in the front offices of many teams, in the media, as PA announcers and umpires, as agents and management professionals, and even as majority owners of professional teams. And our generation just might be the first to see a female GM of a baseball team.

No matter what roles these female executives currently find themselves in, the professional sports world is still dominated by men. So although there are a handful of women in power positions these days, there are still many obstacles to be overcome, glass ceilings to be broken through, and stereotypes to be shattered. We are still left with a number of questions when it comes to the role of women in professional sports, namely:

1. *Women in the Front Office:* Across the board in professional sports, there are not many women in high-powered positions who actually make player or operations decisions. When women are making great strides in many other industries, why is the sports world lagging behind?

2. *Women in the Press Room:* Although they have broken down the locker-room door and there has been some progress for female sports-writers over the past 20 years, there is still only a small percentage of female sports reporters, especially in more senior editorial roles. Why?

3. *Women in the Broadcast Booth/On the Sidelines:* We conducted an informal survey of various sports fans, both men and women from across the country whom we consider to be educated and intelligent, and who have healthy, supportive attitudes towards women. Most of them, regardless of gender, did not like seeing women broadcasters on the sidelines of football games or doing play-by-play of any sport beyond tennis. For the love of Phyllis George, why?!

4. *Women's Professional Sports:* We also asked our group of sports fans, as well as a renowned female sportswriter, why many men and women don't seem to follow women's professional sports, aside from tennis and the Olympics. It's not an easy question to answer. But at least we asked it.

WHY AREN'T THERE MORE WOMEN IN THE FRONT OFFICE?

Life in the front office of a pro sports team: Yes, you're surrounded by men, a lot of ex-players and very few women. But did Erica ever feel disrespected by the men she worked with at the San Francisco Giants? Hell, no. In fact, compared to the female shark-infested waters of magazine publishing in New York City, she always felt the male executives she worked for and with at the Giants did nothing but respect her and elevate her. Sure, there were some "nice rack" comments from some of the old ex-players who worked there. And yes, some of the current players did flirt with her. (She had a boyfriend at the time. Drat!) But this was tame compared to the behavior she witnessed from egomaniacal male publishing execs that dominated a mostly female industry. In all her time at the Giants—and this was in the '90s—there was never a feeling of "You're just a chick. Stand back and let the men do their work and just look pretty."

Granted, she worked in San Francisco—a pretty progressive town. (Remember, they were the first team in baseball history to hire a female public address announcer. And didn't that turn out great? Um, actually, no. Sherry Davis was let go when the Giants moved into the new ballpark. Truth is that many of the fans didn't like her—not because she was a woman, but because she often mispronounced players' names. But "A for Effort," San Francisco! They replaced Sherry with another woman—Renel Brooks-Moon—who is well regarded. The Giants are currently the only team in sports with a female PA announcer.)

Today, the largest non-controlling shareholder of the San Francisco Giants is a woman—Sue Burns, who inherited it from her late husband. And based on the University of Central Florida's 2006-07 report card on race and gender in professional sports, the Giants lead the league in female executives, with seven Vice Presidents. But overall, according to this study, only 16% of all VP positions in MLB are held by women—earning the League a D-minus in this category. The NBA does slightly better with 17% females in VP positions at teams across the NBA. (To be fair, both basketball and baseball's central offices in New York have a greater percentage of female executives—the NBA earned an A-minus in this category, while MLB earned a B. We hope this will lead to a "trickle down" affect.)

It must be noted, however, that most of these VP positions, in baseball or basketball, are roles such as Vice President of Human Resources, Creative Services, Community Relations or Communications. In other words, these are not positions where the real baseball decisions are being made. There are a handful of senior-level Finance, Business Operations and General Counsel positions, but not many. In baseball, there are two women holding the CEO/President position: Jamie McCourt of the Dodgers (but we say she doesn't count because her husband owns the team) and Pam Gardner, the President of Business Operations for the Houston Astros. In basketball, Susan O'Malley was the only executive at this level, serving as the Washington Sports & Entertainment president, overseeing all business operations for the Washington Wizards and Washington Mystics until she resigned in 2007.

In auto racing, you have some powerhouse females, including Lesa

France Kennedy who is on the Board of Directors of NASCAR and the President of the International Speedway Corporation, the company that owns many of the country's top raceways. You also have Kelley Earnhardt Elledge, who is the Vice President and GM of JR Motorsports—Dale Earnhardt, Jr's racing company. If these ladies' last names sound familiar, it's because Lesa is the granddaughter of Bill France, Sr., the founder of NASCAR, and daughter of Bill France, Jr., the executive who turned NASCAR into what it is today. Kelley is the sister of the racing league's most popular driver, Dale Earnhardt, Jr. We're not taking away from any of their accomplishments, but they were born into the business, and that's different from choosing a career and battling your way up the ladder on your own.

Speaking of which, the most exciting development for women in powerful sports roles has to be the career of Kim Ng. She is currently the Assistant General Manager of the Dodgers, and also held the same position with the Yankees organization. She is one of only two women to hold the Assistant GM position. The other is Jean Afterman, who took Ng's spot in the Yankees' front office.

Ng (pronounced ANG) started her career as an intern with the Chicago White Sox. She went on to work fulltime for the Sox for six years, followed by a short stint with the American League, and after that, four years with the Yankees, under GM Brian Cashman. While in New York, she was responsible for negotiating the contracts of some of the Bombers' brightest stars, including Mariano Rivera, Derek Jeter and Paul O'Neill. Plus dealing with Steinbrenner's whims.

After her contract expired, Ng was lured over to the Dodgers, possibly because she felt she might have a better chance to be a full-fledged GM. In fact, when the spot opened in late 2005, she became the first woman to ever interview for a General Manager position. She didn't get the job, but there is still hope. When asked in an interview with *Asian-Week* if she would seek out another GM spot, she said, "At some point, yeah, but not right now. My focus is I'm being as good an assistant GM as I can be. I don't think I've topped out at that level in any way. There's a lot to learn. I've learned something every day, that's what this game is about and that's just the way I approach it." Many think that she could be the one to break the female barrier—and Asian barrier—for the GM position. And with her old colleague Joe Torre now at the Dodgers, there is every reason to believe she still has a chance.

However, Ng has had her share of obstacles. And you can bet that if she does become the first female GM, there will be backlash. Not just because she's a woman, but also because of her ethnic background. There was an incident in November 2003, when Bill Singer, a Mets' scouting consultant and special assistant to the GM (one of these special jobs concocted for former players), mocked Ng's Chinese ethnicity by asking her what country in China she was from, in a bad Chinese accent that rivaled Mickey Rooney's Japanese accent in *Breakfast at Tiffany's*. The *New York Daily News* reported that Singer blamed his behavior on a low-carb diet, combined with alcohol, which caused a chemical imbalance. Nice try. Singer was quickly fired by the Mets. However, in November 2006, he must have proved remorseful to the folks in the Washington Nationals' front office. They hired Singer to coordinate in scouting operations in, of all places, Asia.

Notice we have been remarkably silent about the good old NFL. It's not because they hire so many women in high positions that it's not worth discussing. It's because for the past three report cards, the NFL has chosen not to participate in the University of Central Florida's study. Interesting. According to the University of Central Florida, "Unlike the other professional leagues, the NFL League Office does not participate in the Racial and Gender Report Card . . . Without League Office data, The Institute was left with less sufficient data on gender and, therefore, we did not issue a grade on gender. The record of NFL teams regarding the hiring of women remained poor, especially compared to the significant progress on race." With a little digging, though, it's not hard to see that the NFL would receive a low mark. Is there such thing as an F-minus? If so, they would receive an F-minus, would not be able to go to the prom and would undoubtedly be grounded. For years.

There are only 18 female Vice Presidents across the entire NFL, and only four teams have more than one female VP. Beyond that, Amy Trask of the Oakland Raiders is the only female President/CEO of any NFL team. And Christine Procops serves as the VP/CFO of the New York Giants. Beyond that, the NFL is not a great place for women to excel. Maybe that's why they won't share their data.

But here's the real secret, ladies: if you have lots of money and buy or inherit a team, they have no choice but to let you in. You're a team owner. And everyone has to do what you say!

Currently, there are three female owners in the NFL:

Denise DeBartolo comes from a sports family and she took over the 49ers from her brother Eddie DeBartolo, Jr., who was suspended by the NFL on suspicion of corruption and tax fraud. He eventually paid a $1 million fine and took a plea deal where he pleaded guilty to a felony in federal court. Meanwhile, Denise and her husband John York have owned the Niners since 2000, and they receive mixed reviews (at best) from fans and the media. But there is no denying that Denise is one of the most successful businesswomen in sports. She got her start as the president of the Pittsburgh Penguins. Yes, it was because her family owned the team, but she proved herself. She was instrumental in bringing Pittsburgh its first-ever NHL All-Star Game and many credit her with helping to save the Penguins by bringing them key players, including Jaromír Jágr and Mario Lemieux.

Delores Barr Weaver, wife of Wayne Weaver, is a co-owner of the Jacksonville Jaguars. We're not really going to dwell too much on her, because her husband bought the team and holds the reins, while Delores focuses on the Jaguars Foundation, the charitable arm of the Jags organization. We will note one interesting thing: Wayne Weaver made his fortune in the women's shoe business—he owned Shoe Carnival and Nine West.

Virginia Halas McCaskey is the principal owner of the Chicago Bears. Her father was legendary Bears coach George Halas, from back in the day when many owners were coaches, too. She inherited the team in 1983 when she was 60, and she currently controls 80% of the team, along with her children and grandchildren. Virginia is now 85 years old and holds the title of "Secretary of the Board of Directors." (Maybe Virginia still thinks the "Secretary" title is real neat and doesn't realize that many feel that the term is derogatory and it has nearly been banished from the American vernacular.)

And until she passed away in January 2008, Georgia Frontiere was also a female NFL owner. We had already penned our tribute to Georgia, but found it mildly amusing when we saw all of the candy-coated pieces about her broadcast during the playoffs that year. We found that she was certainly more controversial than the NFL would have us remember— glossing over the fact that she was married seven times and banished her stepson from a job he loved, shortly after his father died. We certainly don't want to disparage the woman—who turned out to be a very popular owner—and we want to let her rest in peace. But her story is quite fascinating, and captures the spirit of the early days of the NFL.

GEORGIA ON OUR MINDS

A native of St. Louis, born in 1927, Georgia Frontiere had a colorful past, to say the least. By the time she turned 30, she had five husbands under her belt. But it was her sixth husband who turned out to be a real winner, and catapulted her to the fame and fortune she had always sought. In 1957, during her dancing days in Florida, she was living life in the fast lane and hanging out with a glitzy crowd. It was that year that Joe Kennedy (yes, the father of JFK, RFK, Teddy and the rest) introduced Georgia to Carroll Rosenbloom at the Kennedy estate in Palm Beach. Carroll was an NFL owner (first the Colts, then the Rams). Both Georgia and Carroll were married to other people at the time. But after having a decade-long affair, the couple was married in 1966—they already had two children together at the time. However, their story did not end happily ever after.

In 1979, Carroll—an avid swimmer—drowned while swimming in the ocean, under mysterious circumstances and wide speculation. When the dust settled from the drama surrounding Carroll's death, it was discovered that Georgia was the new owner of the Rams. Allegedly, Carroll left the team to Georgia only for tax purposes and intended that his son Steven—who started off as a kid doing the team's laundry and worked his way up to become a head-office executive—run the team. But that's not how Georgia saw things. She took complete control and dismissed her stepson Steven from the organization.

The '80s and half of the '90s were a tumultuous time for the Rams, with infighting and claims about the deterioration of the organization at the hands of Georgia. In 1986, Georgia's seventh husband Dominic was indicted on tax charges after being caught in an illegal scheme of selling comp Super Bowl tickets from the Rams 1980 appearance. Georgia divorced him a year after he was released from prison.

Then, in 1995, the same year the LA Raiders moved back to Oakland, it was Georgia's decision to move the Rams from Southern California to her hometown of St. Louis—which was quite risky at the time. However, after the move, the team was somewhat successful, winning their first and only Super Bowl in 1999 with Kurt Warner at the helm. They made a Super Bowl appearance again in 2001, losing to the Patriots.

Georgia was quite quirky, as far as owners go. In her obituary, *The New York Times* reported that while on the sidelines, Frontiere would often plant kisses on players after they played well. She bought each player his own Cabbage Patch Kid, back when the dolls were a hot commodity. And she had been known to draw up astrological charts for some of her, ahem, star players.

Georgia spent the later years of her life as a philanthropist and producer of Broadway plays, perhaps trying to relive her dancing and singing days. In 2004, she was diagnosed with breast cancer and she died just over three years later at age 80, leaving behind two children, six grandchildren and her companion of nearly 20 years, Earle Weatherwax. (At least she learned, by the end of her life, to stop marrying and just have "companions.") Despite all of the controversy, we'll miss Georgia. For better or for worse, they just don't make 'em like her anymore.

In basketball, there are three women who have majority ownership of NBA franchises: Irene Pollin, who is the co-owner of the Washington Wizards with her husband Abe, as well as Colleen Maloof and her daughter Adrienne Maloof-Nassif, part of the Maloof gaming entertainment empire that owns the Sacramento Kings. Again, these women married or were born into a sports franchise, so we won't focus on them too much.

Currently, there are no female majority owners in baseball. We think we know why.

AN ODE TO MARGE SCHOTT

She was the first woman to own and operate a Major League Baseball team. She was our chance. She could have paved the way. Instead, she was forced out of baseball because she made racial and ethnic slurs. And did we mention that she insisted on allowing her dog, Schottzie, to run around during pre-game practice and crap on the field? But as crazy as she sounds, when she died in 2004, the *Cincinnati Enquirer* reflected the conflicting emotions of the city, when tales of "Good Marge" and "Bad Marge" emerged.

Marge was a Cincinnati native and the daughter of a wealthy businessman. She married Charles Schott, a member of another affluent Cincinnati family, in 1952. When he died suddenly of a heart attack in 1968 at age 42, Marge inherited her husband's car dealerships—Schott Buick—but says that she really had no skills and no idea what she was doing. She also had no children to care for. Although she had never really worked a day in her life, Marge had no choice but to take control of their estate, valued at just over $3 million. At first, General Motors didn't believe she could run the dealership, so they tried to revoke her franchise. She fought against what she called the "good old boys club" and won. She was the first female car dealer in a major market. And she was successful. Very successful.

Marge built up the business and in 1981 she decided to buy a minority stake in the Reds. At the time, the team was not thriving. Many of their top players, including Pete Rose and Tony Perez, were gone, and Johnny Bench was playing part-time. But in 1984, the same year she paid $11 million for a controlling stake in the Reds, Pete Rose returned as player/

manager. Not one to stay in the background and let others run the show, Marge became the high-profile CEO of the team the following year. Make that a heavy-drinking, chain-smoking CEO with a raspy male voice. One of the first things she did to solidify her "Good Marge" persona was to ensure that the Reds would stay in Cincinnati. And by 1990, Schott's Reds had World Series rings on their fingers, after sweeping the A's. The people of Cincinnati loved Marge . . . for a while.

Over the next few years, there were many instances when "Bad Marge" came out. She quickly became known as a cheapskate—selling employees day-old donuts, turning off the lights in the front offices to save money, and threatening to fire all of the scouts because she thought all they did was sit around and watch baseball games. But fans loved her, as she welcomed children into her owner's box regularly and only charged $1 for hotdogs. Eric Davis did not love her, because after he was injured in the 1990 World Series, he reportedly had to pay his own way home from the hospital. She also came under fire for calling male employees and reporters, "honey" or "sweetie." (Which is certainly better than "nice rack," don't you think?)

But in 1991, a Reds' executive accused her of refusing to hire African-Americans. During the lawsuit, many ugly Marge-isms came out. According to members of the Reds' front office and around the league, she used racial and anti-Semitic slurs on a regular basis, and kept a collection of armbands with swastikas at home. She allegedly referred to two of her star players, Eric Davis and Dave Parker, as "million-dollar 'n'-words" (except she used the real word). She was also overheard saying "sneaky god damn Jews are all alike." The final straw was when she told a reporter, "Hitler was good in the beginning, but he went too far." She claimed she was joking. Although the Reds executive lost the suit, Major League Baseball slapped her with a $25,000 fine and a one-year suspension from baseball in 1993—a move that was extremely well-received from those around the league, including one of her most outspoken critics, Hank Aaron.

Then things started spiraling out of control for "Bad Marge." When umpire John McSherry dropped dead of a heart attack during Opening Day in Cincinnati in 1996, she didn't want to postpone the game, knowing she'd lose money. She also didn't want to post scores of other games at the ballpark, questioning why Reds fans would want to see other teams' scores. Her controversial comments kept coming, this time directed at homosexuals (stating that "only fruits wear earrings") and Asians (claiming that she didn't know that the term "Jap" was offensive). Meanwhile, the pro-Hitler comments continued, as well. Bad, bad Marge. She also fired three General Managers in eight years, while Manager Lou Piniella quit in disgust (maybe he was tired of posing for photos with Schottzie?). The League was fed up; she was banned again from baseball in 1998.

When General Motors came after her again—this time, for falsifying sales figures—she sold the dealership. Shortly thereafter in 1999, she sold her controlling interest in the Reds for $67 million. "Good Marge" spent the rest of her life giving away much of her money to places like the Cincinnati Children's Hospital Medical Center and the Cincinnati Zoo, while many speculated that she was trying to buy a place in heaven.

This much can be said about Marge: She went from a spoiled housewife to the first woman to run a baseball team. She was outspoken and outrageous. She was clearly confused about what was appropriate and inappropriate, but to some diehard Cincinnati fans, she was kind of like the Grinch: a despicable character, but when it came to kids and her dogs, her heart grew three sizes.

It's really impossible to make the claim, as Marge often did, that this male-dominated world wanted her to fail. She did so many horrible things, they had no choice but to kick her out. Marge did do a disservice to women who are trying to make their way into sports. And when people refer to female owners, Marge's name is at the top of the list—rather than other trailblazers like Joan Payson, who played a large role in the creation of the New York Mets as one of the founding owners back in 1960. But these days, our money is on Kim Ng to make a real difference for women. And the difference will come from a woman who knows her stuff, has proven herself and has fought her way up the ladder on her own—not a women who wrote a check from her late husband's bank account. (Note to readers: Both Chris and Erica are just jealous because they wish they had spouses with big bank accounts so they could buy a team.)

"I think being in the position that I am lends itself to being, obviously, a very visible figure in baseball," Ng said in the *Asian Week* interview. "I think it's heartening for a lot of young girls . . . and for a lot of fathers and mothers as well, where they can point to someone and show their daughters that change is happening."

And that's what it will take: A few generations until little girls start thinking, "When I grow up, I want to be the GM of a baseball team." And a few generations until little boys don't make fun of them for thinking it. And this is exactly the issue that faces women sportswriters and broadcasters.

WHY AREN'T THERE MORE WOMEN IN THE PRESS ROOM OR BROADCAST BOOTH?

We did not see smart, credible women covering sports in our youth. We saw the lovely Phyllis George, former Miss America, who appeared on CBS' *NFL Today* from 1975 to 1984, when she left for maternity leave and did not return. George was not a trampy, big-breasted trollop; however, she was not really adding anything substantial to the conversation. Then, five years later, *NFL Today* brought renowned *Boston Globe* sportswriter Lesley Visser onto the show for four years. They haven't featured a female host since Visser left in 1993. After *NFL Today,* she moved to ABC/ESPN to contribute to *Monday Night Countdown* and *SportsCenter.* In 1998, Visser became the first female sideline correspondent for *Monday Night Football.* And in 2008, well-respected basketball analyst Doris Burke became a color commentator for the NBA Playoffs—becoming the only woman to cover men's professional sports as a TV announcer, not a sideline reporter. When you look back and see that it's really only been 10 years since women have been invited into the fold at *MNF* and, even more recently, that they've been invited behind the microphone and off the basketball court, it's a little disheartening. And this is why we think that the otherwise evolved and intelligent men and women we surveyed have a hard time respecting female broadcasters—even today.

Is it simply that we disregard women's opinions because they have never played professional sports? If so, why do we respect people like

Bob Costas, Greg Gumbel, Chris Berman—or even the late Howard Cosell—none of whom have ever played the game?

Do we disregard women because we hold them to higher standards than men? Most of the men we polled just cared if the women knew their stuff. Many felt that the reason some sideline reporters come off as stupid is because they are forced to ask stupid questions, by virtue of being on the sidelines rather than in the booth, analyzing stats and discussing strategy. (And we should point out that there was a high level of disdain for all sideline reporters and broadcasters, regardless of gender!)

A few of the guys said the first thing they did when judging a female sportscaster was to decide whether they would sleep with her or not. (Okay, maybe not all of these guys were evolved.) One man said, "Main goals [for a female broadcaster]: Look good, dress well, don't have too much personality, report quickly on the facts, kick it back to the booth in 10 seconds or less." Another described an early act of self-love, involving the aforementioned Phyllis George, which we will not detail in these pages. And yet another said, "Perhaps I'm not as lucid in my analysis of [a female sportscaster's] performance if her cans [gazongas] are busting out of her top—I'll admit to that." But generally, the guys had more thoughtful analysis on women sportscasters, knew their names and had strong and fair-minded opinions on whether they were good or not. It was the women we polled who were the tougher critics.

"As a woman, I hate to say it, but they look out of place on the field. Everyone is drenched in Gatorade and they are worried about their hair sticking to their lip gloss," said one woman we interviewed. Two others said that women sportscasters made them nervous: "Is she a dippy-doo spouting off nonsense? Is she manly and not feminine? Is she trying too hard to be one of the guys?" While another said, "I don't care one way or the other that [female broadcasters] are there, but there is always a little trepidation that they are going to sound stupid and embarrass us all." Women don't seem to have faith in their fellow women. At least on the airwaves.

In print, it's a different story. It seems the writing speaks for itself.

Across the board, men and women rarely paid attention to whether the writer was a man or a woman. They just cared if the writer knew his/her stuff.

This is echoed by Vicki Michaelis, lead Olympics reporter and Denver bureau sports reporter for *USA Today*, and former president/current board member of AWSM, the Association for Women in Sports Media. Right out of college at *The Palm Beach Post* in Florida, she was assigned to the high school sports beat. She had no intention of covering sports before then, so she had to be a quick study. "I soon figured out that the way to gain the respect and confidence of coaches, athletes and others was to know my stuff," she said. "That of course also holds true for male sports journalists, and journalists overall. But I think it's especially critical for women in sports media. It helps to soften, rather than reinforce, any bias."

And why does she think men—and women—have a hard time accepting female broadcasters? "I believe this has deep cultural roots," says Michaelis. She describes the bonding that men have over sports: the tradition of fathers and sons at the baseball game, fraternity brothers gathered around the television or best friends with NFL season tickets. "Naturally they view it as their domain . . . As such, I believe many men see women as newcomers to the conversation. What could we possibly know or add to enhance it? And why are we intruding on their turf?"

It's their club. And they think we want in. It's not going to be easy. It hasn't been easy. But Michaelis sees progress. "I see acceptance growing every day," she says. "Because of Title IX [the 1972 Federal Law that prohibited sex discrimination in schools], many more men who are athletes, coaches and male sports journalists today grew up with athletic sisters and female friends. They're used to having women be part of the conversation. They welcome us to it as equals."

Michaelis and her fellow writers have undoubtedly come a long way. It's these writers who have put up with shockingly sexist behavior and have busted their way into men's locker rooms, where no woman had ever been before.

In 1977, Melissa Ludtke broke down that locker-room door. She was a writer for *Sports Illustrated* at the time, and was forbidden to enter the New York Yankees locker room. She and *SI* sued the Yankees for equal access to the clubhouse in a groundbreaking case. They won, allowing female sportswriters everywhere to receive the same access as their male counterparts. Great news. But it wasn't exactly rainbows and puppy dogs for the women who actually tried to do their jobs in these legendary locker rooms. Things were going to get ugly.

LADIES IN THE LOCKER ROOMS

Lisa Olson covered sports for the *Boston Herald,* and in 1990 she got a plum assignment—covering the New England Patriots. During one of her first interviews in the locker room, a group of players started taunting her. They started playing with themselves, simulating masturbation. They then crowded around her, holding their junk in her face. In 1991, she sued the team and the players involved—Zeke Mowatt, Michael Timpson and Robert Perryman. Olson eventually was awarded $250,000 in a civil suit against the team, but the incident sparked a national discussion about the roles of female print journalists in male professional sports—and marked an important milestone in the progress of female sports journalists.

When the buzz died down, things did not get better for Olson. She received hate mail and even death threats from Patriots' fans. Her bosses at the *Herald* gave her a transfer to Australia to cover sports for *The Daily Telegraph* and the *Sydney Morning Herald,* then owned by the same company. In 1998, she came back to the states to work for the *New York Daily News*. In one of her first columns after returning, she indicated that she still received death threats—but insisted that she would not give up the job she loves. However, after a dispute that was reportedly caused by fellow *Daily News* columnist Mike Lupica during Super Bowl week in 2008, Olson was not included on the list of the paper's 35 sports reporters who would attend New York's biggest sports story in years—the Giants-Patriots match-up in Arizona. Olson quit on the spot. We applaud her for once again taking a stand and hope she ends up somewhere soon so we can keep reading her smart columns.

"Baseball is a fraternity, a fraternity of men. And you will never understand that or be a part of that because you are a woman." This is what a ballplayer said to sportswriter Susan Fornoff in 1986. This was shortly after she had received pretty pink box, containing a rat wearing a tag that said, "My name is Sue." It was sent by Dave Kingman of the Oakland A's. Classy. Afterward, he was fined $3,500 (chump change for these ballplayers). In her book, *Lady in the Locker Room,* Fornoff described the ups and downs of covering the Oakland A's for the *Sacramento Bee*. While she faced many obstacles, including the rat incident, she did also feel that she was able to get a very different story out of players than her male counterparts. She felt that the players often spoke to her in a different way than they spoke to male reporters, allowing her to cover the game in a way no man could. At the end of her memoir, she comes to the conclusion that she became accepted as one of the guys without ever having to become one. Interestingly enough, she left sports in 1992 because, "I was, frankly, beaten down by the maleness of the locker room," she said in an interview. She also cited the crazy hours and travel schedule as a reason that she now writes for the home and garden section of the *San Francisco Chronicle*.

Former sportswriter for *The New York Times* and *Washington Post* Jennifer Frey was working as an intern for the *Detroit Free Press* in 1990. She attempted to speak to pitcher Jack Morris for an interview while in the Tigers clubhouse—she had just interviewed him three days prior. But he must have had an audience this time. "I don't talk to women when I'm naked unless they're on top of me or I'm on top of them," he reportedly told her.

In 1985, sportswriter Paola Boivin, who was 25 at the time, headed into the St. Louis Cardinals clubhouse for a post-game interview after a match-up against the Dodgers. As she made her way through the players, a Cardinals player stood in front of her, blocking her path, asking whether she was there to interview someone or to look at some guys' penises. Before she could even speak, a sweaty jock strap came sailing through the air, hitting the young reporter in the head. Boivin ran away and claimed that the incident came close to ending her career. Instead, she became an award-winning sports columnist for the *Arizona Republic,* and is a former president of AWSM.

Before we start channeling our inner Helen Reddy and joining in a refrain of "I am woman, hear me roar!"—we should point out that not all men and players are pigs. Each of these women cite many supportive male bosses, fellow writers, players and executives who have helped them along the way. People like Vince Doria, Senior Vice President and Director of News at ESPN. The network was the first to hire women as sports anchors and incorporate them into reporting teams for high-profile events, like the World Series and the Super Bowl. Women like Gayle Gardner, Robin Roberts and Linda Cohn, who paved the way and knew their stuff.

"I have hired a lot of women. It always seemed to me to be the right thing to do," said Doria in an interview for the book *Women and Sports in the United States.* When he was a young reporter with the *Boston Globe,* Doria was one of nine male sports editors to contribute $100 each to help jump-start AWSM. In an interview with the *American Journalism Review,* he noted that men are inundated with sports clichés from an early age and tend to look for the expected, traditional angle. Women often provide a fresh perspective. "Today female sportswriters are [working] all over the place," said Doria. "No one gives it a second thought."

Well, we might not go that far, but there is definitely progress. "Our working conditions definitely have improved. We no longer have to fight for locker-room access. We no longer have to brace ourselves for harassment at every turn," Michaelis says. "I believe that is because there are more of us and because there are more men among our sources and colleagues who accept us as equals." Excellent. But there is a but. There is always a but.

"But we still have gaps to bridge," Michaelis says. A survey of 305 newspapers commissioned in 2006 by the Associated Press Sports Editors found that women made up just 12.6% of sports staffs, and that 90% of sports editors and 84% of sports columnists were white males. (These are stats, but they relate to women, so we like them!)

Michaelis says that yes, much of the deficit is about gaining entry in a male-dominated world and about breaking through glass ceilings (or glass locker rooms). But some of it is also about figuring out how to find a balanced life in that world. "Jobs in sports media require you to work long hours, nights and weekends," she says. "Reporters travel constantly." It's a lifestyle that's not necessarily conducive to having a family. This is an issue that many industries are facing—not just sports.

A recent study by researchers at Penn State's Center for Sports Journalism found that women stay in the business an average of 10 years. "That means we're not staying long enough to advance into the top positions," Michaelis says. Among AWSM's new challenges is to lobby managers and to help women negotiate working situations that would facilitate longer career spans.

WHO'S YOUR DADDY?

One way to achieve balance as a sports reporter would be to intertwine your professional life and personal life. Kind of like Samantha Stevenson did. The sportswriter, who wrote for publications like *The New York Times* and *Playboy,* covered the Philadelphia 76ers in the late-'70s. During that time, she had an ongoing affair with Julius "Dr. J" Erving—who had been married since 1972, and was widely thought of as a stand-up family man. (Sorry, Chris!) Stevenson kept the affair—and Dr. J's love child, who was born in 1980—under wraps for 20 years. It wasn't until their daughter Alexandra was competing on the pro tennis circuit that a Florida newspaper uncovered the 6-foot-tall, emerging tennis star's birth certificate. Her daddy was indeed Dr. J. The case caused a stir among female reporters. "That was the number-one thing people said: 'Oh, women in the locker room, all you want to do is see guys naked and date them,'" said Diane Pucin, a sports columnist for the *Los Angeles Times* Orange County edition in an interview with *Salon*. "We've all fought for so long against that perception that we're all just voyeurs and trying to get dates with athletes. And there are still people who think that's the case. All it takes to bring that back is for one person to have done that, even if it was 20 years ago."

Now we know why there aren't more women in the front office, the press room and the broadcast booth. We all know that there is strength in numbers—and by just encouraging young women to pursue these roles, progress will be made. Children will see strong female personalities throughout sports and there will increasingly be room for a female perspective in this male-dominated world. But there is still one outstanding question. An important one. And it's a question that many people don't want to talk about.

WHY DON'T WOMEN'S PROFESSIONAL SPORTS STACK UP?

There are many schools of thought on this topic. Along the lines of Michaelis' comment, it's probably true that passion for sports teams and personalities starts at a young age. And because Title IX—the law that outlawed sex discrimination in schools, and required publicly-funded educational institutions to give women the same opportunity to play sports as men—didn't take effect until 1972, there simply have not been many prominent female athletes and women's professional teams to follow up until recently. Men's sports, firmly rooted in popular culture, has had a huge head start.

And in our beauty-obsessed society, our survey reflects that the level of attractiveness of the female athletes is also a factor. Perhaps this is why women's tennis, beach volleyball and certain Olympic sports have stronger followings than other sports. Some guys we surveyed claim that LPGA and WNBA players are not all that attractive (except, they tell us, for golfers Natalie Gulbis, Paula Creamer, Annika Sorenstam and Michelle Wie). Tennis, we're told, is a more feminine sport. The women wear skirts. There is more graceful play. And in women's beach volleyball, they're wearing bikinis, for God's sake! In tennis and volleyball, there does seem to be a larger number of attractive, feminine-looking chicks to choose from when guys are fantasizing and contemplating self-love. (Remember the guys from the survey who commented that the first decision they make when looking at a female broadcaster is whether or not they wants to sleep with her? Same goes with female athletes.) This sucks, but shouldn't surprise anyone.

But the most prevalent comment in our informal survey was the level of play. One male sports fan who used to cover women's basketball and softball for his college newspaper, said, "I have to confess: women's basketball was horribly, relentlessly boring . . . Softball was only slightly more entertaining. But for me, it had nothing to do with 'traditional gender roles,' whatever those are. Aesthetically, women athletes—at least for hoops and baseball/softball—don't look as fluid as male athletes. I don't want to spend two hours of my life watching what I perceive to be a bunch of people awkwardly playing games that require extreme skill." This is the reason he says he doesn't watch high school sports of any kind, stating that high school kids, for the most part, are not as gifted athletically yet. "And maybe that's why tennis is different," he says. "The difference in how men and women look while playing the game is minimal."

The women, once again, were tough critics. "I don't like watching female sports because it doesn't feel like a 'real game,'" said one female fan. "But is it because we're programmed to think that? Because we didn't follow women's sports growing up? I can't pinpoint it." It's a complicated issue for women. "Individual sports are watchable," said another woman. "But women's team sports just look amateurish." This coming from a woman who played on women's sports teams growing up!

Across the board, the women we interviewed loved the fact that Danica Patrick is taking on male Indy drivers, head to head—and were ecstatic over the fact that she won her first Indy race. They definitely loved it when Billie Jean King kicked Bobby Riggs' ass in 1973. And they really want to see golfer Michelle Wie win against the guys. "As long as they can compete against men, it's fine. We just don't want our gender to be perceived as playing in a 'powder puff' league or playing by different rules," one female fan said.

Despite the guys' comments about the skirts, tennis is a sport that successfully integrates male and female athletes, not only in mixed doubles, but also at the actual sporting event. When you go to watch the US Open or Wimbledon, you can see men's matches and women's matches—together. Same goes for Indy Racing and the Olympics. But none of the other pro sports are really capable of that male/female integration.

But we think the root of the issue goes back to how differently men and women watch sports. For women, watching sports is inspirational and communal. They want to gather with a group of people and watch a really exciting game, with loads of drama and back-story. But for men, watching sports seems to be a bit more aspirational. Men want to be blown away by these amazing athletes, doing things that ordinary men couldn't achieve themselves.

After the men we surveyed told us that they weren't fans of the WNBA because most of the women can't dunk, we asked them how many of them could dunk. You guessed it: Not one of them can dunk a basketball. "Not anymore," said one guy, trying to blame his age. (But we don't think he could ever really dunk.) We believe that men are less interested in watching women compete because, for many men, a large part of the appeal of sports is the "fantasy" element—not fantasy as in porn, but the fantasy that they could have played in the pros. All the men we surveyed played sports as kids. And each had admitted to having the male fantasy of becoming a professional athlete at one moment or another in their childhood—even if for a fleeting moment, and even if that moment was in Little League or even Tee Ball. For many of these guys, being an avid sports fan allows them to recapture that brief moment in which they felt they really could have been a contender. If only he had been a few inches taller, if only his parents had pushed him a little harder, if only that coach hadn't been such a jerk, if only he hadn't screwed up his knee.

So if these aspirational fantasies play a key role in most men's love of sports, why would they give a crap about watching a woman who can't dunk or a chick who can't hit a ball 400 feet? (And we say: "Because she could probably still kick your ass, that's why!") Somehow, women—real women—don't have a place in this sports fantasy world. When women come on the scene—whether they're on the field, on the sidelines, in the locker room, in the front office, in the owner's box, even at a sports bar— they are somehow intruding on the fantasy. The bubble is burst. With real women in the picture, the male fantasy is not nearly as . . . fantastic.

As for women who don't watch women's sports, it's a little more complicated. "It's not that I don't want to watch women play," said one woman we surveyed. "I feel like if they showed more women's sports on TV, I would watch it more. It just seems hard to find." Well, that's a chicken-and-egg scenario right there. The networks won't start air- ing women's sporting events until there are more viewers who want to watch them. It's quite a dilemma.

So where does this leave us? We told you this book was not going to cover women's professional sports, and it doesn't. But researching this really opened our eyes about attitudes toward women in sports—both on the field and off. There have been great strides, but there are still trails to be blazed, big-time.

These issues are not often discussed and they're not easy to explore—especially when they reveal ugly truths about our own atti- tudes. So as a result, are we running out to catch a WNBA game right now? In all honesty, probably not. But the next time we flip past Sheryl Swoopes on ESPN2, now playing for the Seattle Storm—we're both going to give it a chance. Why? Because these women, and others like them, have ignored criticism and fought hard to change people's perceptions because of their love of the game.

We can relate to that here at *GameFace*. Plus, as ESPN's Vince Doria might say: It just seems to be the right thing to do.

1 YOU TALKIN' TO ME?!: *Famous Feuds, Rivalries & Pranks*

IT'S HAPPENED A LOT LATELY. WHETHER WE'RE AT MADISON Square Garden in New York or across the country at San Diego's Qual-comm Stadium, we've seen it all too often in recent years.

You've probably noticed it, too: You're watching two rival teams who supposedly hate each other go at it. "There's no love lost between these guys," the newspapers tell you for the umpteenth time, and you're fired up to be there in person. Then the game ends and . . . you suddenly have an uneasy realization as the players mill around. You see that the players from BOTH teams are talking. Together. Even more, they're laughing and clowning around. With each other! You start thinking . . . That guy just lost a tough game, shouldn't he be upset? Wait . . . are they exchanging cell phone numbers now? Are those two guys who talked trash at each other in the papers all week really hugging and waving their thumb and pinky as if to say, "Call me, bro?" It makes you wonder: Did I just drop a $100 a ticket to watch a hard-fought competition? Or was it just a millionaires club doing an elaborate cardio workout? You have a sneaking suspicion it's the latter, especially after watching the virtual love-fests after some ballgames. You might even have an epiphany of sorts, just like Jimmy Fallon did in *Fever Pitch*. Sit back, because it's a toughie: "I might care more about this 'rivalry' than the players actually do." One word sums up this feeling: Ouch! Oh, it's not like a kid finding out there's no Santa Claus. Actually, it might be even worse—like learning that Santa runs a porno studio in the back of a North Pole toy factory, or that he's been cheating on Mrs. Claus with Carmen Electra.

You get the point. For the diehard fan, there are few thoughts (about the players, not Santa) that are more painful. It wasn't always like this. You hear stories about old-school competitors, like tough-as-nails Frank Robinson, who truly didn't know other baseball players very well in the '50s and '60s because he wouldn't talk to them if they wore a different uniform. It's just not like that anymore. Topping the list of reasons why is free agency. Players simply move from team to team a lot more, which means they all know each other better and are on friendlier terms. More than ever, players are loyal to themselves first and the team second, which means they have less invested in their franchise's history and tradition. "I can't hate that guy, we've got the same agent." No one has actually been quoted saying that, but would it surprise you if they did? (For the record, we like free agency. We wouldn't want to have zero options and be stuck in the same crappy, relatively underpaid job for years, so why should the players? Still, free agency has had some lame, unintended consequences, such as the above.)

Whoever called sports the original reality show was a genius. (Wait, that was Erica in the introduction!) Well, it's true. Televised ballgames were the first unscripted dramas, back when being *The Biggest Loser* had a whole different meaning. Nowhere are storylines of sports better than when they're created by arch rivals. Their history and back-stories are just as juicy and complex as anything you'll find in a daytime soap opera. (Which sort of makes Peyton Manning the NFL's Susan Lucci.) For instance, when the Colts play the Patriots, lurking around the stadium is the whole bloody, hard-fought history between them. That day's game is really just an evolving book telling the story of this entire era of NFL football. And Tom Brady and Manning both are well aware of it. They know that each victory is one more argument in their favor when sports historians—and drunken fans in sports bars—debate over who was better. So the ante keeps getting upped every time they play. Now *that* is a modern-day rivalry, and that's great news. It's nice to know that some still exist.

With college teams, it's easy to keep rivalries going because the players come and go every few years while the institution and its tradition always stays the same. In pro leagues, it's a little different, mainly because there is more emphasis on the individual. In the old days, a heated NFC East division match-up would have had you thinking Cowboys vs. Eagles.

Nowadays, that same bill would be Donovan McNabb vs. Terrell Owens. Come to think of it, the feud was McNabb vs. Owens when they were on the *same* team! (More on that trend later.) Perhaps that change is not surprising. The pros are filled with driven egomaniacs who have scratched and clawed (or "grinded," to use an eyebrow-raising word that Buccaneers coach Jon Gruden loves to use) their way to the top of a multibillion-dollar business. It's almost natural that there would be clashing egos, infighting and petty jealousy. And that's just with the cheerleaders!

Fortunately, some pro team rivalries have survived, and not just the Patriots and Colts or Red Sox and Yankees. But watching ex-Red Sox hero Johnny Damon switch sides to the hated Yankees for a slightly bigger contract in 2006 is Exhibit A of what we're talking about. If he had gone to the Mets like Pedro Martinez did, it would have been no big deal. But the rival Yankees? Damon even cut his trademark long hair and shaved his beard to fit in with his new team's clean-cut dress code. On the Sellout Meter, maybe the only comparable scenario is if the late Jerry Garcia had quit the Grateful Dead and taken a 9-to-5 job at IBM. Then Deadheads might have known how nauseating Damon's departure to "The Evil Empire" was for Boston fans. But to our everlasting delight, there still are plenty of simmering, long-standing beefs in sports—only these days they're less about ball clubs and more about one-on-one feuds. This is dedicated to sport's most memorable *mano-a-mano* conflicts, where rivals get personal both on and off the field. The first one we'll look at is the granddaddy of them all.

COMMISH CLASH
The Gangster vs. The Game-Show Host

Whoever said opposites attract never met Al Davis and Pete Rozelle. Davis was the Brooklyn-raised tough guy who settled out west in blue-collar Oakland with the American Football League, an upstart group that challenged the National Football League in the 1960s. Rozelle was the glib, savvy insider who started his career across the Bay in well-heeled San Francisco before moving east into the NFL's tony Park Avenue offices in Manhattan. Their decades-long rivalry spawned a hatred that culminated in the mother of all sports lawsuits.

Rozelle became NFL commissioner in 1960, when the league was in disarray and had mediocre attendance. Rozelle changed all that. He convinced the big-market owners to share profits with small-market teams, which, to this day, allows every NFL team an equal chance to win each year. This is a big reason why the NFL today is king, having long surpassed baseball's popularity. Rozelle, a former PR exec, looked like he should be hosting *The Price is Right*. Politically connected, the tan and stylish smooth operator moved through Madison Avenue and both aisles of Congress with ease. Davis was the opposite. Sure, he had an undeniable charisma and a certain charm. But as Howard Cosell wrote in his memoir, *I Never Played the Game,* Davis was "always tense, charged up, his eyes working a room as if he were looking for snipers." The late broadcaster described a night out with Rozelle as being warm and relaxed, while dinner with Davis was quite different. "By the time the check is deposited on the table . . . you're shell-shocked," Cosell wrote. "That's Davis' style."

While Rozelle had short hair and always dressed in a three-piece suit, Davis grew his mane long with a pompadour and still wears loud Raiders sweatsuits that come in two colors: black or white, with silver trim. When Davis donned a tie and jacket, he looked like the mobsters in the Broadway musical *Guys & Dolls,* and certainly nothing like Rozelle or his slick Park Avenue business pals. Sure, the outfits kept Davis off the cover of *GQ,* but they also lent to his reputation that he was an eccentric maverick who was not to be effed with.

Davis got his first head-coaching job with the Oakland Raiders in 1963, and just three years later, he made the quantum leap to AFL commissioner. Founded in 1960, the AFL struggled at first. But it wasn't long before it cut into the NFL's business, stealing fans and outbidding it for marketable stars, such as Joe Namath. With both men at the helm, the two leagues were on a collision course and there was but one solution to avoid destroying each other: Join forces. But Davis reportedly opposed that idea. According to some, he wanted the AFL to stay separate and keep competing against the NFL. With a merger seeming imminent, he resigned as AFL commissioner. The two leagues soon agreed to become one in 1967, and then they made it official in 1970. But the NFL—and Rozelle—got the upper hand in the deal. The NFL kept the name, and the AFL teams were herded into the AFC, one of the league's two new conferences. More importantly, the NFL kept Rozelle as commissioner. By then, Davis was back in Oakland, where he had the Raiders winning with an unproven coach named John Madden. But before the decade was over, Davis would have another disagreement with league officials, one that grew so heated it would make the merger talks look like a spring picnic.

When the Los Angeles Rams moved to nearby Anaheim, Davis was intrigued. He envisioned selling out the Los Angeles Coliseum's 90,000 seats, building cash-cow luxury boxes there and profiting from LA's huge TV market. But Rozelle blocked the move. So, Davis sued the NFL—an unprecedented maneuver at the time. The animosity between the two men, simmering under the surface for years, exploded into a full-blown blood feud. Rozelle then became "obsessed" with stopping Davis, according to Cosell's account.

For all the heart-stopping games the Raiders were known for back then, just as much drama was found off the field; including the thick tension in their champagne-soaked locker room after winning Super Bowl XV. Davis' and Rozelle's courtroom battles had already started, and sports reporters had wondered all week how ugly it might get when Rozelle had to award the Lombardi Trophy to Davis on live TV. Would they talk more trash than pro wrestlers? Would Davis give a *Godfather*-like speech about honor and revenge? Would Rozelle clock Davis with the trophy? As it turned out, everyone's imagination was more fertile than reality. Both guys took the high road and behaved graciously to each other during the postgame show.

But a year later, Davis scored another big victory—in the courtroom. He won the lawsuit, moved to Los Angeles and then collected a $17 million settlement from the NFL. Davis had gotten revenge on his archenemy, but he also paid a price for it. Simply put, it never worked out that well for the Raiders in Los Angeles, where they played from 1982-94. True, they won a Super Bowl in their second season there, but it was with mostly the same Oakland players and coach, Tom Flores, who had won Super Bowl XV three years earlier. After a short time, they struggled on the field, rarely sold out the LA Coliseum, and stadium officials never did build those lucrative luxury boxes for them. Instead of creating the next NFL dynasty, the Raiders joined a long, notorious list—from James Dean to Britney Spears—of those who went south after going Hollywood. So, Davis went north. He made the historic move of bringing the Raiders back to Oakland in 1995. No team had ever returned to the home city it once abandoned.

Now pushing 80, Davis is a legendary, albeit controversial, football man. He's won three Super Bowls and is a member of the Pro Football Hall of Fame. He reportedly still runs the Raiders with the same intensity as ever. Rozelle retired in 1989 and passed away in 1996 at the age of 70. Considered by some to be the best sports commissioner ever, his sour relationship with Davis mellowed somewhat over time, but they never fully mended their fences. These driven men always wanted to be the best in anything they did, and their bitter feud is no different. It's still tops in league history.

FAMILY AFFAIR

In the history of American business, family squabbles are as legendary as the millionaires these companies created. Just look at the bickering Mondavi clan in Napa Valley's wine industry, or Barron Hilton going to court years ago to take over his family's hotel empire. Why should sports be any different? Truth is, it's not. A prime example occurred in 2007, when years of bad blood within a legendary NASCAR family divided them, probably for good.

Son of a Legend vs. Evil Stepmother

It kind of sounds like a Disney movie: Our hero's daddy dies in a terrifying crash and now our hero has to contend with his stepmother. With his sister at his side, he endures what he considers years of mind-games, only to finally escape in search of a happy ending. Our hero, of course, is Dale Earnhardt, Jr., and Teresa Earnhardt stars as the mean stepmother, according to some accounts. It all started back in February 2001, when NASCAR legend Dale Earnhardt was killed in a fiery crash at the Daytona 500, leaving the world stunned. It was then that Dale Sr.'s wife Teresa took over as the CEO of Dale Earnhardt, Inc. (DEI), a company that the two co-founded back in 1980.

Dale Jr. says himself that his relationship with his stepmother is "black and white, very strict, in your face . . . it ain't a bed of roses." Maybe that's why, in June 2003, he turned down a lifetime deal with DEI, saying if he had taken it, he was "always going to wonder what it would be like to drive for somebody else."

Those in Dale Jr.'s camp say that he just wants to win. He is the most recognizable NASCAR driver and yet he has never won a NEXTEL Cup. And he feels he can't win with Teresa at the helm of DEI, especially after a few controversial decisions she made, like deciding to switch Dale Jr. and teammate Michael Waltrip's crew chiefs and cars in 2005.

Those in Teresa's camp say that she's strictly making business deci-sions that she feels are best for DEI. However, she has also taken a few personal jabs at Junior, like the comment she made to the *Wall Street Journal* in 2006, stating that "[Dale Jr. has] to decide on whether he wants to be a NASCAR driver or . . . a public personality." After that, the relationship completely fell apart.

In the summer of 2007, Dale Jr., represented by his sister Kelley Earnhardt Elledge, announced that he was leaving DEI completely and joining Hendrick Motorsports. After intense negotiations, Teresa would not let Dale Jr. keep the rights to his signature Number 8. She claims that she offered the number to Dale Jr., but wanted to retain the rights to the number after he retired.

Junior called this decision "upsetting as hell," and will now drive the Number 88 car, sponsored by Mountain Dew Amp energy drink and the National Guard. He joins Hendricks—with teammates Jimmie Johnson, two-time defending champ, and Jeff Gordon, a four-time champ—in his quest for the Cup. And he's hoping for that happy ending, one that includes a championship for himself. That's something that undoubtedly would make daddy proud.

BORDERLINE RIVALS

If you've ever seen British soccer hooligans violently tear through a town—as Chris did in St. Etienne, France, during the '98 World Cup—then you know that some of them have to take it down a notch just to be considered unnervingly insane. But it's not just the ticket buyers overseas who have all the fun. There are plenty of team rivalries, where centuries of political squabbling sometime bubble to the surface after a match. No better example of this happened in 1969, when, incredibly, a brief war started between Honduras and El Salvador after the two nations met in a soccer game. (And you thought the Dodgers and Giants hated each other.)

The 2006 World Cup also escalated tensions between two other countries sharing a border. There was no warfare, thankfully, but there is no hint the bad blood will go away anytime soon. We are talking, of course, about Italy and France and a shocking on-field altercation during the Cup final. Is there ever a *right* time to head butt someone during a game? Hmmm, let's take a look . . .

Zidane vs. Himself: The Materazzi Manifesto

How tense and dramatic was the 2006 World Cup final game? Put it this way, we've seen plenty of fans cry in a sports bar after an emotionally draining game. But this was the first time we've seen anyone shed tears *during* a match. And if you think that person was Chris, well, that is absurd and patently ridi- . . . Okay, we admit it, it was Chris. C'mon, it was dusty in there!

All that emotion was flowing even before the violent, bizarre ending between Italy's Marco Materazzi and France's Zinedine Zidane, whose head-butt attack was the tournament's infamous lasting image. Unless you were living in a cave that weekend, you know what happened: With just 10 minutes left in overtime in a 1-1 tie, Materazzi grabbed Zidane's chest as they both jumped to head the ball. As the ball bounced away, Zidane said something to the Italian defender, who said something back. Suddenly, Zidane slammed his head in the chest of Materazzi, who hit the ground like he'd been shot by Dick Cheney. Zidane was ejected, and about 20 minutes later, Italy won on penalty kicks.

Soccer-haters had a new joke: "Finally, something exciting happened during a match!" But this was serious business for the rest of the world. While Italy spent days celebrating its fourth World Cup title, many in France saw it differently. People from French political groups to Zidane's mother herself blamed not Zidane for hurting his team, but rather Materazzi for "provoking" their hero into disgrace. Our response? Oh, boy. Zidane's supporters' version went like this: There is no way that someone as dignified and heroic as Zidane would have lost his cool, unless *something* horrible was said to provoke him. Right? RIGHT?! Well, that's a theory. But you need proof, folks. Which we're still waiting on.

(Quick note: We are no French bashers. We *love* France and we think Paris is one of the world's most amazing cities with people who are much nicer than advertised. Also, the Kentucky-fried clown who coined the term "Freedom Fries" should be impeached immediately. Now, back to the story.)

Some lip-readers quickly came forward, accusing Materazzi of saying something heinous about Zidane's mother. Or his sister. Some even said Materazzi had referenced Zidane's Algerian roots, calling him the "son of a terrorist whore." Whoa! That certainly upped the ante. Around the globe, people hopped on the Internet to see for themselves what happened. Did he actually say it? Can you read his lips? And God, who the hell had time to make all these spoof head-butt videos, let alone watch them all? No one could say for sure.

What pundits did say right away was how "out of character" Zidane's fury was. But that really wasn't true. In fact, Zidane's loss of temper was frequent and well-known. Sure, he wasn't the French Roger Clemens or anything. But he had been suspended before for on-field violence in the 1998 World Cup, and again in 2000 in Italy's Serie A league. Nevertheless, Zidane's supporters trotted out other myths that week in defense of his attack, such as:

▶ Zidane was justified because Italy fouled him all game with rough play.

Please. First of all, soccer is a rough game. Just ask Italy, which was one of the most-fouled teams during the 2006 World Cup. We can point to countless examples of international players from any country who were fouled a lot but never retaliated.

▶ France would have won the game had Zidane not been ejected.

Probably not true. Forget about Zidane, the two French players just as notably missing were Franck Ribery and Thierry Henry. They were ineligible to take any penalty kicks because French coach Raymond Domenech made a bad decision by removing them earlier in the match. As it was, David Trezeguet, one of Europe's best scorers, missed the kick that cost France the title. Zidane there or not, Trezeguet still would have taken his turn, and likely still would have missed. France still would have been 3 for 4 on kicks, while Italy was 5 for 5.

Ultimately, a sincere "sorry" from Zidane would have cleared up the whole mess. Too bad we're still waiting for one. Zidane finally appeared on French national TV a few days after the final, offering roughly half an apology. He conceded he was wrong to physically attack someone, but added he would do it again because of the harsh words that provoked him. Huh? Hey, if we wanted that kind of confusing double-talk, we'd just call our congressman.

Materazzi didn't help himself much at first, either. He didn't reveal what he said to Zidane, which only made people more suspicious. But more than a year after the incident, Materazzi finally gave his version, claiming that after he grabbed Zidane's chest, the French star turned to him and said, "If you really want the shirt, I'll give it to you after the game." Then came the much-investigated comment. "I'd rather have your whore of a sister," Materazzi said he replied. The head-butt then followed, all of which is a version that Zidane has never refuted. An investigation by FIFA, soccer's world governing body, corroborated Materazzi's version. Which means that this entire controversy likely occurred over trash talking that, though it won't win you Miss Congeniality, is as common in soccer as a corner kick.

Also, a lawsuit settled nearly two years after the incident supported Materazzi's version. *The Daily Star,* a British tabloid, publicly apologized to the Italian defender and paid him an undisclosed amount of damages, while acknowledging that its initial report accusing Materazzi of racist verbal abuse was "wholly untrue." If Materazzi's comments had any kind of racial element to them, then we would definitely join his list of critics. But they didn't, according to FIFA and, belatedly, the press. In addition, Zidane has had plenty of chances to make that same accusation that the tabloids did. But he never has.

Looking back, we have a lot of sympathy for Zidane. Hey, we all make mistakes (Chris' 1988 mullet, for example) and Zidane should only be judged by what he did to mend the damage, not the mistake itself. Does he take responsibility? Does he make amends? Heroes answer "yes" and "yes" to those two questions. But Zidane didn't. And still hasn't. End of story. Or that part of the story anyway. The other part is that the France-Italy rivalry has only grown more heated. France felt it should have won the World Cup, while Italians seethed that FIFA suspended Materazzi for two games for his role in the incident—an unprecedented "punishment" for a victim. (Zidane was suspended for three games.) Since then, France and Italy met twice more in feverish, hard-fought matches in 2006-07, and a third time in the 2008 European Cup.

Today, Zidane still is beloved in his country. And why not? He was pure magic on the field, and almost single-handedly (single-footedly? single-headedly?) thrust France into soccer's worldwide limelight in 1998, after years of playing the perennial bridesmaid. Unfortunately, he will always bear the stigma of "The Incident." For every highlight that features him shredding a team's defense, there will always be a snarky headline or damning video footage of that unforgettable loss of cool. It's always going to be on his professional epitaph.

"How could this happen to a man like you?" the French newspaper *L'Equipe* asked the day after the World Cup final. It's a question Zidane fans probably will ponder forever.

WHEN TEAMMATES ATTACK

Rivalries forming between opposing teams is a phenomena as old as Keith Richards. But a weird trend has developed in the last couple of decades: Feuds between guys on the *same* team. Sure, tension in the clubhouse isn't so unusual—having a couple dozen of wealthy egotists who have been coddled all their lives will do that for a business. For example, Pete Rose and Johnny Bench, two old-school Cincinnati Reds teammates, did not care for each other at all. But they—along with a complicit local media—kept it almost entirely out of the public eye, allowing their fans the happy delusion that their boys were one big united Red Machine. Blissful ignorance? Maybe. But after watching dozens of ballplayers in recent years break up great teams over diva-like hissyfits that would have embarrassed Naomi Campbell, we think that the old days weren't so bad. If you had to choose the poster children for this, it's a crowded field these days. Just look at ex-Giant Tiki Barber and quarterback Eli Manning, who traded barbs in the New York tabloids in 2007. Or even Jason Kidd and Jim Jackson with the Dallas Mavericks, whose fight over singer Toni Braxton in the mid-1990s broke up the team. But maybe it's perfect that the ultimate example of feuding teammates played together in the town that also gave us Joan Crawford vs. Bette Davis. One legendary catfight, after all, deserves another.

Shaq vs. Kobe
(Or, I Went to Los Angeles and All I Got Was This Crappy Teammate)
For those of you too young to remember, there once was a guy living in Southern California who infamously uttered the words, "Can't we all just get along?" We guess Shaquille O'Neal and Kobe Bryant didn't get

that memo. These Los Angeles Lakers teammates were superstars that led their team to multiple NBA titles, just as Magic Johnson and Kareem Abdul-Jabbar did in the '80s. But while Magic and Kareem made a point of buddying up so they could keep winning, Kobe and Shaq went the other way. They feuded over just about everything from Kobe's ball-hogging to Shaq's habit of showing up overweight and out of shape each preseason. What should have been a never-ending dynasty instead imploded like those drug-addled rock bands from VH1's *Behind the Music*.

At first it looked like Kobe was the good guy in this squabble. In 1996, his arrival in Los Angeles made instant history, as he became the first NBA guard to be drafted out of high school. He was a likable 18-year-old rookie who was intelligent, polite and even worldly—probably from having traveled through Europe with his dad, Joe "Jellybean" Bryant, who played pro hoops overseas. As a result, Kobe is not only fluent in Italian, he speaks English better than some of the TV announcers. At the time, Erica and Chris joked about how long it would take for the Hollywood fast-lane to corrupt a nice teenager turned millionaire. Time would answer that faster than you can say Mary-Kate Olsen. To boot, Kobe's basketball skills are awesome. He is Jordan-esque in his intense competitive desire and ability to create open shots by himself. Key phrase, "by himself." Because doing too much on his own was a problem that sometimes turned off his own teammates. Check that, it bugged ALL of his teammates at one time or another. Barry Bonds has less of a rep for being self-absorbed.

Meanwhile, Shaq was older and more gregarious. He didn't limit himself to being an All-Star center, measuring in at a giant 7-feet 1-inch and weighing 325 pounds. He created a multimedia empire—making kids' movies and cutting rap albums. (Never mind that most of his entertainment projects ranged from the merely crappy to embarrassingly awful.) Also, he had an annoying habit of giving himself nicknames, including The Diesel, Shaq Fu, The Big Aristotle and Shaq Attack. Apparently, The Big Mouth was already taken. But at least he had personality. Shaq would clown around with the press and teammates, while Kobe rarely did, which only cemented his aloof reputation.

There was a disconnect on the court, too. Despite all their talent, they couldn't win the big games. That is, until coach Phil "Zen Master" Jackson took over before the 1999-2000 season, after which the Lakers reeled off three championships in a row. But that magical run ended after the 2002-03 season and the tension between Kobe and Shaq kept building. But it wouldn't stay that way for long. In fact, it was about to get worse. Much, much worse.

In the summer of 2003, Kobe went to Colorado to have surgery performed on an injured knee. What happened next is open to debate. Kobe, who got married at the tender age of 22, was accused of raping an 18-year-old woman who worked at the resort where he was staying. He denied the accusations, saying that it was consensual sex, and charges eventually were dropped when the young woman refused to testify. Meanwhile, Kobe made headlines back in Los Angeles when he bought his wife Vanessa a $4 million ring as an apology. Wow. That made his Colorado trip the most expensive summer vacation in NBA history.

Worst of all, a bombshell was dropped that promised to launch an earthquake in the Laker locker room. Police revealed that, during questioning after he was first taken into custody, Kobe told Colorado cops about Shaq's own alleged extramarital affairs. Kobe complained that he should just do what Shaq does, which he said included paying off ex-mistresses to go away quietly. True or not, talking about that broke the unspoken rule of teammates: What happens with the stewardess in the airplane bathroom stays in the airplane bathroom—or something like that. And even if it wasn't true, that little news tidbit by Kobe probably didn't please Mrs. O'Neal very much, no matter how much Shaq publicly denied it. And Shaq probably cursed Kobe's name each night he slept on the couch after the news broke.

That juicy personal info that Kobe weirdly passed along to the cops, who then gossiped about it to the world like Joan Rivers, showed just how poisoned his relationship with Shaq had gotten. Even when he was faced with a career-ending felony conviction and prison time, Kobe still found time to compare himself publicly with Shaq. Amazingly, it didn't destroy the Lakers. Not immediately, anyway. With Jackson serving more the role of marriage counselor than coach, he got Kobe and Shaq to play together enough to make it to the 2004 NBA Finals. But they lost there to the Detroit Pistons. Then the real fun started. The following offseason was a bizarre one that included farewells to the team's aging roster, and to Jackson, who did not return as coach. Kobe was a free agent and, though he denies it to this day, it is assumed by most that he gave Laker management an ultimatum: Either Shaq goes or I go. Lo and behold, before the summer was over, Shaq was traded to the Miami Heat and Kobe re-signed with the Lakers. He was the last man standing in a power play that had some wondering if he was more of a sociopath than an All-Star. But Kobe got what he wanted; he was king of the hill. Meanwhile, Jackson later criticized Kobe in his book on his last season in LA, though he returned in 2006 to coach the Lakers and his "uncoachable" superstar once again.

But Shaq may have gotten the last laugh. He signed a $100-million contract and then won an NBA title with the Heat in 2006, proving he didn't need Kobe to win the big one. In 2008, Shaq joined the Phoenix Suns and they continue to be one of the NBA's best teams. Unfortunately for Kobe, for a long time he couldn't make that boast about his Shaq-less Laker teams, which floundered in mediocrity to the point where the Lakers almost traded him. That is, until the 2007-08 season, when the Lakers finally contended for the NBA title again. Maybe the biggest shocker is that Kobe and his wife Vanessa are still married, and now have two daughters. In the meantime, Shaq and Shaunie Nelson, his wife and the mother of four of his kids, divorced in 2007. It wasn't Shaq's first public split. Just ask Kobe and the Lakers.

OWNERS VS. PLAYERS

One of the oldest types of sports feuds is a simple one: Owner vs. player. It usually comes down to money, power, money, ego and . . . did we mention money? In the mid-'70s, it was Charlie Finley vs. Catfish Hunter. Even in the '50s, it was Brooklyn Dodgers owner Walter O'Malley vs. Jackie

Robinson. Wait, who couldn't like Robinson and what he did for baseball? Well, that O'Malley was quite the charmer. But the ultimate owner/player feud took place in the '80s with a different New York baseball owner: George Steinbrenner. The hard part about including Steinbrenner in a section on feuds is just narrowing down the list. Today, he is pushing 80 and has been slowed so severely by failing health, his sons Hank and Hal now run the Yankees. However, Steinbrenner in his prime was a different animal, sometimes literally. The best sports owners hire great people to run the show and then get the hell out of the way. Steinbrenner always got the first part right. The second part? Not so much. His management style was like that of an overbearing stage mother—on steroids. He fought with a lot of his employees and even burned a bridge with baseball's cuddly, somewhat confused, mascot: Yogi Berra.

All of those bad break-ups paled against the trouble Steinbrenner was embroiled in by the late '80s. This scandal tainted his name and almost got him kicked out of baseball for good. It involved a low-level gambler with mob connections. It also involved one of his own high-priced players, superstar Dave Winfield, who came to know better than anyone why the Yankees are known as The Bronx Zoo.

George Steinbrenner vs. Dave Winfield

In John Helyar's excellent book about the history of baseball owners, *Lords of the Realm,* he explains how George Steinbrenner wooed free agent players the same way Casanova courted women. He would turn on the charm and offer you the world if he wanted you. But once the object of his desire said "yes," it wasn't long before he'd turn on you and toss you away for another. Basically, he was baseball's Colin Farrell—just without the humor, good looks and sex appeal.

But how was Dave Winfield to know all that when he came to the Yankees in the prime of his career? He was just about to turn 30 and he was one of baseball's best players. He spent the 1970s playing for the Padres in mellow sunny San Diego, which—as Erica and Chris can vouch for after going to college there—is certainly no place to prepare you for The Big Apple, or the special hell of working for a young George Steinbrenner. But money is always a good carrot and Winfield's 1981 contract—$23 million over 10 years—was baseball's biggest ever. Today, that same contract would insult a superstar; it's well below the Major League average. But back then, that salary was a king's ransom. In Winfield's first year in New York, he and Reggie Jackson led the Yankees back to the World Series in a strike-shortened season. The Yankees quickly won the first two games against the Dodgers and they were halfway to a sweep and yet another world title. And then it all fell apart. The Dodgers won the next four games and the championship. Winfield had a disastrous series, getting just one hit in 22 tries for a paltry .045 batting average. Steinbrenner hit the roof. Later, the owner would humiliate Winfield with an infamous line, comparing him to Jackson, whose postseason heroics earned him the nickname of "Mr. October." So Steinbrenner called Winfield "Mr. May," accusing him of failing to come up big when it mattered. (And there went his "Boss of the Year" candidacy.)

Jackson knew all too well what Winfield was in for. His own clashes with Steinbrenner and manager Billy Martin were so legendary that more than a few books were written about them. The topic was even covered in a 2007 ESPN miniseries, *The Bronx Is Burning,* based on a Jonathan Mahler book. Jackson had once been "the straw that stirred the drink" in New York and, before that, in Oakland, where his A's teams won three consecutive World Series. But now he was 35 and past his prime. He also was expensive. Steinbrenner let him go to the California Angels in the offseason, figuring that Winfield was now the Yanks' well-paid leader. The move backfired. The Yankees would not make it back to the postseason for another 13 seasons.

It was no fault of Winfield's, who played excellent ball in the Bronx throughout the 1980s and was well on his way to the Hall of Fame. But every year the Yankees failed to make the playoffs, Steinbrenner got edgier and edgier. So, he made his best player and highest-paid star take the brunt of his frustration. He also hated Winfield's agent, Al Frohman, reportedly for two main reasons: 1) Frohman antagonized Steinbrenner by badmouthing him to the New York tabloids, and more importantly, 2) Steinbrenner failed to understand a cost-of-living clause that Frohman negotiated between the Yanks and Winfield. What The Boss originally thought was a $16-million deal, quickly turned into $23-million one. Steinbrenner felt that Winfield and his agent screwed him. The relationship between superstar and owner, so warm at the beginning, quickly soured. It wasn't long before both sides lawyered-up. If it was a marriage, they would have gone to Mexico for a quickie divorce. But the contract was for 10 years, practically an eternity that allowed both sides to dig in and fight. And you can bet they fought, even over tiny parts of the contract. It called, for example, for the Yankees to pay $300,000 each year to Winfield's charity for needy kids. But one year, Steinbrenner just stopped the payments and started haranguing Winfield almost weekly about the issue when Winfield complained. Courts ordered Steinbrenner to pay the foundation, but he ignored them, and their relationship went from bad to toxic. Instead of competing together against other teams, they bickered and ended up suing each other for hundreds of thousands of dollars, generating tons of tabloid headlines and distracting the team from its job.

By 1987, it was hard to imagine how things could get worse between them. Enter Howard Spira, a friend of Frohman's and a shady guy with big gambling debts. Spira wanted to exploit the Winfield-Steinbrenner feud by telling Winfield he could give him damaging information about Steinbrenner. Winfield turned him down, so Spira immediately went to Steinbrenner and said he had dirt to dish on Winfield. The smart and classy move would have been to reject Spira. But why be smart and classy when you can be George Steinbrenner instead? He wanted to embarrass Winfield so badly, he took the bait. He paid Spira for the info, which turned out to be the details of a pretty innocuous loan that Winfield had given Spira years earlier. But Steinbrenner reportedly kept

Spira around, asking Spira to dig up information on Winfield's charity with the hopes of embarrassing the slugger for allegedly mismanaging the charity's funds.

Anyone need a shower yet? We feel grimy just writing this stuff. But wait, there's more.

The Yanks owner should have known better than to get involved with a sleazoid like Spira. Steinbrenner had already been suspended from baseball in the mid-1970s for making illegal campaign contributions to President Richard Nixon, who soon would have his own legal problems. The group was called the Campaign to Re-Elect the President, or CREEP, a perfect name for both of these gents. In 1989, President Ronald Reagan pardoned Steinbrenner for his dealings with Nixon. But by then, The Boss was already knee-deep in this new mess with Spira and Winfield. Eventually, Steinbrenner's ties to Spira backfired. In 1990, MLB Commissioner Fay Vincent suspended Steinbrenner from the Yankees for more than two years for associating with a known gambler and for trying to cover up his scheme to discredit Winfield. Spira eventually served 26 months in prison for trying to extort money from Steinbrenner. Winfield—largely the victim in this whole sleazy affair—didn't emerge from the mess with his reputation totally intact. Some fans and press actually took sides against Winfield, even though he was but one guy on a lengthy list of baseball people who locked horns with the pinstriped megalomaniac. Marge Schott must have looked at Steinbrenner and wondered, "And you guys think *I'm* bad for baseball? What's this guy gotta do to get kicked out of the club?"

But poetic justice was served. In 1992, while Steinbrenner was banished and Spira sat in prison, Winfield won his first and only World Series title with the Toronto Blue Jays. "Mr. May" finally could celebrate in October.

WHAT A RACKET!

"You must be joking! Are you kidding me?! Two tennis legends go head-to-head for half a decade and you put 'em last? You're horrible! You . . . cannot . . . be . . . serious!"

That's what a young, fiery John McEnroe might say to us, while he rested his hands indignantly on his hips and his big curly hair flapped in the wind, after seeing where we placed his own rivalry in this chapter.

The Hothead vs. the Robot

As far as unforgettable opponents go, John McEnroe vs. Bjorn Borg had it all. They were the two best players in their sport. They had very contrasting styles on and off the court. And just about anytime they competed against one another, they crafted classic, emotionally draining, epic battles that had the sports world buzzing the next day.

McEnroe was the hothead with the big mouth that you either absolutely loved or hated. Was he a radical, or just an abusive jerk? His fans (and apologists) would defend his antics, calling him a rebel with a cause who merely couldn't stomach incompetence, whether it was from an official blowing an obvious call or his own play on bad days. Fans also argued he was a rough-around-the edges New Yorker simply fighting for tennis justice—one stuffy, visually-impaired umpire at a time. His detractors would roll their eyes at such talk. Sample this line about McEnroe from the British tabloid called *The Sun*: "He is the most vain, ill-tempered, petulant loudmouth that the game of tennis has ever known." His critics would point out that plenty of other tennis stars, especially the quiet Borg, somehow managed to navigate all the bad calls without acting like a three-year-old. And was he really being a "rebel," or just a spoiled brat? They often mentioned that maybe that "drive for perfection" was really just a sense of entitlement the size of Long Island Sound, which was near the wealthy suburb in which he grew up—not exactly the Big Apple's mean streets. Either way, it made for great television. Whether you thought he was breathing new life into the sport or was simply an emotional train wreck, you couldn't stop watching.

Borg wasn't nearly as entertaining, unless you were a knowledgeable tennis fan. C'mon, let's be frank, if people wanted knowledge they'd have gone to a library. Nope, they paid the not-exactly-cheap tennis match tickets to be entertained. Borg's game was incredible and he had his own type of appeal; some went crazy over his long blond hair, omnipresent headband and Scandinavian looks. But he was so mild-mannered that, for others, he was an insomnia cure on legs.

McEnroe had other rivals, including American tennis' original bad boy, Jimmy Connors. But his biggest foe was Borg, the stoic Swede. He was 2½ years older than McEnroe, but sometimes it felt like they had a 30-year age gap. Borg was more of a taciturn grandfather than a big brother, given how glum and expressionless he could be. As a result, he was the old guard's favorite. He was viewed as classy and polite in a sport that valued decorum. And he often won on tennis' oldest, grandest stage: Wimbledon.

Meanwhile, McEnroe burst onto the scene in 1977 like a tousled-hair Johnny Rotten, part new-era athlete, part punk rocker. He excelled on the US Open's clay courts at Flushing Meadows, where he fed off of the volatile energy of the New York crowds. But Borg's and McEnroe's most memorable tête-à-tête (that's the great thing about tennis: we can use these $10 words and not feel like pretentious jerks) came at the 1980 Wimbledon finals. It was a five-set marathon with umpteen tie-breakers. Borg won on the grass surface, to the delight of the sports establishment, and the British tabloids that created a cottage industry in tracking all of McEnroe's moves.

Who could blame them? McEnroe was different. Even his style of play was more jarring and aggressive than Borg's. McEnroe would serve and volley, and loved to attack the net to force the action. Borg, meanwhile, was content to methodically, even robotically, peck you to death, lacing shot after perfect shot to his opponent's backhand, forcing them to run from line to line until they were exhausted. The closest thing we have to these two today is Roger Federer and Rafael Nadal, who might be the two best ever. (We also really like Novak Djokovic, the charismatic Serbian who loves karaoke and does hilarious impressions of other tennis stars.)

However, Borg vs. McEnroe together had something indescribably special. When the dust settled on their careers, their record against each other was perfect: a 7-7 draw. You would expect nothing less from evenly matched rivals. And no, McEnroe, we . . . are . . . not . . . joking.

PRANKS FOR THE MEMORIES

Kyle Kendrick was shocked. And with good reason. The boyish 23-year-old had just been traded from the Philadelphia Phillies. To Japan. For some guy named Kobayashi Iwamura, a player he'd never heard of. At least that's what Charlie Manuel, the Phillies' crusty silver-haired manager, told him. Kendrick had a great rookie year in 2007 and he had been in Spring Training the following season for just three days when he got the bad news.

The trade didn't make sense to the poor kid, and Kendrick looked like he was stuck in a bad dream. But it had to be true the team's assistant GM Ruben Amaro, Jr. confirmed it. Hell, even Kendrick's own agent, Joe Urbon, was on the phone, trying to cheer up his young client about the prospects of taking a 14-hour flight to Tokyo the next morning. Finally, Kendrick acted like a true pro in the clubhouse and grimly faced the local media, who peppered him with questions about the mind-boggling deal. That's when his teammate Brett Myers chimed in with an opinion that Kendrick will never forget.

"You know what I say?" Myers said to Kendrick. "You just got punk'd!"

Laughter erupted among the sports reporters and Phillies teammates gathered in the clubhouse. And suddenly, the fuzzy picture from Kendrick's bizarro day became clearer. There was no trade. There is no pitcher named "Kobayashi Iwamura"—in fact, the name was inspired by real-life hot-dog eating champ, Takeru Kobayashi. It all was just an elaborate prank. Kendrick would not be going to Japan or anywhere else for that matter. As the laughter continued, he just smiled and let out a huge sigh of relief. The good-natured Kendrick was too relieved to be mad at playing the victim. He even happily appeared with Myers on the *Today Show* a few days later to discuss the hoax. Clubhouse tricks have been around forever, but thanks to YouTube, omnipresent cameras and hundreds of baseball blogs, this one had become an instant national classic.

Major League Baseball is filled with men paid millions to play a game with the passion they had as boys. Maybe it's no surprise then, that more than any other sport, a lot of them never stop acting like kids. That's part of its appeal. It's also probably why they play so many pranks on each other. They can be young only once, but the game allows them to be immature forever. Let's be honest. In the game, there is so much time spent standing around, sitting around, spitting around and, yes, scratching around, that making your teammate look foolish isn't just a cure for boredom, it's a time-honored tradition.

Crazy Hazing Days of Summer

Our favorite baseball prank comes in the form of rookie hazing, which the veterans usually save for the end of the year. That's when 10 to 15 Minor Leaguers get called up for a few weeks in the big leagues during what is termed the "September Call-ups." Just before the team sets foot on the team bus that will take them to the airport for the last road trip of the season, all rookies are forced to wear goofy outfits. Let's be more clear here—the rookies are given clothes too flamboyant for Elton John. Yes, you guessed it, within the National Pastime, there is another national pastime: cross-dressing. Veterans force rookies to wear dresses and wigs, sometimes even elaborate costumes you only see on Halloween, like a French maid or a slutty nurse ensemble. It's bad enough to hop on the team bus like that, but things get even better when these humiliated guys are sprung onto the unsuspecting public. You can imagine the awkward conversations at the airport food court or the team hotel. "Daddy, why is my favorite new ball player dressed like Catwoman?" (Long pause.) "Eat your dinner, son. Eat your dinner."

Each year baseball players visit a Chicago statue honoring Civil War hero Philip Sheridan, who is depicted there riding a horse. Then they paint the animal's private parts. Why? The best answer probably lands somewhere between "boys will be boys" and "God only knows." Whatever the reason, it has become a longtime, and undeniably strange, baseball tradition. It usually starts with veterans inviting rookies out for a night of drinking followed by the paint job on the statue horse. But that's just one part of the prank. Part two involves the hungover rookies being visited the next morning by the Chicago police, who tell them they are headed to jail for vandalism. The team manager might even play a role, begging the cops to keep his players out of jail, which only freaks out the athletes even more. That is, until—you probably guessed it—one of the veterans finally admits that the "cops" are fakes. Lesson learned, rookie.

A more staid and old-fashioned baseball prank is the "hot foot." One guy surreptitiously attaches matches to a player's cleats and then lights them on fire. Once the unsuspecting player sees his shoe about to spontaneously combust, he usually dances and jumps in a mad panic to put out the tiny flames—all to his teammates' delight. You get bonus points if the guy starts screaming like a child. Cruel? Not as cruel as having to spend eight months with the same 24 guys in locker rooms, airports and dugouts while traveling the country. The good news for victims is that the never-ending season allows for all kinds of chances for payback.

Another dugout trick calls for taking your bubble gum after blowing a bubble and slyly tossing it on top of another teammate's hat while the game is going on. The trick is to have the gum land softly enough on the teammate's hat so that he doesn't notice a thing. Some have gotten as many as five or six bubbles onto a victim, er, we mean beloved friend and teammate, before he notices anything. If done well, the TV cameras will catch it long before the joke's target does. Meanwhile, one our favorite gags is straight out of a Marx Brothers movie: Throwing a pie into the face of the game's big hero during his TV postgame interview. Problem is, some teams have started banning this because the players often fill the pie container with shaving cream, which stings the eyes and can injure them. Of course, they could easily switch to whipped cream to make it safer and keep the tradition going, but hey, no one said these guys are all brain surgeons.

Here is one of our least favorite: Andrew Brackman, the New York Yankees' 2007 No. 1 draft pick, found a surprise in the clubhouse one day during 2008 Spring Training. A teammate had slit Brackman's baseball underwear exactly down the middle, according to *The New York Post*. They did the same to six of his cleats. C'mon, is that the best the Yankees vets could do? The best pranks require a certain amount of creativity and hard work. Not to mention, a little acting skill. Which is why we don't like the kind of gags that happened to Brackman. What's fun about just ruining a guy's stuff? Look at the time San Francisco Giants teammates spray-painted Will Clark's cowboy boots a bright shade of orange during his rookie season in 1986. Bay Area fans still aren't sure if it was a prank or a seriously passive-aggressive dig from jealous veterans who resented Clark making it to the bigs after spending barely any time in the Minor Leagues. At the very least, they could have pretended he got traded to some faraway exotic land—an act now forever known as the "Kyle Kendrick Treatment."

Lastly, why should the players have all the fun? The Topps trading card company even got into the act when they released a "Future Stars" card in early 2008. One of the prospects they featured was a hard-throwing pitcher named Kazuo Uzuki, a 16-year-old nicknamed "The Uzi." But the first hint that the ball player was a fake could be found in his name. "Kazuo Uzuki" in Japanese means "first son of April." Perfect for an April Fool's Joke, which the fictional hurler most certainly was.

GOTCHA!

And that's just baseball. Check out these hoaxes, dirty tricks and pranks that prove sometimes it's not whether you win or lose, it's how much you've made a fool of someone!

TICKET TO RIDE

Dion Rich, a retired property owner, has the best hobby in the world. He sneaks into sporting contests. Not junior-high field hockey, either, which would be, now that we think about it, a little creepy. Nope, Rich goes ticket-free to the biggest events in sports including World Series games, Triple Crown horse races and the Olympics (not to mention the Academy Awards). Or he used to, anyway. We tracked down Rich, who is around 80, at his San Diego-area home. He told us that he doesn't crash those big events so much anymore, mostly because their post-9/11 security forces are beefed-up and increasingly humorless about his escapades.

"The NFL and Major League Baseball have clipped my wings," Rich said. Friendly and jovial, Rich said he still crashes events for "the thrill of doing it, the rush," but now he's just aiming a bit lower. Instead of going to the Academy Awards like he did in the old days, now he just crashes the after-show parties. Likewise, he bought a ticket and legally attended Super Bowl XLII in Glendale, Arizona, when the New York Giants upset the New England Patriots. But not before reportedly sneaking onto the media bus leaving University of Phoenix Stadium "to save myself cab fare," he told the *North County Times,* a San Diego-area newspaper.

He said a new edition of a book about his exploits, *Confessions of the World's Greatest Gate Crasher: Dion Rich*, will be published soon. Rich also does charity work, such as taking 50 handicapped kids each year to either a ballgame or the San Diego County Fair. But gate-crashing will always be his true legacy. His specialty for many years was the Super Bowl. He says that he couldn't be stopped even immediately after 9/11, when Super Bowl authorities reportedly spent $7 million to protect the Superdome in New Orleans. "It took me less than six minutes to get inside," Rich boasted.

As a result of his famous hobby, Rich has become the sports world's Forrest Gump, showing up in the photos of unforgettable athletic moments throughout the decades, whether it's the winner's circle of the Kentucky Derby or helping to carry Super Bowl-winning coaches off the field. With a mixture of cool nerves and fail-safe strategies, Rich had one of sport's most impressive and long-running streaks. "Wherever I go, I dress the part," he confided. "If I'm at a luau, I'll wear shorts, sandals and a Hawaiian shirt. If I'm at the Academy Awards, I'll wear a tuxedo. At the Super Bowl or at Major League Baseball games, I'll wear a suit, so I can pass as either an owner or someone more distinguished."

But, just like the Patriots' attempted perfect season and Warren Beatty's bachelorhood, his streak of Super Bowl gate-crashing had to end at some point. We asked Rich which Super Bowl was the last one he snuck into, but he proved just as elusive with an exact answer as he was with security guards all those years. He'll only say that it was "several years ago." Some have written that it ended in Jacksonville in 2005, when police nabbed Rich at Super Bowl XXXIX. But Rich told us that was a "simple misunderstanding" where a ticket that he bought with a group of 300 people turned out, unbeknownst to him, to be a phony.

Being held by Jacksonville authorities that day was nothing compared to the treatment he received in Sarajevo during the 1984 Winter Olympics when he tried to sneak into a disco. "Those were Communist police," he recalled with a chuckle. "They detained me for two and a half hours. Now, that was scary."

VICTORIA? VICTORY!

Ah, technology. It has all kinds of benefits. It helps doctors save more lives, and makes our lives more convenient. Oh yeah, it also allows college students to heckle and humiliate opposing players in ways once thought impossible. It is totally fitting that this one occurred just a hooked golf shot away from Silicon Valley. In 2006, some students on UC Berkeley's Rally Committee got the IM address for Gabe Pruitt, a USC point guard. They then pretended to be a sexy UCLA student named "Victoria" who sent him a photo and made it clear "she" wanted to party with Pruitt and his Trojan teammates in Los Angeles. Pruitt responded and the "couple" chatted online all week, giving each other their phone numbers. They could see each other after Pruitt had this little matter of playing a basketball game against Cal in Berkeley. But Pruitt found out the truth the hard way during the game's starting introductions. As soon as the announcer called his name, the Berkeley crowd chanted: "Vic-to-ria! Vic-to-ria! Vic-to-ria!" They then chanted Pruitt's phone number. Needless to say, Pruitt didn't play very well and had an awful shooting night on the floor. Cal won the game by 11 points and Pruitt may one day get his dignity back. No word on whether or not Ashton Kutcher was in the crowd.

IVY LEAGUE HIJINX

Harvard is supposed to be home to the best and the brightest. Supposed to be, anyway. In 2004, they looked more like Animal House when Harvard met Yale to renew their 120-plus years of hating each other on the football field. When Harvard students got to their stadium section, young Yalies posed as the Harvard Pep Squad. Which would be a great group if, you know, it actually existed. No matter, the fake Harvard students passed out placards to real Harvard fans, telling them that at halftime the whole section together would spell out "Go Harvard" with the signs. But when halftime rolled around, those fans merely spelled out, "We Suck." The Harvard fans were probably perplexed as to why their signs elicited more laughter than cheers, but, oh, well. If you are wondering who won the game, our official response is: Who cares? When you get punk'd like that the team should probably just hop on the bus at halftime and head home.

THE BALLAD OF SIDD FINCH

Back to baseball: Don't you wish your favorite baseball team had a pitcher who could throw 168 MPH? Sure you do. Everyone would, if one existed. That's why baseball fans were so excited to read about Sidd Finch, a young Mets phenom with a live arm who played the French Horn and loved yoga. Problem was, it turned out that Finch was merely an April Fool's joke that author George Plimpton played on *Sports Illustrated* readers. One clue about the playful hoax came from Plimpton's 1985 article, in which he inserted a couple of odd sentences: "He's a pitcher, part yogi and part recluse. Impressively liberated from our opulent lifestyle, Sidd's deciding about yoga . . . " Yes, the first letter from each word spells "Happy April Fools Day." When P.T. Barnum said there was a sucker born every minute, he wasn't exaggerating. About 2,000 lonely souls wrote the magazine to marvel about Finch. Nor did it stop a Maine school's baseball team from inviting the fictional phenom to speak at its annual banquet.

The guy who posed as Finch for the magazine photos is Joe Berton, now a junior high school art teacher in his mid-50s. Berton told the *New York Times'* Alan Schwarz that he still gets recognized today, including one memorable moment at a 2003 Cubs playoff game. "I'm lining up for a beer and this guy goes, 'You're Sidd Finch, I can't believe it!'" Berton said in the 2005 *Times* article. "I find that almost everybody loves to recount their moment with the story—where they were when they read it and what it meant to them. It's like they really wanted Sidd to be real."

CRAZY FAST

You'd have to be nuts to run a marathon, we think. But you'd have be especially crazy to fake running one. Well, Rosie Ruiz did that dirty deed twice. First, she ran the 1979 New York Marathon and "finished" in the middle of the pack by taking the subway near the finish line and finishing as an "injured runner." Given the crime-ridden state of the

New York subway in those days, she probably deserved a medal just for making it out alive. But New York race officials didn't catch her because she was just one of hundreds of anonymous people that finished at the same time. Then, as an encore, six months later she almost pulled off the sports hoax of the century. She entered in the 1980 Boston Marathon and she "won"—temporarily anyway. But almost immediately, race officials sensed something was wrong. They wondered: How could this unknown have run the 26.2-mile course with the third-highest time ever for a female? And why wasn't she sweaty or fatigued? They checked with race monitors at various checkpoints and none of them recalled seeing her. Lastly, eyewitnesses came forward to say they had seen her jump into the route about a mile left from the finish line. Race officials eventually took the victory from Ruiz, and gave it to the rightful winner, Canadian Jackie Gareau. Today, the 51-year-old Ruiz lives in Florida and still sticks to her three-pronged post-race strategy: Deny, deny, deny. Yep, she still maintains that she did not cheat. It's that kind of persistence that allows marathon runners to finish such a long exhausting race—that is, for those who actually start at the beginning.

8 AS THE SWAG TURNS:
Sports Wives & Girlfriends

CATTINESS ALERT: WARNING FROM ERICA

Dear reader, you are about to encounter some severe cattiness, sweeping generalizations and superficial critiques that women love to dole out. In short, welcome to *Mean Girls: The Sports Edition*. In writing this chapter, it was easy to resort to this tabloid-ish tone, critiquing sports wives and girlfriends of all types. But what was hard to do was to face why women do this. And even harder, to face why I do this.

I will start with a sweeping generalization about our gender: I do think that we tend to rush to judgment and can be extremely harsh, especially toward other women. I also think that we are constantly sizing each other up: Am I prettier? Are her boobs bigger? Is my butt smaller? Does she dress better? Is she dumb? Is she funny? Did she have Botox? Does she need Botox? And at the root is a basic insecurity. There, I said it. I know that this doesn't apply to all women, and I also know it subsides the older we get. But the green-eyed monster certainly lives inside many of us, and my green-eyed ugliness certainly came out this chapter.

Why? Because part of me wishes I was a sports wife and/or girlfriend myself. And part of me feels like I came pretty close. Not really, of course, but during the time that I worked for the San Francisco Giants, I was asked out by a few players here and there. And, naturally, I *had* to be in a relationship at the time. But looking back, I find myself having those "I could have been a contender" moments from time to time. Just as men feel they could have been a star athlete, I think I would have made a pretty damn good player's wife. Or owner's wife. The envy rears its ugly head, particularly when I'm flipping through magazines and see sports wives and girlfriends on TV. I resort to being *that* girl—sizing up other women, but instead of asking the normal "is my butt smaller" type questions (FYI, the answer is almost always no), I start thinking: If I had that kind of money, I would dress way better than she does . . . If I were her, I would use my abundant time and heaps of money to help make the world a better place . . . And if he was married to me, you can bet your sweet ass that he would never cheat on me/go to a strip joint/hire hookers while on the road! So it's easy to say all of these things, but obviously hard to do. The fact of the matter is that I didn't make it to the Big Leagues of sports wifedom or even girlfriend-dom. I am basically a wannabe, standing on the outside, looking in. And the only thing that might make me feel better right now is sitting at my computer with a bag of mini-Snickers and a big glass of Barolo, being catty towards those women who made it to The Show. Won't you join me?

In the UK, hordes of sports fans and non-sports fans follow the lives and times of footballers' wives and girlfriends. There, they call them WAGs—wives and girlfriends. In fact, being a WAG kind of makes you famous in your own right. There was even a BBC drama about them for a few years called *Footballers' Wives*. But here in the states, we really only seem to follow the famous ones (Jessica Simpson, Carrie Underwood, Elisabeth Hasselbeck, Gisele Bündchen, Angie Harmon). Why is that? Why don't we follow our homegrown sports wives and girlfriends, or SWAGs?

(FYI, SWAG is our adaptation of the British term, and we really want everyone to start using it. Ready? Go! So SWAG, your new favorite word, stands for "Sports Wives and Girlfriends," and it will help us differentiate between other types of wives and girlfriends in America, like PWAGs [politicians' wives and girlfriends, like Silda Spitzer and "Kristen"] and AWAGs [actors' wives and girlfriends, who generally tend to be other actors] and RWAGs [rock stars' wives and girlfriends, like Pam Anderson and the cast of *Rock of Love I & II*.] You get the point. There are a lot of famous people in America. We need several categories of WAGs.)

But that's not the only reason we like the acronym SWAG for this particular type of woman. We like SWAG because it also reminds us of the term for freebies that celebrities and VIPS get when they go to events—bags filled with glitzy watches, sparkling jewels, or the keys to some fancy sports car. Come to think of it, these trophy wives and girlfriends are just like a nice, shiny, free Rolex you get in your SWAG bag—a swanky bauble that looks so nice and sparkly on your arm, until you realize that you have to pay taxes on that motherf-cker. And that all of your buddies and fellow VIPs have the same, exact Rolex. Oh, and that the shiny Rolex has fake boobs and is as dumb as a rock.

In the US, it seems from the outside that most players' wives just sit by the pool, spend their husbands' millions, and consider their next plastic surgery procedure. (Chris to Erica: Jealous much? Erica to Chris: Shut it!) But back in the UK, the WAGs have turned themselves into a PR machine. They hang out together, go shopping together, go clubbing together, travel with the team together, get drunk together and sing *I Will Survive,* while standing on tables in the posh German spa town of Baden Baden . . . together. These chicks have formed the ultimate "clique" and they thrive on the limelight—as the British public follows their every move, every collagen injection, every pound gained, every new handbag purchase.

But here in America, there doesn't seem to be too much SWAG camaraderie. There's definitely a bond between NASCAR SWAGs, because they actually hang out in the pit together, and travel with their driver and crew every week for nine long months. As a result, there's also a bit of cat fighting down in the pit and some dating of ex-girl-friends among drivers here and there. Other than that, there's not too much SWAG action in American sports. And we'd like to see a little more of that, to be honest.

So Alyssa Milano or Tara Reid, the next athlete you date, we respectfully request that you gather some of your famous friends—Alyssa, maybe the *Charmed* girls, and Tara, maybe Paris, if she's talk-ing to you these days—and have them start dating some of the other guys on your boyfriend's team. We think you should travel with the team and trash a few hotel rooms. We'd also like you to go on double dates with Eva Longoria and Tony Parker, or Tony Romo and Jessica, or insert-girlfriend-name-here. Alyssa/Tara, you and your fellow SWAGs could hang out at Butter in NYC with Tom Brady and Gisele, or go to Sundance with Reggie Bush and Kim Kardashian—and be sure to call the paparazzi and tell them where you're going, like those British WAGs do. (On the same trip to Baden Baden back in 2006, the hotel where the WAGs were staying put up special protective screens to keep the paparazzi away, as the ladies lounged and frolicked by the pool. The WAGs asked that the screens be removed, in order to give the paps a better view.)

Okay, before we get too carried away, we need to take the gloves (and the claws) off for a moment. We do like the SWAGs that actually have a life beyond their famous athlete husbands—the ones who have jobs of their own or do a lot of charity work, using their stature to help others. Because truth be told, being the wife of a pro athlete isn't all that easy either. It basically means being a single mom while your husband is on the road, possibly screwing other women every week in a different town. There's definitely a flip side to being a SWAG: That big fancy mansion and that American Express Black Card comes with a price.

When Erica was a writer for *Giants* magazine, she wanted to do a piece on all of the players' wives—their careers, their charitable endeavors, lives outside of their famous husbands. Instead, she ended up interviewing one player's wife—the wife of now-deceased pitcher Rod Beck, who was deeply committed to children's AIDS charities. This was because, from the research Erica did, Stacey Beck was one of the few wives who was doing something interesting, outside of being a player's wife. But the sad reality is that Rod Beck died at the age of 38 in 2007. And according to Stacey in an *Arizona Republic* article, he died because of his addiction to cocaine. She knows more than anyone that there can be a dark side to being a player's wife.

The schedule alone and time on the road is brutal. In Major League Baseball, they play 162 games in the regular season and in the NBA and NHL, they play 82 regular season games. In pro football, there are only 16 regular season games, but it's still no picnic. For all of these athletes, half of the games are on the road, and they also have preseason training camp, PR and charity appearances, and, if they're lucky, the possibility of post-season play. So if you're a young SWAG and don't have kids yet—this schedule can be fun. You're traveling with your famous boyfriend or hubby, living the good life. But when kids come into the picture, you're stuck at home, wondering how your famous husband is spending his days (and nights), while you're feeding kids and attending PTA meetings. It's also hard when daddy is in the news all the time. It can be great if he had a good game, but horrible if he sucked the week before . . . or if he had a wild night on the road with his buddies. Good times for good old wifey back at home when she has to explain that to the little ones. (Just ask Shaq's now ex-wife.) Or try to explain to the kids why the people on TV or fans or blogs are saying that daddy's an idiot or a has-been or that he stinks. And what about the fear that your husband is going to break his neck and be paralyzed if he's a football player? Crash his car and die if he's a racecar driver? Or get injured and ruin his career in baseball, basketball or hockey? How about never really settling into a city, because you could be traded or cut at any moment?

And how about the stereotypical way we (mostly Erica) portrayed SWAGs earlier? These women are perceived as ditzy gold-diggers whose main purpose in life is to go shopping and get plastic surgery. In her 2006 book, author and sociologist Shannon O'Toole—who is married to former NFL player and current USC assistant coach John Morton—paints a more accurate picture. In *Wedded to the Game: The Real Lives of NFL Women,* she provides an insider's perspective on the ups and downs of being an American football player's wife. "It was my anguished face caught by the cameras and plastered on the JumboTron interplayed with [John] being slammed backward on a kickoff return, with such force that his shoulder separates," she said in an interview on the Psychology of Sports website. "But, it was also me as a 20-year-old, driving a brand-new, loaded Blazer back and forth to college because that's what my NFL boyfriend lent me." In the book, she interviews many NFL wives and provides a unique portrait of what life is like for the girlfriend of a rookie free agent—as well as the wife of an NFL legend. It's not always a pretty picture.

Another NFL wife, Gena James-Pitts, formed the *Professional Sports Wives Association,* and started the *Professional Sports Wives* magazine in 2006. "I'm not a wife who only shops, watches TV and waits for my husband to come home," she told the Associated Press in an interview. "I'm more than that." James-Pitts is trying to create a community for these 500,000 women who are or have been married to professional or minor league players, coaches and even sports execs. (Chris to Erica: Guess you can't join that association. Erica to Chris: SHUT IT!) "We're like single parents," said James-Pitts, wife of former NFL defensive lineman Mike Pitts. "While our husbands are gone nearly 10 months in a year, we run the household and are financial planners. Some people think we have maids, but not all of us do. These wives are really hard workers."

The magazine features profiles on inspiring sports wives, as well as columns and articles on financial planning, career counseling for players after they retire, household management and marital guidance— which is important because the magazine reports an astounding 80% divorce rate among professional athletes. While the magazine contains a lot of rah-rah stories about wives building houses in New Orleans or running in "Races for the Cure," there is some honest, raw content. "I am beginning to feel as if my husband is cheating on the road," one reader writes. While another says, "My husband is retired and it seems as if he has lost all passion in his life! He doesn't seem to know who he is." Another article contains a profile on Alison Mahay, wife of Kansas City Royals' pitcher Ron Mahay, who started a line of children's sports-related clothing with three other Major League wives. While another offers advice from author and therapist Angela Wilder, former wife of Lakers star James Worthy, who thought she had a dream marriage to the NBA star, until he was arrested for soliciting a prostitute in 1990. "I've been through the struggle and lived through it," she said in an interview with MSNBC. "Now, I can help other women because not only can I talk the talk, but I can walk the walk."

Before we start going back to begging Alyssa Milano to go trash some hotel rooms—we are happy that there's a community for these women. Despite all of their perks and all of Erica's pettiness, we know it's got to be a hard life. And even though "regular" women go through stuff like this all the time, it can't be easy when your husbands' antics are described on the evening news, or splattered all over the internet. It's easy for us to sit here and make fun of their cushy existence, but not all SWAGs are vapid, materialistic women. Not all of them are just after fame and fortune—obsessed with the spotlight and with their husband's fame, so much so that they turn into crazy bitches and completely lose their minds. Not all. But some. And of course, those are the ones we want to talk about.

Here, we present the "GameFace Gallery of the Greatest SWAGs in the History of Mankind." Some are nuts, others behind bars. Some are famous in their own right and others are media whores. And yes, some are actually normal, down-to-earth chicks who we might be friends with. But we assure you, all of these SWAGs are downright entertaining.

Swags Who Stood By Their Men

Take it from Tammy Wynette: Sometimes it's hard to be a SWAG, givin' all your love to just one man. You'll have bad times. And he'll have good times. Doing things that you don't understand. These SWAGs learned just to turn the other cheek and ignore their husbands' indiscretions. 'Cause after all, he's just a man.

Tawanna Turner: The Hilary Clinton of the hardwood. A sympathetic character, Mrs. Allen Iverson has had to deal with more than a few indignities. In 2002, her NBA guard husband locked her outside their Philly mansion while she was half-naked during an argument. The next night, he went looking for her at a cousin's house, with a semi-automatic gun in hand. And in 2006, her husband's name turned up in groupie Carmen Bryan's tell-all book, *It's No Secret.* The latest news? Tawanna had lunch with Juanita Jordan, Michael's ex, who gave her some advice. Recent reports state that after years of turning the other cheek, Tawanna and Allen are indeed on the rocks.

Kathie Lee Gifford: America's sweetheart—former star of *Name That Tune* and *Regis and Kathie Lee*—married former NFL player and commentator Frank Gifford in 1986. He was 23 years her senior. She enjoyed a decade-long love fest from the press and fans, but soon her sugary, Carnival-Cruisey image reached complete saturation. So after she was accused of hiring 13-year-olds to make her Wal-Mart apparel in South American sweat shops in 1996, and after a 1997 video was released of her husband's tryst with a former stewardess, Americans reacted with open *schadenfreude,* chuckling at her demise. In 2000, Kathie Lee announced she was leaving Regis for good to undoubtedly spend some time away from the spotlight. We kind of feel bad for her and think that maybe she'll have some type of Martha Stewart-esque resurgence, now that she's hosting the fourth (!) hour of the *Today Show.*

Cynthia Scurtis Rodriguez: It can't be easy to be married to heartthrob Alex Rodriguez, the Yankees third baseman. And it's not easy when he's spotted by the paparazzi, hanging out with a 30-year-old stripper from Scores. It's one thing for your husband to have random sex with these tramps, but quite another when he starts flying them around with the team and taking them on dates. Cynthia, mother of A-Rod's two kids, wore a brave face—and a tank top that said "F-ck You" (without the hyphen) on the back to the next Yankee home game. It is unclear as to whether that message was directed toward the media, Yankee fans, her husband, or to her husband's mistress. After looking at photos of A-Rod's girlfriend Joslyn Morse, as well as photos of his wife Cynthia Scurtis, we have some other questions, though. (And Bill Simmons of ESPN agrees with us.) If A-Rod has a thing for masculine-looking, muscular blondes, can an affair with Hulk Hogan be far behind? *UPDATE:* Actually, Hulk Hogan may have to wait his turn. As we go to press, reports indicate that A-Rod has moved on to another muscular blonde: Madonna.

Millie Corretjer: It seemed like boxer Oscar de la Hoya finally settled down. After being a bachelor for a while, he married Puerto Rican singer and actress Millie Corretjer in 2001. They had a son in 2005. She was pregnant with their second child, in the spring of 2007, when some crazy-ass photos were released of Oscar wearing women's underwear . . . while he was in a Philadelphia hotel room with a Russian model/stripper. Many claim—no one more adamantly than de la Hoya himself—that the photos were doctored. Regardless, Millie turned the other cheek, and we're sure she turned her eyes away from these disturbing photos of her husband in fishnets, thongs and pumps, whether they were real or not. She delivered her second child in late 2007.

SWAGS WHO SHOULD JUST LEARN TO SHUT UP

Some SWAGs were meant to be seen and not heard. The sooner these women learn that they are just meant to be arm-candy, the better. They are not supposed to mouth-off—and potentially damage their husbands' careers.

Julie Romanowski: The wife of linebacker Bill Romanowski—who was known as "Romo" probably before Tony Romo was even born—seems more involved than most NFL wives. Involved in drug scandals, in spilling the beans about her husband's 'roid use and in obnoxiously pimping her husband's book, that is. Back in 1998, she was accused of illegally forging Romo's name in order to get prescription diet drugs and steroids. Those charges were dropped. But the following year, she told investigators that her husband obtained human growth hormone from BALCO. During their appearance on Howard Stern in 2005, Julie pimped her husband's new book so obnoxiously that Stern started insulting her on the air. Bill, may we suggest this jewel-encrusted muzzle for Julie's Christmas gift this year?

Brenda Warner: This former marine and loudmouth wife of QB Kurt Warner used to have her own radio show in St. Louis, where she spent a lot of air-time telling the Rams to play her husband more, commenting on his injuries, and even asking to be traded. She also has been known to call other radio shows to talk about her husband's on-field skills. She seems to have quieted down a bit since Kurt's move to Arizona, where he now shares the QB role with young phenom Matt Leinart. Random things you might like to know: Brenda and Kurt met at a country western bar while both were working at a grocery store. Kurt was a stock boy, having taken the job after he was cut from the Green Bay Packers. Brenda was a checker, a bit older, divorced and had two children, one of whom was a special-needs kid. Kurt married Brenda five years later, adopted her two children, and then the duo went on to have five more kids together—for a total of seven. Maybe she just has less time to call into radio shows these days?

Anna Benson: We mentioned her before in our gallery of gold diggers, but her big trap earns her a spot on this list, too. To recap, she is married to pitcher Kris Benson and is thought to be responsible for the Mets trading him to Baltimore in 2006, thanks to her outlandish comments and some say due to her risqué choice of dress to the Mets holiday party. As of 2008, Kris signed with the Phillies, but he's at the stage in his career with he'll be fighting for a spot in someone's rotation—and, as a result, Anna seems to have quieted down. But what fun is that? We miss you, Anna. Here, some classic quotes from the past: "We hadn't had sex for a few days so we got into the back seat of our SUV in the parking lot at Three Rivers Stadium and while we were doing it fans were beating on the windows. We finished screwing, then Kris got out and greeted the fans," she told *Player* magazine. "Hell, I'm not stopping sex with my man so some overzealous fan can have an autograph!" And in a 2006 interview with FHM, she lamented that her husband will not have sex with her on a day he's pitching or the day before. "If you add in Spring Training games, that's like 82 days out of the year you won't [bleep] me. And when I can't have it, that's when I really want it." Let's see which team is lucky enough to pick up the Bensons next season.

SWAGS IN TROUBLE WITH THE LAW

Sometimes the crazy lifestyle led by these famous athletes turns their wives into crazy bitches. But honestly, no amount of cheating or beating should cause this behavior . . .

Deidra Lane: In 2000, this 25-year-old shot and killed her husband, former Carolina Panthers running back Fred Lane, who had just been picked up by the Indianapolis Colts. He came back from training camp and was shot at close range as he entered his house. His key was still in the door. Deidra claimed she put up with years of abuse, but prosecutors think she was trying to get his $5-million life insurance policy. Some friendly advice to any would-be SWAGs: If you kill your famous spouse yourself, you are not entitled to the life insurance money.

Daniell Harper: According to a 2006 police report, Daniell without an "e" claims that she took a filet knife out of the kitchen drawer and "accidentally stabbed" her husband, NFL cornerback Nick Harper. It should be noted that he "accidentally hit" her back in 2005 and was arrested for it. According to MSNBC, Daniell Harper told police that she got the knife out because she was upset that her husband would not speak to her. (In his defense, maybe he was focused on the big playoff game between his Colts and the Steelers the very next day. Maybe he was a bit moody.) Regardless, Daniell began waving the knife over Harper while he was lying on their bed in their suburban Indy home. Nick ended up with a gash in his leg that required three stitches. We will refrain from Lorena Bobbitt jokes and just say that we think he got off lucky.

Kendra Davis: It was a tough decision whether to put the Knicks Antonio Davis' outspoken wife Kendra Davis in the "KEEP THEIR MOUTHS SHUT" category or the "TROUBLE WITH THE LAW" category. She is a big mouth. No doubt about it. Just ask Latrell Sprewell— she verbally attacked him during a playoff game when her husband was on the Toronto Raptors. The former Miss Illinois Teen USA continued to demonstrate her inability to shut her trap in 2006, when her husband was playing for the Knicks. In a game against the Bulls in Chicago, it was first reported that several Bulls fans harassed her at a game she attended with her kids. Her husband rushed into the stands to protect her and break up the fight—he was suspended for five games. It later came out that it was Kendra who was talking trash, waving her finger in faces of other fans and instigating the whole thing herself. And just a few weeks later, she was charged with misdemeanor battery for throwing a cup of hot coffee at a woman during a traffic altercation. Girlfriend needs to chillax.

CELEBRITY SWAGS THAT DIDN'T GO THE DISTANCE—AND WE WISH THEY HAD

Sometimes it takes someone with incredible talent and a true understanding of the pressures of the media to really be able to "get" an athlete. That's why we really thought these celebrity SWAGs were going to make it work with their men. Damn we hate it when we're wrong.

Marilyn Monroe & Joe DiMaggio: Marilyn might be the very first celebrity SWAG, truly paving the way for the rest. And we really wish these two kids could have worked it out. But their relationship did seem doomed from the beginning. When they were married in 1954, they were at two different points in their lives—Marilyn's career was on the rise, while the life-long Yankee had retired and was ready to slow down. Joe was notoriously jealous and Marilyn was notoriously flirty—not a good combination. There are reports that he became furious at the crowd reaction as Marilyn was filming the famous *Seven Year Itch* scene, in which her skirt blew up. Take after take, the fans went wild. And Joe went wild with jealousy. The couple is reported to have had a shouting match in the lobby of the NYC theater where they were filming. Just over nine months after they were married, Marilyn filed for divorce, citing "mental cruelty."

Just like a modern-day Jeter, Joe was then linked to every star-let under the sun, including Lee Merriweather and Marlene Dietrich. Marilyn, of course, went on to hang with the "Rat Pack" and ended up marrying Arthur Miller. But Joe came back into Marilyn's life after her marriage with the famous playwright was ending. He helped her battle back from depression, even getting her out of a mental hospital. The couple was back together for a short time and it was rumored that she became pregnant with Joe's baby, but it was stillborn. According to biographer Maury Allen, Joe had grown tired of her destructive behav-ior and the company she kept, and decided it was time to take action. On August 1, 1962, he quit his job with a military store supplier and had plans to ask Marilyn to remarry him. She was found dead just four days later. It was Joe who claimed her body from the morgue and made funeral arrangements, not allowing Hollywood-types to attend. For the next 20 years, he had red roses delivered to her grave, three times a week. And in an even more romantic gesture, he refused to talk about their relationship in public. Ever. And he never remarried.

Vanessa Williams & Rick Fox: Okay, maybe former NBA star Rick Fox was a philanderer—photos were taken of him kissing another woman in the summer of 2004. But these two are just about the most attractive cou-ple ever. They have a daughter together. We really thought they were going to work through everything. There were rumors in 2005 about a possible reconciliation and the exes recently reunited on Williams' hit show *Ugly Betty*, as Fox guest-starred as Williams' bodyguard in two episodes that aired in late 2007. Regardless, their split was amicable, and the two con-tinue to raise their daughter together and support each other's careers.

Sheryl Crow & Lance Armstrong: We were hoping he was strong enough to be her man. After all, the legendary cyclist had been through cancer himself. Sure, the fact that he left his first wife after she stuck by him during his horrific battle with testicular cancer gave him the poten-tial to be an asshole. But something just seemed right about Lance and Sheryl. We all thought they were in it to win it when they got engaged in September 2005. But then, they split suddenly in February 2006, just two weeks before Crow's breast cancer diagnosis. After she told him she had cancer, he wanted to be by her side, but she refused—saying she needed to surround herself with people who were going to stand by her for the long haul. The couple did not get back together. Sheryl has since survived her cancer and went on to adopt a baby in 2007. Armstrong has been hanging with Matthew McConaughey, designer Tory Burch and Ashley Olsen, of the Olsen twins. No comment on which one we think is the douchebag in this scenario.

CELEB SWAGS AND ATHLETES THAT DIDN'T GO THE DISTANCE—AND WE'RE GLAD:

Sometimes a celebrity couple can't survive when one person's career is flourishing, while the other's is floundering. Others cave to the pressures of chasing success and having their lives scrutinized by the media. Still others are just plain nuts. Here, couples who thankfully called it quits, saving us from more trashy tabloid tales.

Halle Barry & David Justice: We hear he was a wife-beater. She says she tried to kill herself back in 1997, after their marriage fell apart. We really just want Halle Berry to be happy. After one more horrible marriage, we think she seems in a good place with her new beau and baby. And in what can only be described as karma, David Justice's house burned down in the San Diego fires in October 2007, and just two months later, his name was mentioned in the Mitchell Report.

Robin Givens & Mike Tyson: Where do we begin? We already discussed what an animal this guy is—biting ears off of men and attacking women, such as former Miss Black Rhode Island in 1991. How did our dear little star of *Head of the Class* end up with this brute, describing her life with him a "pure hell" on Barbara Walters' couch? Luckily, after a year of marital strife from 1988 to 1989, Givens got out and ended up with $8 million, as reported by *Sports Illustrated.*

Shockingly, a doctor named Monica Turner agreed to marry Tyson in 1997 and they had two kids during their six-year marriage. They divorced in 2003, and between this divorce settlement, along with the estimated $30 million he has paid over the years to various women in paternity suits and civil suits stemming from improper sexual behavior—he's now broke.

Givens has not been much luckier in love. After her marriage to Tyson, she was romantically linked to Brad Pitt, Howard Stern, Marcus Schenkenberg and rapper Ginuwine. In 1997, she had a short-lived marriage to her tennis instructor Svetozar Marinkovic, and then two years later, had a baby boy with tennis star Murphy Jensen. Now, Givens appears to be single—but has been spotted around NYC with Major League Baseball's Executive VP of Baseball Operations Jimmie Lee Solomon. It seems this girl has sports in her blood—for better or for worse.

Carmen Electra & Dennis Rodman: This quickie Vegas wedding and nine-day marriage was ridiculous, and these two are ridiculous—even though we really want to like Carmen Electra. She's adorable, once dated Prince, and we love her "Aerobic Striptease" DVDs, where she gives great advice like, "Never underestimate the power of the finger in the mouth." She and her rock-star husband Dave Navarro split up in 2006, and Rodman told the press it's because Carmen is still in love with him. To that we say ha! If she's still in love with you, then why have we heard rumors that she's dating Joan Jett . . . and David Spade. Wait. Maybe she is still in love with you.

As for Rodman, he says that Madonna tried to have a baby with him—thankfully that didn't happen. He did have two kids with his third wife, Michelle—the two live separately in Newport Beach, California, which oddly, kind of makes sense. Professionally, Rodman's hoping he makes it into the NBA Hall of Fame, but his antics off the court aren't helping his image too much. Lately, he has appeared on the UK version of *Celebrity Big Brother,* served as a spokesperson for an online casino, hosted a show for Mark Cuban's HDNet called *Geek to Freak,* made appearances at his Miami nightclub "Rodman's Rehab," checked into real rehab in May 2008, and yes, he has continued to dress in drag every now and then.

Lisa "Left Eye" Lopes & Andre Rison: We really loved "Left Eye" of R&B girl band TLC, and were shocked and saddened when she died in a car accident in Honduras in 2002, especially because it seemed that she had really gotten her life together after a rather tumultuous time in the '90s. Who could forget her 1994 attempt to burn down Atlanta NFL star Andre Rison's $2 million mansion? She told police that she originally had "decided to barbeque his tennis shoes" in response to his reported infidelity. But instead, the fire got out of control and nearly burned his house to the ground. "Left Eye" was charged with arson, paid a $10,000 fine and was given five years of probation. Surprisingly, the two reunited in 2001 and had plans to be married, but the wedding was called off. We all know about the fate of "Left Eye"—but what about Rison? According to reports, he's a dead-beat dad—owing thousands of dollars to his ex-wife, as well as a former girlfriend/baby-mama—and in 2007, he filed for bankruptcy.

Tawny Kitaen & Chuck Finley: Remember Tawny Kitaen? She was the girl from *Bachelor Party,* who was once married to David Coverdale, the lead singer of Whitesnake. You know, the chick with the big hair who writhed all over the hood of his car in that video. Well, she ended up marrying pitcher Chuck Finley in 1997—nice, cute California couple, right? Wrong! After five years of marriage and two kids, she was arrested for battery and assault for attacking her husband while he was driving—including kicking and gouging him with her high heel and twisting his ear! He filed for divorce three days later. Tawny blamed the incident on her addiction to prescription drugs for depression and migraines. She was sent to rehab, anger management and had to make a donation to a battered-women's shelter. (Why not a battered husband's shelter, we ask?) After this stint in rehab, things got worse. Tawny appeared on *The Surreal Life* in 2006, where she verbally attacked Florence Henderson (who attacks Mrs.

Brady!?!) and had a complete meltdown when she found out her fiancé was having an affair with her manager. Later that year, she was charged with possession of cocaine in her Orange County home, while her children were home. In December 2006, she entered a six-month rehab program in exchange for the dismissal of the felony drug charge. Here she goes again on her own. Goin' down the only road she's ever known . . .

CELEBRITY SWAGS THAT FOUND A WAY TO MAKE IT WORK—SO FAR:

How do these couples keep it together? When the marriage is made up of two stars, the media spotlight shines twice as bright. But despite it all, these couples seem to be surviving—and thriving.

Hilary Duff & Mike Comrie: We don't really get Hilary Duff, but then again, we're probably the wrong demographic. But we do know that she is dating pro hockey player Mike Comrie of the New York Islanders. There were rumors running wild on the celebrity gossip websites a few years ago that Comrie was traded from the Edmonton Oilers because he allegedly slept with his teammate's wife. But now, Hilary just brushes off those rumors, and she and Mike seem like a normal, happy couple—just like the rest of us! They live in NYC and jet around the world. They frequent Manhattan's exclusive Waverly Inn restaurant. They go shopping at chic boutique Scoop. They get bottle service at nightclub Tenjune. Oh, and Mike bought Hilary a Mercedes-Benz G-Class SUV, worth more than $100,000, for her 20th birthday. (That reminds Erica of her 20th birthday, when her boyfriend bought her a Cassingle of *Every Rose Has Its Thorn* by Poison.) See, they're just like us!

Janet Jones & Wayne Gretzky: It is actually remarkable that these two have stayed together. They met on the set of *Dance Fever* in 1984, where Gretzky was a judge. The story should end here, maybe with a one-night-stand. Instead, the two became the royal couple of Canada, exchanging vows at a million-dollar wedding in July 1988 that was televised throughout the country. The ceremony was held at St. Joseph's Basilica in Edmonton—even though neither Jones nor Gretzky were Catholic, and even though Jones was four months pregnant at the time. Just weeks later, it was announced that Gretzky would be traded to the LA Kings, after a nine-year career in Edmonton. It is widely believed that Gretzky engineered the move himself so that his new wife could focus on her acting career. Ah, love. It does make you do crazy things. Gretzky broke millions of Canadian hearts so that Jones could continue to star in such film treasures like the *Police Academy 5* and *American Anthem,* co-starring Olympic gymnast Mitch Gaylord.

Needless to say, her acting career never really blossomed (unless you count the infomercial she hosted for Jackie Chan's Cable Flex resistance system). But her husband, known as "The Great One," after initially being called a traitor by the entire country of Canada, retired with much fanfare in 1999 and is regarded as the best hockey player in history.

Flash forward to 2006. With her lackluster career, it's not too surprising that Jones might have turned to some other form of income. But it was surprising when she was implicated in an underground gambling ring, along with the assistant coach of the Phoenix Coyotes. Yes, that would be the very NHL team that Gretzky now coaches. Suddenly, "The Great One" distanced himself from his wife, denying any knowledge of her gambling and any association with gambling whatsoever. Several weeks after the scandal broke, it was announced that neither Gretzky nor Jones would be charged.

Victoria & David Beckham: They were once Britain's favorite tabloid topics, and now they've come to LA in search of more fame, fortune and glory—if they can succeed in making Americans give a damn about soccer. If anyone can do it, these two media whores can! In fact, they remind us of a certain couple named Wayne and Janet, who moved from Canada to LA, in hopes of glitz, glamour and turning Americans on to hockey. Let's take a look at the similarities, shall we?

▶ Posh and Becks met at a charity football match in 1997 and were married a few years later at Luttrellstown Castle, in an over-the-top wedding in which they sat in golden thrones and received tremendous media coverage. Met trying to get more media attention? Check. Obnoxious, fairytale-type wedding? Check.

▶ Posh and Beckham's four-month-old son Brooklyn served as the ring bearer in the ceremony. Premarital sex? Check. Complete disregard for birth control? Check.

▶ The Beckhams have three boys with cloyingly hip names (Brooklyn, Romeo and Cruz), while the Gretzkys have three boys with cloyingly alliterated names (Ty, Trevor, Tristan). Check! Okay, full disclosure, the Gretzkys also have two girls with non-annoying names (Paulina and Emma).

After that, the similarities end, we're afraid. That's because the Beckhams did things differently. They waited for Becks to get old and injured and slightly past his prime—and then negotiated a deal to have him join the LA Galaxy. If Becks had left in the prime of his career to defect to the West Coast like Gretzky did, there would have been hell to pay—maybe an LA Tea Party or a boycott of McDonald's by the Brits. But Becks did the right thing. He gave his country the best years of his life on the field, and then he sold out—riding off to LA in the sunset. And with the mini-Spice Girls reunion tour, a co-branded David & Victoria Beckham clothing collection, her appearance on *Project Runway* and in the Marc Jacobs campaign, and her 2008 selection as "World's Sexiest Mom" by Victoria's Secret—we think Posh has a much better chance than Janet at making it big in Hollywood.

Ashley Judd & Dario Franchitti: Ashley has always liked the sporty types—she dated baseball player Brady Anderson and actor Matthew McConaughey, who sure likes to jog with his shirt off. But in 1999, she fell for IndyCar driver Dario Franchitti. The two became engaged and in 2001, were also married in a castle (Jesus! Some originality here, people.

Please!) They now divide their time between Scotland and Tennessee, which has got to be quite a contrast. We like Ashley because despite her busy career, she's very involved in her husband's racing and is always seen down in Gasoline Alley—especially when he won the Indy 500 in 2007. We also like her because she's got a big charitable heart *and* she's a big sports fan, regularly attending University of Kentucky basketball games. She even served as a guest columnist for a Kentucky paper, covering the NCCAA tournament. Let's see how she does as her husband makes the shift to stock cars. She might give those NASCAR SWAGs a run for their money down in the pit.

Jewel & Ty Murray: This singer/songwriter and her nine-time bull riding champ of a boyfriend seem to have found a way to make things work—they've been together for nearly 10 years. They're both private people who prefer small-town living. So they live on a farm in Stephenville, Texas, and lead a relatively quiet life—even though Ty is the President of the highly entertaining Professional Bull Riders association and Jewel released a new album in 2008, now making a shift into country music.

Angie Harmon & Jason Sehorn: Another very attractive couple, these two were very much in the spotlight in 2000—in fact, they were the toast of the Big Apple. Jason was the "hot New York Giants cornerback" and Angie was the "hot *Law & Order* chick" at the time. Plus, everyone remembers Sehorn's very cute and very public wedding proposal, in which he made a surprise visit to the *Tonight Show,* where Angie was appearing as a guest. Insert "Awwwww" here. Since then, Harmon's been busy cranking out two babies, filming a few movies and starring in ABC's *Women's Murder Club.* Sehorn is a panelist on *Fox Sports Net.* They live in LA and, from all accounts, still seem to be Super Couple.

Elisabeth Hasselbeck & Tim Hasselbeck: Okay, they're known for their conservatism and cuteness. We'll give them that. They were college sweethearts, married in 2002 and have two kids. She's the right-winger on *The View*. He's a backup QB, who most recently played for the Arizona Cardinals, and is also a sports commentator on FOX (natch). Her brother-in-law is first-string QB Matt Hasselbeck of the Seahawks. Pretty standard stuff. The only thing we find weird about this whole thing is that she was a designer for Puma, then went on *Survivor* and now seems to be everywhere? How did that happen? She better be careful not to become America's next Kathie Lee. Beware of success, saturation and *schadenfreude,* dear Elisabeth.

Enrique Iglesias & Anna Kournikova: This tennis star has been bashed for having more style than substance as a player—and the same could be said for the talents of her crooning boyfriend. But they stuck in there when everyone thought they were a flash in the pan. Despite the on-again/off-again rumors you hear on a daily basis, the two have been romantically linked since 2002. That's a long time in both the celebrity and sports worlds. A tidbit you may not know? There are reports that Kournikova was once married to the NHL's Sergei Federov in 2001, when she was just 20—and he was 32.

Candace Cameron & Valeri Bure: You stole our hearts as D.J. Tanner in *Full House*. You didn't seem to mind it that your brother Kirk was more famous than you were. Or that those Olsen twins went on to be mini-moguls while you were still in high school. We must admit that when you got married to an NHL hockey player at age 20, we thought you were headed in the wrong direction—just like your co-star Jodie Sweetin who played Stephanie and turned out to be a meth-head. But Candace, you proved us wrong. You've been married to now-retired hockey player Val Bure since 1996, and you're raising three adorable kids. We also know that you're super-religious now—along with your brother Kirk, with his hardcore Christian multimedia empire—but we prefer child-stars-turned-religious-fanatics to child-stars-turned-drug-addicts any day!

MODEL SWAGS AND THE
ATHLETES WHO LOVE THEM

The superstar athlete paired with the supermodel is an archetype that goes back to high school, when the quarterback and the head cheerleader are supposed to be perched atop the homecoming float, smiling and waving. Cute as they are, ever notice that there's something a little too plastic about them? We think that's God's way of saying that people can't be athletic, hot *and* smart. It just wouldn't be right. Except if that person is named Tom Brady, that is. (Chris: I thought we hated him and his fellow Patriots? Erica: I'm trying, Chris. I'm really trying.)

Gisele Bündchen & Tom Brady: These two would be your typical jock/beauty queen story—if it weren't for all that juicy baby-mama drama. We are curious to see if Tom has any role in the upbringing of the little fella with model/actress Bridget Moynahan. And we do hand it to Gisele for showering Bridget with chic baby gifts—from Baby Dior, Burberry, and Gucci, of course.

Jennifer & Joe Montana: The Niners legend, also known as "Joe Cool," met his would-be wife—model and actress Jennifer Wallace—while they worked on a Schick razor commercial together. They've been married for nearly 25 years and have four kids—and are generally thought of as the Golden Couple.

Bridgette Wilson & Pete Sampras: Bridgette is an actress, model and former Miss Teen USA. She married tennis star Pete Sampras in 2000 and they have two sons. See, we told you. Nice people, but nothing too juicy.

Patti McGuire & Jimmy Connors: This one's got a little spice to it! Somehow, it's been forgotten (at least to us) that back in the '70s, tennis great and current Andy Roddick coach Jimmy Connors was engaged to another tennis great—Chris Evert. They called it off, and seven years later, Connors married *Playboy* model Patti McGuire. They are still married and have two kids. Better, but still a little lackluster.

Heather Kozar & Tim Couch: Here's a good one. Nothing like a good old love triangle to spice things up. Enter Heather Kozar—Playmate of the Year, one of Barker's Beauties on *The Price Is Right*, and a St. Pauli Girl. She had been happily dating then-Cleveland Browns QB Tim Couch. Until he introduced her to his buddy, then-Bears QB Cade McNown—a guy who has been banned from the Playboy mansion for stealing Hef's girlfriend Brande Roderick. Forget yelling at Mrs. Brady—who steals Hef's girlfriend in his own house? And who would introduce their own Playmate-girlfriend to a known Playmate-stealer? True to form, McNown wooed Heather. He showered her with flowers, gifts, even a Porsche. She fell for it and moved to Chicago for him. But it was short-lived. She returned to Couch and he took her back. They were married in 2005 and had a little boy named Chase the same year. That's a good name for the little tyke, because it pretty much sums up their relationship.

Carmella DeCesare & Jeff Garcia: Another Playmate of the Year, another quarterback. Ho-hum, right? Nope! Ho-mo! Former teammate Terrell Owens implied that Garcia was gay in an interview with *Playboy* magazine. T.O. has since denied the comment and we're not really sure why anyone would believe a word T.O. said anyway—but next thing you know, everyone is calling this hot playmate Garcia's beard! She stands by her man and said in an interview, "I can attest 100-percent that he is not gay." All we know is that they were married in 2007 and had a child in 2008. But keep an eye on these two, because there is the potential for some crazy antics. In 2004, Carmella was charged with assault after an altercation with one of Garcia's ex-girlfriends in a Cleveland nightclub. According to a newspaper report, she "launched" herself at the ex several times, and then "karate-kicked" her in the head.

Ingrid Vandebosch & Jeff Gordon: Gordon met his first wife Brooke—one of NASCAR'S Miss Winstons—in Victory Lane after he won a Busch race. They were married in 1994 and were, by all accounts, happily married—until Brooke found out that Jeff had been cheating, primarily with a stripper named Deanna Merryman. The divorce provided plenty of juicy fodder for the tabloids throughout 2003, and when the dust settled, Brooke walked away with $15 million. Gordon then began dating Belgian supermodel Ingrid Vandebosch, a statuesque brunette who was a year older than Gordon. Jeff and Ingrid announced their engagement in 2006 and at that point, it is widely believed that if Gordon did not get his wife-to-be to sign an ironclad pre-nup this time, he is a complete moron. The two were married in a private ceremony in November 2006—Ingrid was already pregnant with their first child. Not very "NASCAR" of them, was it? Actually, maybe it was.

IN A CATEGORY ALL HER OWN:
SUPERMODEL & SUPER COUGAR SWAG

This one goes out to all those athletes who marry their high school sweethearts, then dump them for *Playboy* Playmates . . .

Carol Alt: At nearly 50 years old, she's still got it! Her modeling career has spanned 27 years—and some claim she was the very first supermodel. In 1983, Alt married New York Rangers defenseman Ron Greschner. After 13 years of marriage, they split up. But that's not the relationship we're intrigued by. She's currently in a committed relationship with Russian hockey player and former NHL center Alexei Yashin, who is 13 years younger than she is. Nicely done! She also recently appeared on *Celebrity Apprentice,* alongside the likes of Gene Simmons and Stephen Baldwin, which made us lose a little bit of respect for her, but we still like her.

ABUSIVE SWAGS AND THEIR
ABUSIVE ATHLETE HUSBANDS

These stories are so ugly, they make us wonder just how people—no matter how rich and famous they are—can be so awful to each other. There are always two sides to every story, but it seems that in these cases, both sides have some explaining to do . . . especially to their kids!

Joumana Kidd & Jason Kidd: Via damning court documents, NBA star Jason Kidd duked it out publicly with his wife of 10 years as they filed for divorce in 2007.

He said: *I am the victim here.* Kidd claims that his wife had become increasingly controlling and manipulative—and that she has kicked, hit and punched him repeatedly over the course of their marriage. He went on to detail his accounts of "extreme cruelty," including Joumana throwing household objects at him, placing tracking devices on his cars and using their son as a pawn when she asked the boy to take his dad's cell phone from his locker.

She said: *That is complete bullshit.* Back in 2001, Kidd was arrested for punching Joumana in the mouth during an argument in Arizona. And aside from the "years of abuse," including claims that Kidd broke her rib and smashed her head into the dashboard of a car, Joumana also describes extramarital affairs with television reporters, strippers, a Nets season ticket holder, a Nets employee and a cheerleader. She also claims that the cell phone she got from Kidd's locker contained lewd text messages and nude photos sent by other women. Oh, and she also said he's a binge drinker and excessive gambler.

Eventually, the Kidds worked out a somewhat amicable settlement—even though Jason can't seem to stay out of trouble. It was reported in late 2007 that he is being sued by a 23-year-old model who claims he grabbed her ass and crotch at Manhattan nightclub Tenjune. Just a month later, Kidd announced that his new girlfriend Hope Dworaczyk—who has been described as a model, groupie and a former Ms. South-Texas Co-Ed Junior teen—is pregnant and due in late 2008.

Sherrie & John Daly: These two seem to deserve each other. Renowned golfer John Daly and his fourth wife Sherrie filed for divorce in 2007, yet were still living together in Memphis when tempers flared. John called police, claiming that his fourth wife attacked him with a steak knife, stabbing him in the cheek and scratching his face. "I just want my fans to know one thing—I am the victim in this," he told SI.com in an interview in 2007. "My wife is a liar, a liar. I'm tired of being a victim of all this crap. She beats me up when I go to sleep. Every time I go to sleep she throws her fists on me. I just married the wrong woman." Daly's wife—who served time in prison last year after a drug and illegal gambling investigation—shot back with charges of sexual assault, claiming that Daly fabricated the entire the knife attack, and that he stabbed and scratched *himself* in an attempt to cover up his own drunken attack. Daly is known for his heavy drinking and serious gambling debts—he has been suspended from the PGA. But Sherrie's no prize either. We just hope these two crazy kids can work it out, so they can keep their craziness to themselves.

A Swag Who Has Her Husband by the Balls

No introduction needed, really. Ladies and gentleman, the swaggiest SWAG around . . .

Jackie Christie: So controlling that she had husband, former NBA star Doug Christie, giving her hand signals during games that meant "I love you," while she sat in the stands, to let her know he was thinking of her. So possessive, she reportedly tried to have a female Sacramento Kings employee fired for leaving a work-related phone message at their home. So annoying that she complained about female reporters getting too close to her husband. So crazy that she is known for yelling at female autograph-seeking fans trying to talk to her husband. So over-the-top that she and her husband get married again every year on their anniversary, in a lavish ceremony.

The only thing good about these two is that they seem to have a sense of humor about their public image—his of a whipped husband and hers as a control freak of a wife. BET did a reality show about them called, *Committed: The Christies,* they wrote a book called *No Ordinary Love,* and they made their own film called *The Christies Un-Cut,* which spoofed their life together. To promote their empire, they took photos that show Doug on all fours, wearing a dog collar and leash, which is held by an S&M-looking Jackie. Doug is now a free agent, so they spend much of their time working together to run jackiechristie.com and all of their ventures. Wait a minute. Isn't he the NBA star? Why isn't it doug-christie.com? Guess he is whipped after all.

Swags Who Are Athletes Themselves

Couples that play together, stay together it seems. We've got soccer player Mia Hamm and her husband LA Dodger Nomar Garciaparra. Softball player Jennie Finch, who married pitcher Casey Daigle. Volleyball phenom and model Gabby Reece, married to pro surfer Laird Hamilton. Tennis great Venus Williams, now reported to be engaged to golfer Hank Keuhne. And soccer player Heather Mitts is giving Alyssa Milano a run for her money these days—she has dated Phillies left fielder Pat Burrell, Eagles quarterback A.J. Feeley and tennis player James Blake. Here, we share a couple of the juicier athlete match-ups:

Steffi Graf & Andre Agassi: These two make a great couple—and this story is really only juicy because Agassi was such a bad boy in his youth with that straggly long hair, earring, flashy style and rebellious attitude. We all know he was married to Brooke Shields for a couple of years—but many forget that he dated Barbra Streisand, something we still find a bit shocking. But Andre claims that always had a thing for Steffi—her style, her attitude, her athleticism. They met years before, but were married in 2001 and Steffi gave birth to their first child just four days later. Although tennis great Steffi had retired in 1999—Andre made a final run for glory, giving us one of the most exciting US Opens ever in 2005, when he beat James Blake in the quarter-finals in a match that kept 20,000 fans in the stands until 1am. He retired the next year at the US Open, where he received an 8-minute standing-o, and gave a goose-bump-raising farewell speech. He and Steffi now live in Las Vegas and have two kids, Jaden and Jaz. Sure their kids' names are a tad nauseating, but nothing can make us stop loving these two!

Chris Evert & Greg Norman: At first, this duo seems like the perfect power couple—an amazing merging of tennis and golf greatness. And they have known each other for decades. Want to know how? Chris' husband of 18 years, skier Andy Mills, was best friends with Norman, the Aussie golfer. Ouch. These sports legends each left their spouses in order to be together. Chris actually got off pretty easy in the divorce settlement, agreeing to pay Andy $7 million. He seems like a class act, telling *People* magazine, "These two people have really meant a lot to me for a long time. At this point I just wish them great happiness." Norman's divorce from his wife of more than 25 years wasn't quite as pretty. Laura, a former flight attendant, and Norman battled it out in the press and she stands to get a lot more money—as Norman is estimated to be worth anywhere between $300-$500 million. Meanwhile, Norman and Evert announced their engagement in late 2007.

REPEAT OFFENDERS: THE SWAG HALL OF FAME

These sensational SWAGs haven't settled down and picked which athlete they're going to stick with just yet. We know, ladies—there are so many to choose from! Just be sure to pick one soon, none of you are getting any younger.

Tara Reid: This hot mess with a highly-publicized botched boob job has been linked to the NFL's Tom Brady, Kyle Boller and Jeremy Schockey, as well as the NHL's Sergei Federov, and even Aussie tennis player and star of that awful *Age of Love* show Mark Philippoussis.

Alyssa Milano: Okay, we've been giving her a lot of shit in this chapter, and here's why: She first dated the NHL's Wayne McBean, then moved on to the MLB where she has been linked to pitchers Carl Pavano, Barry Zito, Brad Penny and Tom Glavine! Wowza! Plus, she didn't agree to be interviewed for this book. But truth be told, we still like her. We really do. And here's why:

- She's a child-star-gone-good.

- We like her blogs on baseball and hockey.

- We applaud her for starting a clothing line for women who are tired of horrible fan fashions and the color pink.

- She seems pretty down-to-earth, accessible (to her fans, not us, obviously) and knowledgeable about sports—but still not afraid to admit she still has stuff to learn.

- She's a GameFace girl at heart. We know it.

Tyra Banks: We really didn't want to include Tyra in this section because we love her. (At least Erica does.) Honestly. She's smart, sassy, savvy and using her talents for the common good. That being said, she's been romantically linked to a ton of athletes, so we had to acknowledge her. Only God—and Perez Hilton—knows if these rumors are true, but Tyra has been connected to the NBA's Michael Jordan, Rick Fox and Kobe Bryant, and had a three-year relationship with Chris Webber. She was also linked to golf's Tiger Woods, sprinter Michael Johnson and the NHL's Mark Messier. These days, it seems she has the athletes out of her system and has turned to another interest of hers—business. She's now rumored to be dating the head of an NYC-based investment bank, John Utendahl.

Paris Hilton: The girl we love to hate—and hate to admit that we sort of love. (Full disclosure: Erica loves her song *Stars are Blind* and Chris kind of thinks she's hot.) Sure, she seemingly has no talent at anything, but she does have a talent for being romantically linked with random men, from all walks of life and all corners of the globe. Even athletes. Again, who knows how much of this is truth or tabloid, but here are the athletes Paris has been linked with: boxer Oscar de la Hoya, linebacker Brian Urlacher, quarterback Matt Leinart, cricket player Kevin Pietersen, hockey player Jose Theodore, and tennis players Mark Philippoussis and Andy Roddick, who, in our opinion, should know better.

Kim Kardashian: She's a Paris-wannabe on paper—famous father, no discernible talent (except her website says she is a closet-organizer to the stars, including the Hiltons, Kathie Lee Gifford, Cindy Crawford, Serena Williams and Kenny G). Whatevs. But this dark diva, with an LA face and an Oaktown booty, is on a mission for fame, fortune and a pro-athlete boyfriend. First she tried to dig her French-manicured claws into QB Ben Roethlisberger. Now Kim, the star of *Keeping up With the Kardashians,* has moved on to Reggie Bush. The two were seen canoodling and collecting a lot of free swag from Sundance in early 2008. "Getting free stuff is the best," Bush said. Oh Reggie—remember what we told you about SWAG of all types! It's never free . . .

PLAYERS WHO ARE . . . PLAYERS

If you are an aspiring SWAG (or an aspiring SHAB: sports husband and/or boyfriend), you might want to avoid these athletes. But remember: Don't hate the player, hate the game, baby!

Maria Sharapova: Practically the only person on this list NOT linked with Paris Hilton, Maria Sharapova is currently the "it" girl of tennis. She has been linked with tennis players Juan Carlos Ferrero and Andy Roddick, as well as Maroon 5's Adam Levine and Portuguese footballer Cristiano Ronaldo.

Andy Roddick: Dated Mandy Moore, linked with Maria Sharapova and, yes, Paris Hilton. He's now engaged to swimsuit model Brooklyn Decker—

who is only 20. We're keeping him on our "player" list because we think they're really young and have a feeling that things might not last.

Matt Leinart: Linked with Kristin Cavallari (KC from *Laguna Beach*), Brynn Cameron, a USC basketball player with whom he had a baby, and yes, Paris Hilton.

Tom Brady: We think he and Gisele will last, and we've already covered his baby-mama, but Brady's worth mentioning again, since he's been linked to Tara Reid, actress Jeri Ryan, entertainment correspondent Maria Menounos and porn star Jenna Jameson.

Tony Romo: We think he's kind of a doofus—especially after seeing him sing *Sweet Child of Mine* on stage on YouTube—but we must be wrong, since he's been linked to beauties Jessica Simpson, Britney Spears, Carrie Underwood and Sophia Bush.

Reggie Bush: Before he started keeping up with Kim, he was linked to pop singer Ciara.

Serena Williams: She's been linked with a diverse selection of men, including film director Brett Ratner, actor Jackie Long and rapper Common.

Rick Fox: Okay, we already know about Vanessa Williams and Tyra, but Fox was also linked to Alicia Keys, Sharon Stone and Mariah Carey—and most recently, *Sex in the City* star Kristin Davis. Oh, Charlotte!

Brady Anderson: This retired outfielder used to date Ashley Judd and Ingrid Vandebosch before they turned to racecar drivers—but most recently, he admitted that he has turned to online dating. He also recently sent a cell phone picture of his six-pack abs, along with some racy text messages, to a girl he met online. The girl happened to be friends with a TMZ-staffer—and the photo was soon all over the Internet.

Derek Jeter: It's hard to keep up with Jeter, as he's been rumored to be dating several members of *Maxim*'s 2008 "Hot 100" list, including Vanessa Minnillo, Jessica Alba, Scarlett Johansson, Jessica Biel and Gabrielle Union. Impressive. But our favorite was his short-lived romance with another "Hot 100" honoree, a one Ms. Mariah Carey. It all began with a hot-and-heavy courtship during Spring Training in 1998. And ended at a P. Diddy party later that year, when Jeter turned his back while Carey was speaking and blurted out, "You're crazy." Which, as we all know, turned out to be true. At least for a while.

But when it comes to love, which of us hasn't been a little crazy? (Erica to Chris: Before you even say anything—just shut it!)

9 GAMEFACE GRUB: *The Fusion of Food & Sports*

THERE IS SOMETHING ABOUT SPORTING EVENTS THAT MAKES a woman who only buys organic milk and hormone-free chicken toss all of her beliefs out the window and shove a hotdog made of unidentified meat into her mouth and down a cheap, light beer in a plastic bottle as a chaser. Yes, our love of sports makes us eat the nearly inedible. But luckily, there is much more to choose from these days than hotdogs, peanuts, pretzels and Cracker Jack.

Truth be told, much of our love of sports does revolve around food. Aside from the joys of eating at the ballpark, we love tailgates that last for days, and nothing's better than having people over for the big game, while a big pot of chili is simmering on the stove.

While the Web is crawling with lists of America's best ballpark food and the most popular tailgate cuisine, compiled by ESPN, FOX and even *Maxim* (who wants to take advice from these guys on food?!)—we are uniquely qualified as experts in this field:

▸ Chris comes from a huge Italian family that lives on a vineyard. He knows how to mangia!

▸ Erica spent four years working in marketing at *Gourmet* magazine, eating her face off.

In fact, Erica spent five Super Bowls wearing a headset and overseeing *Gourmet's* "Big Game Bash" party at Blue Smoke in New York City. (The first year, the party was called the *Gourmet* "Super Sunday Bash" and the NFL sent the magazine a cease and desist letter, stating that the magazine could not use the word "Super" in the title of our little event for a couple hundred people. Oh, NFL, pick on someone your own size!) While the Super Bowl party was a blast, and featured some of NYC's top chefs preparing their favorite tailgating fare, and Wine & Spirits Consultant Michael Green mixing up some incredible football-inspired cocktails—Erica really would have preferred to host her friends and family in her very own living room, with that simmering chili and the semi-creepy referee piñata that she bought at Target as a table centerpiece.

All that said, we know good GameFace grub when we taste it. Here, we share our thoughts on food inside the stadium, in the parking lot and in the comfort of your very own abode.

BALLPARK EATS

It's mostly baseball stadiums that are getting fancy with ballpark food. Football stadiums know that people are going to tailgate and go nuts with their own concoctions, so they don't bother too much with specialty cuisine. And with NFL stadiums only playing host to eight regular season games a year—why would they? Most football stadiums offer your standard dogs, pretzels and nachos with that horrible cheese that gets cold by the time you get to your seat. There are a few exceptions, like the University of Phoenix Stadium, where they served controversial glasses of red wine to Gisele Bündchen during Super Bowl XLII, and Lambeau Field in Green Bay, home to Curly's, where they serve planked walleye and the traditional Belgian soup/stew known as "booyah" . . . we just like to say it. Booyah!

But it's baseball games these days that offer an appetizing array of choices. With all the new ballparks built in the late-'80s and -'90s, the trend of serving local "street food" began, in an effort to create unique experiences at each ballpark. At first, Camden Yards began offering crab cake sandwiches and mid-Atlantic specialties. Pretty soon, other ballparks, even the older ones, started following suit.

Here, we list some regional specialties and signature "dishes" (if you can call them that) you'll find at your favorite MLB ballpark.

Angel Stadium of Anaheim: We're sorry that we have to start off with Angel Stadium, because the only thing to like about this ballpark is the big A outside the stadium. Other than that, the food is quite standard and they were given 118 vermin violations in 2006/2007—that's compared to two violations at San Diego's Petco Park and seven at Dodger Stadium in the same period. We suppose if you're into fast-food chains, this could be your Valhalla. You'll find Wienerschnitzel, Domino's, Panda Express and Carl's, Jr. We are not glass-half-empty kinds of people, though, so we will point out that they do serve Sapporo, and beer prices are cheap—under $7!

AT&T Park in San Francisco: Gorge yourself on Gilroy Garlic fries, Gordon Biersch brews, chowder in a bread bowl, Niman all-beef hot-dogs, crab-meat sandwich, splits of sparkling white wine, made-to-order caramel corn, Ghirardelli hot fudge sundaes—and the best San Francisco treat? Hot chocolate on a cold summer day. AT&T was nominated by the Food Network for the first-ever Best Ballpark Eats award in 2007. Plus, we like them because they had a food-related mascot named Crazy Crab in 1984.

Chase Field in Phoenix: Nothing too crazy here at the home of the Diamondbacks—but we do like their "Visiting Team Special," in which they include a specialty menu item and specialty beer from the home-town of their visiting guests.

Citizens Bank Park in Philadelphia: You'd best fast for days before a visit to see the Phillies. Be sure to try a Philly cheesesteak from Rick's Steaks, a pulled-pork sandwich from Tony Luke's, or a hoagie from Planet Hoagie (don't be scared—a hoagie is just another name for a sub sandwich). And if you have absolutely no regard for your health whatsoever, why not head over to Harry the K's Bar and Grille, named after Phillies broadcaster Harry Kalas, and attempt to eat "The Schmitter," a cheesesteak with three types of cheese, fried salami, special sauce, lettuce, cheese and tomatoes, all on a special bun. No wonder Citizens Bank Park won the 2007 Best Ballpark Eats award from Food Network.

Comerica Park in Detroit: Although many are still lamenting the demise of Tiger Stadium, Comerica has a lot to offer, including the Coney Dog—a hotdog smothered in beanless chili with onions, cheese and mustard. You can also snag some Little Caesars pizza (or rather Pizza! Pizza!), which was founded in Michigan.

Coors Field in Denver: Known for its onsite brew pub, where you can find Fat Tire and Sandlot beer, alongside your typical Coors selections. You can also choose from a plethora of beer-battered cuisine—including Rocky Mountain Oysters. Don't ask, just eat.

Dodger Stadium in LA: Dodger Dogs are as polarizing as Ann Coulter—you either love 'em or hate 'em. But there are legions of rabid fans who crave these LA legends, whether they're boiled (yuck) or grilled (better). But even though the dog is rather skinny, it's longer than the bun, which you won't find at all parks. If you're not in the mood for dogs, try the new Dodger Stadium outposts of SoCal classics Ruby's Diner or Canter's Delicatessen. And look throughout the park for some great Japanese fast food—grab some sushi, eat it in the stands with chopsticks, wear over-sized, Nicole Richie sunglasses, and you'll be *so* LA

Dolphin Stadium in Miami Gardens: Joe Robbie, Pro Player Park, whatever the hell you want to call this thing, you probably are not going to have a very memorable eating experience. You'll find standard ballpark fare here at the home of the Marlins, the Miami Dolphins and now the University of Miami Hurricanes, except for a Cuban sandwich and conch fritters, which give you a bit of local flavor.

Fenway Park in Boston: They do serve classic Clam Chowder from Legal Seafood, but it's the Fenway Frank that gets rave reviews. Sure, it's a boiled dog, but it's served on a split-top New England-style bun. The Italian sausage with peppers, washed down with a bottle of Sam Adams, is also a favorite.

Great American Ball Park in Cincinnati: This stadium might have a strange Riverboat theme, but when you're there, don't miss out on their signature hotdog called the Big Red Smokey, or some delicious Montgomery Inn barbecue. And if you stop by Foul Pole Desserts, you can have deep-fried Twinkies or deep-fried cookie dough. "Foul" is right. Maybe you should stop by the United Dairy Farmers stand for a malt, where at least the ingredients seem a bit more natural.

Progressive Field in Cleveland: Definitely try a dog topped with Bertman's Ballpark Mustard, but you can broaden your horizons with *paninis,* Reuben sandwiches, and sushi . . . in Cleveland? We'd stay away from the sushi. And we'd also stay away from their *pierogies* because we all know that REAL *pierogies* are from Pittsburgh.

Kauffman Stadium in Kansas City: Grab a beer from Boulevard Brewing Co. and save room for plenty of Gates BBQ, a genuine institution in KC.

McAfee Coliseum in Oakland: The A's might be moving closer to San Jose in a few years. Until then, this old ballpark serves delicious Miller's Coliseum Dogs and Saag's Sausages. The park also features a pretty extensive beer selection, including Widmer, Red Hook, Sierra Nevada, Pyramid, Stella Artois and Tecate.

The Metrodome in Minnesota: You're in a ballpark that many claim is the worst in the majors. What can you do but embrace the dome, grab a beer from Wally the Beerman (who even has his own baseball trading cards) and sink your teeth into a pulled-pork sandwich and corn on the cob from Famous Dave's, a local favorite.

Miller Park in Milwaukee: There are a few specialties at Miller Park: Klement brats with "Secret Stadium Sauce," butter burgers (a hamburger served on a buttered, grilled bun), classic cheese curds, and, of course, Wisconsin fish fry. Many beers are available from the Miller family, of course, but there are a few great microbrews from Wisconsin's own local breweries, including Capitol, New Grist and New Glarus Brewing Co.

Minute Maid Park in Houston: You'll find as much Minute Maid as you'd like, natch, along with brisket, Texas dogs (with chili, cheese and jalapenos), and the ultra-popular BBQ stuffed baked potato, filled with cheese, pulled pork and barbecue sauce.

Nationals Park in Washington, D.C.: Although the food at RFK Stadium was notoriously horrible, they seem to have turned things around at the new Washington Nationals Park, where they devote a whopping 64,200 square feet of space to restaurants. But our favorite feature is the fact that they include a food selection for each National League team: Mets fans can find knishes, Padres fans can sink their teeth into fish tacos and Dodgers fans will, of course, find sushi.

New York City Stadiums: In 2009, both the New York Mets and the Yankees will have new stadiums to call home. And because New York is never to be outdone, instead of taking casual hometown eateries and bringing them to the ballpark like they do in other cities, some of Gotham's finest chefs will be stepping up to the plate (sorry) at the new Citi Field, home of the Mets, and the new Yankee Stadium. At Citi Field, restaurateur Danny Meyer of Gramercy Tavern, Tabla and The Modern fame will bring his renowned Shake Shack cuisine to fans. And Dave Pasternack, chef at the swanky seafood eatery Esca, co-owned by Mario Batali, will lend his expertise in opening an upscale fish shack at the park. No chefs have been announced yet for the new Yankee Stadium, but we're sure Steinbrenner & Co. will try to steal the Mets' thunder. It's what they do. In the meantime, see below for a recipe for a gourmet take on the classic Arnold Palmer from Shake Shack, in case you can't make it out to NYC anytime soon.

The Shake Shack's Arnold Palmer

SERVES 8 (MAKES ABOUT 3 QUARTS)

You can create a spiked Arnold Palmer by adding a jigger of vodka per serving.

> *6 regular or decaffeinated tea bags*
> *11¼ cups water, divided*
> *1¼ cups sugar*
> *Zest of three lemons (using a vegetable peeler makes it easy)*
> *1 cup freshly squeezed lemon juice, strained of pulp*
> *Lemon verbena or mint sprigs for garnish*

In a small sauce pan, combine 1¼ cups water, sugar and lemon zest and bring to a boil, stirring occasionally until sugar is dissolved. Remove from heat and strain, discarding zest. Refrigerate lemon syrup until ready to use.

Bring 6 cups water to a boil and add tea bags. Steep tea, letting water come to room temperature. Remove tea bags. Add cooled sugar syrup, remaining 4 cups of water and lemon juice and stir to combine. Chill until ready to use.

Serve over ice, garnished with lemon verbena or mint.

Oriole Park at Camden Yards: Get your fill of lump crab cake sandwiches, but save room for brisket, pulled pork, ribs and turkey at Boog's Barbecue, owned by former Oriole John "Boog" Powell, who still hangs around and gives autographs. Camden Yards—the birthplace of this fancy ballpark food trend—was also nominated by the Food Network for Best Ballpark Eats in 2007.

Petco Park in San Diego: Don't miss Rubio's fish tacos or shrimp avocado salad from Anthony's Fish Grotto for a true taste of SoCal. Wash it all down with a yard-long margarita.

PNC Park in Pittsburgh: Yinz goin' dahn de the Bucco's game, an' at? (Translation: Are you going down to the Pirates game, and that?) Since they'll probably lose, drown your sorrows with I.C. Light, pig-out on a famous Primanti's Brothers sandwich (which includes an egg, fries, coleslaw—all on the sandwich), and don't forget a side of deep-fried *pierogies*. And save room (somehow) for some Manny's BBQ, which is owned by former Pirate Manny Sanguillen, who attends every home game. Wait. You're not done yet. Be sure to make a pit stop at the ever-popular and delicious Quaker Steak & Lube for some famous wings. Those yinzers like to eat.

Rangers Ballpark in Arlington: Barbecue is king here and you'll find BBQ turkey legs, beef sandwiches and lots more. You'll also find a nice selection of Tex-Mex food, as well as fried catfish. Be sure to try a Shiner Bock, from the Spoetzl Brewery in Austin.

Rogers Centre in Toronto: Grab a Labatt Blue and sink your teeth into a grilled Blue Jay dog. This all-beef frank is slit several times during the grilling process and is served on a poppy seed roll. Word on the street is that it's one of MLB's best. Another specialty is the Back Bacon Sandwich (which is pretty much slabs of Canadian bacon on a bun), and be sure to try a potato latke on the side.

Safeco Field in Seattle: Aside from baseball, this park doubles as a giant food court. You'll find Ichi rolls (spicy tuna sushi), cedar-planked salmon and Sea Dogs (a "hotdog" made out of cod meat, which is then battered, fried and served in a hotdog bun). Or pick up noodles from our favorite Safeco concession stand: Intentional Wok (not kidding). They also have a slew of West Coast microbrews for your sipping pleasure. Safeco was also nominated by the Food Network for Best Ballpark Eats in 2007.

Tropicana Field in Tampa Bay: Sorry, not much to love here at the Tropicana Dome. The only standouts are the Ybor City Cuban Sandwiches (made with ham, roasted pork, salami, Swiss cheese, mustard and pickles on Cuban bread, then grilled), followed by a microbrew from the Budweiser Brew House, and maybe some boiled peanuts, another Tropicana Field specialty.

Turner Field in Atlanta: In The House that Ted built, some complain that there is not enough Southern cuisine. You can find baby-back ribs and boiled peanuts, along with standard ballpark fare, but the truly memorable thing about "The Ted" is that they offer more than 20 different dogs—including the Bison Dog.

US Cellular Field in Chicago: Our sources tell us that new Comiskey Park (our sources refuse to call it US Cellular) has much better food than Wrigley. Here, you'll find the best kosher hotdogs, polish sausage and bratwurst, served with sauerkraut and grilled onions. They also have specialty carts that Mexican food and Greek pita sandwiches. And to wash everything down, try to catch the attention of the roving margarita guys, who walk around with a huge container of margaritas on their backs, and use a hose and nozzle to shoot your purchase into a plastic cup!

Wrigley Field in Chicago: The city that claims to have the best hotdogs in the world had better serve good hotdogs at Wrigley, right? Some say no. Instead, pre-load on hotdogs at the Wiener's Circle, in nearby Lincoln Park, where you receive complimentary insults with your dogs. Or head up to Wrigleyville hours before game time, you'll have your choice of decent bar food and drunk fans at packed joints like the Cubby Bear or Murphy's Bleachers. But once you've made your way into Wrigley, grab an Old Style beer and just soak in one of the best, old stadiums around—and enjoy it while it's still called Wrigley. (The Cubs owners have announced that they're willing to sell the naming rights to one of the most beloved ballparks. Don't even get Chris started on this . . .)

Some ballparks have started a one-price, all-you-can-eat ticket, which is pretty scary and reminds us of when Red Lobster started their all-you-can-eat crab promotion. The executive who came up with the brilliant idea was fired because they could never have predicted how much Americans could eat when presented with an "all-you-can-eat" challenge. Be on the lookout for this special eat-till-you-vomit ticket at Dodger Stadium, Turner Field in Atlanta, Kauffman Stadium in Kansas City, Orioles Park at Camden Yards, the Metrodome, the McAfee Coliseum in Oakland, Rangers Ballpark in Arlington, even at some basketball, hockey and football venues, not to mention lots of Minor League parks. You can gorge on as many hotdogs, popcorn, nachos and sodas you can shove in your GameFace—and in some cases, ribs, burgers, sausages and baked beans.

So far no one has been dumb enough to do an all-you-can-drink night—especially after the disastrous 10-cent beer night in Cleveland in 1974, which resulted in crazed fans, a riot and a forfeit for the Indians. However, there are still $1 beers at some Minor League games. And speaking of dumb: the Gateway Grizzlies, a Minor League team in the middle of Illinois, offers a 1,000-calorie Krispy Kreme bacon cheeseburger. It consists of cheddar, two slices of bacon and a burger in a bun made out of a Krispy Kreme cut in half. Sounds disgusting, but part of us wants to try it (and the part of us that wants to try it is Chris).

A Tribute to The Famous Sausage Race

We must give a food-lover's shout-out to Milwaukee's Miller Field and their Famous Sausage Race. In the middle of the sixth inning, you'll witness a thrilling race run by five 7-foot-tall sausages: Brett Wurst, a bratwurst wearing lederhosen; Stosh, a Polish sausage wearing an odd choice of dark sunglasses and a polo shirt; Guido, an Italian sausage wearing a chef's outfit; Frankie Furter, a hotdog wearing a baseball uniform; and Cinco, the newest sausage, who is a giant chorizo wearing a sombrero. Nothing like reinforcing ethnic stereotypes in the name of diversity! Just kidding. We like this promotion. We also like it because various employees of the Brewers dress up as sausages and actually run the race. There have also been some famous runners, including ballplayers Mark Grace and Hideo Nomo, as well as a few sports journalists and former Green Bay Packers wide receiver Javon Walker.

You also might remember the Famous Sausage Incident back in 2003, when Randall Simon of the Pittsburgh Pirates thought he was being funny and hit one Ms. Mandy Block, dressed as Guido, on the head (not her head, but on the top of Guido's chef's hat) with a bat. Guido fell down onto Frankie Furter, but Stosh the Polish Sausage helped them both back up and they all finished the race. End of story? No.

Brewers fans and executives were outraged and wondered what kind of human being could do something like swing a bat at an innocent sausage! Randall Simon was arrested, suspended for four games and fined $432. He profusely apologized, and a down-to-earth Mandy Block (a.k.a. Guido) didn't press charges or go sue-happy. She simply asked Simon for the signed baseball bat he used in the incident and said, "I'm just a sausage, guys. It's not a big deal. I'm fine." A whole line of T-shirts, hats and pins came out with a new slogan: "Don't Whack our Weiner!" Simon was later traded to the Cubs and when he returned to Miller Park, fellow players pretended to hold him back during the Sausage Race as a joke. Simon even bought a bunch of Italian sausages for random fans at the game.

And in an attempt to make nice with the Brewers fans, the Pittsburgh Pirates, who host their very own "Mrs. T's Great Pierogi Race," fly Jalapeño Hannah (who sports a green hat), Cheese Chester (yellow hat), Sauerkraut Saul (red hat) and Oliver Onion (purple hat) to Milwaukee once a year for the great Pierogi and Sausage Race.

TAILGATING

Sometimes the food inside the park is so overpriced and lousy that you're inspired to do a little tailgating. For some reason, it seems to us that most people tailgate for football games, some never even entering the stadium. And some tailgates—primarily college—have been known to go on for days. And of course we know that NASCAR tailgates have been known to go on for a full week!

All that said, tailgating goes way beyond burgers, brats and beers—and is now an art form of sorts. Did you know there is an American Tailgaters Association and a United States Tailgating Association? Did you know that there's an annual tailgating trade show, where they showcase different tailgating products? Did you know that there is something called "The Ultimate Tailgating Vehicle" (UTV for short), which is 43-feet long, has four flat-screen TVs, two bathrooms and features a commercial kitchen? But tailgating doesn't have to be fancy to be fantastic: some have taken old school buses, '70s vans, nondescript RVs and even old ambulances, and turned them into over-the-top, tricked out tailgating vehicles. It's not about how elaborate you get, but the spirit of your tailgate that counts.

Some say that the Ole Miss tailgate at the Grove and the LSU tailgate at Tiger Stadium are the best in college football. They both start on the Thursday before a Saturday game, and feature incredible Southern cuisine—not to mention crazed fans drinking all sorts of crazy concoctions. (Don't tell that to the Penn State faithful, who tend to love their crock-pot dishes as much as they love Joe Paterno. Or the UCLA and Michigan tailgaters, who fancy the fact that they can tailgate on a golf course. And please, for the love of God, do not tell that to the Army/Navy/Air Force tailgaters, who would likely start World War III if they knew we didn't pick them as college football's top tailgaters.)

In the NFL, there is something about teams in notoriously bad weather regions that causes them to be diehard tailgaters. Maybe there's nothing to do during the winter but to plan an elaborate tailgate? Many rank the Buffalo Bills the top tailgaters in the league (possibly because you can come as early and stay as late as you want), followed by the Kansas City Chiefs (with their incredible selection of grilled meat), the Green Bay Packers (cheese, glorious cheese), and the New England Patriots (with their lobstah and chowdah). But the warm weather folks have a better selection of ingredients to choose from year round, allowing them to earn their place as top tailgaters: The Niners are known for featuring incredible wine and cuisine at their tailgates (so they can feign having an upscale experience at notoriously downscale Candlestick Park). Chargers fans at Qualcomm Stadium are known for their incredibly fresh ingredients—especially seafood—as well as authentic Mexican fare. And in Houston, where their cuisine is influenced by the South and the West, tailgaters go over-the-top with barbecue and Tex-Mex cuisine.

But in New York, you can find many of the best chefs in the world, some of whom are avid football fans. In fact, in the parking lot of the Meadowlands, you just might find the dynamic duo of Brad Thompson and Brett Traussi. According to a piece in *The New York Times,* the two met at Restaurant Boulud, one of Daniel Boulud's signature restaurants in NYC, where Brad was a sous chef and Brett is still Director of Operations. Even when Brad moved to Phoenix for a few years to become head chef of the renowned restaurant Mary Elaine's, he would still fly back for every New York Giants home game so they could prepare their gameday feast—a tradition that began back in 1998. As described in *The Times,* their gourmet spreads are inspired by the team the Giants are facing, which does keep things exciting week in and week out. And of course, since most tailgaters spend a good 12-plus hours in the parking lot, there is more than one meal to consider. For instance, when the Giants played the Arizona Cardinals, Brad, Brett and friends started the day with breakfast burritos, complete with scrambled eggs, green chili, hash browns and chorizo. And in keeping with the Southwest flavors, the next course included duck confit and *huitlacoche* quesadillas, as well as pork shoulder with mole sauce, over moist cornbread. And then, of course, the guys prepared fried red birds—symbolically deep-frying the Cardinals, in hopes that their beloved Big Blue would do the same. And sure, the chef's beverage of choice while cooking is a good old Bud, but when it came time to eat, they busted out an extravagant magnum of Gaja Barolo. The next home game, against the Saints, called for gumbo, crawfish *étouffée* and *beignets.* That's a twist on tailgating that we can appreciate.

Another great NYC chef and buddy of ours is Kenny Callaghan of Blue Smoke, where the Gourmet Super Bowl party was held for five years. It was recently announced that the Mets' new Citi Field will include its very own Blue Smoke restaurant—great news for 'cue-loving New Yorkers. But back to Kenny: This man knows his barbecue and also loves to tailgate. In fact, he grew up in New Jersey and has been a lifelong Yankees, Giants and Rangers fan. He says if he could have any athlete as a special guest at his tailgate, it would be Mark Messier, and if he's busy, Kenny would invite Derek Jeter. Here, he shares with us some of his barbecuing tips, perfect for your next tailgate, as well as his mouthwatering recipe for Herb Marinated Hanger Steak, one of Blue Smoke's specialties.

Kenny's Shopping List of Tailgating Food & Beverages

- Slow-Smoked Baby Back Ribs

- Kansas City Spare Ribs

- Beer

- Dijon & Balsamic Marinated Lamb Chops for the Grill

- Herb Marinated Hanger Steaks for the Grill

- Grilled Lobster Tails with Garlic Butter

- Shrimp Cocktail

- Burgers with raw onion, sliced tomato, dill pickles, ketchup, mayonnaise

- Good quality hotdogs with split-top buns and deli mustard

- Sweet & Spicy Sausage, roasted red & yellow peppers and onions, onion rolls for sandwiches

- Tequila & Lime marinated Chicken breasts

- More Beer

Kenny's Tips on preparing meat ahead of time:

- ▶ Butcher and trim all meats at home, before arrival at the game.

- ▶ Marinate everything that needs to be marinated before arrival.

- ▶ Do as much prep-work ahead of time so that at the game you are only cooking, slicing and assembling.

- ▶ Use cuts of meat that are user-friendly to tailgaters (i.e. precooked ribs, lamb chops, burgers & dogs).

Kenny's BBQ tips:

- ▶ Always have plenty of table space to work on and a designated trash bag.

- ▶ I generally use hardwood charcoal, as it burns quicker and hotter.

- ▶ Make sure you have all your grill tools, knives, plates, napkins, silverware, condiments ready to go before the meat hits the grill.

- ▶ Always begin cooking on a clean grill. Burn off any old stuff and scrape the grill clean before you begin. I usually take it one step further and wipe the grill surface with a wad of paper towels to clean off any residual carbon left behind by the grill brush.

- ▶ Season your meat appropriately before placing on the grill.

- ▶ I grill most of my meat over high heat for a short amount of time. This allows the meat to sear on the outside while sealing in juices on the inside.

- ▶ Let your meat rest for at least 5 minutes before slicing.

Blue Smoke Herb-Marinated Hanger Steaks

SERVES 8

You can easily expand this recipe to fit a larger crowd by adding 1 sprig of each herb, 1 additional clove of garlic and ¼ cup olive oil per additional steak.

> *Eight 6-8 oz. hanger steaks, trimmed of visible fat*
>
> *8 large sprigs fresh rosemary*
>
> *8 sprigs fresh thyme*
>
> *8 sprigs fresh sage*
>
> *8 cloves garlic, lightly crushed*
>
> *2 cups olive oil*
>
> *Kosher salt*
>
> *Fresh ground black pepper to taste*

Place steaks in a large bowl or shallow glass baking dish with the herbs and garlic. Pour olive oil on top and toss all ingredients lightly, using your hands or a set of tongs. Cover with plastic wrap and let steaks marinate a half hour before they go into the fridge. Then, let them marinate in refrigerator for 12 to 36 hours, tossing occasionally. (Olive oil may solidify; don't worry about this.)

Remove dish from refrigerator and let stand at room temperature until olive oil is no longer solid, about 30-45 minutes. Remove steaks from marinade, discard oil-herb mixture, and allow most of the oil to drip away from the steaks. Season steaks liberally with salt and pepper.

Preheat a gas grill or cast-iron grill pan until hot, about 5-6 minutes. Cook steaks until edges are charred and steaks are medium-rare in center, 3-4 minutes per side. Remove from grill and let rest 5-10 minutes. Transfer steaks to a cutting board and slice steaks against the grain into ⅛-inch slices.

Another NYC chef friend of ours is Jody Williams, formerly of Gusto and Morandi, and now chef at Gottino. While she is known for her incredible Italian cuisine, she also shared with us her love of tailgating from back in her college days. Here is her ideal tailgating plan that involves a raw bar, plenty of Anchor Steam and a snowman as a bartender. And who would be her special tailgating guest? As a tribute to her love of horseracing, her guest would be Seabiscuit.

"So what I usually choose to do for a big game, whether it be field side, in a stadium lot or at home, is a huge raw bar. Best-case scenario would be pitch side for any rugby game. It is all about the set-up and shopping. Ice, ice and more ice—or if you are lucky enough, it will snow.

"A typical pre-game raw bar will include: Malpeque oysters, steamed Dungeness crab, lobsters, shrimp cocktail, a dozen thermoses of New England clam chowder, my mother's clam dip, celery sticks, sourdough bread (flown in with the crabs from San Francisco), aioli, cocktail sauce and oyster crackers. To drink: Anchor Steam, sparkling wine and wine.

"Most of the prep, I get out of the way the day before. With a couple of pots, I manage to steam the lobsters and crabs, and boil the shrimp for the next day. The shrimp are peel-and-eat and simply boiled in beer, so that is easy. Lobsters and crabs are boiled with Old Bay seasoning, and left halved in the shell to munch on.

"The most coolers I have ever brought to a tailgate like this was six— and that was just food. It's very easy to pre-pack the coolers, so when they are opened your raw bar looks great and is in operation. A box of kosher salt helps stabilize the ice from melting too fast. And to make things even easier, keep the cocktail sauce and aioli in squeeze bottles.

"You need to make a minor investment in lobster crackers, oyster knives and bar towels so every guest is self-sufficient. Somehow it always turns into an oyster-eating competition and I have seen piles of oyster shells knee high.

"Can you imagine a nice little patch of snow, outlined with lemons and seaweed, to dump your raw bar on? How about a snowman bartender standing guard over the Anchor Steam?"

Yes, Jody. We can imagine. And we want to know when and where we should show up.

By now you know we love lists. We hereby present our list of practical tailgating advice:

Common Sense Tips:

▶ Make a list, check it twice. We will assume you are not an idiot because you bought this book, but we are going to start with the basics. Make a master list for everything you will possibly need. Take a look at Kenny's list above as a guide. We all know that once you are in the parking lot and you're counting down to the game, you can't send someone down to the grocery store to pick up some aluminum foil or the beer you forgot (not that you would ever forget the beer!). But you catch our drift.

▶ Start planning as early as possible and ask for help. You might be a control freak like Erica, but there's nothing fun about taking all of the responsibilities on yourself, slaving away for weeks, and spending the entire tailgate serving everyone. The whole idea of tailgating is about group bonding and bringing fellow fans together. And honestly, nothing brings people together more than making them feel they are a part of the planning and execution.

▶ This may seem like a no-brainer, but check the weather as you get closer to the tailgate. For cold-weather tailgating, bring extra layers, scarves, hats and waterproof gear, because chances are some of your guests, probably the male ones, will forget. For warm-weather tailgating at a NASCAR race or baseball game, try bringing a tent for shade, and maybe even plan a little water-balloon toss or squirt-gun battle, especially if there will be kids. But do not wear a white T-shirt with a sheer bra, and tell everyone that if they get any water on you whatsoever—ESPECIALLY YOUR HAIR—the children will get no food and the adults will get no beer.

▶ Try to streamline and simplify your menu. This goes for all types of entertaining. Instead of coming up with a complicated menu with a dozen side dishes, stick to one or two main courses and just a couple of sides. Don't overdo it. Most tailgaters will eat anything. You'll see. Oh, and try to prepare food that can sit out for a good deal of time without spoiling. Avoid mayo-based dishes and don't leave anything sitting out for more than two hours.

▶ And just as tailgaters will eat anything, they will make a mess out of everything. So bring extra water, baby wipes, paper towels, napkins, re-sealable plastic bags, and a ton of garbage bags. Also, be sure to have the least amount of stuff to clean up and bring home—so use throw-away aluminum pans and aluminum foil for cooking everything, and paper plates and plastic cups/utensils for serving everything. Don't forget to recycle all your aluminum, cans and bottles.

▶ Keep the raw and the cooked separate. Plan on several coolers, like Jody—a couple for all beverages on ice; others for all prepped/cooked food that is ready to eat; and separate ones for all raw meat and food that will be cooked.

▶ The best way to keep food warm is to bring it, piping hot, in aluminum pans (maybe insulated in yet another cooler, layered with some kitchen towels). Don't forget to keep stirring your dish so your food doesn't stick to the bottom of the pan. Also, people have been known to bring their crock-pots to keep food warm. This is fine, as long as you can plug it in to your car lighter, or use another alternate form of power.

▶ Cook for an army. Make sure you have enough food for your group, as well as sharing with others—after all that's the spirit of tailgating. And there is nothing that will kill the spirit of tailgating faster than running out of food—or worse, beer! (Okay, speaking of beer, this might be a good time to bring this up: Have a designated driver. Or if that's no fun, hire someone to drive you and your friends home in a van or bus, or find some other way for everyone to get home safely. We're all adults here.)

▶ Check the rules at the stadium to find out how early you can arrive (you should plan on getting there at the very least 3 or 4 hours prior to game-time) and find out when you have to vacate your spot. If you're in another city, be sure you chat up your tailgating neighbors to find out if you are in someone else's regular spot. Sometimes there are unspoken rules of tailgating.

▶ Make sure your main course is served no later than 1½ to 2 hours prior to the game, giving yourself enough time to eat, clean up and get ready to enter the stadium. Don't forget to package up the leftovers and make sure the food and drink are accessible after the game, in case you want to continue the tailgate and wait for traffic to die down.

▶ Try to leave your area spotless and be sure to dispose of any charcoal properly. (There have been reports of some ~~jackasses~~ people who have put their grills under their cars, so no one will steal them . . . then return to a fire truck putting out flames that have engulfed their car.) First, close the vents of the grill to stop the flow of oxygen—this will start the cooling process. Then, when your charcoal is completely cool, look for specially marked receptacles for used charcoal.

Now that we have all the common sense things taken care of, here comes the fun part.

Tips for Making Your Tailgate a Unisex Success

▶ While some think that beer is the beverage of choice throughout the tailgate, we think it's fun to start with a signature cocktail to set the tone. Start with a Bloody Mary in the morning, to symbolize the blood your team will draw that day, and maybe continue with some pre-mixed themed cocktails like: Seahawks Sangria, Pats Punch or Colts Caipirinha—or for warm weather, perhaps our spiked Arnold Palmer cocktail from Shake Shack.

▶ Do what chef Brad Thompson and Brett Traussi do: have your feast take on the theme of the visiting team. Or special-order beer or other specialties from the opposing team's city—like ordering some Abita Light and pralines for a game against New Orleans, or Old Style beer and deep-dish pizza for a game against Chicago.

▶ If you have some money to burn, there are insane tailgating vehicles that you can rent for the day. Some have full kitchens, others have hot tubs. OR for a low-rent version of this idea, you could rent a U-Haul and put in an old couch and coffee table so you can feel like you're in the comfort of your own home! (Don't forget a flat screen TV and a PlayStation 3 to keep your friends occupied until game-time.)

▶ We are always fans of dressing up in costumes, and luckily, the NFL and college football seasons overlap with Halloween, during which you can dress up as anything. And the season also coincides with Thanksgiving, when you can dress up as pilgrims or turkeys, if you are so inclined. Or, you can tell all of your guests to come dressed as their favorite all-time players. Maybe have everyone dress as gorillas or Elvis. Or perhaps just hire an Elvis impersonator. We're not sure what Elvis has to do with football, baseball or racing, but we feel you can never go wrong with an Elvis impersonator at any event.

▶ If costumes aren't your bag, come up with a name and logo for your tailgating group, download your artwork to CafePress.com, and each member of your gang can order their own custom banners, pins, T-shirts, sweatshirts, trucker hats, aprons and even thong underwear!

▶ We're not into body paint that much, but we are into temporary tattoos. You can design your own—with your favorite team's logo, player's name or team slogan—and print them out on special temporary tattoo paper on your printer. We're also into professional face painters, who can be hired to come paint cool things on your faces. Other ideas? Hire masseuses to give people neck and back massages (the masseuses will bring their own chairs). Or hire a manicure technician to give your female fans the perfect mani, topped off with their team logo or team name on their nails. Goofy, but fun. And people will be waiting in line for it. Guaranteed.

▶ Create a photo-op for your group and other fans nearby. Bring a life-size stand-up of your favorite player, and create instant souvenirs with a Polaroid, or use your digital (be sure to get your fellow fans' e-mail addresses so you can send the pix to them . . . and create your very own tailgating network, while you're at it).

▶ Some people bring ping pong and foosball tables, play horseshoes, create themed mini-golf holes or try their hand at a game of Tailgate Twister—which is weird because 80% of tailgaters are men, according to tailgating.com. We're more apt to host a chili cook-off between several guests, then declare a winner. Or start a little harmless football pool, charging a buck a box, with winners after the first quarter, halftime, the third quarter and final score. What's a little harmless gambling among friends? And back to that 80% men stat: If you are out to meet a man, this is not a bad place to start. It's hard to beat this male-to-female ratio, and chances are, you'll meet someone who's rooting for your favorite team—which is always a plus and sometimes a must.

▶ We've covered pretty much everything: food, drink, temporary tattoos, Elvis impersonators . . . what's left? Ahh, music. If you're in the mood for something a little more exciting than plugging in your iPod and playing your "Totally Over-the-Top Tailgate

Mix," ask a musician friend or favorite local band to play at your tailgate. Make things easier and keep it acoustic, so you're not worrying about woofers and tweeters. Next year, we might just ask our country-music-singing friend Cooper Boone to play an acoustic set at our next sports gathering—especially because he wrote a song called *Love at a Tailgate*! And if he's busy, we'll just plug in the old karaoke machine and let others have at it—if they can wrestle the microphone out of Erica's hands, that is.

HOME FIELD ADVANTAGE

Sometimes the big game is not a home game, and instead, you're hosting a gameday bash in your own home. In one Cleveland neighborhood, according to the Ultimate Tailgater site, an away-game against their rival Bengals doesn't deter these Browns fans from tailgating. Instead, they bring their grills out on their driveways, hang up their flags, bring the wide-screen TVs into the garage, and tailgate throughout the neighborhood—visiting, cheering and offering food, drink and support to their neighbors (the Browns usually lose in this match-up). The best thing about this idea: ice cold beer right out of the fridge, and no drinking and driving!

But for many of us, why stand out in the cold in a parka when a comfy couch is calling? Having the gang over to your house also gives you many more choices for the type of food you are going to prepare, because you have all the amenities of your kitchen and don't have to rely on a barbecue. We like a hearty meal that you can have simmering on the stove, or keep warming in the oven, so that guests can serve themselves . . . because we don't like missing any of the game!

As kids growing up, both Erica and Chris almost always watched games on TV, whether they were home or away. With big families and the cost of going to a pro game a little on the extravagant side, our moms would instead prepare football-inspired feasts, while our families gathered around the tube, fiddling with the bunny ears to ensure a clear picture. Erica, with her Myron Cope (may he rest in peace) Terrible Towel, and Chris, with his child-sized leather Raiders biker jacket, would sit right in front of the TV, risking radiation poisoning, or whatever it was that our mothers told us so that we would not sit so damn close to the TV.

Erica's mom used to cook out of a collection of Steeler cookbooks, a series of little spiral-bound cookbooks containing recipes from the players, coaches, owners and their wives that benefited the Multiple Sclerosis Society. Honestly, it looked like someone created this thing on their Apple IIc and bound them all by hand. But that's why we still love, and use, these cookbooks. The recipes are classic party fare, but the best part of the whole experience is reading the little descriptions above each recipe, like: "John loves this," wrote Flo Stallworth, about her favorite recipe called "Husband's Delight," in honor of her Hall of Famer hubby. Or defensive end Dwight White's description of one of his favorite cocktails: "Dwight's Piña Colada. An excellent drink in the summer, by a fireplace, in the shower, or whatever!"

We love the thought of the players' wives, gathering in bad '70s outfits at one of the player's homes, surrounded by handmade macramé décor, cooking for each other and watching their husbands play in the big game. And when the guys got home from the game, their wives would serve them Piña Coladas in the shower! Times were so much simpler then. Nowadays, these spoiled SWAGs, like our pals Jessica Simpson and Kim Kardashian, aren't doing any home-cooking. Are you kidding? Instead, they're getting blow-outs, buying stupid pink apparel and slipping in last-minute Botox injections before they go sit in a luxury suite, sipping Cristal. Sigh.

Here is a Boeke-family favorite, adapted from the 1982 *Super Steeler Cookbook*. It's a one-dish wonder that you can eat for lunch at the 1pm game and again later for the 4pm and 8pm games. We never seem to get tired of this dish. Serve it up with a big Caesar salad and a great loaf of Italian bread . . . open up a bottle of Chianti or a couple of Peroni beers . . . and your gameday feast is complete. (Just tell people it's a tribute to famed running back Franco Harris, who is half Italian.)

Sharona Boeke's Super Steeler Spaghetti Pie

SERVES 8 HUNGRY PEOPLE

Kosher salt

¾ lb. angel hair or other very thin spaghetti-type pasta

½ cup shredded or grated Parmesan cheese

3 eggs, well beaten

4 tablespoons good-quality olive oil, divided

1 large red onion, chopped (about 2 cups)

¾ lb. sliced mushrooms (about 4 ½ cups)

1 teaspoon salt, divided

½ teaspoon fresh ground black pepper, divided

3 cups sour cream

¾ lb. lean ground beef

¾ lb. mild Italian sausage (turkey, beef or pork), casings removed

one 26 oz. jar marinara sauce, any vegetarian variety,
plus more if desired

24 oz. of shredded mozzarella or provolone cheese

Preheat oven to 350° F. Fill a large pot with salted water and bring
to a boil. Break pasta in half and cook until barely tender, about 5-6
minutes. Drain and transfer to a large bowl. Combine parmesan and
eggs; toss with warm spaghetti.

Grease the bottom of a roasting pan or lasagna pan (minimum 10" x
14" x 2") with 2 tablespoons olive oil. Spread spaghetti mixture over
bottom of pan and set aside.

Heat 1 tablespoon olive oil in a large sauté pan over medium-high
heat. Add onions and sauté, stirring often, until soft and translucent,
about 6 minutes. Add mushrooms and sauté until mushrooms
reduce in size and release most of their liquid, 5 to 6 minutes. Season
with ½ teaspoon salt and ¼ teaspoon pepper and transfer to a bowl.

Add the sour cream to vegetables and stir to combine; spread evenly over spaghetti mixture.

Heat remaining 1 tablespoon olive oil in a large sauté pan over medium-high heat. Add ground beef and sausage and cook, stirring to break up lumps, until nicely browned, about 7-8 minutes. Season with remaining ½ teaspoon salt and ¼ teaspoon pepper. Add marinara sauce and simmer for 5 minutes. Remove from heat and pour evenly over sour cream layer.

Bake uncovered for 25 minutes. Remove pan from oven and raise temperature to 400°F. Spread shredded cheese evenly over the top and return to oven until cheese is melted and golden brown around the edges, 20-25 minutes. Remove from oven and let rest for 5 minutes before serving. Serve with additional spaghetti sauce on the side, if desired.

Chris' mom had to cook for an army, since she had six kids to feed. It didn't help that Chris used to eat so much of this dish that he vomited, on two occasions. But please, don't let that gross you out. It's really, really good!

Mama De Benedetti's Outrageous Oakland Raider Macaroni Salad

SERVES 8

One 1-lb. box macaroni pasta (any shape)

1 cup chopped celery (2 large stalks, trimmed)

1 bunch scallions, greens and whites included, chopped (about 1 cup)

1 cup sliced canned black olives (about 6 oz.)

2 cups mayonnaise

1½ teaspoons chili powder, plus more to taste

1 ½ teaspoons garlic salt, plus more to taste

½ teaspoon black pepper, plus more to taste

Cook macaroni according to package directions, drain and rinse with cold water. Transfer macaroni to large bowl and add the celery, scallions and olives. In a medium-sized bowl combine mayonnaise, chili powder, garlic salt and pepper, and stir with a fork until smooth; add to macaroni and toss well to combine. Refrigerate for at least 2 hours and up to 8 hours. Season with additional chili powder, garlic salt and black pepper to taste.

But before we go, Kenny Callaghan and Jody Williams gave us two other fan favorites for your next at-home tailgate.

Jody Williams' Mom's Clam Dip

SERVES 8 (ABOUT 2½ CUPS DIP)

This recipe can be made using either fresh or canned clams.

IF USING FRESH CLAMS:

    3 lbs. Manila clams or cockles, rinsed well in cold water to remove sand

    2 garlic cloves, crushed

    ¼ cup olive oil

    1 ¼ cups dry white wine

    ½ cup water

IF USING CANNED CLAMS:

    two 6 ½-oz. cans minced clams

FOR BOTH RECIPES:

    1 clove garlic, cut in half

    12 ounces (1 ½ packages) cream cheese, at room temperature

    4 teaspoons fresh lemon juice

    2 teaspoons Worcestershire sauce

    ¼ teaspoon Tabasco, or more to taste

    ¾ teaspoon salt

    ¼ teaspoon pepper

IF USING FRESH CLAMS:

Heat olive oil in a large, high-sided sauté pan over medium heat. Add garlic and cook until fragrant and softened but not browned, about 3-4 minutes. Add wine, water and clams and bring to a simmer. Cover and cook until all clams are opened, about 6-7 minutes. Remove from heat and drain, reserving ¼ cup of the cooking liquid. Mince clams and reserve.

IF USING CANNED CLAMS:

Drain clams, reserving ¼ cup of liquid.

FOR BOTH RECIPES:

Rub a medium serving bowl with the garlic halves and discard garlic. Add cream cheese and beat with a fork until smooth. Add remaining ingredients and the reserved ¼ cup of clam broth or canned clam juice and blend well. Cover and refrigerate for at least 1 hour. Serve with crackers, chips or celery.

Blue Smoke Deviled Eggs

SERVES 6-8

10 large eggs

7 tablespoons mayonnaise

2 teaspoons Dijon mustard

1 teaspoon Champagne vinegar or white wine vinegar

½ teaspoon mustard powder

¼ teaspoon cayenne pepper

1/8 teaspoon each salt and fresh ground pepper

¼ teaspoon curry powder (optional)

Place eggs in 4-quart saucepan and cover with 1 inch of cold water. Bring eggs to a boil over high heat, then lower heat and simmer eggs for exactly 9 minutes. Drain eggs and run under cold water to cool, about 20-30 seconds. Gently crack shells and peel eggs under cool running water. Cut a very small sliver off each end of each egg, so they lie flat on a plate.

Slice the eggs in half width-wise, being careful to make halves as equal in size as possible. Gently remove the yolks directly into the bowl of a food processor and arrange whites on a platter, like small upright cups.

To the food processor add mayonnaise, Dijon mustard, vinegar, dry mustard, cayenne, salt and pepper, and curry powder, if using. Process until smooth, scraping down sides and bottom of bowl if necessary.

Using a spatula, transfer egg yolk mixture into a pastry bag with a star tip, or into a 1-quart Ziploc bag with ¼ inch snipped off of one corner. Pipe 1½ teaspoons mixture into each egg half. Refrigerate until ready to serve.

   Mmmm, deviled eggs. We could go on about food and sports forever. We haven't even touched upon athlete-owned restaurants and bars . . . or great sports bars across the country, especially those that are particularly female-friendly. No worries. We have all this and more on GoGameFace.com. And we can't wait to hear your feedback (and get recipes from some of your favorite gameday dishes). Because the only thing we like more than eating and sports, is talking to other people about eating and sports.

10 THE BATTLE OF THE BOBBLEHEADS: *How Marketing Is Ruining (& Saving!) Sports*

- -

YES, WE SPLIT UP ONCE BEFORE FOR THE NASCAR RACE. BUT for the first time in *GameFace* history, the collective "we" is going to split up for an entire chapter, as we tackle something that we vehemently disagree on: Marketing and Promotions in sports. Chris is a purist. Period. End of story. Erica certainly respects tradition, but doesn't mind some innovations and funding from sponsors, if it helps make the fan experience better. Who's right? You make the call.

CHRIS' ANTI-MARKETING RANT

- -

"You can hold onto something so tight, you've already lost it."
—U2, *Dirty Day*

It was a night where anything seemed possible. What else is there to think when Larry Hughes is out-dueling the all-world Kobe Bryant. Yes, that Kobe Bryant. Even more amazing, the then-god-awful Golden State Warriors were holding their own against the World Champion Los Angeles Lakers. It was 2000 and the 21-year-old Hughes was the only bright spot on yet another unwatchable Warriors team.

When Hughes had 30 points at the end of just three quarters, long-suffering hoops fans in Oakland finally had a moment they could get excited about. The Warriors were on the verge of upsetting the hated Lakers and the fans were gearing up for a wild 4th quarter.

"Lar-ry! Lar-ry! Lar-ry!" they chanted.

After years and years of embarrassing losses, nearly 20,000 fans were rising up in unison in the kind of organic, impromptu explosion of noise found only in great sports moments. Was it a one-time highlight? Or maybe something more significant—perhaps a dramatic sign that the long-moribund franchise was finally turning the corner and headed for respectability? No one could say for sure. All they knew was that it felt good again—finally!—to watch Warriors basketball, if only for this fleeting moment.

"Lar-ry! Lar-ry!" the fans continued. And they would have kept going deep into the Oakland night, if allowed.

But they weren't allowed to. They were sabotaged by the Warriors front office. Inexplicably. Sadly. Frustratingly. Oh, they weren't "sabotaged" intentionally, of course. But the fans indeed were drowned out by some soulless music turned way up in the P.A system, which was the intro music for the team mascot's trampoline dunking performance. And no, we're not making up that last part.

Here's what happened:

Somewhere in the Arena in Oakland (as it was cumbersomely titled back then), someone on the promotions staff had a tight, pre-planned schedule to keep. He or she turned up the music real loud while Thunder, the Warriors team mascot dragged out a trampoline so he could do some acrobatic fake dunks between quarters three and four.

That's right, Erica. In lieu of the *real* energy and passion the fans were showing while creating one of those electric memories for which sports exists, the team instead piped in canned fun, MTV-style, replete with sound effects and a mini-light show. Meanwhile, some underpaid stranger in a blue muscle suit playing the role of "Thunder" waved his arms and exhorted the crowd to make some noise(!) like, ya' know, they already were doing before he crashed the party.

The crowd responded with a collective yawn. Sure, no one sat there with their arms folded, giving the "thumbs down" sign like the guy at the puppet show in *Spinal Tap*. But still, it was depressing.

Even worse, when the quarter started, the miffed crowd sat on its hands. Incredibly, the fans had been taken out of the game by their own organization. All the momentum with which the third quarter ended had been squandered. The Warriors lost the game. Moment ruined. Game over.

"So, it's come to this, has it?" That's what any longtime diehard fan must have been thinking that night. The larger problem is that just about every NBA team has this stuff. And it's running rampant in other sports, too. How the hell did we get here?

ERICA'S PRO-MARKETING RANT

> "The world don't move, to the beat of just one drum.
> What might be right for you, might not be right for some."
> — Theme from *Different Strokes*

Take it from me and Abe Lincoln—you can't please all of the people all of the time. And that's exactly what we're experiencing here. I guarantee you, Chris, that for every fan who was annoyed at the mascot and his jumping antics, there was another fan who enjoyed it. Sure, that person wasn't a diehard fan like you. Or maybe he or she had kids. Or maybe he or she is a dummy. But in this day and age, great action on the court—or the field or the baseball diamond—isn't enough. Americans have severe ADD. It's not enough to see their sports heroes appearing before their very eyes, playing their best, setting records. In the old days, watching sports was so exciting because there was nothing else to do! There were no televisions, let alone iPhones, Wii's or YouTube. Nowadays, you had better jump through hoops to attract fans' attention. Actually, you'd better jump through flaming hoops.

Oh, and you need at least a D-List star to sing the national anthem or maybe a couple famous fans in the stands. Next, you need fancy food in luxury suites, with bottle service, or the ability for fans in box seats to electronically order so they never have to move their spoiled asses out of their seats. Then, you need WiFi service so fans can follow along with their computers. And of course, you need cheerleaders and/or mascots for those with little to no interest in the game, and you also need T-shirts shot out of an airgun to keep people amused. Blame it on the dumbing down and sheer laziness of Americans—don't blame it on sports. These promotions are simply a reaction to this trend of complete stimulation overload and utter excess. I'm not saying it's right, I'm saying it's a response to the American consumer.

Let me guess—the mascot was jumping on a trampoline that was branded "Coca Cola" or something, right? Before you start bashing the sponsors, you should thank them. Yes, to a certain degree having their logos shoved in your face cheapens the experience. Look, I don't like to hear James Brown (J.B.) welcoming us to the "Doritos Halftime Show" either. And before we start thinking that this is a new development, let me take you back to the sign at Ebbets Field that said "Hit Sign, Win Suit" sponsored by Abe Stark's clothing store back in the '30s and '40s— promising a new suit to whatever player would hit the sign. Sponsors have always been part of the fabric of sports. Without their big bucks, teams couldn't afford to operate their lovely new ballparks, the War- riors would not be able to afford Baron Davis and all the players they replaced Larry Hughes with, and you bet your sweet ass that the Lakers couldn't afford Kobe. If you strip sports of all of these things that you deem to be extraneous—all sponsors, promotions, frills and filler—I'll tell you what you're left with: about three fans sitting in a dilapidated stadium (Chris and his two brothers), crappy players, no fancy luxury suites—and to many, that means no fun.

CHRIS'S IDEA OF FUN

Fun? You think a grown man in an animal suit jumping on a trampoline is fun? For whom?

Erica, let's just start with mascots. The aforementioned "Thunder" has become the Bay Area's worst mascot since the Crazy Crab in the early '80s got booed out of Candlestick Park by San Francisco Giants fans. But at least the Crazy Crab was a Letterman-like in-joke, an inten- tionally bad idea done with a wink by the creative execs who brought you the Croix de Candlestick, a badge of honor for the fans who braved Candlestick's notorious Arctic breezes. Likewise, the lustily hated Crab was invented with a wink—he was lovable precisely because he was so hateable; he was an ironic anti-mascot that parodied all others. But with "Thunder," the Warriors brass is serious. Painfully serious.

As we write this, the Warriors have undergone a renaissance, of course. Led by general manager Chris Mullin and coach Don Nelson, the team is again an exciting winning team with a charismatic cast of characters, castoffs and yes, some convicted criminals. But hey, a "W" is a "W."

But in 2000, no Warrior was either colorful or good. And no one on the team's business side had any faith in what the Warriors' should have been selling—winning basketball! To counter this, they seemed to trot out more gimmicks and sales pitches than Al Pacino in *Glengarry Glen Ross.*

Tired of the humiliating losses? Who cares, Thunder is going to come out and break dance with the rich kids who sit courtside! Is the other team laughing at yours by the 2nd quarter? Don't fret, something called "The Hoop Troop" (read: teenage interns working for free or damn near it) will come out and slingshot T-shirts into the crowd! Is your team losing by 30? It's cool! Just a few buckets more, and it's free *chalupas* for everybody! Are we having fun, yet? Ugh. What's a real fan to do?

The presence of mascots and these "teams" of canned fun is a sign of mindless herd mentality. ALL the other teams have a mascot, so we have to have one too, right? Wrong. These mascots and "hoop troops" are inventions of some marketing executives who have the goal of "relating" to little kids and casual visitors who aren't basketball fans. And therein lies the problem. These trends have nothing to do with basketball or the sport's many rabid fans.

Wait, Erica, you're probably asking, why would a basketball team do something that takes away from its own fans' favorite game experience? Because team officials don't have any faith that a good chunk of the people are there just for the basketball. Wait again, you might ask, why wouldn't people attending a basketball game be there for the basketball? The answer, as usual, is tied to money and big business.

For starters, these days ticket prices for NBA (and NFL and MLB) games have become so expensive that regular folks often cannot afford to attend them. You may be a loyal and passionate hardcore fan, but unless your wallet is as big as your heart, you're shut out. So, many, perhaps most, of the "fans" at the arenas and stadiums are part of the corporate crowd that so many of these teams cater to. They're there to be seen or because it's a hot ticket, not because they really are fans of the team or the sport.

So, the goal isn't to create a cool scene where magical moments between team and fan flow organically and whereby great sports memories are created. Nope, instead, it's all about keeping as many things as bland and canned as possible.

Rule No. 1 is: Don't offend anyone. Rule No. 2 is: For God's sake, don't let them get bored. Check that, don't let them even think about getting bored. Check that again: Don't let them even think. Rule No. 3 seems to be: However loud the music is, turn it up one more notch.

ESPN.com's Bill Simmons once argued that TV executives too often come up with bad ideas simply because they have to justify their jobs. The same could also be said about sports marketing executives. To make sure they keep up with the other NBA Joneses, franchises will hire a marketing team. They don't come cheap, so the only bad idea is no idea. They have to justify their existence in a visceral way. It doesn't matter if their ideas are particularly good, or if they obtrude on the game action or on the fan's time of visiting with whomever they attended the game.

Nope, like a ball-hog who refuses to pass to his open teammates, you best get out of the way of these guys because these execs are going to do what's good for them and only them. They have to have *something* to justify their paycheck. So they end up trying to fix a lot of things that were never broken. They come up with ideas like new, gaudy uniforms that threaten a team's tradition, and new cheerleaders and dancers in places where they just don't fit, like the ridiculous Knicks City Dancers at New

York City's Madison Square Garden. They come up with free pizza give-aways if the team scores 100, causing "fans" to cheer wildly at the end of the game, even if their team is getting trounced. They come up with team-hired hyper kids who, looking like Ellen DeGeneres on speed, dance with perplexed fans in the stands during timeouts. And yes, they come up with mascots using trampolines to do somersault dunks.

ERICA'S IDEA OF FUN

Now you just wait one cotton-pickin' minute. I understand that you feel the teams' marketing and promotion squads should be more connected to the actual game being played than their schedule of kissing sponsor's asses and distracting people who aren't that into the game. But I have to stop you right here and discuss some of the amazingly creative, fantasti-cally fun promotions that have actually enhanced the fan experience. Have you ever placed a magnetic schedule on your fridge? Ever sung *Take Me Out to the Ballgame*? Ever put a bobblehead of your favorite player on your desk? Ever take your free mini-bat and use it to beat up a rival fan in the parking lot? That's what I thought. Read on for the best sports promotions ever!

Long Live Bobbleheads: Who knew that the bobblehead craze of the '60s would rear its ugly, bobbling head again in the new millen-nium? Since 2000, bobblehead giveaways have run rampant through many of the professional leagues—and the little dolls are collectibles sold on eBay, kind of like Beanie Babies. But why stop at your favorite player or coach, when you can get a bobblehead of comedian Bill Mur-ray from the Charleston River Dogs, a Minor League team in which Murray is a co-owner? Or why not get a set of former president bobble-heads—including George Washington, Thomas Jefferson, Abe Lincoln and Teddy Roosevelt—from the Washington Nationals? (Some think that the team doesn't have any star players, so they have to give away bobbles of dead presidents. It's just a theory!) Or at Portland's PGE Park,

Minor League fans received a "Bob L. Head" bobblehead, created to look like an Iowa man named Bob Leroy Head. Or pay a visit to the Minor League Lowell Spinners game, where they gave away Jack Kerouac bobbles, as well as bobbles of 19th century artist James Whistler, who painted "Whistler's Mother." Hello, culture meets kitsch. How can this possibly be a bad thing?

Before you answer that, answer this: Why even get a bobblehead when you can get another bobbling part of the body—like a Curt Schilling bobble-ankle after he played in the 2004 World Series for the Red Sox with a bum ankle that bled through his sock? Truth be told, the popularity of bobbles in declining in recent years. So what's next? In Chicago, they gave away Cubs Mr. Potato Heads in 2007, and the Minnesota Twins even gave away finger puppets. But word has it that painted figurines, commissioned by artists and numbered for fans, are the next big thing.

Make Some Noise: That was easy to do back in 2006 with the Tampa Bay Devil Ray Cowbell Night or in 2007 with the Florida Marlins Kazoo Night. To that we say, "More cowbell, people!"

Fashion Plate: In Oakland, they had Necktie Night, designed by then-A's pitcher Barry Zito, and sponsored by Macy's! And at Wrigley, they had Budweiser Floppy Hat Night. Who doesn't look good in a floppy hat?

Cheap Beer & Free Money: We have already mentioned the ill-fated 10-Cent Beer Night back in 1974—an attempt by the Cleveland Indians management to bring fans out to see their miserable team play the Texas Rangers. See Chris, sometimes you don't have a winning team to draw in fans, so why not try 10-cent beer? Aside from that one woman who flashed the crowd from the on-deck circle . . . oh, and that father/son mooning incident . . . and the fans who kept coming on to the field and shaking outfielders hands—everything went fine! Until the ninth inning. With the game tied, the fans went wild—throwing cups of beer, rocks, golf balls, batteries, anything they could find onto the field. One fan ran down and took the Rangers' right fielder's glove. The Indians forfeited the game and 10-Cent Beer Night was never repeated. But, since then, marketing folks have really learned how to do it right . . .

And these days, what gets people more riled up than cheap beer? Yep, that's right: Free money! Fast-forward 32 years to 2006, when Detroit's Single-A team, the West Michigan Whitecaps, had a helicopter drop $1,000 in various denominations after a game, with kids lining up to scoop up the cash. Sure, a couple kids got roughed up, including a 7-year-old who got trampled and taken to the hospital. But he was later released with a few bruises. When asked for a comment, the team spokesperson told *USA Today,* "It's for fun and games. This is why we have everyone sign a waiver."

But the Cleveland Indians seem to have redeemed themselves from the 1974 debacle by coming up with their own take on "Free Money Night" at the ballpark. Each fan walks into the park and receives an envelope—they could end up getting $1 or $100 or even $10,000! That's pretty cool. Chris, are you convinced yet? Wait, there's more. For the very best and creative promotions, we must return to the Minor Leagues!

Diamonds Are a Girl's Best Friend: Who knew that this $10,000 diamond ring giveaway would end up destroying the Sonoma County Crushers' very own diamond back in the '90s? The promotion, sponsored by a local jeweler, involved burying a fancy diamond ring somewhere in the infield dirt. After the game, all of the women in attendance were supposed to go out and dig in the dirt to retrieve their coveted prize, using wooden "sporks" they were given upon entering the ballpark or using garden trowels that they brought from home. Our friend Ed, who was in attendance, reports: "I swear, I'm not making this up . . . they must've been out there for half an hour, in 105-degree heat. And all the guys in the stadium were all gathered in the shaded seats behind home plate laughing their asses off. The men were all just sitting back there, yelling at the women 'Move left!' and stuff like that, as the girls sweated and toiled away and dug enormous potholes in the infield." Now, normally I would cry sexism here and say that this perpetuates the stereotype of women being gold-diggers (or in this case, diamond-diggers). However, I have to take off my PC hat for a moment and declare that this is a hilarious and brilliant promotion—kind of like when women go nuts in that Filene's Basement "Running of the Brides" promotion, brutally attacking each other (and knocking over the *Today Show's* Al Roker) in the quest for deeply-discounted wedding dresses.

McDreamy Night: Every Thursday, the Hagerstown Suns have "Ladies Night." So how do you get women to come out to the ballpark on the same night their favorite TV show is on? Simple. You hire five Patrick Dempsey look-alikes, host a fashion show with models clad in doctors' scrubs, hold a medical spelling bee and have a "McDreamiest" hair competition, in which a panel of nurses chooses the winner.

FILL 'ER UP: In Birmingham, Alabama, the Minor League Barons are in touch with the daily trials and tribulations of their fans. To show that they felt the pain of high gas prices in 2007, fans could buy general admission tickets for the current price of unleaded gasoline, which was about $2.90 per gallon at the time. They also offered box seats for the price of premium unleaded per ticket, around $3.50, and raffled off a $250 gas card as part of the promotion.

Billy Donovan Night: Down in Fort Myers, they keep up with current events. Their Minor League squad, called the Miracle, planned a promotion around the flip-flopping of Florida Gators basketball coach Billy Donovan. Back in June 2007, Donovan took a job coaching the NBA's Orlando Magic, but the very next day he changed his mind, returning to the Gators. The Miracle came up with a few ideas to help celebrate Donovan's change of heart: they allowed fans to "opt out" of their tickets if they weren't having a good time by negotiating with a local attorney . . . they served waffles at concession stands . . . and had someone named Billy Donovan scheduled to throw the first pitch, but of course, he changed his mind at the last minute and didn't show up to the game.

The same people who came up with this idea came up with Tonya Harding mini-bat night and Vasectomy Night, in which all male fans could enter to win a free snip job. (Thankfully, someone pulled the plug on Vasectomy Night before it came to be.) But who is the brain behind these crazy ideas? Who else but Mike Veeck, the son of legendary MLB owner and promoter Bill Veeck, who had a career of crazy baseball antics that spanned from the 1940s to the 1980s. Yes, that Bill Veeck, the same man who placed a secret PA microphone in Harry Caray's announcer's booth in 1976, as he sang *Take Me Out to the Ballgame,* broadcasting it to the entire crowd at Comiskey Park—starting the tradition of leading the crowd in song that Caray brought with him to Wrigley. I say we need more guys like the Veecks. Chris, I hope by now that you are seeing that some of sports' greatest traditions began as marketing stunts.

CHRIS' REBUTTAL

Funny you should mention Veeck, Erica. I really liked Bill Veeck. He was a great owner and promoter exactly because he didn't take himself or the game too seriously. But, as amusing and fun as your above anecdotes are, I need to remind you of a few fiascos:

Disco Demolition Night: The year, 1979. The place, Comiskey Park. The game, a doubleheader between the White Sox and the Detroit Tigers. The Bill Veeck-concocted theme? The death of disco. A local radio station had recently gone to an all-disco format, leading to the firing of popular DJ Steve Dahl. So Veeck, his son Mike (mentioned above) and Steve Dahl came up with the idea that fans should bring old disco records to the park in exchange for a 98-cent admission price (representing the station's location on the dial). The records were to be collected and destroyed on the field in between the day's two games. Sounded like a harmless enough plan. And at least it didn't involve secretly signing a little person to the team and having him jump out of a cake before taking the field, which the elder Veeck did in 1951.

The first problem with Disco Demolition Night was that the Veecks did not realize how many people really hated disco. Close to 100,000 people showed up to the park, which had a capacity of 50,000—and many of those fans were turned away. But these disco-haters were not to be deterred. They climbed over the walls of the stadium to get in. The inebriated fans started using the records as Frisbees, throwing them around the stadium, along with beer and firecrackers. And when the demolition moment arrived, Steve Dahl marched out to the crate of records dressed in army fatigues, as the crowd chanted "Disco sucks!" He triggered an explosion that was quite a bit bigger than expected—it ripped a hole in the grass of the outfield. Thousands of fans took to the field, rioting, throwing things, burning whatever they could find, stealing the bases and even destroying Comiskey's batting cages. Manager Sparky Anderson and his Tigers refused to take the field—out of fear for their lives—and the White Sox forfeited the second game. The only good thing to come out of this hair-brained promotion was the fact that it demonstrated the increasing hatred toward disco and contributed to its demise.

Ball Night: In 1995, Dodger fans were invited to Ball Night, where fans would receive a souvenir baseball. Brilliant idea . . . at least for the first six innings. In the seventh, the Cardinals right fielder bobbled a ball, causing fans to throw their precious giveaways at him. Then with one out in the ninth, Umpire Jim Quick made a questionable strike call against Raul Mondesi, who argued and was tossed from the game. Tommy Lasorda came out of the dugout to continue the argument, and he was tossed out of the game, as well, causing fans to throw their souvenir balls onto the field. The game was called and the Dodgers forfeited—the first forfeit in the National League in 41 years.

Salute to Indoor Plumbing: You're right, Erica. Stupid promotions can be found in places other than the Majors . . . Minor League baseball has plenty. Like this great idea from the folks at West Virginia Power, the Brewers affiliate. In a May 2007 game, their plan was to make fans appreciate indoor plumbing by closing all the restrooms and forcing fans to use portable toilets. Sounds fun to me! When faced with health-code violations, the team's employees instead dressed in overalls and mashed up brownies in order to have a "Poo Toss." Poo toss? That's the one thing spitballer Gaylord Perry was never accused of!

It's as if they have decided that we all have attention spans the size of a flea's eyelash and if they give us a single second of silence or non-action then we're going to storm out of the stadium. Since they don't have enough Ritalin for 20,000 people, they treat the stadiums and arenas as one big pinball machine and their crappy ideas are the silver ball that is randomly, annoyingly heading our way all night. We've left ballgames with a headache after experiencing this stuff.

Like big-budget Hollywood movies and bigger-budget presidential candidates, almost all teams have convinced themselves (erroneously, by the way) that the best way to capture the most dollars is to distract fans from the actual game and keep things as mindless as possible. Meanwhile, the sport and the athletes who are the crux of the league oddly take a backseat in many of the ad campaigns. Sure, sometimes in the big leagues, stars like LeBron James or Tom Brady are featured. But far too often you get saccharine, Prozac-inspired slogans such as the Warriors' slogan: "It's a Great Time Out!"

Here's how these kinds of ad campaigns are inherently dishonest. Sometimes attending a game is decidedly NOT a good time out. Sometimes you walk out of a stadium after a loss feeling like you got kicked in the groin. I take that back. Sometimes you walk out of a stadium feeling like you got kicked in the groin *and* everyone is laughing at you *and* someone just stole your lunch money. (Can you tell I've had my heart broken by my teams once or twice or 209 times?)

It's part of the manic-depressive gig that makes being a fan so exhilarating. Feeling that low when your team loses is why you feel so high when they win. I wouldn't say it's always "fun." Dramatic, yes. Entertaining, usually. "A Great Time Out?!" Sometimes, yeah. But not always. And no amount of "Poo Tossing" is going to change that.

Another example of this is when you're at the stadium/arena in person and your team has blown a game they should have won. You've been to funerals with happier crowds. The outcome is already decided, but there is still a minute or so on the clock. A smart in-stadium producer would shut it down, turn down the volume on the PA, cancel the commercials on the JumboTron and just let 70,000 people stew in their juices. But for a variety of reasons, some due to contractual obligations or a set production schedule or simply because they just can't help themselves, these teams never leave well enough alone. Never mind that thousands of pissed-off fans are on the verge of committing group hari-kari, or are calculating just how much of their kids' college fund they robbed to pay for the pricey game tickets. No, instead the public address announcer will come on in the same cheery, game-show-host voice to pitch a product or plug the next game or to remind them that, gosh, they're the greatest fans in the world. It's like being at a dysfunctional holiday dinner that ended in a fight and, instead of just pouring a stiff drink or letting people head to their cars, here comes cheery Aunt Peg with a fake smile: "Hey, who wants a Triscuit?"

ERICA TO CHRIS: CAN'T WE ALL JUST GET ALONG?!

I agree with you on this front. I used to like it at Yankee games when they played *New York, New York,* by Sinatra after a win . . . and *New York, New York* by Liza Minnelli after a loss. It allowed fans to grieve, just a little bit, knowing that Liza is no Frank. And I do agree that for all of these goofy promotions, it would be great if they had a bit more to do with the game. Some of my greatest memories of going to games with my dad included keeping score together on my scorecard. It made every play important. Every pitch. And now, with the razz-matazz, jazz hands and constant tap-dancing by the promo team—as fun and kitschy as I think it is (except for that "Poo Toss" thing)—it's nearly impossible these days to just settle in, focus on the game and enjoy the luxury of having several hours of uninterrupted time with your dad or sibling or friend or significant other. But don't blame it on sports. It's a societal issue. And sports teams—from the Majors to the Minors and everyone in-between—are just trying their best to adapt to a changing consumer.

SOMETHING ELSE CHRIS AND ERICA CAN AGREE ON

We may be split on whether or not we like goofy promotions, but there is one thing we agree on: Mascots are pretty lame. They're just another maddening way that the leagues' overproduction of games often threaten our enjoyment of them, even though that's the last thing they're trying to do. We think. Please allow us to reunite as one, and shift our rant to team mascots. They are supposed to entertain, to cheer on the team, to distract bored kids. But how can you explain this behavior?

When Mascots Attack: First, a disclaimer: There are some longtime traditional mascots that we both like. USC's Tommy Trojan or Notre Dame's Leprechaun come to mind. So does St. Joseph University's Falcon, who has to flap at least one "wing" for the duration of an entire game, which makes him the hardest working mascot in college sports. And don't forget baseball's Phillie Fanatic, Pirate Parrot (not the one involved in the 1985 cocaine scandal) or the San Diego Chicken (we can't hate on a mascot that used to steal scenes from Tommy Lasorda on *The Baseball Bunch* show). And Erica must give a shout out to Ferrous and FeFe of her Lehigh Valley IronPigs. We know it's not an easy job. It's hot inside that damn costume and you basically have to humiliate yourself night after night after night—for little pay and no glory.

But over the last couple of years, a few mascots have taken their role in the game a bit too far. We find their actions not only offensive, but also downright nauseating. Sample:

Lascivious Louie the Laker: The mascot for Grand Valley State University in Allendale, Michigan, is Louie the Laker—a commercial fisherman. A very horny commercial fisherman, apparently. In November

2007, he was caught on TV doing a touchdown celebration that, thankfully, Terrell Owens hasn't thought of. He grabbed the goalpost and was caught jubilantly humping it before he realized he wasn't in his living room watching Skinemax. The TV announcers tried to ignore it and the cameras quickly cut away. But thanks to YouTube, his act of goalpost-erotica will live on forever. Behind him, a stadium ad had the slogan: "Get this close . . . without the bruises." No comment.

The University of Oregon Dirty Duck: Ever take the kids to a wholesome college football game in a small town and an episode of *Oz* breaks out? That's what happened in Eugene, Oregon, on Sept. 1, 2007. The University of Oregon Duck mascot didn't just tackle the Cougar mascot from the University of Houston. The dirty Duck pummeled the cowering Cougar, sitting on him and then doing a couple of bumps and grinds on top of him before University of Houston cheerleaders broke up the melee. He was later suspended for the attack, which might have been the first R-rated assault between mascots in sports history.

The Driving Force Behind the Tennessee Titans: If Michael Vick got 23 months in jail for abusing dogs, what should the Tennessee Titans' mascot get for abusing backup quarterbacks? T-Rac, as the Titans' mascot is known, was driving a golfcart on LP Field on August 12, 2006, at a preseason game between the Titans and the New Orleans Saints. Problem is, T-Rac was driving worse than Billy Joel after an office party. At least that's what quarterback Adrian McPherson alleges in a $20-million lawsuit he filed against the Titans. McPherson claims that the mascot hit him with the golfcart while the rookie QB was warming up at halftime. McPherson had battled back from having his college career at Florida State tainted by a check-forging and betting scandal, and was trying to make the Saints after the team drafted him the 5th Round in 2005. But he never got that chance. The golfcart accident injured the player, and just weeks later the Saints put him on the injured reserve list, ending his season, the lawsuit states. Now McPherson is out of the NFL and playing in the Arena Football League.

San Francisco Giants' Lustful Lou Seal: We're not sure if San Francisco Giants' Lou Seal is forced by law to introduce himself to neighbors whenever he moves; but it wouldn't surprise us. Lou Seal, who has been the Giants' mascot since they moved into AT&T Park in 2000, is known for standing on top of the dugout, doing pelvic thrusts and pretending to, there's no other polite way to say this, slap booty. Maybe all those Viagra ads on MLB telecasts are getting to him?!

Da Bull-Shit: Quick, some team should sign Da Bull of the Austin Toros to a contract. The mascot for the minor league basketball team in Texas got suspended for two games in the NBA Development League after running onto the court and dunking an alley-oop pass *during* game action.

Boomer Boo Boo: In March 2007, Boomer, the Indiana Pacers' cat-like mascot, did a bird-brained thing. He tackled a fan who had just taken part in a halftime shooting contest. Problem is, the man had just had back surgery and Boomer's tackle re-injured him. A future lawsuit isn't a question, it's a formality.

To once again show a united front, we have compiled a list of things we both loathe and love about marketing, promotions and technological advancements.

A List of Marketing/Promotions/ Technological "Advancements" We Loathe

▶ Longer and more frequent TV timeouts during NFL games.

▶ The corporate naming of pretty much every stadium in America—and the fact that these companies always seem to be merging or cursed to bankruptcy, forcing us to call the stadium something new every year.

▶ Baseball executives threatening to extend the divisional series to seven games so they can make more advertising revenue—meaning that the World Series will be played in November, rendering the term "Mr. October" useless.

▶ Music turned way up at all times so that you can't talk to your friend/family member.

▶ The goofy gopher-cam on Fox's NASCAR coverage, as well as the NFL robot on Fox, recently given a name: "Cleatus" (Erica agreed to let Chris put this here, but she secretly likes the robot).

▶ Austin Powers sound effects (Erica agreed to let Chris put this here, but she secretly likes these sound affects).

▶ Overly commercial marketing schemes, such as the attempt to put *Spiderman II* ads on bases and the on-deck circle during games, like they tried to do back in 2004—thankfully, the baseball world retaliated and canceled the promotion.

▶ More and more teams leaning on their radio and TV affiliates to just be their propaganda arms, leading to overly-biased coverage of teams.

▶ The Los Angles Angels of Anaheim: Worst name ever; though the Utah Jazz (formerly the New Orleans Jazz, which makes a lot more sense) and the Golden State Warriors (formerly the Philadelphia Warriors and the San Francisco Warriors) are close.

▶ Overkill with the fantasy numbers and crawls during a game. These guys can use the damn WiFi and go online to see how their pretend teams are doing.

▶ The NFL "Football Night in America" red-carpet intro that we must endure each week—can't they change it up each week?

A List of Marketing/Promotions/ Technological "Advancements" We Love

▶ The yellow line for first downs on football TV telecasts.

▶ Coaches' Challenges and Instant Replay.

▶ Baseball players getting to pick their own song before batting.

▶ Rock music between innings for baseball and before introductions at football games.

▶ The use of AC/DC's *Hells Bells* intro to get crowd riled up in between plays.

▶ Playing the *Rocky II, Hoosiers* and/or *Animal House* pep-talk scenes in the 9th inning when the home team is down.

▶ Throwback unis, "Turn Back the Clock" Days and Old-Timer's Games.

▶ Despite our disdain for pink, we do like the cute Mother's Day and Father's Day promotions, including pink and blue wristbands in honor of moms and dads—and especially the pink Louisville Slugger "Going to Bat Against Breast Cancer" promotion.

▶ Incredible Super Bowl Halftime Shows that are not lip-synched— Prince in 2006 rocked. (However, we do not like how this type of entertainment has now spread to Conference Title Games and Season Openers, like that awful Faith Hill debacle in 2007, where she sang *This Kiss* prior to the first game of the season—what does that have to do with football?! They should have had Faith sing a cover of Pat Benatar's classic *Hit Me With Your Best Shot* or something like that. Or if they HAD to stick with one of her songs, how about *Mississippi Girl,* but changing the words to talk about her love of football? Come on NFL and NBC, you can do better!)

▶ The tradition of fans singing *Sweet Caroline* in Boston.

▶ Guest singers who lead the Wrigley crowd in *Take Me Out to the Ballgame*, since Harry Caray passed away in 1998.

▶ Fireworks nights.

▶ Dollar Beer Nights/Dollar Dog Nights at Minor League games.

▶ The *YMCA* performance by the grounds crew and the completely out-of-place, but much loved playing of *Cotton-Eyed Joe* at Yankee Stadium.

▶ Kiss-cams. Awwww.

11 ROAD TRIP:
Let the Away Games Begin

- -

ANOTHER WAY IN WHICH MEN AND WOMEN ARE QUITE different when it comes to sports is this: Women like to plan. Most men are content just winging it. In fact, Erica and her sister recently went to a Steelers vs. Jets game and encountered a group of guys who just showed up at the game, not dressed for the weather at all, who had just decided to wing it. They took a one-way car service to the game, brought a 12-pack in a paper bag, scalped tickets and then tried to hitch a ride back to Manhattan from the sisters—who of course had bought tickets months prior, complete with a parking pass, and happened to have extra scarves/Terrible Towels, just in case! Since the aforementioned guys were pretty good-looking guys from the good old 'Burgh—the girls agreed to drive them home. (WARNING: Do not try this at home. Leave it to the professionals).

But it did get us thinking: Not about the dangers of driving strange men home, but the fact that chicks would never just show up somewhere with no plans, no gloves or scarves in 30-degree weather, with no plans on how to get home. Just wouldn't happen. And this got us thinking about some of the trips we have taken that were sports-centric, and how a little girlie, type-A planning turned the sporting event into a really fun vacation. For instance: Spring Training in Arizona is a ritual for both of us. Erica and her sister also try to travel to one Steeler game in a cool, "away" city each season so they can mix a little eating, drinking and shopping with their tackling. And when Erica went to the NASCAR race in Phoenix, she turned it into a weekend of R&R (that's Racin' & Relaxin'), by staying at a luxe resort with a visit to the spa. And we both are already planning our trip to South Africa for the World Cup in 2010!

Here, we detail some incredible ways to fuse your love of travel and love of sports into an action-packed vacation. (Bring your significant other for an incredible trip that is guaranteed to win his undying love. Or, if you're single, these trips are great for groups of girlfriends—the male-to-female ratio is heavily in your favor and you're guaranteed to score with a fellow fan, if that's your goal!)

MLB Spring Training: Let's start with our favorite annual getaway. When March rolls around and we're getting serious cabin fever, we plan a trip to sunny Scottsdale to check out our favorite baseball team, as well as many other teams in action. Personally, we prefer the Cactus League in Arizona to the Grapefruit League in Florida—mostly because both of our teams play in Arizona, but also because we get to see lots of other teams while we're there. The Grapefruit League teams are a bit more spread out, so it's harder to see several teams without a long drive or a short flight. But don't get us wrong—if your team is playing down in Florida, you'll still have a great time. And, with the Dodgers and Indians abandoning Florida for Arizona in 2009, you can bet that these small sleepy Florida cities are going to be building up in an effort to keep up with Phoenix and ensure that the current Grapefruit League teams stay there. So go ahead and plan your trip to the Sunshine State. But if you're looking for us, we'll be in Scottsdale, probably at the Salty Señiorita.

We plan a trip for at least four to five days, and book a room at one of the area's incredible resorts. The Sanctuary is über-chic, but The Phoenician, Royal Palms, Westin Kierland and the Four Seasons are also upscale, and right up our alley. The Hotel Valley Ho is a fun and hip choice, as well. Next, we plan some fun dinners in Old Town Scottsdale—including the Pink Pony and Don & Charlie's, where all the Giants and front-office people go. And we set aside time for spa treatments, pool time and shopping at the cute Old Town galleries and shops. Another epicurean ritual for Erica is a daily trip to the Coffee Bean for an Ice Blended Vanilla and at least one trip to In-n-Out for a Double-Double with cheese and well-done fries, Animal Style—because she doesn't have either one of these hugely popular culinary institutions on the East Coast.

Oh, yes, and then there's the baseball. All of the ballparks are intimate and accessible—some shiny and new, some old and historic, all fun. It's your chance to see your favorite ballplayers in a small-town setting, with other fans who are serious about their baseball. Attendance runs anywhere from 7,000 to 10,000 fans per game during Spring Training versus 30,000 to 40,000 fans per game for most MLB teams during the regular season. And Spring Training tickets are cheap—around $10 to $15 for general admission or bleacher seats, slightly higher for better seats if you get them early enough. Otherwise, try StubHub.com. Parking is easy breezy. It's always sunny in Scottsdale and if it isn't, well, it will be sunny soon. Life at Spring Training is good.

We usually hit brunch before the game, bring a blanket (or towel from the hotel room . . . don't tell), find a seat in the grass and settle in for some sun, hotdogs, cold beer and sizzling baseball action. After the game, Old Town Scottsdale is teeming with fans grabbing a post-game beer or cocktail out on the patio. It's a big party and a great way to meet fans from all over. There are tons of West Coasters, and at times, it does feel as if the entire city of Chicago comes down to see their Cubbies and Sox (they're the fans with the really white legs).

Whether you decide to spend your spring in Arizona or Florida, here is a list of which Major League teams play where.

Grapefruit League in Florida

Atlanta Braves, Lake Buena Vista
Baltimore Orioles, Fort Lauderdale
Boston Red Sox, Fort Myers
Cincinnati Reds, Sarasota
Detroit Tigers, Lakeland
Florida Marlins, Jupiter
Houston Astros, Kissimmee
Minnesota Twins, Fort Myers
New York Mets, Port St. Lucie
New York Yankees, Tampa

Philadelphia Phillies, Clearwater

Pittsburgh Pirates, Bradenton

St. Louis Cardinals, Jupiter

Tampa Bay Rays, St. Petersburg (until 2009, when they move to Port Charlotte, Florida)

Toronto Blue Jays, Dunedin

Washington Nationals, Viera

Cactus League in Arizona

Arizona Diamondbacks, Tucson

Chicago Cubs, Mesa

Chicago White Sox, Tucson

Cleveland Indians, Goodyear (starting in 2009)

Colorado Rockies, Tucson

Kansas City Royals, Surprise

Los Angeles Angels, Tempe

LA Dodgers, Glendale (starting in 2009)

Milwaukee Brewers, Phoenix

Oakland Athletics, Phoenix

San Diego Padres, Peoria

San Francisco Giants, Scottsdale

Seattle Mariners, Peoria

Texas Rangers, Surprise

NFL Football: Since the Super Bowl is nearly impossible to get tickets to if you're a regular fan, you could head to Vegas for the big game—which has become almost as big of a party as the Super Bowl itself. Personally, we'd rather watch at home and avoid the crowds. So if we're itching for an away game, as we mentioned before, we pick a fun city where our team is playing and make a weekend out of it. Here are some ideas:

▶ Miami is always a good choice for a little sun and spice (and based on their 2007 season, your team is almost guaranteed a win against the Dolphins!)

▶ San Francisco is an amazing choice with wine country nearby, incredible restaurants and lots of fun outdoorsy stuff to do. Except you'll have to watch the Niner game at Candlestick Park—a place that's near and dear to Erica's heart, but not exactly the best stadium to catch a game. You might be better off to try a Raider game and join some of their hardcore fans. If you do, you should try to borrow a Harley and definitely wear black.

▶ New Orleans makes for an emotional and inspiring trip (and delicious and debaucherous, if you'd like to go that route). We must note, though, that we still are shocked at how quickly the Superdome got up and running after Hurricane Katrina, and felt that the NFL could have done a little bit more to get the city back on its feet, rather than the Saints. But you should do your part and go for a visit as this resilient city continues to rebound. It could use your support. And so could the Saints, based on their losing record in 2007.

▶ We wouldn't really recommend coming to New York City to see the Giants or Jets. It's a pain to get out to The Meadowlands (just ask those guys we met) and you feel really detached from Manhattan, anyway. But you should come out for some US Open tennis action. We'll talk about that later . . .

▶ San Diego makes for a fun away-game trip. Play in the Pacific and frolic on Mission Beach, stroll around the Hotel Del, check out the zoo, and even hit surf camp while you're there.

▶ Philadelphia can actually be really quaint, with its great restaurants and charming Rittenhouse Square. (We had a joke in here about packing heat while in Philly, but thus far in 2008, the murder rate has dropped by a whopping 25%. Way to go "City of Brotherly Love"!).

▶ The Big D makes for a fun trip to see the Cowboys (and the DCC). Be sure to hit Primo's Bar & Grille, and check out the Sixth Floor Museum, devoted to the JFK assassination. You can look out the window of the former Texas School Book Depository, which now houses the museum. Step outside to look around Dealey Plaza for yourself, and stand on the grassy knoll, which is both eerie and fascinating.

▶ Chicago is a great choice, because the city is packed with amazing restaurants, museums, bars and live music, but we might recommend going to an early season football game or else you'll be freezing your tits off! Literally. (Seriously.)

▶ Arizona would be a nice choice, except we think their team is boring and we already went there for Spring Training and for NASCAR. Enough already!

▶ And what about good old Beantown? Oh, forget it. We hate the Pats. Just kidding. We're just jealous. We admit it. Boston is a great city. We'll talk more about it later.

▶ How about LA? Oh yeah, they don't have a football team. Doh!

Our favorite idea involving football, though, has to be digging out the old passport and hitting one of the international NFL games. Although these games are an effort to convert the world to the NFL religion and we already think the NFL is scary enough now—we still like the idea of watching good old American football in a completely new city. (Even though part of us does feel like this is a bit like going to Paris and dining at the Hard Rock, but still.) You say the word and we'll hop on over to Europe, catch a regular season NFL game with nearly 100,000 Euro fans and then make a longer trip out of it. In 2007, the NFL hosted their very first regular season game in Europe, when London played host to the New York Giants and the Miami Dolphins in October. Whilst it was a bloody boring game, it was still a huge success, as the game was sold out and was mostly attended by Brits and other Europeans. In 2008, the NFL returns to London, where the New Orleans Saints will serve as the "home team" as they face the San Diego Chargers in October. In addition, the Buffalo Bills will play one regular season game per year in Toronto, from 2008 to 2012. And the NFL also plans to host regular-season games in future seasons in Mexico and Germany—and to that, we say, "Achtung, baby!"

Basketball: Okay, we do like basketball and we suppose you could plan a trip around an NBA game, but for some reason, traveling for a regular season game doesn't sound all that exciting. But if you're feelin' it, go for it. Maybe somewhere like Portland or LA—cities that don't have football teams. Or head to Phoenix in February 2009 for the NBA All-Star Game (maybe just stay through March for MLB Spring Training!)

If we were planning a basketball-centric trip, we would go to Vegas during NCAA finals. You get to watch all the games in the sports book, while eating, drinking, gambling and clubbing the rest of the night away. This is definitely a good one for the single ladies, as Vegas is crawling with men during March Madness. We stay at the Wynn or Bellagio, we "heart" the sports book at Caesar's, and we like to hang out at the Hard Rock—in our opinion, Vegas is the only city where it's acceptable to hang out at a Hard Rock.

Tennis: Many people don't get the thrill of watching live tennis. We are not like those people. We love live tennis. We love the civility of it. We love how the announcers shush you. We love the sheer athleticism of the athletes, the fact that you can see men and women playing at the same sporting event, we even love Sharapova's groaning/sex noises. And we sure love to see what Federer and the Williams sisters are going to wear, count how many times Nadal picks his ass, and see who Djokovic is going to imitate next. And we like to see it live. Join us, won't you? Head to New York at the end of August to check out tennis' biggest stars at the US Open. Plus, you can explore Manhattan when it's pretty empty and mostly everyone has vacated the city for the Hamptons, Upstate, Fire Island or the Jersey Shore. If you are up for mixing hot tennis action with steamy, sultry weather and smells you've never experienced before—this is the perfect trip for you! It's easy to get to the US Open via subway or the Long Island Railroad (unlike the New York-area football games) and you can choose from day or night sessions. It's an upscale event, so tickets are not cheap and neither is the food! But that's New York for you. Throughout the summer, the US Open Series also visits nine other cities in North America, leading up to the big event in NYC. They are: Los Angeles; Indianapolis; Palo Alto, California; Washington, D.C.; San Diego; Montreal; Cincinnati; Toronto; and New Haven, Connecticut. Pick one and make it a weekend. (We would do Montreal. We *aime* Montreal. It's a short flight, you can pretend you're in Paris and use that high school French—plus, the people, architecture, cuisine and shopping are all *magnifique*!)

Another great tennis-related trip is possibly one of the hardest tickets to get in sports: Wimbledon. Our British friends tell us it's harder to have breakfast at Wimbledon than to get into the Super Bowl. But if you plan early and pay through the nose, you can make it happen. It's held in late-June/early-July and is the oldest and most prestigious championship in tennis. So wear something nice. Don't embarrass us.

Or, if you're really feeling the tennis love, try one of the other two Grand Slam tournaments: The French Open held in late-May/early-June in Paris, or the Australian Open, which kicks off the tennis season in January in Melbourne.

NASCAR: NASCAR makes it easy to catch a race and experience the fast and the furious for yourself, with races across the country during their extra-long season, from February through November. Many of the cities where NASCAR races are held, however, don't feature many other activities to experience while you're there. And look, we do like NASCAR, but one day of racing is enough for us. We're not going to spend Thursday through Sunday at the speedway—unless we're in Robby Gordon's tricked-out trailer. Therefore, here are the NASCAR cities we think are weekend-worthy:

▶ **Las Vegas:** No explanation needed. Make it a weekend of racing and raucous behavior.

▶ **Atlanta:** Although the track is in nearby Hampton, Georgia, stay in Buckhead, check out some great restaurants and make it a weekend in Hot-lanta.

▶ **Talladega, Alabama:** There's probably not much else going on in Talladega than racing, but since we love Will Farrell's *Talladega Nights* so much, this is a must on the NASCAR circuit. It's a super-speedway, so the track is huge and there is so much to do that you'll be kept busy all weekend. When there, please shout, "I'll get you Ricky Booby!" from the stands, with a Borat accent. Thanks.

▶ **Phoenix:** We've spent a lot of time telling you how great Phoenix and Scottsdale are. There's a ton of stuff to do, and it's always hot and sunny. And we still think this is a great NASCAR destination. We stayed at The Wigwam, which sounds goofy, but it is a lovely old resort that recently underwent a multi-million dollar renovation. It's charming, really close to the race in Avondale, Arizona, and there's an Elizabeth Arden Red Door Spa, as well as a great steakhouse called Red's. Lots of NASCAR folks stay there, and this is the hotel with the helicopter service from the front lawn of the hotel directly to the race for only $150 round-trip. With all that traffic, it may be worth it.

▶ **Martinsville/Richmond, Virginia:** Virginia is beautiful. No doubt about it. Take a trip through the state's burgeoning wine country, hit Virginia Beach, or make your way through the Blue Ridge Mountains en route to Martinsville or Richmond. Both of these raceways feature short tracks, and NASCAR only has three of these, so they're both worth checking out. In Richmond, they race on Saturday night rather than Sunday afternoon, which is rare and really cool.

▶ **Charlotte, North Carolina:** Charlotte represents the very essence of NASCAR. It's the birthplace of the sport, and home of many NASCAR legends, including Dale Earnhardt and Richard Petty. While here, be sure to hit the North Carolina Auto Racing Hall of Fame Museum and the Richard Petty Museum. Or, if you happen to be visiting when NASCAR isn't in town, you can check out the FasTrack Driving School or the Richard Petty Driving Experience, both held at the Lowe's Motor Speedway.

▶ **Dover, Delaware:** No need to go to Dover, really, except to give your regards to Joe Biden. Just kidding. Remember, they do have that lovely air-conditioned casino at the raceway where you can stay overnight and watch the race from your room or the restaurant that kicked us out.

▶ **Sonoma, California:** This is another great weekend trip, where you can mix your motor sports with merlot (not behind the wheel, of course)! It's one of only two road-course races in NASCAR, so you won't be bored by these guys going in endless circles. The turns on this course are tight and winding. Many of the drivers hate driving this course, which in turn makes fans love this course. When you're done at Infineon Raceway, spend the weekend in the heart of wine country by visiting Sonoma and its adorable downtown—be sure to visit Sebastiani and Buena Vista wineries, or Gundlach Bundschu for a quirky, off-the-beaten path winery. And if the Sonoma crowds are driving you crazy, make your way back to the 101 and head up to Healdsburg. The Hotel Healdsburg is on the quaint town square, and there are incredible restaurants and wineries here, just ask Chris. This is his hometown.

▶ **Long Pond, Pennsylvania, in the Poconos:** We'd like to recommend this as a destination, because Erica lives part-time in nearby Bethlehem in the Lehigh Valley. However, even though it's a superspeedway, we have already told you how horrendous the traffic is, thanks to the rural location. And there's really nothing else to do in August, except maybe head to the Poconos when there's no snow. We can't really say it's a weekend-worthy destination. (But if you're in Erica's neck of the woods in August, stop by Lehigh University for the Philadelphia Eagles preseason camp, instead—and while you're there, check out Musikfest, a really cool, 10-day music festival with top performers.)

▶ **Loudon, New Hampshire:** This race is held just a 90-minute drive from Boston in September, so we suppose you could go for the weekend to catch a Red Sox or a Pats game. But why would you want to do that? Just kidding. Enough Boston bashing. Beantown is a really incredible city—great food scene, plenty of cool shops and boutiques, lots of quaint streets and historic sites. If you can somehow manage to catch a NASCAR race, a Sox game AND sneak a peak at Tom Brady, all in one weekend—we'd be really impressed.

▶ **Joliet, Illinois:** You're really close to Chicago, so here's a great itinerary: Arrive in Chicago over July 4th weekend. Attend Taste of Chicago—the Windy City's awesome food and music festival. Spend the rest of the week eating and drinking your face off, hitting a Cubs and Sox game, listening to as much live music as you can, hit a museum or two, eat some more, maybe get tickets to see *Oprah*—then bookend the trip with a NASCAR race up in Joliet. Yep, sounds pretty ideal to us.

▶ **Homestead, Florida:** A NASCAR weekend in Miami is just our speed. Imagine the fusion of Southern flavor with Latino spice, with a healthy dose of Miami heat . . . we're getting hot and bothered just thinking about it! Well, Erica is.

In case you are choosing your NASCAR destination by the type of racetrack that is located there, we present a handy-dandy list of all of the NASCAR Raceways across good old US of A. (Refer back to page 110 if you need a refresher on what exactly a Superspeedway is!)

NASCAR Raceways

Daytona International Speedway, Daytona, Florida: Superspeedway

California Speedway, Fontana, California, (outside of LA): Superspeedway

Las Vegas Motor Speedway, Las Vegas, Nevada: Intermediate Speedway

Atlanta Motor Speedway, Atlanta, Georgia: Intermediate Speedway

Bristol Motor Speedway, Bristol, Tennessee: Short Track

Martinsville Speedway, Martinsville, Virginia: Short Track

Texas Motor Speedway, Fort Worth, Texas: Intermediate Speedway

Phoenix International Raceway, Phoenix, Arizona: Speedway

Talladega Superspeedway, Talladega, Alabama: Superspeedway

Richmond International Raceway, Richmond, Virginia: Short Track

Darlington Raceway, Darlington, South Carolina: Speedway

Lowe's Motor Speedway, Charlotte, North Carolina: Intermediate Speedway

Dover International Speedway, Delaware: Speedway

Pocono Raceway, Long Pond, Pennsylvania: Superspeedway

Michigan International Speedway, Brooklyn, Michigan: Superspeedway

Infineon Raceway, Sonoma, California: Road Course

New Hampshire International Speedway, Loudon, New Hampshire: Speedway

Chicagoland Speedway, Joliet, Illinois: Intermediate Speedway

Indianapolis Motor Speedway, Indianapolis: Superspeedway

Watkins Glen International, Watkins Glen, New York: Road Course

Kansas Speedway, Kansas City, Kansas: Intermediate Speedway

Homestead-Miami Speedway, Homestead, Florida: Intermediate Speedway

As we discussed, there is a lot of controversy over whether or not Indy racing is dying a slow death. That being said, we still think going to the Indy 500 is really cool. There are three weeks of fun activities leading up to the race—from mini-marathons to fashion shows, from concerts to galas—and it all culminates in some wacky traditions, including the winner drinking a glass of milk. Now that's what we call a party! The race is held over Memorial Day, and again, if you plan ahead, you could turn it into a fun weekend and maybe share a dance with Helio from *Dancing With the Stars*.

Many of the other Indy races take place at the same tracks as the NASCAR races do, so you can decide whether you want to experience Indy or NASCAR. However, Indy is a bit more prevalent in the Midwest, so if you find yourself in Wisconsin, Ohio, Kentucky or Iowa—try to check out one of the Indy Car races. Or, if you're feeling really ambitious, Indy heads to Motegi, Japan, once a year for a 300-mile race.

Another race that we think is worth mentioning is the Baja 1000, referenced earlier in the book. The popularity of this anything-goes race down in the desert is on the rise, and this could be a fun getaway for a group of friends. The Baja 1000 is held in mid-November, and the Baja 500 is held in June. The big party is in Ensenada, and a few other cities on the way down to the finish line near Cabo. But if this kind of wild west adventure sounds good to you, head on down and cheer on the Gordon clan! Check out score-international.com for more details.

European Football: Plan a trip to England from August to May and you'll likely be able to see an English Premier League match. Even though you won't know any of the songs, just drink and be merry with the locals. Study up on the rivalries and grab a tabloid to see what the WAGs are up to. Actually, head to your favorite city in Europe, South America, Russia or Asia, hell, even the Caribbean or the Middle East, and you can catch a football match. The only place we would avoid watching football/soccer would be here in the US. Sorry, Becks.

As for us, we are both planning to be in South Africa sometime between June 11 and July 11, 2010, for the next FIFA World Cup. (You know, as research for GoGameFace.com. Wink, wink.) Qualifying matches start in June 2008, so start paying attention now—and by the time the World Cup rolls around, you'll know all the key players and teams. We'll start at the beach in Cape Town, exploring South Africa's painful past and promising future. We'll visit Robben Island, where Mandela was held for 18 years, and of course make time to visit the nearby winelands. Then we'll head up the coast to Durban, to experience the tropical climate, warm Indian Ocean and hip, beach culture. And then it's on to Johannesburg, the bustling economic hub of South Africa, where the final will be held. If you're serious about this trip, you'd better start planning now.

Horseplay: If horseracing is your thing, do the Kentucky Derby in early May. Each year, you see more and more stars flocking to Churchill Downs in Louisville, KY. Join 150,000 others to see the most exciting two minutes in sports. It's a tough ticket, but plan ahead. And you best go to a milliner and have a fabulous bonnet made for the occasion. Again, don't embarrass us.

If you like horses, but prefer things a bit more down and dirty, be sure to hit the Houston Rodeo in March or the Calgary Stampede in July. Along these lines is the World Finals of the Professional Bull Riders in December in Las Vegas—which is actually really fun, whether you're rooting for the bull riders, the rodeo clown or the "animal athletes." Again, if you're lookin' to lasso a cowboy, all of these are great girls trips.

But if you are looking for something completely different, travel to Siena in Italy for Il Palio, held twice a year on July 2 and August 16. This gorgeous Tuscan city, enclosed in medieval walls, hosts a ten-horse race, with bareback riders, each representing a different district of the city. They're all vying to win a silk banner and boasting rights—after all, the race has been going on since the 1700s. There are strange traditions: a horse can win, even if its jockey falls off, which often happens in this race held in the town square. And winners have pacifiers in their mouths, as it feels like they have just been born after completing the race. For four days prior to the race, it's an Italian eating and drinking frenzy. And after the race, the districts that lose go into deep mourning if their horse does not win. (Look for an action sequence taking place during Il Palio in the next Bond movie, coming out in fall 2008, which means that more people are going to find out about this, so book now!)

Other sports-related itineraries:

Golf: Sure, hit The Masters, the US Open, the Ryder Cup or the British Open. But we like our golf with a few celebs and some gambling on the side. We suggest Lake Tahoe in July for the American Century Celebrity Golf Tournament—and traveling to Tahoe is especially important after the big fires they had there. Many think of skiing when they think Tahoe, but it is just as fun in the summer, with its great resorts, outdoor watersports and blackjack! There are dozens of current and former athletes who participate in this tournament (like Michael Jordan, Lance

Armstrong, Charles Barkley, Drew Brees, Tony Romo, Marcus Allen, Brandi Chastain, Jason Kidd, Ben Roethlisberger, LaDainian Tomlinson, John Elway and Mario Lemieux), plus lots of Hollywood types, too (Kevin Costner, Don Cheadle, Ray Romano, Cheech Marin, Jack Wagner), as well as some other randoms (Stone Phillips, Maury Povich, Dan Quayle and chef Ming Tsai). Because Tahoe is so small and intimate, you can see many of these characters around town, while you're at dinner or playing craps, as well as on the golf course.

Hockey: Alright, we need a trip for our avid hockey fans. You could hit the NHL All-Star Weekend in January, but we suggest going to a regular-season game in Canada, where people are serious about their stick. Try Toronto or Montreal. Both are amazing, beautiful and cultural cities filled with Canucks who love their hockey. The Hockey Hall of Fame in Toronto is really cool, and you can see the original Stanley Cup—before it found its way to Scores—and check out the new NHL Zone. And have we mentioned that we love Montreal's incredible restaurants and great shopping? *Mais, oui!*

College Football: If your college alma mater didn't have a football team, like us, college football can seem a little daunting. But if we're going to plan a weekend where we start tailgating at 6 AM and learn school songs about a place we didn't even attend, we're going down South to adopt a new college team. We'll choose 'Bama, University of Tennessee, Ole Miss, University of Georgia, Clemson, Texas A&M, LSU, University of South Carolina. We don't care. But here's what we do care about: marching bands, ladies getting dressed up for the games, and the fact that everything is fried or contains bourbon. And then, if our adopted team is having a winning season, we might even head to a Bowl game: Rose, Orange, Fiesta, Holiday or our favorite: Chick-Fil-A in Atlanta (formerly known as the Peach Bowl). Mmmmm, Chick-Fil-A. Mmmmm, Chargrilled Chicken Club Sandwich. Sorry, for a minute, we thought we were still in the *GameFace Grub* chapter. Moving on.

The Olympics: We have a friend who travels, with her entire family, to as many winter/summer Olympics as they possibly can. It's a huge undertaking, but well worth it to root on your nation's team and see some of the world's best athletes in action. You have to sign up for a lottery to buy your tickets, so start thinking about Vancouver in 2010, London in 2012, and Sochi, Russia, in 2014.

Surfing: If you live in California or are independently wealthy and can get anywhere with a few hours notice on your private jet, you have to check out the Mavericks Surf Contest. Mavericks is an infamous big-wave break, located a half mile off the coast of Half Moon Bay, just south of San Francisco. In this contest, 24 of the world's best surfers have just 24-hours notice to come battle the big wave. From December to March, when the "window" is open, check your email or cell obsessively to find out when the official "Greenlight" message goes out. Then get your ass to Half Moon Bay, book a spot on one of the tour boats and get ready to witness a truly awe-inspiring, big-wave surfing experience. Beware: it's freezing, wet and you must have a strong stomach. But it's truly one of the coolest sporting events anywhere.

Visit GoGameFace.com for links to more info on all of these sporting events and information on how to book your next sports-centered trip. Ladies, start your planning!

12 THE BIG LEAGUES MEET THE BIG SCREEN: *Sports & Hollywood*

"WHERE'S YOUR HAT?"

It's the greatest line in sports movie history, even though it has nothing do with winning or losing. If you want to know why *Rocky* is as beloved by women as it is by men, look no further than the moment when Adrian falls into Rocky's arms right after his life-changing bout with Apollo Creed. She has just pushed her way through the raucous crowd, losing her red beret in the process, while Rocky, bruised and swollen, stands alone in the ring looking for her. When she finally arrives, he doesn't talk about himself or what he's just accomplished. He only wants to know what happened to her hat.

Really, who wouldn't fall in love with a guy who holds his own in a fight and still likes helping his girl accessorize—especially when he does it after a uniquely rough day at the office?

It took Erica just one viewing to notice the line, while it took Chris about 30 times. (Typical man!) It's an unpredictable, almost goofy thing to say to somebody just moments after getting beaten to a pulp for 15 rounds. But it's also why *Rocky* is the kind of sports movie that we *both* love. While action-movie fans are enthralled by the boxing at story's end, we liked the *other* game being won by the heroes. Rocky, played by a pre-steroidal Sylvester Stallone, may have lost the big match, but he and Adrian had won something much rarer than a boxing title. She found a good man to love while he discovered his self-respect. Together, they had breathed life into each other's dreams—which, of course, dwarfed whatever the boxing judges' final tally was. Win or lose, Rocky had met his meager but near-impossible goal of just "goin' the distance" with Creed. Yet, even in the heat of that moment, he had but one thing on his mind as his swollen eyes desperately searched the crowd. Yep, you guessed it: "Adrian! . . . Adrian!"

As for the beret? Ah, Rocky probably bought her another one the next day in South Philly. But in sports movies that followed, this was the problem: There was no *hat*. In other words, no heart and soul to give all that sports action real emotion and meaning. We know when this trend started—in 1980 with *Rocky II*, when Rocky finally beat Creed. Since then, almost all sports films have followed its formula rather than that of the first *Rocky*. With an eye solely on big box office, filmmakers want to let the viewers have their cake and eat it too, sending them home with a story where the hero wins the big game *and* the girl. Which is fun enough, but also predictable and a little tiresome. It's sort of like watching Britney Spears on *Entertainment Tonight*—you know it's always going to end with a pink wig, running mascara and an ambulance. Instead, we like our sports movies to shake it up a little bit and give us the kind of great characters we will root for long after the big game—win or lose—is over.

Fortunately, Hollywood has been making sports movies for about a century, or at least since Charlie Chaplin met his first groupie. So, there are all kinds of stories about all kinds of athletes made in just about any era from the last 100 years or so. A lot of them are good. A lot of them are bad. A lot of them land in our favorite category: So-Bad-They're-Good. Amazingly, a lot of the same faces pop up—from Burt Reynolds (Erica's favorite) to Michelle Rodriguez, and even Jerry Lewis (embarrassingly, one of Chris' favorites). And the day you see all three of them in the same movie, fix yourself a stiff drink because it can only mean the end is near! Until that fateful day, here are the best—and some of the worst—sports movies of all time.

Top 10 Baseball Movies

Make them and they will come. That must have been Hollywood's slogan during the late-'80s and early-'90s, when it seemed like every other movie released had a baseball theme. Not that we're complaining. If you love baseball as much as we do, these movies below provide no better way to mark the winter days until pitchers and catchers report to Spring Training each February.

The Bad News Bears (1976): They have an alcoholic coach, a parent-less motorcycle-riding superstar, a foul-mouthed girl pitcher and a team of sad-sack Little League nobodies. Hey, look, everyone, it's the '62 Mets! Just kidding. This movie is actually much more entertaining than any real team. Also, setting the team's horrible defensive bloopers to the music from the opera *Carmen* is pure genius. While it stars Walter Matthau, Tatum O'Neal and Jackie Earl Haley, it's Vic Morrow who steals the show as the meanest coach in Little League history.

Field of Dreams (1989): Kevin Costner, appearing in the second of his three baseball-themed movies, plays Ray Kinsella, who builds a baseball diamond in the middle of an Iowa cornfield after hearing an invisible whisper: "Build it and they will come." Weird. But it only gets stranger when real-life—and long-dead—old ballplayers like Shoeless Joe Jackson emerge from the cornstalks to play ball on the field. The sentimental movie moves from a one-glove flick to a double-hankie one when Kinsella's late father arrives at the field to play catch with his son just one more time. Of course, if he built it now, Costner's dead career probably would materialize from the cornstalks.

Bull Durham (1988): Nuke LaLoosh, Baseball Annie and Crash Davis. With names like these, who even needs a plot? Luckily for us, this Ron Shelton-directed movie does have a great story, along with electric chemistry between Tim Robbins (Nuke), Susan Sarandon (Annie) and Kevin Costner (Crash). Nuke is a raw phenom with the "million-dollar arm and a ten-cent head." Annie is a groupie with class and an almost metaphysical belief in the game. Crash is a Minor League lifer, too good for the minors but rarely getting his shot at The Show—their slang for the Major Leagues. However, he does get a shot at love with Annie and, unlike his cup of coffee in the majors, he doesn't waste it.

A League of Their Own (1992): A baseball movie with Madonna, Jon Lovitz and Rosie O'Donnell? Sounds like a formula to sweep the Razzies awards for worst film of the year! But no worries, it also stars Tom Hanks and Geena Davis, who carry this comedy about a real-life all-female baseball league. Whenever you hear the cliché, "There's no crying in baseball," you can thank Hanks, who made the line famous with his perfectly exasperated delivery while playing the team's boozy, down-on-his-luck manager.

The Sandlot (1993): Okay, enough of this R-rated stuff, isn't baseball supposed to be a family game? This movie is. It has James Earl Jones and a subdued Denis Leary, but the real stars are the little kids who play ball every summer day on a suburban sandlot in the early 1960s. Their biggest worry is the scary dog belonging to Jones, a mysterious neighbor who turns out to be a kindly, ex-Negro League star.

Pride of The Yankees (1942): Staying in the G-rated zone, this tear-jerker has stone-faced Gary Cooper playing stoic Yankee legend Lou Gehrig. Babe Ruth even appears as himself, showing off pretty good acting chops along the way. And of course, there is Gehrig's own real-life retirement speech, which echoes in every fan's memory bank as much as it did around Yankee Stadium that day. Cooper's performance will put a lump in your throat as he calls himself "the luckiest man on the face of the earth," even when everyone knows Gehrig soon will die from the disease that now bears his name.

The Natural (1984): Phenom Roy Hobbs (played by Robert Redford) has his promising career cut short by a sexy but pistol-toting female fan. Years later, Hobbs makes a middle-aged comeback, carrying the fictional New York Knights in a 1940s pennant race. Before anyone gives him a steroids test, Hobbs falls for Kim Basinger, who is in cahoots with the team's evil owner. Hobbs' final at-bat has become film legend—he literally knocks the hide off the ball, sending it soaring into the lights, creating a stadium pyrotechnic celebration as he rounds the bases. The soundtrack is played in every stadium nationwide, even though many players' muscles today aren't exactly "natural."

Fever Pitch (2005): Has the passion you show for your favorite sports team ever ruined a romantic relationship? It certainly did for Jimmy Fallon in this Farrelly Brothers version of Nick Hornby's autobiographical book about his obsessive love for a British soccer team. In this version, Fallon falls in love with Drew Barrymore in Boston, but is there enough room in his life for her *and* his beloved Red Sox? She doesn't think so and gives him his walking papers. But maybe, just like the miracle 2004 Red Sox, there is one last hope for them? The original screenplay was written assuming the Sox would lose. But during filming in 2004, the team looked like it was on the way to a curse-breaking, history-making season—which led the filmmakers to quickly change the ending of the movie. Fallon and Barrymore's makeout scene was captured during the real on-field celebration by the Red Sox at Busch Stadium in St. Louis. All of this caused Nick Hornby to quip, "Please tell the people of Boston that I am claiming personal responsibility for this."

Major League (1989): This one is like a July afternoon game at Wrigley—wild, off-color and chock-full of dumb fun that you'll never forget. Charlie Sheen, Wesley Snipes, Tom Berenger and Corbin Bernsen—wow, that reads like the roster of a bizarre Learning Annex seminar: "Bad Decisions 'R' Us: Go from the A-List to the B-List in Three Easy Steps." They all carry the sad-sack Cleveland Indians to victory, in spite of the evil team owner.

Eight Men Out (1988): Baseball players misbehaving, a bad commissioner and amoral owners looking the other way. The Mitchell Report on steroids? Nope, it's about the 1918 Chicago White Sox—forever known as the scandal-marred "Black Sox" because some of them allegedly fixed the World Series. Starring John Cusack, Charlie Sheen and D.B. Sweeney as Shoeless Joe Jackson, the movie takes a sympathetic look at the players, who despised cheapskate owner Charles Comiskey enough to ruin their reputations by taking money in exchange for losing on purpose to the Cincinnati Reds.

BEST BASEBALL MOVIE YOU'VE NEVER SEEN

Bang the Drum Slowly (1973): Would you believe Robert De Niro as a hillbilly baseball catcher dying of cancer? Once you see him in this underrated gem with a Southern accent and a mouthful of chew, you will. Co-star Michael Moriarty plays De Niro's roommate, a smart but moody All-Star pitcher for a fictional New York team unmistakably based on the Yankees. As you might imagine, there's no happy ending for De Niro's ailing character, who is faced with a game he just can't win.

TOP 10 FOOTBALL MOVIES

Hollywood and football have been linked together as far back as the silent-film days, and we're not even talking about that nasty rumor about 1920s actress Clara Bow having sex with the USC football team. Whatever the era, these movies below are a surefire way to get your football fix during its long offseason.

North Dallas Forty (1979): No, this is not about Jessica Simpson's bra size. It is, however, one of the first sports movies to show the dark side of professional football's business, warts and all. Nick Nolte and Mac Davis play the hard-partying wide receiver and quarterback tandem of a Texas pro team. Based on the book by former Dallas Cowboy Peter Gent, it also stars football wild man John Matuszak, who didn't have to stretch his acting muscles too far to play a semi-crazy, fun-loving defensive end.

The Longest Yard (1974): We're going to pretend the Adam Sandler remake never happened. You should, too. Instead, check out the original with Burt Reynolds starring as Paul Crewe, a has-been quarterback tossed into prison after shaving points and driving his girlfriend's car into the bay. Once behind bars, he gets recruited to lead the prisoners' team against the guards. Yes, the inmates play football against the prison guards. What could go wrong there?

Heaven Can Wait (1978): Warren Beatty stars as a guy who gets reincarnated into a Los Angeles Rams quarterback and promptly leads them to the Super Bowl. As the writer/director, Beatty also quarterbacked this remake to the Oscars—it was nominated for Best Picture. Rounding out the squad is a great cast, including Julie Christie, Jack Warden, Charles Grodin and Dyan Cannon.

Any Given Sunday (1999): Like a lot of recent Oliver Stone movies, this one is kind of a mess. But it's an entertaining mess, and one that put Jamie Foxx on the map as a serious actor. Foxx, playing a backup quarterback, holds his own in scenes with Al Pacino, who seems to think that most pro coaches dress like an out-of-work New York theater actor. No matter. Cameron Diaz is great as a tough, smart team owner. And NFL legends Jim Brown and Lawrence Taylor surprisingly shine, while Pacino delivers an unforgettable, scintillating pregame speech about this game of inches.

Semi-tough (1977): Ah, the weird and woolly 1970s. What other era would feature a football movie featuring game-show king Bert Convy as the leader of an "alternative religion," a trend at the time? Burt Reynolds was in the prime of his career, and this was just a few years after posing nude in *Cosmopolitan,* a photo that Erica used as her MySpace.com profile picture for a while, until she decided it was in poor taste. Reynolds is a star running back whose best friend is the team's quarterback, as played by Kris Kristofferson. They both vie for the affection of the thinking man's sex-symbol of the decade, Jill Clayburgh.

Jerry Maguire (1996): We promise we won't mention this movie's played-out catch phrase. The Cameron Crowe film is fresh and unpredictable, with lines of dialogue that have become an indelible part of pop culture. ("You had me at hello.") It's less a sports movie and more of a smart love story, with Tom Cruise wooing Renee Zellweger and her little bespectacled son. As a sports agent, he also has to woo a bunch of athletes, including Arizona Cardinals wide receiver Rod Tidwell (Cuba Gooding Jr. won an Oscar playing him) who just wants Jerry to show him the mo—okay, stop! Phew, that was a close one.

All the Right Moves (1983): Tom Cruise—back when he was considered a nice, normal guy—plays a high school football player desperate to use the game to escape his dying Pennsylvania steeltown. Problem is, he clashes with the megalomaniacal coach, played with authentic prickdom by Craig T. Nelson. Much like *Friday Night Lights,* this movie does a good job of capturing the angst of big-time high school athletics in a small town.

That's My Boy (1951): Dean Martin and Jerry Lewis? In a football movie?! They play the cheerleaders, right?! Yeah, it's not Shakespeare. Hell, it's not even the Farrelly Brothers. But this silly, wholesome 1951 film is a fun guilty pleasure. Lewis' ridiculous pregame pep talk before the big game—like a Bill Murray scene on speed—is worth the rental alone.

Rudy (1993): The same guys who made *Hoosiers* pull it off again with *Rudy,* whose lead character dreams of just one chance to play on Notre Dame's hallowed field. Based on a true story, Sean Astin plays Rudy Ruettiger, a college walk-on who was too small to play football but still earned the respect of his teammates with his hustle. Charles S. Dutton steals the show with his classic tough-love speech: "You're 5-foot nothin', ya' weigh 100-nothin', not a speck of athletic ability!" Which, oddly enough, is what Chris and Erica say each day to get pumped up for their writing sessions.

Brian's Song (1971): Who'd a thought that the mother of all tear-jerkers would involve the Chicago Bears, but wouldn't include bumbling quarterback Rex Grossman, who has made Bears fans cry for years? Nope, this true story is about the friendship between Hall-of-Fame star Gale Sayers and his teammate Brian Piccolo, an easy-going running back who bravely fought his terminal illness before dying in 1970 at the age of 26. Piccolo, who was white, and Sayers, who is black, became friends in the 1960s when segregation was a hot issue. Starring an understated James Caan and Billy Dee Williams, this TV movie and its haunting musical score was an instant classic.

BEST FOOTBALL MOVIE YOU'VE NEVER SEEN

TIE: BUFFALO '66/FIGHTING BACK/GUS

Buffalo '66 (1998): We don't know what's more impressive: That Vincent Gallo made a sports movie with virtually no sports action, or that it's a critically acclaimed film co-starring faded has-beens Jan-Michael Vincent and Mickey Rourke. Gallo's bitter lead character is released from prison after being convicted of a crime tied to a big bet he lost because of a Buffalo Bills placekicker's big Super Bowl miss. (Paging Scott Norwood . . . Paging Scott Norwood.) Anjelica Huston shines as Gallo's mother, a diehard football fan who makes it quite clear that she loves the Bills much more than she loves him.

Fighting Back (1980): This TV movie starring Robert Urich as Rocky Bleier could have been cheesy. Instead, it's a fun, realistic look at Bleier's incredibly courageous story of coming back from being an injured Vietnam vet, who was told he'd never walk again, to becoming a star fullback in the Pittsburgh Steelers' 1970s dynasty.

Gus (1976): If you ever needed proof that drugs were rampant at various times in Hollywood, then just read the synopsis for this movie. A pro football team called the California Atoms hire their team mascot, a mule named "Gus," as the squad's placekicker. Yes, Gus is a kicking mule that can kick the ball through the uprights from any distance, which means the team scores every time it has the ball. Then again, when your team is coached by Don "Barney Fife/Mr. Furley" Knotts, as the Atoms are, you probably need all the help you can get.

TOP 10 BASKETBALL MOVIES

For some reason, basketball movies are where sports filmmakers get a little weird. Maybe because they're not weighed down by baseball's National Pastime bluster or that John Wayne-like talk in football about discipline and toughness—basketball has none of those trappings. Even more, it's the only sport where the athletes get compared to artists and musicians. Some say it's like jazz music, for example, because it allows individuals to improvise while still playing with a group. Except for the New York Knicks, who are more like the kids in Menudo: Painfully bad and sure to be gone in a few years.

Teen Wolf (1985): We're not saying the plot is ridiculous. C'mon, who didn't have a basketball-playing werewolf at their high school? Michael J. Fox is the high school hoopster who's experiencing just a little more than the usual burst of teen hormones. When Fox turns into the werewolf, his classmates are more fired-up than scared because he plays like some insane combo of Michael Jordan and Magic Johnson—only better and with more hair. But all he wants is to be normal again. Making matters worse is his coach, who offers Fox these gems of advice: "Never get less than 12 hours sleep." And, "Never play cards with a guy named after a city." Thanks, coach. Lotta help.

Fast Break (1979): What *Stripes* did for the Army—namely, mock it with its special formula of smart-ass characters, drug humor and unforgettable one-liners—this movie did for college basketball. Gabe "Mr. Kotter" Kaplan plays a New York-bred basketball coach who takes over a small Nevada college team and immediately schemes on how to make the program a national success. Kaplan brings with him some talented but shady Big Apple hoops stars, including two played by real-life UCLA All-American, Michael Warren, and future NBA stud, Bernard King.

Glory Road (2006): This film is based on the real-life Texas Western college team, which was the first NCAA team to start five African-

American players. Josh Lucas plays Coach Don Haskins who bucked social pressure in 1966 and didn't factor race into forming his basketball team's roster. It may sound crazy now, but as recently as 40 years ago, some college coaches like Kentucky's Adolph Rupp were not too keen on racially integrated teams.

Semi-pro (2008): Will Ferrell plays American Basketball Association owner/coach/player Jackie Moon in this comedy about the hoops league that invented the three-point shot, the slam-dunk contest and red-white-and-blue basketballs. Defunct since 1975, the ABA has since gone the way of bell-bottoms and giant Afros. But Ferrell, along with Woody Harrelson and OutKast's Andre 3000, revive its anything-goes spirit while playing for the Flint Tropics. Yes, that is a fictional team based in Michigan, but their name is still better than the real-life Utah Jazz. Ferrell may be making too many sports movies these days, but this one had us laughing.

Hoosiers (1987): Gene Hackman is a bad-tempered coach looking for redemption in an Indiana backwater after he lost his old job. Fortunately, he finds Hickory High and their sharp-shooting stoic star, Jimmy Chitwood. Together, they lead the tiny school to the state finals. Dennis Hopper plays a bombastic substance-abuser (what a stretch!) who drunkenly storms the court in one game, which might be the one and only kind of tantrum that Bobby Knight never threw.

The Fish That Saved Pittsburgh (1979): Have you ever heard of the Pittsburgh Pisces, a sad-sack team mired in incompetence? Probably not, because the franchise doesn't exist, except in the twisted minds that made this B-movie. Julius "Dr. J" Erving plays Moses Guthrie, the Pisces' lone star player. They're an awful team, until they start following the charts made by astrologist Stockard Channing. Our favorite scene is when Dr. J takes his girlfriend on the worst date of her life: He puts on a slow-motion dunking exhibition at a playground as a forgettable R&B

song plays over the soundtrack. Our second favorite is when the Pisces arrive for the championship game in a futuristic, funkadelic hot-air balloon that looks straight out of a George Clinton video.

The Basketball Diaries (1995): Ex-UCLA basketball coach John Wooden used to give his players his "Pyramid of Success," a sheet listing his suggested habits for achievement. Somehow we don't think "Inject yourself with heroin" made the cut. But don't tell that to the characters played by Leonardo DiCaprio and Mark Wahlberg in *The Basketball Diaries.* Long before they would clash as angry Boston cops in *The Departed,* they starred together in this movie about drug-addicted high school hoops stars.

Hoop Dreams (1994): A great documentary about two Chicago teenagers, Arthur Agee and William Gates, who dream of making it to the NBA. It examines life in America's inner-city and in the high-stakes universe of college sports. Neither world is a pretty picture.

He Got Game (1998): NBA superstar Ray Allen plays a blue-chip prospect delving into the dirty world of big-time college basketball recruiting, while his ex-con dad (Denzel Washington) tries to reenter his son's life. With Spike Lee directing, the action is hot and dirty, and that's just the threesome that Allen has with women provided to him by shady recruiters.

White Men Can't Jump (1992): Racist title? Or just the truth? This movie doesn't take itself seriously enough to care, and neither should you. Woody Harrelson and Wesley Snipes play Los Angeles pick-up-game hustlers who need to win to pay off Harrelson's big gambling debts. This film was written and directed by Ron Shelton, who has made a career out of sports movies like *Bull Durham* and *Tin Cup.*

The Best Basketball Movie You've Never Seen

Love & Basketball (2000): It's all about chemistry, whether we're talking winning teams or, yes, even love. Ahhh, that was deep. Omar Epps and his female lead Sanaa Lathan are friends and rivals who have a love-hate relationship while growing up in urban Los Angeles. Still, the sparks fly onscreen between Epps and Lathan—kind of like when Magic Johnson played against Isiah Thomas, only with less kissing on court.

Top 5 Boxing Movies

Boxing is the perfect sport for the silver screen. It has a ton of blood-and-guts action, and there's no scarier villain to conquer than the boxer threatening to pummel you for 45 minutes straight. Also, its ugly history of fixed fights makes for classic moral dilemmas for proud athletes: Do I take the easy money and hate myself forever or do I do the right thing and maybe get blackballed? (Actually, that's the dilemma in just about any job, isn't it?) Throw in the fact that most fighters come from the wrong side of the tracks, and you have the instant underdogs who movie viewers love so much. Besides, wouldn't it be great if any conflict could be solved with a boxing match? How much more fun would the Donald Trump-Rosie O'Donnell feud have been if they could have settled it in the ring? (We would bet the ranch on Rosie, by the way.)

Raging Bull (1980): This classic Martin Scorsese film about real-life fighter Jake LaMotta was shot entirely in black and white and features incredible boxing scenes. Robert De Niro famously went from a buffed fighter in his prime to a bloated ex-champ, gaining more than 50 pounds for the role and winning a well-deserved Oscar along the way. It was also Joe Pesci's first movie, playing LaMotta's brother. Pesci deserved some kind of award, if only for having to hear De Niro/LaMotta ask him about 1,000 times, "Did you f*ck my wife?"—a question bound to ruin any family gathering.

When We Were Kings (1997): This amazing documentary looks at the stranger-than-fiction legendary bout, The Rumble in the Jungle, which pitted an aging Muhammad Ali against a young George Foreman in the African country of Zaire (now called Republic of the Congo). Experts thought Foreman would not only win, he might end Ali's career. Instead, Ali scored one of the biggest upsets in boxing history by using his "Rope-a-Dope" strategy; he leaned against the ropes and absorbed Foreman's punches, waiting to attack until after his opponent was exhausted. Authors George Plimpton and Norman Mailer also share their colorful memories of the 1974 classic match. Another great documentary on this boxing legend is "Muhammad Ali, the Greatest" (1969), written and directed by William Klein.

Million Dollar Baby (2004): It's a simple formula. Make Hilary Swank look as unattractive as possible and she gets an Oscar. When we do that, all we get are quiet Friday nights. What gives?! Meanwhile, this Clint Eastwood movie about a female boxer is excellent, until it takes a surprising, and somewhat disappointing, plot twist toward the end. Still, it has excellent characters portrayed by an A-plus cast, including Eastwood and Morgan Freeman.

Girlfight (2000): The title may be every guy's fantasy, but roughneck chick Diana Guzman is no dream. Played by Michelle Rodriguez (from Lost), she is anyone's nightmare when she puts on the gloves. Rodriguez has had her share of controversy offscreen, drawing a jail term in 2007 for DUI arrests. But this gritty low-budget independent film won rave reviews and put Rodriguez—a rare combo of toughness and beauty—on the map.

Rocky I & II (1976 & 1979): We've already covered how much we love these movies, even if the four(!) sequels that followed don't measure up to the first two. The actors alone make this movie shine: Talia Shire as Adrian; Burgess Meredith as Mickey the trainer; Burt Young as Paulie, Adrian's loser brother; and of course Stallone, who touted the underdog spirit back then as much as he promotes the benefits of human growth hormone today.

Best Boxing Movie You've Never Seen

Somebody Up There Likes Me (1956): A tough Italian-American boxer with shady ties redeems his loser life through boxing and a girl's love. Sound familiar? About 20 years before Rocky Balboa, there was this biopic about Rocky Graziano, a real-life fighter who went from criminal to champ by stepping inside the ring. Paul Newman gives one of his sterling career's greatest performances as Rocky, and Pier Angeli, best known as James Dean's ex-girlfriend, plays his shy love interest. A couple of others to note: a classic called *The Set-Up* (1949) and the Ken Burns documentary on Jack Johnson, *Unforgivable Blackness: The Rise and Fall of Jack Johnson* (2004).

Guilty Pleasures, Innocent Fun

One surprising thing about rooting for a horrible team is that it can be kind of fun. Yeah, the losing is discouraging. But you learn to enjoy all those pressure-free games because the team is out of the playoff hunt from the season's outset. Bad sports movies can be like that, too. Very early on, you recognize that you're watching trash and you can laugh at it while you're barely following it. Low risk, high yield. Perfect for a lazy Sunday. Or unemployed writers, which, ahem, we know a thing or two about. We pay tribute to such gloriously horrendous sports movies with our list below.

Top 5 Sports Movies That Are So Bad They're Good

One On One (1977): Short little Robby Benson is supposed to be a blue-chip basketball recruit? What's next, Zac Efron as the lead in *The Muhammad Ali Story*? Actually, Benson is surprisingly athletic and his youthful innocence kind of works for a story where his character quickly gets disillusioned with the politics of big-time college sports. G.D. Spradlin plays the creepy coach, which is not be confused with Spradlin's performance as the creepy senator in *The Godfather II* or his creepy football exec in *North Dallas Forty* or the creepy army general in *Apocalypse Now.*

Bingo Long Traveling All-Stars & Motor Kings (1976): It's got a great cast: Billy Dee Williams, James Earl Jones and Richard Pryor. It also has a cool topic: the Negro League-era teams who barnstormed through towns to play local baseball teams. Pryor is hilarious as a guy who pretends to be Cuban so he can break the Major Leagues' color-line. Come to think of it, the movie isn't so terrible, but good God, can we please do something about that title?

Hustle (2004): Picture this phone call when this ESPN original movie started filming:

"Hi Pete Rose, it's your agent. No, not your probation officer."

(Pause)

"Hey, they're making a movie about you and maybe it'll finally set the record straight."

(Pause)

"No, Pete, Ron Jeremy isn't right for the part. Nope, the good news is Tom Sizemore is playing you. Yes, they let him out of rehab for this. Nah, he's not doing it just for the money. It's probably for the drugs! Guess they got the biggest dirtbag in Hollywood to play the biggest dirtbag in baseball! Kidding, kidding."

(Pause)

"Bad news is, I've seen the dailies, and the hairpiece they gave Sizemore is straight out of the 'Moe from Three Stooges Collection.' Seriously, the hair's so bad it makes your 19th century 'do look like Andy Garcia's. But that can be a good thing, right, Pete? Right?"

(Pause)

"Hello?!"

The Kid From Left Field (1979): Simply put, the best Gary Coleman baseball TV movie ever made in San Diego! Co-starring Ed McMahon. Seriously. Robert Guillaume (of *Benson* fame) plays Coleman's dad, who starts the movie selling concessions at Padres games but, incredibly, later leads the team to the World Series as the team manager. The only thing less realistic is if they'd had Coleman win the Series with a game-winning home run. Wait, I think I smell sequel here.

Fear Strikes Out (1957): Anthony Perkins plays a mentally-unbalanced Boston Red Sox player, and no, it's not Roger Clemens in the 1990 playoffs. Three years before playing Norman Bates in *Psycho,* Perkins played real-life headcase Jimmy Piersall, a ballplayer who suffered a nervous breakdown. The movie means well, but the scenes where the decidedly unathletic Anthony Perkins is asked to throw and catch are laughably bad.

THE BEST OF THE REST

Although we've covered some of Hollywood's favorite sports— football, baseball, basketball and boxing — we like all kind of sports and all kind of sports movies. Here are some other favorites:

TOP 3 GOLF MOVIES

Caddyshack (1980): Not just the king of golf films, this might be the granddaddy of all sports movies. The unforgettable cast includes: Bill Murray as Carl Spackler, the insane and possibly brain-damaged groundskeeper; Ted Knight as the sleazy Judge Smalls; Chevy Chase as rebellious Ty Webb; Michael O'Keefe as the story's working-class hero, Danny Noonan; and, of course, Rodney Dangerfield as the wonderfully obnoxious Al Czervik. And its cultural impact has been enormous. Starting with the fact that most men wouldn't be able to talk with each other if they didn't have memorized *Caddyshack* lines to lean on whenever the conversation hit a lull. Seriously, how many awkward holiday dinners were salvaged with a Bill Murray quote? Maybe only a million.

Happy Gilmore (1996): "The price is wrong, bitch!" It's not so surprising to find that line in an Adam Sandler comedy. But it did raise an eyebrow when the line was delivered by game-show host extraordinaire, Bob Barker. This might be Sandler's best movie, which, we admit, is kind of like choosing Milli Vanilli's best CD. Sandler plays a failed hockey player who brings his bad temper to the links in order to make enough money to save his Grandma's house. Includes hilarious supporting roles by Carl Weathers and Kevin Nealon.

Tin Cup (1996): Kevin Costner's career is filled with sports flicks ranging from cycling to baseball to golf. In this romantic comedy, Costner re-teams with his Bull Durham director Ron Shelton, playing another down-on-his-luck athlete. This time, he's failed West Texas golfer Roy McAvoy, trying to win the heart of Rene Russo and beat his rival, Don Johnson. It's not as good as *Field of Dreams*. But it's not as bad *Waterworld*, either.

BEST GOLF MOVIE YOU'VE NEVER SEEN

The Greatest Game Ever Played (2005): We love underdogs, especially in this movie where the lead character crashes golf's upper-crust, exclusive circles. This film is based on the true story of the 1913 US Open, where working-class golfer Francis Ouimet, played by then-baby-faced Shia LaBeouf, came out of nowhere to compete for the title.

TOP 3 SOCCER MOVIES EVER

Bend It Like Beckham (2002): No, this has nothing to do with the Brit soccer star's faux-hawk. It's a coming-of-age story about a girl raised by orthodox Sikh parents from India who rebels against her strict upbringing by playing soccer in Britain. Co-starring Keira Knightley just before she became England's "It Girl."

Gracie (2007): This one gets three stars, but you'll need at least four hankies. This tear-jerker is based on a true story about actress Elisabeth

Shue, whose older brother was a high school soccer star who died in a car accident. She channeled her grief by becoming the first girl to make the high school men's soccer team in suburban New Jersey, conquering chauvinism and opening minds along the way.

Victory (1981): Sylvester Stallone, Michael Caine and Pele in a World War II movie. Could there ever be an equally weird casting combination? Maybe something like . . . Harvey Keitel, Richard Simmons and Randy Moss together in a gymnastics film. Whatever, somehow they make it work and this solid movie has our heroes, who are Allied prisoners of war, escaping the Nazis after they play a soccer game against German soldiers.

BEST SOCCER MOVIE YOU'VE NEVER SEEN

TIE: Zidane: A 21st Century Portrait/Ladybugs

Zidane: A 21st Century Portrait (2006): This documentary shows the French soccer star, Zinedine Zidane, playing with typical brilliance as 17 cameras track his every move. The film has a unique flavor, offering no interviews and very little talk—just exciting game action while he played for the Spanish-league team, Real Madrid. While the cameras capture his on-field genius, he also gets ejected for getting into a shoving match late in the contest. (Sound familiar? See 7 for more.)

Ladybugs (1992): We don't know whether to laugh or call the police on this one. We've got Rodney Dangerfield helping his girls' team win by recruiting a young boy and making him dress like a girl. To sum up, we have the "protagonist" breaking the rules and potentially scarring a kid for life. Who's coaching this team, Bill Belichick?

TOP 3 HOCKEY MOVIES

Slapshot (1977): The mother of all sports comedies is this movie about minor league hockey. With a screenplay by Nancy Dowd, the wildly irreverent story is alternately hilarious and violent. It also drops almost as many F-bombs as *Scarface*. Paul Newman stars as the team player/coach. But this movie's scene-stealers are three long-haired triplets who wear nerdy eyeglasses and love to fight. They are forever known among hockey fans as the Hanson Brothers, as played by real-life brothers Jeff, Steve and David Carlson. And once you've seen *Slapshot*, you won't ever again be able to hear Maxine Nightingale's disco classic, *Right Back Where We Started From*, without thinking of this flick.

Miracle (2004): Do you STILL believe in miracles? Yes! (As announcer Al Michaels, who did the play-by-play for the real game this movie is based on, might have said.) Kurt Russell stars as real-life hockey coach Herb Brooks, who incredibly led a ragtag group of American college players to defeat the great Soviet hockey team at the 1980 Winter Olympics before winning the gold medal.

Mystery, Alaska (1999): A look at small-town life in a hockey-crazy Alaskan town chosen to host an exhibition game against the New York Rangers. It stars Burt Reynolds and Russell Crowe—just before he exploded onto the Hollywood scene as a box-office star and respected actor.

BEST HOCKEY MOVIE YOU'VE NEVER SEEN

Youngblood (1986): This cast is straight out of *I Love the '80s*. It stars Rob Lowe, with supporting roles from Patrick Swayze and hockey-loving Canadian Keanu Reeves. Lowe goes to Canada to play hockey and falls in love with Cynthia Gibb. The movie came out just a few years before his sex video temporarily slowed his career. God, it's weird to think there was a time when a sex tape actually *hurt* a celebrity's career.

TOP 3 RACING MOVIES

Talladega Nights (2006): A NASCAR parody with Will Ferrell, Sascha Baron "Borat" Cohen and John C. Reilly. Ferrell is Ricky Bobby, a dim-witted NASCAR driver who loses everything—his wife, riches and No. 1 ranking. Cohen plays a gay, French, espresso-sipping racer. And Reilly is Cal Naughton Jr., Bobby's ex-friend turned rival. Tucked away in all the gags are gentle jabs at auto racing's red-state tendencies.

The Cannonball Run (1981): We know you are sick and tired of Burt Reynolds by now—but this movie is a reminder why he once was the biggest star in the world. Reynolds is at his good-ol'-boy-peak here in this action-comedy about an illegal cross-country race. The supporting cast is like a time capsule, featuring Dom DeLuise, Farrah Fawcett, Jamie Farr and former James Bond actor, Roger Moore.

Days of Thunder (1990): It's not a NASCAR parody, but watching it almost 20 years after its release, it sort of feels like it. Tom Cruise plays Cole Trickle, a racing novice who takes the sport by storm after being mentored by Robert Duvall. Just like *Talladega Nights*, it co-stars Reilly, along with one of Cruise's future wives, Nicole Kidman. Reportedly based on Tim Richmond, a real NASCAR driver who died from AIDS in 1989.

BEST RACING MOVIE YOU'VE NEVER SEEN

Heart Like a Wheel (1983): Long before Danica Patrick and Leilani Münter, there was Shirley Muldowney, a pioneering female drag-racing champ. Bonnie Bedelia gives a great performance, capturing Muldowney's guts and talent in this underrated racing story.

Top 3 Non-Mainstream Sports Movies

Kingpin (1996): Who couldn't love an Amish bowling comedy about a bad-luck loser with one hand? For us, this is one of the best comedies ever, sports or otherwise. The Farrelly Brothers were in their prime with this mean-spirited, cynical movie about bowling and forgiveness—and isn't that what every great film is about? Maybe not. Either way, Bill Murray brings his A-game as despicable phony and bowling legend Ernie "Big Ern" McCracken. Woody Harrelson was never better as the bitter, none-too-smart Roy Munson and Randy Quaid is perfect as Ishmael, the Amish bowler who loves the nightlife.

Ice Castles (1978): More Robby Benson. This time as an ice skater helping a female skater make a comeback after being hurt in a nasty accident. If you love sequins, tight shiny pants and storylines so sickly sweet they may give you diabetes, this is your movie.

The Karate Kid (1984): The *Rocky* of the '80s. Ralph Macchio plays a New Jersey teen getting bullied by karate students after moving to Southern California. But Pat Morita plays an old Japanese man named Mr. Miyagi who helps him fight back. Co-starring Elisabeth Shue, it made Macchio an A-lister for a while and it spawned an ungodly number of sequels, including *The Next Karate Kid,* starring a younger Hilary Swank.

Best Non-mainstream Sports Movie You've Never Seen

The Endless Summer (1964): This surf documentary by Bruce Brown was released at the perfect time, right when The Beach Boys were writing hit songs about the surfing lifestyle (even though only one of the Boys could actually surf). It's also when all those awesomely corny surf movies starring Frankie Avalon and Annette Funicello were released. If you've never seen a surfing movie, *The Endless Summer* is the best place to start. Its real-life footage, with surfers navigating mind-blowing massive waves, is really unforgettable.

Top 5 Sports TV Shows

The White Shadow (1978-81): Bruce Paltrow gave the world three nota- ble things: a) the hospital drama *St. Elsewhere,* b) his daughter Gwyneth and, most impressively, c) *The White Shadow.* Ken Howard plays a white ex-NBA player coaching a multiracial basketball team in inner city Los Angeles. This show took turns being funny, witty, heartwarming and unpredictable—tackling serious issues while never being preachy. It could also be a lot of fun, like when the players sang classic doo-wop songs in the shower. Looking back, there's nothing homoerotic about that. Nope, not at all.

The Baseball Bunch (1982-85): This was the perfect Saturday morning show for kids in the '80s. Low-budget and corny, it starred ex-Reds all- star Johnny Bench and Dodgers ex-skipper Tommy Lasorda hamming it up as The Dugout Wizard, who dispensed baseball tips to kids. Then- superstars like Andre Dawson and old-timers like Ted Williams also would stop by to share their wisdom with viewers.

Friday Night Lights (2006-Present): This solid TV show is based on H.G. Bissinger's best-selling and beloved book about Texas high school football. A 2004 feature film also based on the book starred Billy Bob Thornton and Tim McGraw. As good as the movie was, the TV version might be even better. It features that rare combination of realistic foot- ball action and solid storylines, ably dissecting the issues of small-town America, not to mention the pressures of living in that fishbowl of rural Texas football.

Sports Night (1998-2000): It didn't last too long, but this "dramedy" (God, we hate that word) about a highlight show similar to ESPN's SportsCenter was smart and fresh. It also springboarded the careers of writer Aaron Sorkin, who created the megahit, *The West Wing;* actor Peter Krause, the star of *Six Feet Under;* and Felicity Huffman of *Desper- ate Housewives.*

Coach (1989-97): If it were about hoops coach legend Bobby Knight, it would have been called Psycho Jerk. But thankfully it's only about Hayden Fox, played by Craig T. Nelson, the football coach for the fictional Minnesota State University team. Believe it or not, this sitcom was on TV almost as long as *Seinfeld*, lasting eight seasons and almost 200 episodes.

BEST SPORTS TV SHOW YOU'VE NEVER SEEN

Bay City Blues (1983): Of course you didn't see it. It only lasted one year. But it was a great show about a Minor League baseball team from the guys who brought you *NYPD Blue* and *Hill Street Blues*. The cast included future stars: Sharon Stone, Dennis Franz (of *NYPD Blue*), Michelle Greene (*LA Law*) and Mykelti Williamson (*Forrest Gump, Heat*). Unfortunately, this one-off will best be remembered as a noble TV failure.

TOP 10 ATHLETE ROLES IN MOVIES AND TV

Reggie Jackson, The Naked Gun (1988): We can't forget the baseball slugger walking slowly out of right field in his Angels uniform, brainwashed and muttering, "I must . . . kill . . . the Queen." Looking back, it's still hilarious. The movie also co-stars O.J. Simpson. Looking back, O.J.'s not so hilarious.

Barry Bonds, Beverly Hills 90210 (1994): Long before he got in trouble allegedly fibbing to the Feds, Bonds tried a different type of lying: Acting. He played a fictional ballplayer named Barry Larson, competing against Ian Ziering in a father-son golf tournament. Bonds later appeared in Don Johnson's *Nash Bridges* and *Renegade,* the entertainingly tacky '90s-era Lorenzo Lamas action show. Maybe Bonds will return to acting, now that his baseball career seems be near its end.

Kareem Abdul-Jabbar, Airplane! (1980): This glum and emotionless NBA center's cameo role as an airline pilot pretending hard NOT to be Kareem Abdul-Jabbar was as surprising as it was genuinely funny.

Cam Neely, Dumb & Dumber (1994): The Farrelly Brothers have made a ton of unpredictable, off-color comedies and they always put their favorite Boston sports stars in them. Neely, a Boston Bruin hockey hero, is legendary in the role of Sea Bass, a violent trucker who attacks Jim Carrey in a roadside bathroom.

Roger Clemens, Kingpin (1996): Another Farrelly Brothers comedy where a Boston sports star, this time the ex-Red Sox pitcher, has a cameo. Here, Clemens plays a redneck who punches Amish bowler Randy Quaid for dancing with his girlfriend. Just think how ballistic the ballplayer would have gone if it had been country singer Mindy McCready, Clemens' alleged real-life teenage mistress!

Brett Favre, Something About Mary (1998): Wow, a Farrelly Brothers cameo with a sports star *not* from Boston. In this 1998 megahit, Favre plays himself, the guy who loses Cameron Diaz to Ben Stiller. Now you know why they call it fiction!

Keith Hernandez, Seinfeld (1992): *Seinfeld* featured several New York athletes, but Hernandez's 1992 two-episode appearance undoubtedly was the best. He played Elaine's boyfriend, and Jerry developed a man-crush on him, especially after Hernandez debunked Seinfeld's and Newman's myth that Hernandez once spit on them at a game. After a *JFK*-like investigation, it turned out to be teammate Roger McDowell.

Mark McGwire, Mad About You (1999): What's more surprising in retrospect? McGwire's 70-homer season in 1998, or that this annoying Paul Reiser sitcom lasted seven years? Also surprising is McGwire's decent acting while playing himself.

TIE: Joe Namath, The Brady Bunch (1973) and C.C. & Company (1970): The Jets' Super Bowl hero only cemented his reputation as the coolest athlete in the world when he appeared in this classic *Brady Bunch* episode, bailing little Bobby Brady out of his lie to buddies that Namath was a family friend. As for C.C. & Company, well, *Time* magazine called it a "Z-grade" movie. But any flick that meshes the world of biker gangs, fashion and a football star can't be all bad, can it? Namath plays C.C. Ryder, a motorcycle gang member who turns his back on his biker pals in order to save a fashion journalist (played by Ann-Margret) who gets stuck in the desert.

TIE: Terry Bradshaw, The Cannonball Run (1981) and Mean Joe Greene, Smokey and the Bandit II (1980): This is Erica's perfect storm! The Steelers' Terry Bradshaw playing a good ol' boy named Terry, and Mean Joe Greene playing himself—both times with her personal sports-movie God himself, Burt Reynolds.

TOP SPORTS MOVIES WITH MONKEYS (YES, YOU READ THAT RIGHT.)

Erica and Chris have a friend who has wondered more than once if there is a secret cabal of super-intelligent monkeys working in Hollywood who are responsible for the inexplicably large number of movies about chimps, gorillas and other primates. It's a plausible conspiracy theory, who else would be greenlighting this crap? So, here are some sports movies where, yes, there was plenty of monkeying around. (Ouch.) And it's driving us bananas. (Sorry!) I mean, we're really going ape about it. (ENOUGH!) Okay, here we go . . .

Ed (1996): Isn't this the kind of really bad movie that Matt LeBlanc should be doing *now*, instead of at the height of his *Friends* fame? LeBlanc starred in this "comedy" about a monkey that plays for a professional baseball team. It also fulfills what seemed to be a legal requirement at the time that the late Jack Warden must appear in every sports movie between 1960 and 2000.

MVP: Most Valuable Primate (2000): When you think monkeys, don't you automatically think ice hockey? Of course you don't! Because you have a brain. This kids' movie is about Jack, a monkey that has been taught sign language by a doctor before escaping to Canada where the primate finds he also has natural hockey skills. Let's see, he's bilingual and athletic—that makes him more talented than most real NHL players! It also had a basketball-themed sequel called *Most Vertical Primate*. Get it? Get it?!

Every Which Way But Loose (1978): Clint Eastwood plays a boxer in this B-movie. However, Ruth Gordon steals most scenes in this box-office hit by playing an unforgettably foul-mouthed old lady. And don't forget "Clyde," a beer-drinking orangutan. No, we did not make that up. Eastwood didn't have a hard-living sidekick like this again, until Charlie Sheen co-starred with him in *The Rookie* in 1990.

At this point, you would think we had reached a new low by providing you with our picks of the greatest sports films featuring monkeys, apes and/or orangutans. But if you really want to hear about athletes hitting rock bottom, read on . . .

13 THE DARK SIDE OF SPORTS: *Crime and Drugs and Cheating, Oh My!*

MAYBE IT ALL STARTED WHEN A STAR QUARTERBACK WENT to jail for something sick like abusing dogs. Or maybe it was when a track-and-field star was forced to return her gold medals after spending more time holding a legal brief in court than a baton on the track. Or it might have begun when the number of baseball's steroid cheats reached close to 100 players.

We're not sure exactly when, but some time within the last few years, it officially felt like the sports world had gone mad.

Legendary ex-*New York Times* sportswriter Robert Lipsyte, a reporter since 1959, said he has seen these kinds of scandals before. "There's always been this stuff going on," Lipsyte told us. "But there has never been this much of it, and certainly not at this kind of celebrity level."

By now, you can probably tell that we're crazy about pro sports and our childhood teams. And we're definitely not the gloom-and-doom types—we like our cups always half-full, preferably with a cold, light beer. But even big fans like us have gotten turned off at times by the continuous wave of crime, drugs and cheating.

To give you a quick taste of what we're talking about, here are just a handful of athletes who seem to keep making trouble for themselves and plenty of negative headlines to go along with it.

CRIME

No one more than these three NFL stars have done more to shift, almost single-handedly, the league's once-stellar image from "community-minded" to "criminal justice":

Adam "Pacman" Jones: The gifted young NFL star is on the verge of wasting his world-class talent with a series of arrests and bad life-choices that led NFL commissioner Roger Goodell to suspend him from the league. He's been a hard guy to like, even with his kick-ass nickname.

Chris Henry: The only NFL player to get in more trouble than Pacman. The ex-Cincinnati Bengals wide receiver lost his job in March 2008 after his fifth arrest. Once called a "one-man crime spree," Henry was one of 10 Bengals to get arrested between 2006-07.

O.J. Simpson: If there is a Hall of Fame for Self-Destruction, then O.J. is a first-ballot inductee. It's fitting that this ex-superstar is back in trouble right now. He's not the first once-adored athlete to turn bad and betray the public. But his fall from grace was the furthest and certainly was the most memorable. Many think he got away with murder in 1995. But O.J. was arrested again just a dozen years later when Las Vegas police charged him with participating in an alleged armed robbery to retrieve sports memorabilia that he thought belonged to him.

DRUGS

However, the NFL isn't alone. Check out these two guys in individual sports who have allowed getting high to bring them oh, so, low:

Aaron Fike: In 2007, this young driver in NASCAR's Craftsman Truck Series was arrested while shooting up heroin. Fike since has cleaned himself up and is back in racing, albeit by competing in slightly less prestigious midget-car competitions. Still, he shocked the racing world in early 2008 when he publicly admitted that, before his arrest, he sometimes used heroin the same day that he competitively raced. Yikes. Who knew you could get a DUI on the racetrack?

Tommy Morrison: This former heavyweight champ and sometime actor—he co-starred in *Rocky V*—has had a career that was by turns triumphant and tragic. He once beat boxing-legend George Foreman to win the title belt, but he also spent more than a year in prison on a drugs and weapons rap. He has also tested positive for HIV. Yet even as he's pushing 40, he's still attempting to resurrect his once-flourishing fighting career.

CHEATING

Don't worry, we'll get to Bill Belichick and "Spygate" soon enough in this chapter. But the Patriots haven't been the only blatant cheaters in sports. Here are a couple others:

Carl Edwards: According to NASCAR rules, there is a new scofflaw in town. Edwards' car failed a post-race inspection after winning the UAW-Dodge 400 in Las Vegas in March 2008. NASCAR officials discovered there that his oil-tank lid was missing, which could give drivers an aerodynamic advantage, according to a *Los Angeles Times* article. That's fancy auto talk for, "Dude, you might have cheated." So, Edwards was docked 100 points for the Sprint Cup Series. But his crew chief, Bob Osborne, got it much worse. Officials fined Osborne $100,000, suspended him for six races and put him on probation until the end of the year. But this wasn't "Cousin Carl's" first time for getting in trouble. Come to think of it, Edwards' car failed the post-race inspection after he won the Dover race Chris and Erica went to in late 2007, too! Does this guy *ever* drive with a regulation car?

Floyd Landis: The American cyclist and 2006 Tour de France winner eventually had his title stripped after he tested positive for a high level of synthetic testosterone. Landis spent more than $2 million in trying to clear his name in the doping scandal, all to no avail. His two-year ban from the Tour de France expires in early 2009.

And that's just the short list. At least one big question remains: Do all of these dark moments constitute a trend? Maybe not. Maybe people have been misbehaving like this since the beginning of time, only now the omnipresent news media and Internet are there to capture it all, 24-7.

Then again, as bad as it's been, maybe the sports world has yet to bottom out, too. "We've reached a watershed [level of scandal], although it could still get bigger," Lipsyte cautioned.

PERFORMANCE-ENHANCING DRUGS: JUST SAY NO! . . . RIGHT?

Quick, write down the names of all the athletes we cheered for who were later tainted by a connection to steroids. The number is staggering. Several professional cyclists have tested positive, including Tammy Thomas, who also was convicted of perjury. Rodney Harrison has won Super Bowls with the New England Patriots, but he was later the focus of a steroid investigation that found he was receiving performance-enhancing drugs in the mail from a pharmacy. Olympic gold medalist Marion Jones went from national hero to teary-eyed disgrace, just before getting sentenced to prison for a steroid-related conviction. And baseball, of course, has garnered the most headlines for scandals around performance-enhancing drugs, with superstars Barry Bonds, Mark McGwire and Roger Clemens leading the pack.

The solutions that most experts tout for policing the steroids problem include increased testing and harsher punishment for those who test positive. But some are suggesting an alternative solution, one that would be cheaper and certainly is the path of least resistance: Should sports simply legalize performance-enhancing drugs? The "pro" argument states that we're never going to be able to catch everybody, so let's just make the drugs, which are obviously already widespread, part of the sporting landscape. Hmmm. Interesting take. At the same time, plenty of people disagree with that view. Those opponents cite the social and human health costs that legalizing steroids would bring. The majority of people, from members of Congress to league commissioners to the athletes themselves, say they want more testing because they want to get rid of these scandals once and for all. Don't they?

PUT TO THE TEST: CAN WE TRULY
GET RID OF STEROIDS?

Go to an NFL game and just look around. The fans have spent most of the day loading up on alcohol. Plenty of the cheerleaders have had plastic surgery. The overworked coaches, with their legendary 20-hour work days, undoubtedly are fueled by coffee or Red Bull. The players? History has shown least some of them are on steroids or human growth hormone. Also, odds are the myriad in-stadium advertising includes Viagra or Levitra logos, pushing the pills that enhance the sexual performance of older men. Meanwhile, Major League Baseball takes the Viagra ads one step further, allowing them to appear quite visibly on the wall behind the catcher during TV telecasts. (Maybe there should be a Linda Ellerbee-hosted special on Nickelodeon for parents: *How to Handle the Kids' Inevitable Viagra Question While Watching Sports.*)

When viewers are done watching a ballgame on TV, they can turn the channel to professional wrestling or Ultimate Fighting Championship bouts and see what steroid-induced weightlifting does to a body. Then they can click the remote to MTV and watch hip-hop stars Mary J. Blige, 50 Cent, Wyclef Jean and Timbaland, who have been linked to steroid purchases, according to an *Albany Times Union* article. A probe by Albany County prosecutors in New York found that those musicians allegedly purchased steroids that were sent to a New York doctor from a Florida pharmacy that also served Major League Baseball players and at least one NFL star.

So, it's official. The use of artificial means to "improve" oneself is *everywhere* in our society. Why should it be any different with athletics? In fact, the line between what is acceptable and what is not may be even more easily blurred in sports than other industries. For instance, some medical treatments that allow an injured athlete to play, such as cortisone, are widespread and legal. As a result, the players are given mixed messages. For example, asking your trainer to inject you with deca-durabolin or androstenedione, to name two illegal steroids, is against the rules. But having your trainer inject you with shots of cortisone or other pain-killers is perfectly legal, and is common practice in every sport, even though that drug is the only thing allowing your injured body to play. That's kind of a thin line to walk, isn't it? Also, until a few years ago, amphetamines were reportedly so common in baseball, clubhouses had little bowls full of them placed out in the open for the players to grab whenever they needed an energy boost. In that world, it's easy to see how some ballplayers could rationalize using steroids or HGH, even though just about all of the athletes know that using them is illegal under the league's guidelines and under federal law.

So, it doesn't seem to make much sense to "tell these athletes they are going to be society's last pharmacological virgins," as John Hoberman said, a professor and author who has written extensively on the issue of performance-enhancing drugs. "There is lots of selective indignation here. There is something crazy about this. Hypocrisy is not quite strong enough a word to describe it."

Baseball officials, the media and Congress all agree on one thing. The steroid scandals have set a horrible example for kids who look up to ballplayers. But it's hard to tell children about the evils of drug use when they grow up in a society where plastic surgery is commonplace, and where legal narcotics, from Prozac to Levitra to Ritalin, are widely advertised and overprescribed. "People say to kids they shouldn't do steroids, but then the kids respond, 'What about daddy's Viagra? What about mommy's Botox?'" Hoberman said.

Hoberman, author of *Testosterone Dreams: Rejuvenation, Aphrodisia, Doping,* said the use of steroids and other performance-enhancing drugs is pervasive not just in sports, but many areas of society—some of which might surprise the average American. For example, he has discovered an underground academic doping culture in universities where students are using Ritalin, not for Attention Deficit Disorder, as is often the case, but rather to stay awake while cramming for finals. Also, aging movie stars reportedly are taking steroids as never before. "Actors in Hollywood are doping more than athletes, they're doing what they need to do to stay relevant," said Howard Bryant, an ESPN.com columnist and author of a comprehensive book on baseball's steroid-use epidemic, *Juicing the Game*.

Sylvester Stallone is proving Bryant right. Stallone didn't go into showbiz to become a paid steroids spokesman. But he's halfway there. Still making action movies at age 61, Stallone was caught carrying vials of human growth hormone in Australia in 2007. A few months after facing possession charges, Stallone defended his drug use and praised HGH as if he just had bought stock in it. He told *Time* magazine, "Testosterone to me is so important for a sense of well-being when you get older. Everyone over 40 years old would be wise to investigate it because it increases the quality of your life." He added, ominously: "In 10 years, it will be over the counter." Stallone is no different than now-disgraced Roger Clemens, who received a $28 million-per-year contract at age 44 in 2007. Likewise, the aging actor garnered a lucrative two-picture deal after *Rambo* scored big at the box office in early 2008. Contrary to what his cop characters might say on the big screen, Stallone's drug-related crime seems to have paid quite well.

PERSONAL GROWTH (HORMONE)

Men usually take HGH to make their muscles bigger and firmer, while women are known to use it mostly as an anti-aging tonic. The synthetic drug differs from so-called bodybuilding steroids, such as winstrol or deca-durabolin, in that it delivers defined muscles, while also allowing for greater flexibility and movement. According to *Game of Shadows*, Lance Williams' and Mark Fainaru-Wada's exposé on Barry Bonds' alleged steroid use, Bonds preferred HGH because it allowed him to build his massive physique with less training. Some also believe that HGH improves eyesight, a crucial part of a baseball hitter's success. Another big factor for HGH's popularity among ballplayers is that Major League Baseball does not test for it yet. Despite that, MLB officials and the Players' Association have responded to pressure from Congress by agreeing to tighten their rules on performance-enhancing drugs and to increase the number of steroid tests administered to players.

Outside of sports, steroid use has been alleged in some surprising circles. For example, Blackwater USA is a multimillion-dollar corporation that contracts with professional soldiers to act as security in the Iraq War and other hot spots around the globe. But Iraqi citizens have filed a wrongful-death lawsuit against the private security company, and one of the more intriguing parts of the lawsuit alleges that 25% of Blackwater employees are on steroids, a charge that the company vehemently denied. But if true, it raises a big concern: We don't really want to give steroids to tired, edgy soldiers in the heat of battle, do we? Some would argue that well-paid private soldiers such as Blackwater's employees—much like high-salary athletes—should look for whatever edge they can find, especially because the ramifications are so much larger for them and the military if they lose on the battlefield.

On the flip side, still others will criticize the idea of private soldiers (supporters call them "contractors," while critics call them "mercenaries") wreaking havoc with their hormones and better judgment by popping steroids while handling serious weaponry at the same time. It might be a matter of time before that combo leads to abuses and even law-breaking on the front lines in Iraq and Afghanistan. War is ugly enough by itself. But adding steroids to the fray might make it worse. Much worse.

Meanwhile, an international police operation dealt steroid distributors a blow in September 2007 in a raid that held implications for the world's athletes. Called "Operation Raw Deal," authorities raided steroid laboratories and clinics all over the United States, in parts of Mexico and other foreign countries. Nearly 125 people were arrested and more than 50 labs were closed. The number of people and international locales showed just how widespread steroid use is in society. All those drugs certainly are not just for the small percentage of people who are pro athletes. Perhaps the probe's biggest finding was the depth of China's involvement in steroids' creation and sales. According to reporter Shaun Assael, an ESPN reporter and author of *Steroid Nation*, most of the world's illegal drugs are made with raw materials in dozens of factories in China, home of the 2008 Summer Olympics.

GOOD COP, BAD COP

Back at home, there are growing steroid-related problems similar to the Blackwater case that will only grow more urgent if it's not addressed. Hoberman estimated that at least 25,000 police officers nationwide are on steroids. Wait. Police officers are juicing like they're Jose Canseco with a badge? . . . Really? Yeah, really. The cops feel like they have to bulk up to go head-to-head with criminals, Hoberman explained. However, just as with Blackwater, the possibility is frighteningly strong that armed police officers in high-stress jobs may do serious wrongs while experiencing 'roid rages. The New York Police Department recently found that nearly 30 of its officers were identified on a client list at a Brooklyn pharmacy that was targeted in a Federal steroid probe, according to *The New York Daily News*. That news came on top of the 2007 report that six NYPD officers were caught buying steroids and tested positive for it.

The potential for problems here is obvious. Namely, the next time there is an egregious police abuse accusation, such as the 1999 case when a New York officer was convicted of brutally assaulting Haitian immigrant Abner Louima with a broom stick, can allegations of 'roid rages—and a multimillion-dollar lawsuit—be far behind? The issue may present still other problems, especially considering that police officers are on the front lines in the government's long-running war on drugs. "Can you wage war on drugs by using cops who are using those drugs?" Hoberman wonders. "Again, we're back to the selective indignation problem. Cops are hard on some drugs, like cocaine and marijuana. But when they're asked to crack down on their own officers using these drugs, they're not interested."

Brian McNamee is a former New York City police officer now caught on the other side of the law. He's in trouble for the work he did as a personal trainer with Major League ballplayers, and he testified under oath that he injected Roger Clemens and Andy Pettitte with HGH while all three of them were employed by the Yankees. McNamee's admission could be found in the Mitchell Report, the probe led by former Maine Senator George Mitchell. Commissioner Bud Selig had asked Mitchell, a Red Sox executive closely associated to the team's owners, to investigate the use of steroids and performance-enhancing drugs within baseball. Major League Baseball paid $20 million for the 409-page report. Released in December 2007, the document listed around 90 players, including Clemens and Pettitte.

Pettitte quickly admitted that McNamee was telling the truth, though he stipulated that he used HGH only "two days" out of his life when he had an elbow injury in 2002. Pettitte later amended that to include a third time in 2004, when HGH had been delivered to him by his father, who had been using the stuff to treat a heart condition.

Clemens, in contrast, came out swinging like a guy on a, well, 'roid rage. Clemens is the guy who angrily threw a broken bat at Mike Piazza during the 2000 World Series, and got himself kicked out of a 1990 playoff game for generally acting like a psycho, screaming at the home-plate ump until he got ejected. After the Mitchell Report listed Clemens, he vehemently denied that he had ever taken any performance-enhancing drugs. He also denied all of McNamee's claims in a tersely written statement, followed by an edgy *60 Minutes* interview and a fiery news conference with reporters. Congress asked all three of them—Pettitte, Clemens and McNamee—and others to testify. Pettitte's testimony matched McNamee's version of events, rather than the version held by Pettitte's buddy, Clemens—a split that strained the teammates' longtime friendship, Pettitte later said.

Meanwhile, Clemens and McNamee continued their he-said-he-said game at a testy televised session in front of a Congressional committee in February 2008. The session quickly, and strangely, divided along partisan lines. The Republicans on the committee favored Clemens, while the Democrats backed McNamee. Some of the details that emerged were bizarre, like Clemens' admission that his wife Debbie used HGH before she posed in a bikini for a magazine photo shoot.

Then things got really ugly. Clemens had filed a defamation lawsuit against McNamee, mentioning that McNamee was a suspect, but was never arrested, in an alleged rape case in 2001. The Yankees reportedly fired McNamee after the incident. But then it was Clemens' turn to have his reputation sullied. Reports from the New York tabloids said that Clemens allegedly cheated on his wife with several women, including a stripper, an ex-wife of troubled golfer John Daly, and country singer Mindy McCready when she was just 15 years old.

And it might get even worse for Clemens. As we went to press, federal authorities were considering charging him for perjury.

Other sports legends snagged in the authorities' net, such as Olympic gold medalist Marion Jones and San Francisco Giants slugger Barry Bonds, have fared much worse. They were customers of the Bay Area Laboratory Cooperative, a company that made and sold cutting-edge performance-enhancing drugs to star athletes. But when the federal government raided BALCO's offices, located just south of San Francisco, the jig was up. BALCO founder Victor Conte served four months in prison for his steroid sales and money laundering convictions. Jones eventually went to jail for six months for lying to federal investigators about her involvement with the BALCO lab. Meanwhile, Bonds was indicted for perjury and obstruction of justice. Just as when he played, Bonds is a polarizing figure. Some cheered the indictment, accusing Bonds of practically daring the feds to indict him while he passed Henry Aaron's home-run record. Still others have criticized the government for going out of their way to "get" Bonds.

Sportswriter Dave Zirin is one of these critics. "You had the US Attorney General, John Ashcroft, personally announcing an investigation into a Bay Area steroids lab—that's insane when you think about the other crimes going on in this country that they could be focusing on," Zirin told us.

On the other hand, anti-steroid activists say a strong message has to be sent or kids will imitate their sports heroes and juice up just to get the same results. In fact, that cat is already out of the bag, said Dr. Denise Garibaldi. As many as five million minors in America have used performance-enhancing drugs, she said. Which is a dangerous proposition for families living with these users, given that the drugs' side effects may trigger irrational rages, mood swings, further drug use and severe bouts of major depression. As if hormonal teens aren't already moody enough. Other side effects due to high steroid dosages may include harmful changes to cholesterol and blood pressure levels, heart disease, liver damage and, for men, shrinkage of the testicles. For women, they may increase body hair and decrease menstrual cycles. Whoa, talk about a deal with the devil!

Garibaldi and her husband Ray know quite well about steroids' devastating effects on a young life. Their son, Rob Garibaldi, once a promising young ballplayer at USC, killed himself at the age of 24. Just a few years earlier, such a development would have been unthinkable to anyone who knew Rob, his family said. He was the strong, silent type, and a hard-working overachiever all throughout his youth. He earned top grades by simply studying longer than most kids and, despite his smallish body-type, he was a great baseball player. He never drank alcohol or tried recreational drugs because he wanted to stay focused on playing baseball, his mother said. And it worked. He was a prep All-American from Petaluma, California. Having grown up in NoCal, he idolized Bonds and the Oakland A's Bash Brothers, Jose Canseco and Mark McGwire. In time, all three superstars, of course, would be implicated in steroid use. After taking a year off of school, Rob excelled at Santa Rosa Junior College in 1999, when the New York Yankees drafted him. "At that time, it was so exciting," Garibaldi recalls. But even then the Yankees repeated to Rob—then just 5-feet 11-inches tall and weighing 150 pounds—what he often heard: Get bigger. The Yankees urged him to attend USC, which was offering a scholarship, to give him time to bulk up.

What Rob's parents didn't know was that he had already started using steroids, having made his first purchase in Tijuana with buddies in the late '90s. "They bought the steroids and were back [over the border] within an hour," Garibaldi said. This is the part of performance-enhancing drugs that is very dangerous, but rarely talked about, Garibaldi said. The kind of drugs that middle-class kids will buy are cheaper and easier to get; they also are low quality and will do the most long-term damage to users. Wealthy ballplayers, in contrast, will get the best that money can buy. "The professionals have the advantage of affording quality substances," she added. "What's coming out of Mexico are veterinary steroids, not the designer stuff."

At USC, Rob's drug use only increased, negatively affecting his personality enough that, after a while, his parents barely recognized him. They first noticed the toll the drugs were taking on him when they came to visit and saw his bedroom had been torn apart. He had done it himself during a steroid-fueled rage. "Everybody was using steroids there," Garibaldi said. "I think [the coaches] were aware." Soon, Rob's personal issues and frequent 'roid rages started to overcome him. He had been suffering from depression, and at one point, he even physically attacked his father when he confronted his son about his drug use. He was spiraling downward and his loved ones felt increasingly helpless. Even an intervention didn't sink in with Rob. Finally, one day in October 2002, he took his own life with a gunshot.

Since then, the Garibaldis have tried to channel their grief by raising awareness about the issue, giving public speeches and doing interviews. They took Rob's story to the nation's capital in 2005, where they testified at a watershed Congressional hearing on steroids in sports.

Unfortunately, there are plenty of other families who have suffered the same type of tragedy. Efrain Marrero, another Northern California teen who played baseball, killed himself after taking steroids. He was just 19. The same was true for Tyler Hooton, a 17-year-old suicide victim from Texas. Since speaking out, sometimes parents, who have children going through the same issues that Rob did, will track down Denise Garibaldi and phone her for advice, she said.

WHAT TO DO?

California politicians also have turned to the Garibaldis for solutions to the steroid problem. They have even worked together on legislation that would require testing for high school athletes. That is one potential answer. What are some of the others? Can the problem ever be solved? The debate is between those who take a zero-tolerance approach and those who are in favor of legalizing steroids and HGH. On one side, the majority of people—from fans to league commissioners to the media— seem to believe that using performance-enhancing drugs is cheating and should be stopped. On the other side, there are the anti-prohibitionists, who argue that adults in a free society should be allowed to use whatever drugs they want.

Marvin Miller, the well-respected founder of baseball's Players' Association, is one who is against drug-testing athletes for steroids. Citing the US Constitution and the Bill of Rights, he likens testing to a violation of American search and seizure laws, which state that authorities must produce evidence to a judge to obtain a warrant to search people or their property. "I have no problem with that procedure," said Miller, now in his early-90s. "But mandatory testing of anybody and everybody in that company or industry without showing any probable cause or guilt? That, I object to. That is anti-people. It's not allowed by government and it should not be allowed by a private employer."

Drug-testing proponents argue that the hands-off approach of the '90s allowed drug use to eventually trickle down to teens. They also believe it's hard to ignore steroids' negative health effects on the human body, given the ugly statistics tied to professional wrestling. Since 1997, dozens of pro wrestlers age 45 and younger have died from health problems connected with steroids and other illegal drugs, according to a *USA Today* study. Just look at the sad case of Chris Benoit, a former WWE professional wrestler who killed his wife and their 7-year-old son before taking his own life. Autopsy results revealed that Benoit had steroids in his body when he died in 2007, though authorities said they did not believe that a 'roid rage contributed to the double-homicide and suicide. Interesting.

Given that they seem so widespread in society, can we truly get rid sports of steroids at this stage of the game? Hoberman says it is possible to reduce the number of users by doing more testing and by trying to persuade and educate the public. Also, more users are getting caught these days—that's the good news. However, "the assumption that we have a fighting chance to produce a drug-free sports culture is fading away," Hoberman said. "The demand for [athletic] performance is accompanied by the demand for performance-enhancers. Given the money, the system of incentives, the athletes' ambitions and the ethics-free zone in which many athletes exist, I don't know how you're fully going to get rid of them."

When it comes to steroid testing, count us more on the side of the prohibitionists. We may never totally eradicate them; authorities are always playing catch-up, especially considering that the drugs are constantly evolving and sometimes they are hard to detect. But in our opinion, each sports league has to try, if only to maintain at least a semblance of their integrity. "I know people who take that Libertarian attitude of, 'May the best team with the better drugs win,'" writer Howard Bryant said. "For me, that's not acceptable because I think there is too much money at stake, and too much hypocrisy."

BASEBALL'S GOOD BAD BOY

Of course, not every drug is a performance-enhancer, and not every substance-abuser is a bad guy. Want proof? Look no further than one of our favorite baseball players ever.

ACID WIT: THE LEGEND OF DOCK ELLIS

It's a warm sunny Southern California day, perfect for relaxing. But Dock Ellis is agitated. He is trying to quiet his barking dog at his home so he can talk on the phone and, at the same time, keep his neighbors from complaining more than they already have about the pet. There is more than a little irony here. The Pittsburgh Pirates pitcher prided himself on always being ready to "buy a wolf ticket"—that is, he was always ready to compete against opponents who talked trash and challenged him and his teammates. But now his neighbors have bought some "wolf tickets" of their own, complaining about the dog's noise out on the golf course on which Dock's home sits. "I'm going to fight them on this," he vows feistily.

It's perfect in a way. Almost 30 years after Dock finished one of baseball's most controversial careers, even when he's just trying to live a quiet normal life, he's still getting accused of making too much noise. It was a frequent complaint by media, management and even some fans when he played Major League Baseball. He was an outspoken African-American athlete at a time when few baseball players spoke up about anything. Despite his controversies, he had an All-Star career that spanned 12 seasons, and featured a solid record of 138-119 with an ERA of 3.46. He played for a total of five teams, but he's best known for his early days with the Pittsburgh Pirates.

Scratch that, he's best known for a foggy night in San Diego when he threw a no-hitter. On LSD. It's no urban legend, Dock says, who is more than eager to talk about it. In fact, when we bring up the infamous game, Dock immediately replies in a cheerful, almost excited voice: "Oh, you mean, the acid no-hitter?"

After just a few minutes talking with the guy by telephone, one thing comes shining through. He will answer absolutely any question and discuss any topic, happily and intelligently. There is no shame in his game, not with his personal life, not about his off-field fights with management, not with his past substance abuse. "The acid no-hitter?" he repeats, savoring the memory of the June 12, 1970, game. Um, yes, Dock, the acid no-hitter.

"I got mixed up on which day I was pitching because of the acid," he explains. "I woke up at my friend's girlfriend's house and she said, 'You're pitching today.' I said, 'No, I'm pitching tomorrow.' And she said, 'I'm reading the newspaper and it says you're pitching today.' And I said, 'You need to take me to the airport.'"

So Dock took the short flight from Los Angeles to San Diego and got to the clubhouse on time. Barely. He followed his pre-game ritual of popping an amphetamine and—wait, what? It's true. Dock says he would pop an "upper" before every game. "It gave me energy, and [it helped me with] dealing with the fear—fear of failure, fear of success," he adds.

Reports of the no-hitter in subsequent years say that he took an amphetamine to level off the effects of the acid. Not true, he says today. It was just his pre-game routine. Part of the story's legend is that he asked his catcher, Jerry May, to put day-glo strips on his fingers so that Dock, still feeling the influence of LSD, could focus better on the catcher signs. That's also not true. He says he asked May do that merely because it was a misty night in San Diego and he just was having trouble seeing his catcher's fingers. "No one knew about the condition I was in, no one on the team," he recalls. "Well, they might have known something was wrong with me probably 'cause my faced looked wilder than normal. If you see pictures of me from that night you can tell something is wrong."

But his pitching was just right. Dock was grooving so well on the mound it didn't even matter that rookie teammate Dave Cash broke the cardinal rule of baseball dugouts by mentioning the no-hitter to Dock in-between innings. His pitching was too strong to be affected by the superstition. And when the game was over, he wasn't shy with the media about what happened or how he did it.

"I said to some [reporters], 'Ain't this a bitch! A f-cking no-hitter on acid!' I said it out loud," Dock says. What did the reporters do? "They just laughed." Dock himself didn't publicly reveal his notorious anti-performance enhancer until a 1984 interview.

He always seemed to be in the thick of controversy during his playing days. Sometimes it was through bad luck, but more often due to his habit of never backing down from a confrontation. That habit earned him a lot of respect—and a lot of trouble. "I was like Mr. Magoo, just walking around and running into things," he says, chuckling. "I crossed all the lines there were to cross: racial lines, socioeconomic lines. I hung out with the poor and the wealthy, it didn't make a difference to me."

Some of his incidents are part of baseball legend. Like the time in 1974 that he hit the first three Cincinnati Reds batters he faced. He plunked Joe Morgan, Pete Rose and Dan Driessen, and then walked the fourth, Tony Perez. Finally, when he almost hit Johnny Bench with two more pitches, his manager Danny Murtaugh mercifully removed him. Dock admitted he did it on purpose. Why?

"They beat us in the playoffs in '72, and when I spent the night in Cincinnati, I saw what the Cincinnati press was saying about the Pirates—that we played dumb, that we were dumb players," he said, harboring still a hint of anger at the 36-year-old memory. It infuriated him at the time and, like a mafia don, Dock never forgot the slight. A year-and-a-half later, he wanted revenge.

"I let it be known to my teammates that they were calling us dumb players, and I told them, 'I'm gonna hit their ass,'" he said. He also was egged on by teammate Kurt Bevacqua, who bet him an expensive bottle of wine that he wouldn't do it. Abusing alcohol and drugs was as much a part of Dock's daily routine as putting on cleats and a mitt. But that's in the past. The 62-year-old has been sober since 1980, and he worked for years as a substance-abuse counselor before recently retiring. He lives with his wife of 16 years, Hjordis ("That was David Niven's wife's name, too," Dock says, an out-of-left-field reference to the late British actor.). They live in a home located in what he calls "the bellybutton of California"—midway between Los Angeles and Las Vegas. It seems like a nice, quiet life. Which is quite the opposite of his playing days, of course.

There was that time in 1976, for example, when he plunked Reggie Jackson in the face with a fastball. That season, Jackson played for Baltimore and Dock was on the New York Yankees. The longstanding rumor is that he hit Jackson as revenge for the memorable, towering home run that Jackson hit off of him in the 1971 All-Star Game.

"Nah, that wasn't it," Dock says. "It's 'cause he was talking shit. [Orioles shortstop Mark] Belanger had come up to the plate. I was exchanging balls with the ump, and one of my throws came close to Belanger. They thought I was trying to hit him. So Reggie came up to the plate and said, 'Why don't you try to hit a big motherf-cker like me?' Reggie was talking shit. He was selling a wolf ticket. And I bought it. I bought a lot of wolf tickets in my time. If it cramped my style, yeah, I was buying. I was there for the shit. In baseball, whatever went down, I was ready."

So Jackson took a fastball to the face, but he was okay. The incident did nothing to diminish Dock's reputation as one of the most intimidating hurlers in baseball. But the next year in Spring Training, Dock met his new Yankees teammate, Reggie Jackson. Tension? "Nah, Reggie was cool. We got it straight. I told him, if any pitcher comes near you, I'll hit everybody in their f-cking lineup."

Another story, detailed in author Donald Hall's entertaining book, *Dock Ellis in the Country of Baseball,* involved a Riverfront Stadium security guard in Cincinnati who denied Dock entrance to the stadium. The guard hassled him because he lacked proper I.D. and then maced him when Dock objected, even though he was with fellow Pirates stars, like Willie Stargell. The security guard also said Dock had a half-empty bottle of wine, a charge that even the Pirates front office didn't believe.

You're probably starting to see the pattern here. Dock is also the first baseball player—and the last—to get in trouble for wearing hair-curlers on the field. This was 1973, but he was ahead of his time in terms of fashion and hair style. In recent years, even tough-guy Texan Roger Clemens has frosted his hair with different colors. Dock was messing around with different styles, too, only this was 35 years ago, when virtually nobody did. Commissioner Bowie Kuhn ordered Dock to stop wearing the curlers. The commissioner was prompted by complaints from Pirates management, Dock says today. The Pirates first told Dock to take out the curlers, but his response was, shall we say . . . *uncooperative.*

"I told them to kiss my ass," he said. So Kuhn sent out a form letter to all the teams saying that they had to conform to the uniform guidelines. Dock asked reporters why Kuhn didn't do the same thing to Joe Pepitone of the Yankees when he wore a long hairpiece under his ballcap. Looking back, Dock sees a racial element to the crackdown. "They didn't understand that that's what the young blacks were doing," he says. "They had no idea about what young blacks were doing, or even that they had a brain." He pauses and then adds, "Motherf-ckers."

Dock grew up in Los Angeles, coming of age in the early '60s. Even though it was a far cry from the South, he had more than his share of racially-charged fistfights growing up. It wasn't totally uncommon for him to hear the "n"-word on SoCal playgrounds if he strayed too far from his middle-class black neighborhood. When he played for Minor League teams in the South in the mid-1960s, many cities still had Jim Crow laws and forced segregation. Dock, the hot-tempered kid from California, didn't exactly abide by those ugly rules.

"They sent me to the South in '65 and it was a trip 'cause I was seeing all this stuff that I'd read and heard about but really couldn't believe," he said, remembering that there were signs that said "White" and "Black" for different water faucets. "I'd drink out of the white one. I didn't know it at the time but the coaches wouldn't let the team bus stop to eat in certain towns because they knew I would go off [in protest of the segregation]."

His alcohol and drug use, which he started as a teenager, got heavier at that time. "I self-medicated just to get through it all," he says. And Dock continued, both in using the recreational drugs and in excelling on the field. He got to the big leagues with Pittsburgh in 1968 at the tender age of 23, and had some outstanding seasons, with his best coming in 1971. He went 19-9 and the Pirates won the World Series that year with a young Willie Stargell and an aging Roberto Clemente leading them on the field. All of the notorious stories about his colorful side probably overshadow the fact that Dock was a great Major League pitcher. True to form, Dock isn't sure if he agrees. "I was a good pitcher when I was down on earth, but most of the time I was in outer space," he says. Steroids were just beginning to become readily available to ballplayers as his career was ending, but they really weren't Dock's style. "I didn't do any because they couldn't get me high," he says.

Looking back on the wild times in his youth, would he do anything differently? "I have no regrets," he says. Or does he think he might be in the Hall of Fame if he had taken better care of himself? To that, he answers with an uncharacteristically short response. "I don't know," he replies, pausing briefly. "You never know."

If his accomplishments have been overshadowed, that's too bad. Because there is way more to the guy than just his wild off-field antics and eyebrow-raising quotes.

Being a baseball rebel who stood on the outside looking in is a role that the legendary Jackie Robinson warned him about. The duo formed a kinship after Dock once introduced himself to the baseball pioneer at the Apollo Theater in Harlem. Before his death in 1972, Robinson started writing the young pitcher notes of encouragement and advice. "He always let me know that he understood what I stood for," Dock recalls. "He'd say, 'Although you're fighting for [other ballplayers], don't rely on them to come to your aid as far as anything in baseball is concerned.'" Robinson also bluntly told him to forget ever working in baseball after he retired. "He'd say, 'It's because you talk too much,'" Dock recalls, adding a hearty laugh. Today, he says he wouldn't mind working for a baseball team, but there have been scant offers. Does he feel that Robinson's prediction was right, that he's been blackballed for being so outspoken over the years? "Oh, yeah," he replies. "They know I can teach the game."

In the baseball movie, *The Natural*, the story's fictional hero Roy Hobbs (played by Robert Redford) laments how there are some mistakes that a person never stops paying for. Dock, a different kind of baseball man from a different time, can relate. He was diagnosed recently as having cirrhosis of the liver. He says that staying sober since 1980 wasn't enough to offset the years of serious alcohol abuse before then. But he seems to be approaching his condition with a positive attitude. "I cheated the game to have lasted this long," he says. "If I didn't quit drinking back then, I would have been gone in five years."

Today, he clearly is still respected by the athletes for whom he paved the way. As we talk, four-time 20-game winning pitcher Dave Stewart telephones to check in and say hi to Dock—one great African-American pitcher from a younger generation paying respect to another. Meanwhile, conversation turns back to his neighbors and how he was fined $61 for his barking dog. Where he used to fight the racial slurs on Southern California playgrounds or go toe-to-toe with baseball's power structure, now he's doing battle on the most suburban of fronts. A loud dog by a lush golf course is about as benign a squabble as a guy can get into. But a "wolf ticket" is a "wolf ticket" and he damn sure is still buying 'em. What else is a born rebel supposed to do?

As our conversation winds down, Dock again mentions his nosy neighbors, comparing them to the old fights of his ballplaying days. "It's like it's the same old bullshit, just older people," he says, half-exasperated and half-chuckling. Dock takes a long pause as if he's searching for the perfect word to explain himself. Finally, he pierces the silence.

"Mother . . . f-ckers."

TRICKS OR CHEATS

If we write one more sentence about drugs in this chapter, we're going to get a contact high. So, we'll stop right now on that subject. Instead, we're going to conclude with stories about three different leagues that are trying to navigate their way through the fallout from three very different cheating scandals. For doing something so wrong, each sport's (alleged) co-conspirators still did something very right: They shocked us—which, in this cynical age, we thought was no longer possible. Here they are:

MATCH (SHAVING) POINT: TENNIS VS. CONTROVERSY

Remarkably, one scandal-marred professional league has enough serious problems that it may leapfrog all the others, in terms of rampant wrongdoing and bad publicity: Professional tennis. Really? It's true. The sport known for its rules on decorum and dress between the white lines has gotten fairly ugly outside of them. What other league has its most famous spokesman openly worrying that the Russian Mafia may be infiltrating the ranks and threatening top players to throw games? What game suspended five players in less than half a year for betting? What sport had one of its best players declaring that his food was intentionally poisoned before a big match? The correct answers would be a) tennis, b) tennis and c) tennis.

Gambling-fueled suspicions about players throwing matches have become almost commonplace. The most noteworthy potential scandal involves Russian star Nikolay Davydenko, a top-five player. The Association of Tennis Professionals has investigated his questionable 2007 loss to Martin Vassallo Arguello. Davydenko lost the match (he quit with an injury in the third set) after winning the first set, just as bets started pouring in. Authorities have asked, why would so many bets be placed on an underdog, especially after he lost the first set? Betting irregularities also trailed a suspicious 2003 loss involving Russian player Yevgeny Kafelnikov, who lost to an also-ran on a losing streak. Meanwhile, several tennis players recently have admitted that they were approached by people to fix matches, or they know of others who were approached.

All of this led retired legend John McEnroe to publicly express fear that the Russian Mafia could be involved in professional tennis. "That's potentially pretty dark and scary. I think that's the side that people aren't really looking at with these match-fixing stories," McEnroe told Britain's *The Daily Telegraph* newspaper. "With a high-ranked guy like Davydenko, he's making so much money to begin with that he'd be risking so much to do it. . . . It would make more sense if they are being threatened in some way and that's why they're doing it."

This isn't to say that tennis is going to go the way of roller derby. It is still going strong with star players. Top-ranked player Roger Federer is dominant, as is his top rival, second-ranked Rafael Nadal. And don't forget Novak Djokovic, whose easy-going charisma matches his excellent No. 3 ranking.

Still, there have been plenty of recent scandals that have seriously stained the sport. Martina Hingis abruptly retired in November 2007 after she tested positive for cocaine at Wimbledon earlier in the year. Once nicknamed "The Swiss Miss," the former No. 1-ranked player angrily denied ever taking drugs at a tearful press conference, and she left without taking questions. In early 2008, Federico Luzzi of Italy was fined $50,000 and suspended for more than six months for betting 273 times on tennis matches within a three-year period. Tennis authorities found that he once bet on himself to win a match, according to *Tennis Week* magazine. Luzzi, ranked 139th in the world at the time, was the fifth Italian tennis pro to be punished for gambling charges within a four-month period.

But the most bizarre incident occurred when Germany's Tommy Haas claimed he was intentionally poisoned when Germany lost to Russia in a Davis Cup semifinal held September 2007 in Moscow. Haas fell ill there and his replacement lost the match. But German teammate Alexander Waske told the German tabloid *Bild* that he spoke to an unnamed Russian man with connections to sports who claimed that

Haas had been poisoned. Waske did not reveal his source's identity. The Russian Tennis Federation said that Haas' claim was laughable, but the International Tennis Federation said it would investigate. Haas later flew to the United States for tests, which showed no traces of poison at all. Haas dropped the issue, but he didn't say his claim was entirely baseless, either. He instead pointed to the fact that two months had elapsed between his illness and the testing. "It's no longer an issue," he said in a statement released by the German Tennis Federation. "The tests gave no results. It was too far in the past."

The sport's leaders hope the same soon will be said about tennis scandals.

BLOWN WHISTLE: THE NBA REF WHO COULDN'T SEE STRAIGHT

One moment, Tim Donaghy was reffing an NBA game. The next moment he was in a *Sopranos* episode, keeping company with gamblers claiming to have ties to organized crime. Only this wasn't fiction. It was all too real. Especially for NBA commissioner David Stern, who in the summer of 2007 had to deal with this sad reality: Federal authorities accused one of his referees of point-shaving and betting on basketball games in which he reffed. That ref was Donaghy. Soon, reporters were asking if any other refs were involved. The whole affair was shaping up to be a huge debacle for the NBA.

Shortly after the story broke, Donaghy pleaded guilty to the charges, also admitting that he gave insider information to gamblers James Battista and Thomas Martino, who used it to bet on NBA games. Battista and Martino, who went to high school with Donaghy, paid the ref up to $5,000 for each successful wager. Both gamblers were convicted, with Battista facing 10 to 16 months in prison, and Martino facing 12 to 18 months. Later, prosecutors also accused Donaghy of betting on more than 100 games that he worked as a referee. His sentencing was delayed several times in early 2008, but he was facing as much as 25 years behind bars.

"How much are they bribing you?!" That's a familiar jeer from sarcastic fans heckling referees who've made a bad call. It's intended usually for a dark laugh more than anything else. But once the Donaghy scandal broke, the joke suddenly wasn't so funny. Now it was an ugly but fair question that threatened the integrity of the entire NBA itself. Faced with the biggest crisis in his career as NBA commissioner, Stern had no choice but to spend the off-season in full damage-control mode. He interviewed each NBA referee and he found a combination of bad and good news. The bad news was that each referee had broken the league's strict rules that banned any and all gambling. The good news was that none of them bet on NBA games or used a legal sports book or an illegal bookie. Instead, their gambling was mostly confined to harmless casino visits or card games with friends that most of us play, according to Stern. So, the NBA commish didn't punish the other refs. Instead, he relaxed the rules and made them more realistic.

"Our ban on gambling . . . is too absolute, too harsh and was not particularly well-enforced over the years," Stern said before the 2007-08 season, according to an ESPN.com article. "It's too easy to issue rules that are . . . violated by $5 Nassau [a golf-related bet], sitting at a poker table [or] buying a lottery ticket."

But as his case wound down in May 2008, Donaghy dropped another bombshell on investigators. He claimed that NBA referees, coaches and players sometimes worked together in ways that "affected the outcome of games."

Stern denied Donaghy's accusations. Illustrating why he is sports' shrewdest commissioner, Stern maintained his consistent response to the controversy, minimizing bad publicity in the face of a league-threatening crisis. Donaghy and his shady pals are gone and Stern essentially has said, "Nothing to see here anymore, folks. Move along now." But the fact remains that the next time we see a horrible call by a referee, we'll be hard-pressed not to think of Tim Donaghy and wonder if there are any others just like him.

Signs, Lies and Videotape:
The Patriots' Film Gets Exposed

"Spygate" might have prematurely ended the New England Patriots dynasty, but it incredibly has involved so much more: Lawsuits from opposing players. A former intern-turned-golf-pro threatening to dish even more dirt. And pressure from a powerful Congressman who has pushed the NFL to investigate more. All plenty-reason why the controversy simply won't go away—even though Patriots officials and the NFL surely wish it would.

It all started during the NFL's first weekend of the 2007 season, when the Patriots were caught spying on the New York Jets during a blowout win. They secretly used a video camera to tape the Jets coaches' defensive signals so that Patriots coach Bill Belichick and his staff could predict what plays were coming later in the game, or later in the season—as the Pats and Jets play each other twice a year, every year. It soon was revealed that the Patriots had been illegally videotaping several opponents for years, and NFL commissioner Roger Goodell quickly fined Belichick personally $250,000, and the New England franchise another $500,000. He then took away the team's 2008 original first-round draft choice, though the Patriots still owned the 49ers' more valuable first-round pick.

Since the controversy started, Belichick has claimed in his defense that he didn't know that videotaping opponents was cheating. But it was indeed illegal.

In the meantime, the Jets likely had more than an inkling they were being spied on—their head coach, Eric Mangini, is a former Patriots assistant coach and Belichick protégé. This prompted angry Patriots fans to argue: How can Mangini make the spying accusation when he benefited from the cheating while with the Pats, only to turn snitch once he was on another team? Good point. But here are some other fair questions bound to annoy New England fans: Did the Patriots spy during any of their three Super Bowl victories in 2002, 2004 or 2005? Or in any other playoff games? And did any of the Patriots players, like superstar quarterback Tom Brady, know about the spying, which would make them accomplices?

The Patriots at first never publicly answered those questions, in part because Goodell never asked them to. Sure, Belichick told Goodell that he had been taping opponents during games since he took over as Patriots coach in 2000. And the Patriots handed over to the NFL notebooks and videotapes from their 2006 season and the 2007 preseason. However, Goodell then promptly, and incredibly, ordered that evidence be completely destroyed. If he was trying to make the bad publicity go away, it backfired, big time. Nagging issues remained, including questions about whether New England taped opponents while winning each of its Super Bowl titles by just three points each time. Did they cheat in those games? For a while, no one knew. As a result, long after the 2007 season ended, the scandal's black cloud lingered.

The Patriots themselves also gave the controversy legs. They often humiliated opponents by running up the score, amassing a perfect 16-0 record during the 2007 regular season. But they somehow still looked miserable doing it. Brady, once an amiable and likable leader, screamed at referees and talked trash to defenders at the slightest provocation. And Belichick's mumbling and surly interactions with the press seemed like he was teaching a yearlong seminar titled, "How to Be an Arrogant Jerk in 10 Words or Less." Over the course of the season, the turned-off public and media started wanting to believe they had cheated. Even so, it looked like the controversy finally had been put to rest as the Patriots got ready to play the New York Giants in Super Bowl XLII.

Enter Matt Walsh, who worked for New England from 1996-2002. Just a few days before the Super Bowl, Walsh's name was connected to a *Boston Herald* story that claimed Patriots coaches asked Walsh in 2002 to videotape the St. Louis Rams walk-through practice shortly before they played New England in Super Bowl XXXVI. The article created a huge stir, not to mention a massive distraction for the team before the biggest game of the season. Belichick and Patriots general manager

Scott Pioli vehemently denied the accusations. But few people outside of New England believed them.

While the Patriots front office has taken a lot of heat, a *Boston Globe* investigation revealed that Walsh is no saint, either. The newspaper found, among other things, that the Patriots fired Walsh in 2002 after the team learned he secretly recorded a work-related conversation with Pioli.

Regardless of Walsh's reputation, the fallout from the story just got worse for the franchise. Former Rams player Willie Gary and some fans filed separate lawsuits against the Patriots. Gary later dropped the case. But Kurt Warner, the losing Rams quarterback from that Super Bowl, said he wanted the league to investigate Walsh's charges.

Warner wasn't the only one. The case drew serious interest from Sen. Arlen Specter, a powerful Republican congressman from Pennsylvania—the home state of the Pittsburgh Steelers (whom the Pats upset in 2002 on their run to win Super Bowl XXXVI) and the Philadelphia Eagles (whom the Pats beat in Super Bowl XXXIX in 2005). Specter was on an honest quest for the truth, or shamelessly trolling for votes, depending on your point of view. Either way, he has criticized the commish for his handling of the case, especially for destroying the evidence. Specter also used his considerable influence to pressure Goodell to further investigate "Spygate" and to meet with Walsh, saying that he even wants to be present if and when the NFL ever interviews the ex-Pats employee. Older Boston residents might remember Specter, who served on the much-criticized Warren Commission that investigated the assassination of New England-bred President John F. Kennedy. More than 40 years since he first entered the national spotlight, Specter has refused to let "Spygate" die until Goodell got to the bottom of it.

Now working in Hawaii as a golf pro, Walsh eventually met with Goodell, but only after the NFL agreed to protect him from any potential lawsuits filed against him by New England. Walsh gave Goodell new videotapes that proved the Patriots taped opposing coaches' signals in at least six other contests, including the 2002 AFC Championship Game in Pittsburgh. As for that alleged pre-Super Bowl Rams walk-through tape, it turned out that it didn't exist, prompting *The Boston Herald* to apologize for their inaccurate story. But Walsh wasn't done. He claimed that he watched the Rams' walk-through practice before the Super Bowl and then passed on what he saw to a New England assistant coach. Walsh also accused the Patriots of allowing players on the injured-reserve list to practice, a clear violation of another NFL rule. Walsh's claim was supported by former Patriots lineman, Ross Tucker.

Meanwhile, the Patriots tried putting the scandal behind them during the 2008 offseason. At an NFL owners' meeting, Belichick and Patriots owner Robert Kraft apologized to their peers, who reportedly responded with applause. Belichick also greeted the media with a rare friendly face to discuss the issue. But finding true closure will be difficult for them. Fairly or not, the national perception of the Patriots is that they truly cheated and their championships are tainted. They failed to win Super Bowl XLII, but they lost their collective soul long before that. Which is why everyone outside of New England was rooting against them in that title game and was thrilled that they lost it, and their bid for a perfect season, to the New York Giants.

In many ways, "Spygate" was the perfect sports NFL controversy for this decade. From Jose Canseco to Marion Jones, the line between champ and alleged cheat has grown thinner and thinner. Now we can add Bill Belichick and his team to that infamous list, because it appears that the scandal may never entirely be laid to rest, no matter how much the Patriots and the NFL wish it would be.

Here's hoping the rest of the sports world has better luck in shedding its notorious image, and we fans can return to talking more about dominant players and dynasties, not the dark side.

14 HOPE FOR THE FUTURE: *Athletes Who Still Give Us a Lot to Cheer About*

IT'S A SMALL WORD WITH HUGE IMPLICATIONS FOR EVERYONE connected with sports. It lurks in every fan's heart when their boys are down by a run in the bottom of the ninth, or when the clock is ticking perilously close to zero and they need a three-pointer to tie. It's also why March is nearly every baseball booster's favorite month, and why football junkies get that goofy grin every August. A new season is about to dawn and, dammit, this just might be the year. All of these emotions can be explained with four simple letters: H-O-P-E.

Hope. It's a simple concept. But it's in frighteningly short supply. Especially in today's sports world, where the stat sheet seemingly has been replaced by a rap sheet. With all the negative sports stories, even passionate fans like us sometimes get cynical and turned off. However, looking beneath the surface, we still see many athletes and teams who give us plenty to root for. Even in these scandal-ridden times, we've compiled a list of sports figures that we are proud to cheer and celebrate. The men and women we admire aren't necessarily the ones who avoid controversy or always say the politically correct thing. Some are household names and some are just regular folks who simply did the right thing when thrust into an extraordinary situation. Still others struggled and toiled in anonymity until they were finally given a small fleeting opportunity, and they turned it into the chance of a lifetime. And we especially appreciate the jocks, be they active or long-retired, who help out those less fortunate, and do so with no cynical PR motives. They just generously give to their community and fans with truly no strings attached. Doing all this good stuff sounds obvious, but these days it actually seems pretty rare. Just like hope itself. Together, these people remind us why we grew to love sports in the first place.

Two Lords of the Ring

Phil Villapiano was looking just to bum a beer in a stadium parking lot. Less than a year later, he was on *Oprah* being hailed for his remarkable generosity. How the hell did that happen?

As first detailed in print by well-respected veteran Oakland Tribune reporter Dave Newhouse, it all started after a Raiders game in October 2001. Villapiano, who played for the Raiders from 1971-79, made the annual trip from his New Jersey home to Oakland watch his old ball-club. After the game, he and a buddy came across Mitch Oellrich, a Raiders fan enjoying a postgame tailgate party with friends. Villapiano asked Mitch if they could have a beer and they started a conversation that would change both of their lives. At the time, Mitch was completely wheelchair-bound after a 1999 swimming pool accident where he slipped off a diving board. After Mitch explained his spinal injury, Villapiano immediately took off a ring he was wearing, only it wasn't just any ordinary jewelry. It was the specially made ring he received for winning Super Bowl XI with the Raiders, an event that Villapiano still describes as being more important to him than his wife and children. No matter. Villapiano gave the ring to Mitch, a stranger whom the NFL legend had known for all of 10 minutes and half a beer. Mitch and his family tried to say no, but Villapiano insisted, telling them there was just one condition: He could give the ring back only after he proved he could get himself out of his wheelchair and walk on his own.

"And that was it, it was decided," said Bonnie Oellrich, Mitch's wife. "That was Phil's thing: Mitch was going to have to walk to give the ring back."

But how? Sure, Mitch admitted that up to that point he hadn't done much to improve his condition. But major physical therapy is expensive and also no guarantee for progress. Their friend John Bailey and a few other of their construction-worker pals had an idea. They came over to the Oellrich home in Livermore, California, an Oakland suburb, and built a homemade contraption in their garage. Bailey and his friends designed a harness with rollers that attached to a pulley that in turn wrapped around a steel beam in the garage. "It was kind of like a bungee, so when his leg gave, the harness would give, too, and it allowed him to sink a few feet without falling onto the ground," Bonnie Oellrich said by phone. So Mitch started going out there a couple of hours per night, battling the chilly winter temperatures in the unheated garage in hopes of being able to walk again.

Meanwhile, back in New Jersey, some of Villapiano's friends and family thought he had lost his mind. "My son Philip said it the best. He said, 'Dad, it was either the best thing you've ever done or it was the stupidest,'" said Villapiano. "But my wife Susan absolutely loved it."

Looking back, the ex-All-Pro linebacker said he had been emotionally moved by seeing Mitch in a wheelchair next to his wife and daughters at the ballgame. The clincher was when Mitch, warming to the idea, said he would model his work ethic after the wildly successful '70s Oakland teams on which Villapiano starred. "He told me that he would work like a Raider. He said, 'I'll work out three times a day just like a Raider, I'll walk.'" said Villapiano, now 59. "And I believed him. So I gave him the ring. I believed in the guy."

As the 2001 season wound down, Mitch continued to do his home rehab work in the garage. And Villapiano kept checking in with encouragement, even stopping by their home with another ex-teammate, John Vella, to share beers with the couple in their kitchen. It was no small visit for the Oellriches. They were big football fans who got engaged to each other in front of 50 friends at one of their own Super Bowl parties. "Being Raiders fans, I can't think of anyone other than Elvis who would have meant more to us than Phil as someone to get to know," Bonnie Oellrich said. "They started telling stories about the old days and it was such a treat, we were just sitting there with our mouths hanging open."

But there was still the matter of when and where Mitch would attempt to walk. Villapiano dreamed briefly of having him take the field at Oakland's McAfee Coliseum during a Raiders game and walking toward The Black Hole, where the rabid fans sit in the south end zone. But finally, it was decided that Mitch would give it a try in the ballroom of a Reno hotel, where Villapiano often throws a Super Bowl party for friends and ex-teammates. In the weeks leading up to the party, everyone involved had high hopes for Mitch—mixed with large doses of anxiety.

"I was excited, and I also was afraid he wouldn't be able to do it," Bonnie Oellrich said. Mitch shared his concerns about it with her, too. They weren't alone.

"I had seen him about a month before [the Super Bowl party], and there was no way he could stand up," Villapiano recalls.

But Mitch kept working-out over the holidays and through January 2002. And on Feb. 3, little more than three months after meeting Villapiano in the parking lot, Bonnie and Mitch went to the Silver Legacy Hotel in Reno. There, they rubbed elbows at the party with NFL legends, such as Hollywood Henderson and Conrad Dobler, whose wife also had suffered a spinal injury. Later came the moment everyone had waited for. Mitch's friends lifted him on the hotel ballroom stage, where he joined Villapiano. The ballroom grew quiet. All eyes were on them. Slowly, tentatively, Mitch took a few steps with the aid of a cane. And then he took some more steps. And he just kept going.

"It all felt like it was happening in slow-motion," Bonnie Oellrich said.

Finally, he made it to Villapiano, and the crowd erupted like they had won the Super Bowl. "About a thousand people are going, 'Mitch! . . . Mitch! . . . Mitch!'" said the football legend. "I looked down at Mitch's mother—she was crying. His two daughters were crying, his wife was crying. I was crying. He was crying. It was so emotionally powerful. It was soooo cool!"

Mitch gave the ring back to Villapiano and the party continued. But that's not where the story ends. Soon thereafter, they appeared on *Good Morning America*. Even producers from *Oprah* came calling, and she featured Villapiano and Mitch in a segment on inspirational people. Oprah herself even paid for a year's scholarship for Mitch to do more physical therapy at Project Walk, a clinic in San Diego, where he did intensive training five hours a day, five days a week. "They helped me a lot," he said.

Today, Bonnie Oellrich said she can see improvement in Mitch's physical condition. He has strengthened his torso and stomach muscles and now is able to stand and sit by himself. And there have been bigger achievements, too, such as being able to walk for short distances. Even that kind of incremental gain makes a major difference with his self-esteem, she added. For example, just the act of parking his van at a supermarket and being able to walk in by himself and greet people without his wheelchair was empowering for him, Bonnie Oellrich said.

About seven years after first meeting, the Oellriches and the Villapianos still stay in touch, sending Christmas cards each year and occasionally surprising each other with a phone call. All because of the symbolic power of a Super Bowl ring and the type of rare kindness from a sports figure that does much to restore even the biggest cynic's faith in the games we watch.

"It was like, wow, he did it," Bonnie Oellrich said, marveling at the memory of that electric day in the hotel ballroom. "He really did it. They did it. With Phil's inspiration, Mitch was really able to do it."

GEORGE MARTIN: ON THE ROAD

Beating the once-unbeatable New England Patriots in Super Bowl XLII was an amazing New York Giants highlight. But it wasn't even the best thing a Giant did in 2008. That feat belongs to former defensive end George Martin, who had the goal of walking more than 3,000 miles to raise money for medical care for the roughly 40,000 first responders to the Sept. 11 terrorist attacks. Martin, who took a leave from his job as the vice president of a New York insurance company, started at the George Washington Bridge in New York City and headed to Southern California.

His fund-raising goal is $10 million and he has enlisted private donors to match him dollar-for-dollar. Which is impressive, especially because this was more than just a nice stroll. Martin, 55, walked dozens of miles per day through the heat of the East Coast's Indian summer and the Midwestern winter during snow, rain and windstorms. It's no wonder that his old Giants coach Bill Parcells once said that if one of his players was going to save the world it would be George Martin.

As we went to print, Martin was in Palmdale, California—just a few hundred miles from the finish line. You can check out more information on his journey, or make a donation, at his website, www.ajourneyfor911.info. He was scheduled to arrive at his final destination in San Diego on June 21, 2008—just in time to take a much-deserved rest before the Fourth of July weekend. It's a fitting finish for a guy we consider to be a true American hero.

THE YEAR OF FORGIVING DANGEROUSLY

Too many people go to the ballpark and act like Tony Soprano—foulmouthed, entitled, aggressive and (occasionally) violent. But for a few months in early 2008, the sports world did an about-face and behaved like Dr. Melfi (Sopranos' TV therapist). That is, it was all about healing and closure. It's true. For some reason, a lot of people were in a forgiving mood, as three sports cities took their painful memories of unforgettable gaffes, horrible luck and bad blood and finally laid them to rest. First, Golden State Warriors coach Don Nelson and aging superstar Chris Webber reunited nearly 14 years after their bitter 1994 feud resulted in Webber being traded and Nelson getting fired, while it left the tattered Warriors with a 13-season playoff drought. The reconciliation in Oakland didn't work out that great—the Warriors failed to make the playoffs and Webber had to retire after just nine games due to a bad knee. But we still tip our hat to both guys for letting bygones be bygones.

Winning the Fall Classic apparently allowed the city of Boston to forgive Bill Buckner, once and for all. On Opening Day 2008, Red Sox fans gave an emotional, long-overdue standing ovation to Buckner, who threw out the ceremonial first pitch. Buckner's fielding error allowed the

New York Mets to win Game 6 of the 1986 World Series against the Sox. When the Mets went on to win Game 7 and the championship, Buckner was unfairly deemed the goat. For years after that, he faced constant fan heckling and public ridicule and became a symbol of Boston's cursed team. Buckner always said he wasn't bothered by the critics. But the tears streaming down his face as Boston fans wildly cheered him on Opening Day told another story. After the Red Sox won the 2007 World Series, their second in four seasons after a 86-year drought, it appeared that any remaining wounds from 1986 finally had been healed.

New York Mets outfielder Moises Alou also had forgiveness on his mind in Spring Training. The ex-Cub tried taking the burden off of Steve Bartman, the infamous fan we covered back in 5 on Curses & Superstitions. More than four years later, Alou said he never would have been able to catch the ball that Bartman touched anyway, adding that Chicago fans should forgive Bartman and forget. Cubs legend Ernie Banks also defended Bartman and said the team should show it has moved on by having him toss out the first pitch before a game. Just like the Red Sox, the Cubs might have to end their own curse and finally win a World Series before all of their fans embrace Bartman again. But, we agree with Alou. C'mon, Cubs fans! To paraphrase Banks, let's bury the hatchet and then let's play two!

THREE CHEERS FOR THREE REFS

It's an old axiom for referees: If the fans aren't noticing you, then you must be doing your job well. But three Kansas referees who made a quick judgment-call at a high school gymnasium on Feb. 2, 2008, have admirably broken that rule. Their separate split-second decisions drew nation-wide coverage, but these are refs that we would never boo. Here's what happened: An official from St. Mary's Academy, a religious high school outside of Topeka, Kansas, refused to allow Michelle Campbell to referee their game. Why? The reported reason was that having a woman in a position of authority over boys violated the school's beliefs. (Apparently, the school has never heard of the concept of motherhood!) Campbell, a retired police officer and former Kansas State player, did the most respectful thing she could think of—she left the gymnasium without incident. She later told the Topeka Capital-Journal newspaper that she was "dumbfounded when she learned of" the school's decision. Meanwhile, Darin Putthoff was supposed to referee the game with Campbell, according to the Associated Press. But Putthoff didn't pander to the school's sexism. He refused to work the game. Then they asked Fred Shockey, another ref at the gym. However, Shockey, who served in the Army for a dozen years, declined when he found out why they needed him.

"I have been led by some of the finest women this nation has to offer, and there was no way I was going to go along with that," Shockey told the Associated Press. Putthoff added that he probably will not work at St. Mary's Academy again due to the incident. "We have to support our fellow officials," he said.

With their quiet and dignified actions, Campbell, Putthoff and Shockey gave the high school students inside the gym some quick but very important lessons on a variety of topics ranging from sexism to loyalty. So no jeers here for these refs, only cheers. We proudly salute the three of them for making the right call on ignorance before the game even started.

ONE STEP AT A TIME FOR KEVIN EVERETT

On September 9, 2007, the first week of the NFL season, Buffalo Bills tight end Kevin Everett fell on the turf on a kickoff tackle, just like he's done hundreds of times. Only this time he didn't get up. Everett, 26, was paralyzed from the neck down due to a serious spinal injury, and at first doctors weren't sure if he could ever walk again. But he made quick progress, rehabbing in private, tentatively making his first steps. Finally, he put fans' and teammates' questions to rest on December 23, when he returned to Ralph Wilson Stadium in Buffalo for the Bills' emotional home finale. He walked up to teammates and greeted them, most of whom he hadn't seen since his frightening injury. "I was speechless, on the verge of tears," Bills quarterback Trent Edwards told *USA Today* about seeing Everett up and walking again in the locker room.

The Bills released Everett in the offseason so he could receive disability and pension benefits, which he would have not received had he stayed on the team's roster. If Everett's next goal is to join a new team out on the field soon for game action, given his progress—and bravery—we're not betting against him.

CARLOS DELGADO'S WORLD

What do this Puerto Rican first-baseman and the Dixie Chicks have in common? Both publicly and firmly opposed the Iraq War from the beginning and paid a big price at first for those opinions. Sports has never been a safe place for political protest. Delgado found that out the hard way in 2004, when the then-Toronto Blue Jay started staying in the dugout during the playing of *God Bless America* during the seventh-inning stretch. He said he had no problems with the song or America, to which Puerto Rico technically belongs. It was the war in Iraq that he rejected, and the song represented the war at the time, Delgado said. About half a decade later, most Americans agree with him about the conflict in Iraq. But at the time, it was not so hip to say so, and Yankees fans booed him for it in New York. "This is my personal feeling," he told newspaper reporters at the time. "I don't want to draw attention to myself or go out of my way to protest. If I make the last out of the seventh inning, I'll stand there. But I'd rather be in the dugout." Some public figures have been buried by an avalanche of negativity after sharing such unpopular views. The list includes singer Sinead O'Connor and NBA star, Mahmoud Abdul-Rauf, who refused to stand for the National Anthem at basketball games in the mid-1990s. But the good news is that Delgado survived the controversy and now thrives in, of all places, New York City. He plays for the Mets. In 2006, he was awarded the Roberto Clemente Award, which each year honors one MLB player for charity work. Clemente, like Delgado, was a Puerto Rican ballplayer with a political mind and a big heart. And these days, Delgado is even ready to make nice. As a gesture of goodwill to New York fans, he now joins his Mets teammates for performances of *God Bless America,* ably showing Americans that one can exercise the freedom our soldiers are fighting for and live to tell about it.

BLADE RUNNER: THE COURAGE OF OSCAR PISTORIUS

Oscar Pistorius is everything that the Olympic Games say they stand for. But for a time, international sporting officials would not allow the South African runner to compete in any Olympiad in the near or distant future.

A medical condition forced doctors to amputate both of Pistorius' legs when he was still a baby. Now 21, he competes in races for the handicapped with artificial legs; they are carbon fiber blades attached just beneath his knee. He holds the world record for amputees in the 100, 200 and 400 meters, earning him the nickname, "The Blade Runner." Pistorius has competed against able-bodied runners recently, and he wants to continue running against them in international, officially-sanctioned contests. "I'm not disabled, I just don't have any legs," he once told the Daily Mail, a British newspaper. His biggest goal was to race the 400 meters at the 2008 Olympics in Beijing. At best, he was a longshot merely to hold his own with able-bodied athletes, especially after a rough showing in July 2007, when he finished last and later was disqualified for running out of his lane. Things would have to go perfectly for Pistorius to even finish an Olympics race, let alone win a medal. Still, in January 2008, the International Association of Athletics Federation rules banned "any technical device . . . that provides a user with an advantage over another athlete not using such a device." In short, they excluded him because they believe his artificial blades give him an advantage over real legs. All together now with a big Bronx cheer: Boooooooooooo!

We didn't really understand the decision at the time, because if anyone exemplifies the courage and grace of the Olympic spirit, it's Pistorius. But just like most dramatic races, this story has a comeback. Pistorius appealed the IAAF decision. And he won. He told reporters that he burst into tears when he got the news. The surprise ruling cleared the way for him to take part in the qualifying races, which took place after we went to print.

Whether he qualified or not, he still had plans to go to the 2008 Beijing games, either at the Olympics or at the Paralympics, a competition for disabled athletes, also held in China. In the 2004 Paralympics held in Athens, Pistorius took home the gold medal in the 200 meters and the bronze in the 400 meters, proving that he is still "the best runner on no legs"—another one of his nicknames.

Pistorius' now-deceased mother probably put it best when she wrote a heartfelt letter to him when he was just a toddler, long before he started racing, of course. According to the Daily Mail, she wrote this for him to read as an adult: "Feet cannot earn a good salary or give us a compassionate and loving heart . . . A loser is not the one who runs last in the race. It is the one who sits and watches and has never tried to run." Hey Oscar, we don't care what any track officials have to say. Here's the deal: You never stop running, and we'll never stop rooting for you. Deal? Deal.

HOT AS A PISTOL: JASON MCELWAIN'S SHOT AT GLORY

Who needs the movie Rudy when Jason McElwain starred in his own basketball version of it? You may have seen his story on TV in 2006, when his high school team, Greece Athena High School, played their last home game of the season. McElwain, who is autistic, had been an enthusiastic varsity team assistant for years at the upstate New York school. The squad's coach Jim Johnson asked McElwain to suit up for the first time ever—it was the coach's sign of thanks to the high school senior for all his hard work. Late in the game, Johnson put him in and the student section cheered in approval. It was a small but nice gesture—a little extra time for the kid. McElwain promptly hoisted a long airball and then missed a layup, not too surprising for a guy who hadn't played in a real game all year. But then, as the final seconds ticked, something just clicked. First, McElwain nailed a three-pointer. The high school gym's fans roared, and his teammates were high-fiving each other. Another nice little moment. But suddenly, it went beyond "nice" and turned into something simply magical. McElwain got the ball and hit another three-pointer. More cheers. And then another three-pointer. And then another!

By now, his teammates were jumping like five-year-olds on Christmas morning, and the student cheering section shook in pure bedlam. Somewhere amidst all the madness, he scored again—an ordinary two-pointer. And then just before the buzzer, he hoisted another three-pointer from the right side. Nothing but net. The buzzer sounded. Game over. Incredibly, McElwain had scored 20 points in four minutes. Practically everyone in the gym stormed the court and placed the kid on their shoulders.

Fortunately, a student filmed the game on a video camera, and soon the footage was everywhere: first the local news, and then the national networks, not to mention ESPN, CNN and the Internet. McElwain eventually won an ESPY Award for "Best Sports Moment," and sold his story's movie rights to a Hollywood studio. He was even invited to meet President Bush. When later questioned by reporters, no one on the team could explain his offensive explosion. McElwain himself put it as well as anyone could have when interviewed by a *CBS News* reporter: "I was hot as a pistol," he said matter-of-factly. That's what we love about sports. Sometimes, the unthinkable, the unimaginable, the impossible actually happens, right in front of our very eyes, reminding us why hope indeed springs eternal.

EXTRA INNINGS:
The End of the Book.
The Start of the Conversation.

GUESS WE'D BETTER STOP THERE. DON'T GET US WRONG. We could go on forever. That's another reason we love sports: every day there is some new controversy to discuss, some news on an obscure player you forgot about, some new rule to follow, and some jackass—or trailblazer—violating that rule.

Not to sound like an after-school special, but we hope at this point, we made you laugh a little. Learn a lot. And even get a bit pissed off at some of our opinions. Or angry that we left out your favorite sport or team. (Hey, we had to leave something for the sequel!) But mostly we hope we reminded you of what made you love sports in the first place: (Hint, it's not stats or analysis.) It's green grass. It's holding your dad's hand. It's butterflies in your stomach. It's cigarette smoke on a hot sunny day. It's that incredible play that you saw with your own two eyes. It's whatever you remember about the day your love affair with sports began.

What we really wanted to do in *GameFace* was to start a new conversation about sports—a conversation where women could share their own distinct point of view, and discuss those views with other smart, opinionated female sports fans (and evolved guys like Chris). Let the stat-heads bicker about their fantasy teams and quiz each other incessantly—we'll be over here at the bar, talking about the good stuff. The juicy stuff. The real stuff that sports is made of.

But most of all, we hope we inspired you to join us in our quest to be enthusiastic students of sport. We will never memorize everything there is to know, but we will never stop asking questions. Why have they always done it that way? How does this affect the bigger picture? And he got what STD from who?!

But don't be sad. (There's no crying in *GameFace*!) You may be done with the book, but the conversation has just begun. Now that we have a voice of our own, it's time to add your voice to the mix. Visit us at GoGameFace.com. We'll be there waiting—delivering our witty, wise and wise-cracking perspective on sports, this time, on a daily basis. Stop by and say hello. We want to be the first to welcome you to the club.

BIBLIOGRAPHY

Allen, Maury. *Where Have You Gone, Joe DiMaggio?: The Story of America's Last Hero*, Dutton, 1975.

Asinof, Elliott. *Eight Men Out: The Black Sox and the 1919 World Series*, Holt, Rinehart, 1963.

Bryan, Carmen. *It's No Secret*, VH-1, 2006.

Cook, William A. *Pete Rose: Baseball's All-Time Hit King*, McFarland, 2003.

Cosell, Howard with Peter Bonventre. *I Never Played the Game*, Avon Books, 1985.

Dravecky, Dave with Mike Yorkey. *Called Up: Stories of Life and Faith From the Great Game of Baseball*, Zondervan, 2004.

Evans, Robert. *The Kid Stays in the Picture*, Hyperion, 1994.

Fenster, Bob. *They Did What!?*, Andrews McMeel Publishing, 2002.

Fields, Sarah K. *Female Gladiators: Gender, Law and Contact Sport in America*, University of Illinois Press, 2005.

Gatto, Steve. *Da Curse of the Billy Goat: The Chicago Cubs, Pennant Races and Curses*, Protar House, 2004.

Hall, Donald with Dock Ellis. *Dock Ellis In the Country of Baseball*, Fireside, 1986.

Helyar, John. *Lords of the Realm: The Real History of Baseball*, Ballantine Books, 1995.

Madden, John with Dave Anderson. *One Size Doesn't Fit All*, Villard Books, 1988.

Mahler, Jonathan. *Ladies and Gentleman, The Bronx Is Burning: 1977, Baseball, Politics, and the Battle for the Soul of a City*, Farrar, Straus and Giroux, 2005.

Maxymuk, John. *Uniform Numbers of the NFL: All-Time Rosters, Facts and Figures*, McFarland & Company, 2005.

McGee, Bob. *The Greatest Ballpark Ever: Ebbets Field and the Story of the Brooklyn Dodgers*, Rutgers University Press, 2005.

O'Toole, Shannon. *Wedded to the Game: The Real Lives of NFL Women*, Bison Books, 2006.

Ritz, David. *Divided Soul: The Life of Marvin Gaye*, McGraw-Hill, 1985.

Shapiro, Michael. *The Last Good Season*, Doubleday, 2004.

Tosches, Nick. *Dino: Living High in the Dirty Business of Dreams*, Doubleday, 1992.

Williams, Lance and Mark Fainaru-Wada. *Game of Shadows*, Gotham, 2006.

Notes are posted on GoGameFace.com